Luminos is the Open Access monograph publishing program
from UC Press. Luminos provides a framework for preserving and
reinvigorating monograph publishing for the future and increases
the reach and visibility of important scholarly work. Titles published
in the UC Press Luminos model are published with the same high
standards for selection, peer review, production, and marketing as
those in our traditional program. www.luminosoa.org

D1714386

The publisher and the University of California Press Foundation
gratefully acknowledge the generous support of the
Sue Tsao Endowment Fund in Chinese Studies.

The Women Who Ruled China

The Women Who Ruled China

Buddhism, Multiculturalism,
and Governance in the Sixth Century

———

Stephanie Balkwill

UNIVERSITY OF CALIFORNIA PRESS

University of California Press
Oakland, California

Suggested citation: Balkwill, S. *The Women Who Ruled China: Buddhism, Multiculturalism, and Governance in the Sixth Century*. Oakland: University of California Press, 2024. DOI: https://doi.org/10.1525/luminos.192

Cataloging-in-Publication Data is on file at the Library of Congress

ISBN 978-0-520-40181-5 (pbk. : alk. paper)
ISBN 978-0-520-40182-2 (ebook)

32 31 30 29 28 27 26 25 24
10 9 8 7 6 5 4 3 2 1

Para Diego,
mi todo.

CONTENTS

ILLUSTRATIONS

TABLE

MAP

FIGURES

ACKNOWLEDGMENTS

I have been so lucky in my life to share not only my vocation of historical scholarship but also my profession as a researcher and teacher at a public university, with my husband, Diego Loukota. So many of the ideas in this book are Diego's, just as was the invite for our first date. Our daughter, Remedios, may be the only third grader in California who knows anything at all about the Northern Wei or who has spent any time imagining the dusty oases of the Tarim Basin. My first acknowledgement must therefore go to them: Diego and Remedios, you constantly inspire me and I love you for it. My second acknowledgement must go to my larger family: To the family I was born into, the family I am married into, and the family I have made from my closest friends—you have all sustained me over the years that I have been writing this book. Now that the book is finished, I think that it is a poor repayment for your many years of service. I really hope you like it anyway.

To James Benn, my teacher: It seems to me an irony that in the scope of one lifetime I cannot repay the kindnesses you have shown me in this very same lifetime. For that, I can only say thank you. And to my other teachers: Rory O'Hagan who taught me to write, Ren Yuan who taught me diligence, Shayne Clarke who taught me precision, and Mark Rowe who taught me the value of challenge, I remain forever grateful. I hope that you all see yourselves in my work.

Many people have directly contributed to the success of this book. Diego has discussed every stage of it with me and has listened attentively to my frequent oration of all the many parts that I am still unsure about. Those who read full drafts and provided insightful comments include Megan Bryson, Keith Knapp, James Benn, Scott Pearce, Matthew Hayes, one other anonymous reviewer, and Eric Schmidt, my editor from the UC Press who has championed this book from day one. James, in particular, has read *many* drafts. Scott, in particular, has saved me from making countless embarrassing mistakes. Megan came up with the idea that formed the first part of the introduction, which is really the coolest part of the book. I have discussed pieces of this work with many colleagues, some of whom have also read chapters, drafts, and translations, or have either invited me to give research talks or responded to my talks in both formal and informal ways. Although there are too many colleagues to name in full, and in addition to those mentioned above, I owe special thanks to Lori Meeks, Kate Lingley, Wendi Adamek, Chen Jinhua, Gil Raz, Rick McBride, Amy Langenberg, Andy Chittick, Eric Greene, Nina Duthie, Yongshan He, and Li Lan.

Finally, though I have never met her and have not been able to track her down, Jennifer Holmgren's pioneering research on the Northern Wei has undeniably provided the motivation for my own research. Dr. Holmgren's work is daring and bold. Her name belongs among the names of the world's top Sinologists. I hope this book somehow finds its way into her hands or the hands of her family.

That I am a scholar at all is entirely a result of Canadian public education; that I am now employed at a renowned public research institution is because of the ongoing support of individual administrators and colleagues who continue to make public institutions essential to social equity. At McMaster University, Doreen Drew is a wonder who probably doesn't know how often I think about her and quietly thank her. At the University of Winnipeg, my colleagues in the Department of Religion and Culture have been my most energetic cheerleaders even though I have traded their adamantine Manitoba winters for the sunny shores of California. At UCLA, it has been a tremendous honor to work with colleagues whose research I admire and whose commitment to academic excellence is matched only by their human-heartedness. In particular, I wish to thank Robert Buswell and William Bodiford for the opportunity to come to UCLA and for the mentorship that they have shown me since I arrived here.

Just as I was finishing this manuscript, my life changed in such a way that I was forced to confront the Buddha's teachings on impermanence and suffering; that I have been able to see this book to publication during my tumult through *saṃsāra* is a testament to the power of community. To those who have sent food and emails, who have made all kinds of support available to me, who phone and who write and who care, and to those colleagues who have taken on extra work on my behalf, I am profoundly grateful.

I understand the word *China* to refer to a geographical area in continental East Asia whose English name is taken from a short-lived but influential dynasty that made its empire there: the Qin (221–206 BCE). China, then, refers to a part of the world centered geographically on the central plains of the Yellow River valley, which has seen cultural continuity for well over two millennia. The people who settled this area of the world are known as the Han; however, China and its tradition encompass a much broader range of peoples, their languages, and their cultures. Therefore, when I use the term *China* it is to refer to the ever-shifting geographical boundaries that mark changing polities through time, and when I use the term *Chinese* it is to refer to a spectrum of cultural practices that have been inherited and reconfigured within these boundaries and by diverse groups of people. In this study, I refer to these diverse peoples and polities through the specific names by which they would have been known in the early medieval period. I also use the etymologically cognate word *Sinitic* to refer to specific cultural, linguistic, and political traditions ultimately derived from this broadly defined China, but when they have been adopted and adapted beyond the boundaries of China itself.

To support the publication of this Open Access volume, I have limited the use of Sinitic characters within the main body of the text and instead have supplied a character index. In some places, where including the characters is essential to understanding my arguments and translation choices, I have retained the characters in the text. All other terms, titles, names of people, and names of medieval cities and villages are found in the index. For titles of texts consulted in this study, please see the bibliography.

All dates are in the Common Era unless otherwise marked with BCE. Where dates from the medieval calendars themselves feature in translations of primary text material, I have also provided the Common Era dates.

DRAMATIS PERSONAE

Taghbach Gui (r. 386–409) was the founding leader of the Northern Wei empire (386–534), a polity formed of Inner Asian peoples from modern-day Inner Mongolia known to history by the reconstructed ethnonym of Taghbach.

Emperor Wencheng (r. 452–65) was a Taghbach leader who ruled the Northern Wei from its northern capital, Pingcheng. On his accession in 452, he declared Buddhism to be the state religion. He also took the Sinitic title of "emperor" instead of the Taghbach title of "khagan."

Empress Dowager Wenming (442–90) was empress to Wencheng though she was not Taghbach. She was a prolific Buddhist patron. She did not mother any sons, but she became dowager to Wencheng's son after his death, and then to that son's son after forcing the first son into retirement.

Tanyao (fl. 450) was Wencheng's personally appointed monastic supervisor. A Buddhist monk himself, Tanyao is reputed to have designed the initial strata of monumental Buddhist grottos at Yungang, which contain representations of Northern Wei emperors in the guise of buddhas.

Sengzhi (d. 516) was a Buddhist nun who originally served the Northern Wei court as the private teacher of the court's women and children but who eventually became the private tutor of the emperor. She used her influence to have her own niece appointed to court: That niece would eventually become Empress Dowager Ling.

Emperor Xiaowen (r. 471–99) was Emperor Wencheng's grandson who was said to be controlled by Empress Dowager Wenming. During his rule, the capital was moved to Luoyang—an ancient Han dynasty capital—and the Taghbach royal house adopted the Han-derived name of "Yuan."

Emperor Xuanwu (r. 499–515) was the son of Emperor Xiaowen. He was a well-known Buddhist patron and his religious teacher was the nun Sengzhi. It was he who took Sengzhi's niece—the future Empress Dowager Ling—as his concubine.

Empress Dowager Ling (d. 528) hailed from a Buddhist family and was herself the most ambitious Buddhist patron of her age. After Xuanwu's death, she is said to have murdered his empress, taken the position of dowager behind her son, and ruled the empire independently until her own assassination.

Emperor Xiaoming (r. 515–28) was the son of Empress Dowager Ling and Emperor Xuanwu. At his father's death, he became emperor at the age of five. His mother was his regent, though there was no shortage of political competition for his favor. He was murdered just as he was coming of age, and his mother was implicated in the murder.

Yuan Yi (487–520) was a prince and the son of Emperor Xiaowen. After the death of Xuanwu in 515, he became the lover of Empress Dowager Ling who was also his sister-in-law, and he died as a result of a coup d'état against her. He was also a known Buddhist patron.

Yuan Cha (486–526) was an ambitious but low-ranking prince who sought to establish his own regency over the child Emperor Xiaoming. He murdered Yuan Yi and staged a coup d'état. Empress Dowager Ling eventually forced him to commit suicide.

Mistress Pingyi (492–557) was Empress Dowager Ling's sister and the wife of Yuan Cha. Although her husband and her sister were engaged in bloody political conflict, she remained loyal to her sister. She collected her sister's body after her assassination and had it interred in a Buddhist monastery.

The Nameless Emperor (528) was the daughter of Emperor Xiaoming and the grand-daughter of Empress Dowager Ling. After the former's death, the latter placed her directly on the throne. She remains the first ever girl or woman in the imperial history of China to be installed as emperor.

Erzhu Rong (493–530) led a rebellion against Empress Dowager Ling. He brought an army to Luoyang, murdered the empress dowager, and staged a mass murder of the imperial house. He was later assassinated.

Emperor Xiaozhuang (r. 528–30) was a puppet emperor placed on the throne by Erzhu Rong but who orchestrated Erzhu Rong's murder after only two years in power. Xiaozhuang was then subsequently murdered in retaliation by Erzhu Rong's nephew.

Gao Huan (496–547) was temporarily allied with the Erzhu Clan in their overthrow of Empress Dowager Ling; however, he broke away from the Erzhu and made his own bid for power. He was successful. His own son became the first emperor of the Northern Qi (550–77).

Emperor Jiemin (r. 531–32) attempted to regain control of the Northern Wei for the Yuan/Taghbach family after the murder of Erzhu Rong and Emperor Xiaozhuang. He was murdered by Gao Huan's faction.

Emperor Xiaowu (r. 532–35) was Gao Huan's puppet emperor, chosen to reestablish the Yuan/Taghbach line. Xiaowu fled from Gao's control and the Northern Wei collapsed. Many historical sources refer to him with a pejorative title: "the emperor who fled."

Emperor Wenxuan (r. 550–59) was Gao Huan's son and the emperor of the Northern Qi, which considered itself the true successor of the Northern Wei. It was under his patronage that the official history of the Northern Wei was compiled and written.

Wei Shou (506–72) was a minor courtier of Empress Dowager Ling but was given a high position at the Northern Qi court, where he was tasked with compiling the official history of the Northern Wei from the perspective of its self-proclaimed successors. His text has been criticized for its political biases.

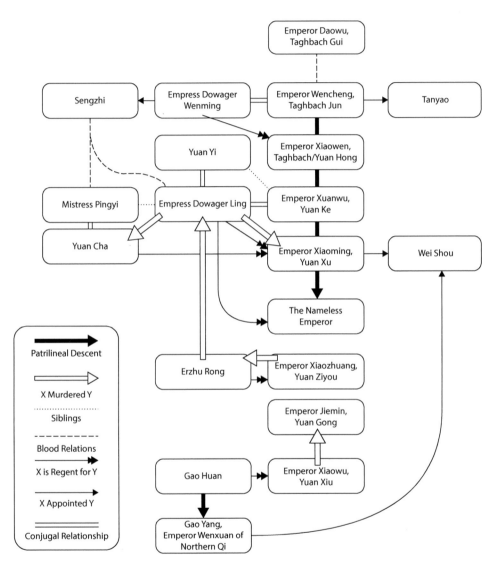

FIGURE 1. Diagram of the relationships of Empress Dowager Ling's immediate associates and family members.

ABBREVIATIONS

B   Beijing tushuguan 北京图书馆, and Jin Shijie 金石组. *Beijing tushuguan zangguan zhongguo lidai shike taben huibuan* 北京图书馆藏中国历代石刻拓本汇编 [*A Compilation of Books of Rubbings from Chinese History Held in the Collection of the Beijing Library*]. 100 vols. Zhengzhou: Zhongzhou guji chubanshe, 1989.

BS   *Bei shi* 北史 [*History of the Northern Dynasties*]. 100 *juan*. Li Yanshou 李延壽 (d.u.), comp. Beijing: Zhonghua shuju, 1974.

HHS   *Hou Han shu* 後漢書 [*Book of the Later Han*]. 120 *juan*. Compiled by Fan Ye 范曄 (398–445). Beijing: Zhonghua shuju, 1965.

I   *Beichao Fojiao shike tapian baipin* 北朝佛教石刻拓片 百品 [*One Hundred Pieces of Rubbings from Buddhist Stone Inscriptions from the Southern and Northern Dynasties*]. Chinese Buddhist Text Authority. Accessed December 2, 2024. https://cbetaonline.dila.edu.tw/zh/.

LYQLJ   *Luoyang qielan ji* 洛陽伽藍記 [*Record of Buddhist Monasteries in Luoyang*]. T no. 2092.

T   *Taishō shinshū daizōkyō* 大正新修大蔵経 [*Great (Buddhist) Canon, Newly Compiled in the Taishō Era*]. Edited by Takakusu Junjirō 高楠順次郎 and Watanabe Kaikyoku 渡辺海旭. 100 vols. Tokyo: Taishō Issaikyō Kankōkai, 1924–32.

WS   *Wei shu* 魏書 [*Book of the Wei*]. 130 *juan*. Compiled by Wei Shou 魏收 (505–72). Beijing: Zhonghua shuju, 1974.

ZC   Zhao Chao 趙超, ed. *Han Wei nanbei chao muzhi huibian* 漢魏南北朝墓誌彙編 [*A Guide to Tomb Inscriptions from the Han, Wei, and Northern and Southern Dynasties*]. Tianjin: Tianjin guji chubanshe, 1992.

ZW   Zhao Wanli 趙萬里. *Han Wei nanbei chao muzhi jishi* 漢魏南北朝墓誌集釋 [*Collection and Explanation of Tomb Inscriptions from the Han, Wei, and Northern and Southern Dynasties*]. Taipei: Dingwen shuju, 1972.

ZZ	Zhao Junping 趙君平 and Zhao Wencheng 趙文成, eds. *Heluo muke shiling* 河洛墓刻拾零 [*A Collection of Tomb Inscriptions from Luoyang, Henan*]. Beijing: Beijing tushuguan chubanshe, 2006.
ZZTJ	*Zizhi tongjian* 資治通鑑 [*Comprehensive Mirror for Aid in Government*]. 294 *juan*. Compiled by Sima Guang 司馬光 (1019–86). Presented to the throne in December 1084. Beijing: Zhonghua shuju, 1963.
ca.	"circa"—designates when the date is approximate.
Ch.	"Chinese"
d.u.	"dates unknown"
fl.	"floruit" (flourished)—designates a time period in which a person lived when precise dates are unavailable.
Kr.	"Korean"
r.	"reign"—designates the dates of a particular reign.
Skt.	"Sanskrit"
trad.	"traditional"—designates traditionally accepted dates when precise dates are uncertain.

Introduction

This book is about a woman who ruled an empire in medieval China, a woman who did so independently, as a man would do. Her capital city, Luoyang, was said to have shone brightly throughout the sky on account of the gold-topped Buddhist temples and monasteries that stood on every corner. Life in her city was teeming with Buddhist persons, ideas, objects, and architecture, all of which the female monarch utilized in the legitimation of her rule while she also connected herself and her reign to pre-Buddhist sites and symbols of political importance from the then-classical Han empire (206 BCE–220 CE), which had also had Luoyang as its capital. As the most prominent patron of Buddhist building projects in her time, she commissioned the construction of a massive, opulent, religio-political complex in her capital, which subsequently (and famously) burned to the ground. The burning was reported to have been a karmically appropriate response to the indulgent expenditures of a female ruler. She also commissioned the building of a massive rock-cut grotto at the Buddhist site of Longmen just to the south of Luoyang, and her own likeness can still be found at the site, forever etched in stone. Buddhist donative inscriptions from the period refer to her rule—as regent to the emperor even though she ruled directly—as that of the "Two Sages" (*ersheng*). This book chronicles the life, reign, and death of the earliest known woman to rule an empire in East Asia as a Buddhist monarch.

But this book is not about who you think it might be about. It is not about the most famous woman in Chinese history, Wu Zetian (624–705), who was the only woman to rule with the male title of "emperor" (*di*). Although Wu Zetian was known as one of the "Two Sages" in a paradigm of corulership, although she made Luoyang her capital city while legitimating her reign through both

1

Buddhist and Han dynastic ideas, texts, and objects, although she built a majestic religio-political complex in Luoyang that was destroyed by fire, and although she was a major patron of the Buddhist grottos at Longmen, where her visage is arguably still seen, this book is not about her.

This book is about a woman whose name is probably unknown to most readers: Northern Wei (386–534) Empress Dowager Ling (d. 528). I argue that the Northern Wei empress dowager served as a hitherto unrecognized predecessor to Wu Zetian/Emperor Wu Zhao. This is an argument largely based in Buddhist sources from the period, which I bring together, analyze, interpret, and translate in order to explore the precise social and historical circumstances that contributed to the accession of this largely unknown woman in the year 515 of the Common Era.

A NAMELESS GIRL

On an unknown date in an unrecorded year sometime in the mid to late 400s, a girl was born in northwestern China to a family of the local gentry. At her birth, the sky was awash in a glimmering crimson glow. Thinking this odd, her father consulted a diviner who made a prophecy for the otherwise unremembered child born far away from the imperial center. Reading the sky's majestic hue as an omen of the girl's great virtue, the diviner declared, "She will become the mother of heaven and earth and will give birth to the lord of heaven and earth."[1] The prophecy proved true on both counts: The child would go on to enter the inner court of the capital, become the favored concubine of the emperor, and provide him with a male heir. After her son's birth, part of her prophecy was fulfilled. The other part she made happen all on her own. As regent to her son, she ruled in her own name and did not relinquish power to him when he came of age. Although we know very little about her birth as a girl from the local gentry, we know much about her death as an empress dowager. In 528, Northern Wei Empress Dowager Ling (regency: 515–20; 525–28) is recorded as having been drowned in the river by invading forces in the capital city of Luoyang, but not before attempting to retire from political life by shaving her head and becoming a Buddhist nun.

How Empress Dowager Ling came to the central court in Luoyang is almost as curious a story as her birth: On the advice of a Buddhist nun, she was appointed to court by Emperor Xuanwu (r. 499–515).[2] The recommending nun was the empress dowager's aunt, a reputed teacher of the Buddhist law known to history by her monastic name, Shi Sengzhi (d. 516). The aunt-nun's name and story are preserved in her biography, which was etched on stone and placed in her tomb.[3] Sengzhi was the private Buddhist teacher of Emperor Xuanwu. More than simply lecturing him on the Buddhist law at court, the aunt used her influence in elite circles to promote her niece's appointment. This appointment raised the profile of their patrilineal clan, the Hu Clan from Anding, which saw their patriarch, Hu Guozhen (438–518), awarded with a position at the central court in Luoyang.[4] As for Hu Guozhen's daughter and benefactor, Empress Dowager Ling, her own trajectory at court is remarkable: Having given birth to the only living direct male heir to the throne, who would himself go on to become Emperor Xiaoming (r. 515–28),[5] the empress dowager ruled as regent after the death of Emperor Xuanwu. Her ascension was not without difficulties. Records indicate that she outlived an assassination attempt from Emperor Xuanwu's official empress, Empress Gao (d. 518).[6] Those same records tell us that Empress Gao did not escape her own assassination at the hands of Empress Dowager Ling, the latter of whom paved her own way to regency by eliminating her competition.[7]

Normative modalities of regency rule appear not to have been what Empress Dowager Ling had in mind when she found herself at the helm of the empire. Hailing from comparatively humble roots but managing to ascend to the highest possible of female ranks, the empress dowager wanted more: direct rule. The dynastic annals of Chinese history tell of a woman who held court in her own name, used the royal "we" (zhen), issued her own edicts, enacted the ancient calendrical rites demarcated for the emperor, placed honors on her patrilineal family, survived a coup d'état in order to resume her regency, and finally murdered her own son in order to retain power. Even more incredible, the empress dowager is said to have placed a female child on the throne after that son's murder. This infant was her own granddaughter, the daughter of the murdered son, and though she was not the only person in Chinese history to have had the honor of being called China's sole female emperor—that honor belongs to Wu Zetian as Emperor Wu Zhao—she was, indeed, China's other forgotten female monarch.[8] Placed on the throne by her grandmother, Empress Dowager Ling, the baby held her status for merely a few days before being displaced by a male heir. Her fate, as well as her name, is unrecorded by history.

Empress Dowager Ling is often characterized as the last independent ruler of the Northern Wei because the empire had suffered irreparable internal division with its move of the capital to Luoyang in 494, and it fell to internecine war during her rule. After the murder of the empress dowager in 528, her murderers set up a puppet emperor and the subsequent remainder of the dynasty was beset by a series of other short-lived puppet emperors installed by competing factions until its final collapse. During the reign of the last of these emperors, the empress dowager was given her posthumous name, "Ling," which is conventionally translated into English as "numinous" and which, in medieval usage, well expresses the historical ambiguity that surrounded this controversial female politician. Although she was granted a posthumous name, she was not given an imperial burial. Not entombed in the cluster of Northern Wei imperial tombs at Luoyang's Mount Mang,[9] the empress dowager's body, as well as the precise circumstances of her death, is—just like her granddaughter's—unrecorded by history.

ARGUMENTS FOR A NEW RECORD

Although the empress dowager's birth name and body have been lost to history, it is my goal in this book to excavate the details of her life insofar as is historically possible. I do so because the many underutilized sources that document her life tell a story that has not yet been adequately told: This is the story of the emergence of public and political roles for women brought about through the arrival of Buddhism to East Asia, the advent of multiethnic states and multicultural cities, and the reinvention of cultural and political traditions that came about as a result.

In chapter 1, "Luoyang Reborn," I begin my deep dive into the historical and social context of the empress dowager by providing an overview of Northern Wei society as it was settled in its final capital city of Luoyang, situated in the central plains of the lower reaches of the Yellow River valley. By providing an overview of Northern Wei history as it relates to the founding of that polity's southern capital and the cultural practices found there, I engage, in some depth, the question of the type of world that the empress dowager was living in and helped to create during her brief but important reign. Northern Wei Luoyang in the sixth century was a dynamic urban center; that very dynamism, however, likely contributed to its downfall. In describing the changing nature of ethnic relations, religious affiliation, and gender norms in this city and at this precise juncture in time, I seek to locate the empress dowager within the historical setting of her precarious but exciting capital.

In chapter 2, "A Woman of Power, Remembered Poorly," I offer a full translation and study of the standard biography of the empress dowager as it is retained in the *Book of the Wei* (Wei shu), which is the official history of the Northern Wei compiled by a scholar named Wei Shou (506–72) approximately twenty-five years after the death of the empress dowager. Before providing the reader with an annotated translation of this work, I discuss the political biases in the text that make it an unreliable witness to the life of the empress dowager and I argue that the genre of dynastic history is not well suited for documenting the lives of women. Following the translation, I provide an overview of the formative tropes that inadequately characterize the empress dowager and that have emerged from her biography, and I argue that such tropes have facilitated the general historical silencing of the empress dowager and her story.

In chapter 3, "Brought to Court by a Nun," I begin the first of three chapters that offer a critical interpretation of the life and reign of the empress dowager and that are informed by her Buddhist practice. Chapter 3 focuses on the very woman who brought the empress dowager to court in the first place: the Buddhist nun Sengzhi, the empress dowager's aunt. In positioning the empress dowager's own role at court within the history of the rise of Buddhist monasticism for women in East Asia, I reveal in this chapter how the empress dowager benefitted from the Buddhist monastic institution in order to achieve her highest status as the last independent ruler of the Northern Wei. Through a study of the entombed biography (*muzhiming*) of the aunt-nun, I investigate the ways in which Buddhist monasticism created opportunities for women in the Northern Wei's court/monastic structure. I argue that women of the Northern Wei court utilized the new social role of the elite Buddhist woman in order to position themselves as eminent persons in high society, thereby enabling themselves to mobilize their relationship with the Buddhist monastic institution as a means to support their own political careers. Finally, I set this argument in the context of the general, cultural openness to women holding public positions across various sectors of society within the social organization of the people who ruled the Northern Wei.

Chapter 4, "A Girl on the Throne," contains the most challenging of all the arguments that I put forth in this book, which is that perhaps the empress dowager knew just what she was doing when she attempted to place her granddaughter on the throne. In the *Book of the Wei* and its derivative texts, the fact that the empress dowager placed a girl on the throne is entirely glossed over, possibly being seen as an example of the general recklessness with which she is said to have ruled. Using Buddhist sources, I argue that this was not the case. I believe that the empress dowager's placement of her granddaughter on the throne was backed by the intriguing possibility that by the early sixth century Buddhist texts had provided textual precedence for rule by women, and that this fact dovetailed with a widespread change in both notions of imperial legitimation and gender dynamics in the period, a change rooted in the rise of multiethnic states like that of the Northern Wei. By surveying Buddhist textual material translated under the auspices of the empress dowager's court, by using entombed biographies and donative epigraphy from the late Northern Wei, and by connecting to comparable Buddhist forms of imperial legitimation flourishing in neighboring polities, I probe the ways in which Buddhist women participated in the Northern Wei court as high-level politicians. I furthermore expose how the empress dowager actively created and supported roles for women in her court—maybe even the role of emperor.

In chapter 5, "No Salvation in Buddhism," I engage the question of the empress dowager's death and legacy. The biography of the empress dowager states that she attempted to evade her own death by becoming a Buddhist nun, as did many women of her time who faced perilous situations like widowhood or loss of title. Her ploy did not work. Despite having the shaved head of a nun, she was murdered by enemy forces invading the capital. Thousands of her courtiers were also murdered, and the nuns of the inner imperium were reportedly raped in their nunnery. In this last chapter, I consider the fact that although the empress dowager came to court and rose in power there—in part through her affiliation with Buddhists, their texts, ideas, and institutions—Buddhism failed to prevent her final downfall. Furthermore, I raise the possibility that in the hands of those who controlled the Northern Wei after her death and informed the composition of the *Book of the Wei*, the type of Buddhism that she ascribed to was one of the sources of her demise. In positioning her as a ruler whose Buddhism diverged from that of her courtiers, I also explore the divergent meanings of her posthumous name, "Ling" among both Confucian and Buddhist audiences and I show how the name functioned simultaneously as a political critique and a form of religious identity. Finally, I argue that the space between these meanings was the space she occupied as a deeply controversial figure in her time.

In the "Conclusion" I consider the question of how the empress dowager's legacy affected the lives of women who came after her. Working from the premise that Buddhism was patronized as a secondary arm of government during the Northern Wei and beyond, I expose how elite women in medieval times were uniquely situated to play central roles in the development, expansion, and policing of state-sponsored Buddhism through to the Tang empire (618–907). In sum, I argue that Empress Dowager Ling provides our earliest known case study of the formation of a type of courtly Buddhism that came to characterize Buddhism as such across much of East Asia: A Buddhism that looked to the buddhas and bodhisattvas as religio-political figureheads, but used court and bureaucratic structures rooted in the administration of Han dynastic forms—structures that, within the multiethnic context of the northern dynasties, had often fallen under the auspices of political women. The gendered angle, I suggest, is what made the Northern Wei unique— that is, it is this angle that ultimately set Northern Wei Buddhism apart from the Buddhism of other medieval polities. Such a Buddhism—female, political, and northern—was similarly seen under the reign of the female Emperor Wu Zhao. I argue that Northern Wei Empress Dowager Ling was a model for the Emperor Wu.

THE MAKING AND THE BREAKING
OF HISTORICAL SILENCE

Empress Dowager Ling is little known outside medieval historiographical sources. To my knowledge, there is not one dedicated, book-length study of her in any modern language.[10] This lack of interest in her life and reign is frustrating. A medieval woman who transgressed the boundaries of culture, station, and gender, who built majestic Buddhist structures including the tallest building in the known world, and who ruled a major urban center in the medieval period—her story should be much better known. What accounts for this silence? And how do we break it?

Influential source materials that document the life of Empress Dowager Ling belong to a genre of historiographical texts authored by a social stratum of elite, literate men who wrote in a literary form of the Chinese language that I refer to as Literary Chinese.[11] These men, who are called the Ru, wrote political and governmental histories throughout China's imperial era, and their histories have shaped a narrative of the dynasties that is concerned with documenting continuity over time. This narrative is androcentric and ethnocentric. Throughout the imperial era, rulers, their advisors, and their courtiers were mainly men. There are very few counterexamples—perhaps just enough to prove the rule. It is the stories of these men and their counterparts that are central in the standard dynastic histories written by the Ru. Women do appear in these political histories, but usually only in the context of biographies of women partnered with powerful men or biographies of women noted for heroic acts of virtue. In addition to this sort of androcentrism, we witness a certain misogyny in the official accounts: When women were depicted as having taken power, they were written about poorly in the dynastic histories, a fact we will explore throughout this study. The Ru scholars belonged to a cultural tradition that is referred to in this study as the tradition of the Han, an ethnogroup that has been the majority population in the central plains of China since antiquity. Following Marc Abramson, who explains that although the term *Han* was not the most commonly used term in the medieval period to express the ethnic Self borne witness to in Literary Chinese writings, it is nonetheless an effective English translation for a variety of other words that express a similar idea,[12] this study uses the term Han to refer to peoples in the medieval period who identified themselves as the primary cultural and ethnic holders of a tradition that was: (1) defined on the basis of historical links to the Han empire; (2) conceived of through classical literature that became authoritative during the Han; (3) located geographically in administrative place names derived from the Han state. The Ru are very much in this tradition. Their texts encode an ethnocentric bias that favors polities ruled over by Han peoples and that considers only those polities to be legitimate dynasties in the unfolding of the Chinese imperial tradition.

Not only was Empress Dowager Ling a woman; she also ruled a dynasty that was famously non-Han, even though she herself was said to be Han. As I will show in the subsequent chapters of this book, the Northern Wei was founded by people who were ethnically different from—"Other" than—those represented by the traditions of the Han and the Ru, a group whose ethnonym has been reconstructed from historical sources as "Taghbach" (Ch. Tuoba) and who trace their origins to what is modern-day Inner Mongolia. Not only did the Taghbach have a different understanding of political order and dynastic succession than did the Han; they also knew different definitions of gender and its performance. By the time of the Northern Wei, the Taghbach were also Buddhist. Arguing that Taghbach cultural traditions helped to facilitate the rise of Buddhist and female politicians at court, I will discuss the Taghbach at length and critically analyze the role that they played in the redefinition of kingship during the medieval period. For now, what needs to be considered is that the empress dowager is doubly disadvantaged in terms of the historical records compiled and written by the Ru: A female ruler of an illegitimate empire, her story has been ignored. Moreover, the empress dowager's story has been ignored because it has become troped. Important sources documenting the life and rule of the Empress Dowager were written by those who benefitted directly from her death. As we will see, the stories of her life that these people compiled serve to characterize her as an incapable ruler and a licentious woman. These same sources also suggest that she murdered her own son, the emperor. Such tropes align with similar descriptions of powerful women in the official histories of the Ru scholars and they have allowed for the minimizing of women's work across the *longue durée* of imperial history.

To reinterpret the historical record, we can return to these same historiographical sources and read them deeply, looking for new ways in and equipped with different questions to ask. In this study, much of the equipment and the questions that I bring to the sources that document the life of the empress dowager are derived from the tradition of Buddhism. As a historian of the Chinese Buddhist tradition, it is clear to me that Buddhist studies has much to offer to the project of women's history because Buddhism was very popular among women in medieval times and because women themselves both created and are documented in many of the source materials that we might call "Buddhist sources." In the case of Empress Dowager Ling, Buddhist sources of all types—texts, epigraphs, architecture, art, and material culture—provide clues to a different history than that offered in the Ru accounts. All those sources will be used in this study to sketch a new and more historically meaningful portrait of the empress dowager. In creating that portrait, this book aims to bring to the surface the history of how Buddhist women came to rule diverse polities in East Asia during the medieval period. I also seek to make a methodological intervention into my discipline of Buddhist studies with the story that I tell in these pages. Reading Buddhist sources in their full context of patronage and audience and with attention to gender and ethnic difference, I show the potential that Buddhist sources hold for offering new forms of historical information. I also suggest a method of historical scholarship that I refer to as Buddhist feminist historiography, which prioritizes historically contextualized Buddhist sources as a means for asking critical questions about women's lives in history.

One other type of source that is often used in this study is a genre of texts known as entombed biographies (*muzhiming*). These are mortuary biographies that contain verses of praise for the dead, and which are inscribed on stone slabs that are located either inside the tomb with the body or outside the tomb near the tomb entrance or doorway. They are a literary genre of the Ru tradition and are bound by specific genre conventions, as well as being subject to the ethnocentric and androcentric biases of other Ru texts.[13] They are also a genre of writing that seeks not only to commemorate the dead but to rank them according to family prestige and individual attainment.[14] In general, historical information that details individual rank and attainment is not information that we have for women in the historical record; however, in the early medieval period, such emerging entombed biographies do document the lives of cultural outsiders to the Ru tradition, both women and ethnic Others. Even though the data that comes from these texts is itself influenced by tropes and genre conventions, this is data that we simply do not have in any other form and it is therefore invaluable for our study, which seeks to ask new questions about women's lives in the medieval period. By critically utilizing these biographies alongside other source materials, we will meet many women of the empress dowager's time who also took up new social roles in society that helped to bring Buddhist women into the mainstream of medieval Chinese political life. With their bodies interned at the cluster of Northern Wei imperial tombs north of Luoyang and their names and biographies etched in stone within, we will meet Buddhist nuns, Buddhist administrators, female bureaucrats of the Northern Wei court, and high-ranking women of the inner chambers who all had some affiliation with Buddhism. We will even meet women who were buried alone in the sixth century without reference to their male kin.[15] Taken together, these women's lives document a tremendous change in how women lived their traditions in the context of urban, Buddhist, and multicultural life in Luoyang, and they track a course toward the accession of the only woman to ever rule China with the male title of "emperor", Wu Zetian or Emperor Wu Zhao. Finally, because this genre of literature seeks to appraise and rank, and because Buddhist affiliation in the medieval period provided a mechanism to adjudicate women and their work, these biographies contain information on the social standing and gender performance of Buddhist women from the medieval period who were deeply engaged in the reinvention of tradition in their time.[16]

Historical studies often highlight "great men of history," a tendency both motivated and described by the nineteenth-century Scottish philosopher Thomas Carlyle's dictum that "The history of the world is but the biography of great men."[17] In turn, studies in women's history have sometimes looked like companion texts, showing that women, too, were great and that women, too, shaped history. Empress Dowager Ling certainly was great. Her work had a long-lasting impact on the development of Buddhism and Buddhist ideas of monarchy in East Asia. I do not, however, write this book as a "great women of history" project. Instead, with this study, I embed the empress dowager deeply within her society to show the complex networks of persons, ideas, and institutions that enabled her to do the work that she did. In so doing, I embrace texts that are on the periphery of normative political history. Sources like Buddhist texts, Buddhist donor inscriptions, entombed biographies, and Buddhist images and statuary allow me to bring to life a political history that, until now, has not been told. To put this differently, the use of sources peripheral to imperial power allows me to tell a story that, until now, has only been told from the center of imperial power itself. In so doing, I join other feminist scholars of history in their insistence that feminist history must not affirm patriarchal modes of power and the dissemination of said power but that it must seek to overturn such ways of thinking about the past and thereby radically reenvision the social structures of the world in which we live.[18]

In the case of Empress Dowager Ling, her physical move from the periphery to the center—from being born without a recorded name at the far edge of an empire to dying as the leader of the court in the capital city—presents an opportune case study in feminist history. As I will show, if we adopt the historical method of reading from the center of power, we see the empress dowager described as licentious, indulgent, and dangerous. If, however, we read from sources that are peripheral to normative historiography, we see her as acutely involved in multifarious ways across networks of social forces that worked to shift that very center of power and thereby make it possible for a woman like Emperor Wu Zhao of the Tang to fully take control of it 150 years later. By adopting the methodology of Buddhist feminist historiography, which highlights social embeddedness and reads from both the center and the periphery of power and history, I tell a bigger story than that of just two women. The story I tell is one of shifting notions of what it meant to be a woman and what it meant to be a ruler in a time of the rapid reinvention of tradition, and I aim to show that this shift—brought about in no small part from the spread of Buddhism in the period—saw the emergence of profoundly new and arguably revolutionary social roles for women, roles that put them at the center of public life.

1

Luoyang Reborn

In the year 515, Empress Dowager Ling commissioned the construction of the tallest building that anybody in the then known world had ever seen. The building was a Buddhist stūpa, otherwise known as a pagoda, and it stood in the center of her capital city, Luoyang. Positioned in front of the palace on the west side of the central avenue, the stūpa was the showcase structure within the palace's own religio-political complex, the Eternal Peace Monastery (Yongning si). Nine stories tall and covered with rich decoration, the stūpa soared high into the sky like a glimmering jewel. Completed in the year 519, this veritable wonder of the world stood for less than a decade. It was destroyed by fire after the empress dowager's murder in 528, when Luoyang was sacked.

The empress dowager's Luoyang must have seemed modern and extravagant to everyone who visited the city; however, in the year 494, when the Northern Wei moved its capital there, Luoyang was in ruins. Having served as the capital city for a number of prior empires—most notably that of the Eastern Han (23–220)—the city of Luoyang was synonymous with imperial rule in early and medieval China. Its very name still evokes ancient capitals and their cycles of rise and decline. For those people in Northern Wei era Luoyang who saw the capital rebuilt, the feeling they had must have been one of tremendous energy and excitement. In the year 515, when the empress dowager began her regency, the city had been resurrected with an imposing palatial complex, with Budddhist monasteries and nunneries of all varieties, and with the late Emperor Xuanwu interred in a luxurious tomb at the imperial burial site north of the city. The neighborhoods and markets of the city were flourishing, and construction at the Buddhist cave site at Longmen had begun. By the year 519, the empress dowager's signature stūpa at the Eternal Peace Monastery was completed, as were many other majestic Buddhist complexes. Construction at Longmen had continued, with cavernous and highly decorated grottos being added month after month. Luoyang was reborn in majestic splendor.

Luoyang was built on the north bank of the Luo River, a tributary of the Yellow River, along a north-south axis and inside an enclosing wall. The palace was at the north end of the city, and its main entrance faced the central avenue, which bisected the city's markets and living quarters. During the Eastern Han, important structures of imperial legitimation were built just outside the city's southern gate, near the river. Two of these structures are important to our story of the formation of rule by Buddhist women in the medieval period: The imperial observatory or the numinous platform (*lingtai*) and the bright hall (*mingtang*). The Eastern Han court entombed their royals at a site east of the city called Mount Mang. The Northern Wei capital at Luoyang maintained much of this structure, burying their imperial dead at Mount Mang, constructing their palace at the northern end of the enclosed city, and building up the site of the Eastern Han numinous platform at the south of the city. Even in their prior northern capital of Pingcheng (modern-day Datong), they utilized the Han court's imperial structures and built a bright hall for the purpose of their own rituals of political legitimation.[1]

As akin to each other as Han and Northern Wei Luoyang were in their bones, two important differences between them remained in their connective tissue. The first of these differences concerned Buddhism. Buddhist persons, ideas, and texts started to arrive in the central plains of China along the Yellow River basin sometime during the Eastern Han period; however, their presence was limited and the Han court never exclusively patronized the Buddhist religion. By the time of the founding of the Northern Wei, Buddhist persons and things of all types had spread rapidly throughout both the northern reaches of the old Han territories and the central plains. Unlike its Han predecessor, then, Northern Wei era Luoyang was a Buddhist city. And, like Buddhism itself, it was also multiethnic. Ruled over by the Taghbach imperial clan and replete with the presence of other Inner Asian traders, translators, and royals, Northern Wei era Luoyang looked, smelled, and tasted differently than Han era Luoyang did. Small glimpses of this can be found in the archeological record, where some statues of men have beards and boots that identify them as peoples from the Inner Asian steppe and where some tombs have identifiably Zoroastrian funerary beds.[2] But even in this Northern Wei multi-ethnic capital, we can discern connection to the Han dynasty. The Han rulers had annexed the so-called "western regions" (*xiyu*), which were accessed from the central plains through the Hexi corridor and included large segments of Inner Asia that we today commonly call the Chinese province of Xinjiang. The Han rulers and politicians were thereby early facilitators of a long process of cultural exchange and confrontation along the

Silk Roads, and their Luoyang was also markedly diverse in terms of its population. By the time of the Northern Wei, trade routes between the central plains and the western regions were well traveled and increasing numbers of peoples of different origin lived in the big cities along them, including Luoyang at the eastern edge of the network.

The empress dowager was born in Anding, a prefecture that would have been at the western edge of the territory occupied by the Han empire prior to its annexation of the western regions. This region, just at the entrance to the Hexi corridor through modern-day Gansu province and along the ancient Silk Roads that connected the Han empire with its Western Protectorate, served as a conduit between the major centers of the Sinitic, Iranian, and Indic worlds. It was a region of the medieval world characterized by ethnic, cultural, and linguistic diversity and hybridity. It was also characterized by Buddhism. Situated geographically between the two most famous centers for Buddhist textual translation that produced the scriptures most germane to the practice of Buddhism across East Asia—Guzang (modern-day Wuwei), where the translator Dharmakṣema (Ch. Tan Wuchen; 385–433) worked, and Chang'an, where Kumārajīva worked (Ch. Jiumoluoshi 334–413)—the region from which the empress dowager and her family hailed would have been a place where Buddhist objects, people, and texts commonly circulated. During the first three decades of the fifth century, this region also saw the creation of early Buddhist grottos that would come to be so important to the Northern Wei's own projects of Buddhist grotto building: Both Tianti shan and Maiji shan, with their colossal Buddhas, are near the well-traversed routes that lead to major centers and cities in the region. Furthermore, if one continues the journey from Chang'an, through the empress dowager's ancestral home, to Guzang, and then beyond, one would eventually encounter Dunhuang, the great monastic city on the Silk Road that Dharmakṣema came from, and much further, the kingdom of Kucha, where Kumārajīva was famously imprisoned and translated Buddhist scripture.

In a sense, then, the empress dowager's own arrival in the capital reflects much of the cultural and demographic change that all the old Han territories were experiencing in the reformation of empire during the medieval period: Just as she came to Luoyang as a Buddhist woman from a culturally hybrid region at the periphery of the old Han empire, so too did the cultural networks that she was embedded in. Having been born in the latter half of the fifth century, just on the coattails of famous Buddhist translation projects and building projects that were formative for the development of East Asian forms of Buddhism throughout the medieval period, she arrived in the central plains as part of a Buddhist vanguard from the regions of the empire where Buddhism was flourishing most impressively. The story of her move to the central plains and her rise in power therefore tracks the movement of both Buddhist ideas and multicultural life to a major center of power: Luoyang. Although the empress dowager likely

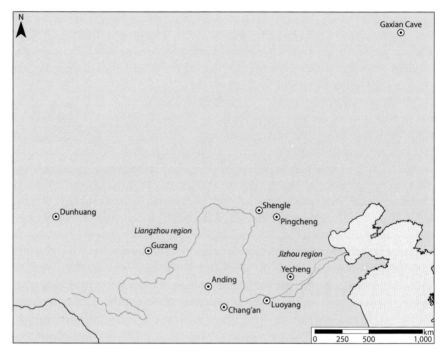

MAP 1. Places and territories discussed that were under Northern Wei jurisdiction in the sixth century and that are important to the peoples and events discussed in this study. © Andrew MacIver.

came directly to Luoyang from her family's region in Gansu, her benefactor at court—her aunt, the Buddhist nun Sengzhi—took a much longer route. With the Northern Wei's political takeover of the empress dowager's ancestral lands in the mid-fifth century, the nun Sengzhi went first to their northern capital of Pingcheng—a trip of almost two thousand kilometers. Hence, when we think about the arrival of the Northern Wei court in Luoyang in the year 494, we need to think not only of those who ruled it but of the collection of people that they ruled over, the people who moved with them and who brought their families and their religions with them to the central plains.

In this chapter we journey to the rebuilt and resplendent capital city, Luoyang. Our aim on this journey is to explore the urban life and culture of the city that both sustained and created the empress dowager and that she, in turn, sustained and created. In doing this, we consider the intersecting vectors of ethnicity, religion, and gender that converged in the capital. We concentrate on these three cultural vectors in order to introduce important characteristics of the world that the empress dowager lived in and therefore to understand this story of the rise of Buddhist women in public and political positions in early medieval China.

LIFE IN THE GLIMMERING CITY

Luoyang served as the Northern Wei capital for a mere forty years, and only in its full splendor for approximately fifteen of those. It was regarded as a wonder of the world in its time, and then it was destroyed. Fortunately for us, one man journeyed back to the ruined capital some twenty years after its demise and wrote a retrospective of the broken city that had been so famed for its Buddhist opulence. This man was named Yang Xuanzhi (fl. fifth century) and his text is called the *Record of Buddhist Monasteries in Luoyang* (Luoyang qielan ji). Yang had worked directly for the empress dowager during the final era of her reign.[3] After her death and the turbulent ultimate demise of the Northern Wei, Yang relocated to the new center of power, a city called Yecheng, and there he served the Eastern Wei (534–50), which is known to have been the successor of the Northern Wei. Yang states in his *Record* that he was sent back from Yecheng to Luoyang in order to write the official memoir of the old capital's most resplendent Buddhist structures after their sacking and demise.[4] His text is less journalistic than it is commemorative; seeking to recall the splendor of Luoyang's Buddhism after its ruin, Yang returned to the destroyed city in the year 547. His record provides the most detailed description of the empress dowager's stūpa at the Eternal Peace Monastery that we have.[5] It is the first building that Yang features in his *Record* and he states that it was built by the imperial decree of Empress Dowager Ling and contained more than one thousand rooms for monks. Various records attest to the structure rising ninety *zhang* in to the sky. This would be approximately 248 meters, or the height of more than two American football fields.[6] The whole structure was embellished with fineries the likes of which dazzled the semimythical founder of Chan Buddhism, Bodhidharma (fl. 6th c.), who had seen the entire Buddhist world in his lifetime and considered the monastery to be without comparison.[7] Regarding the workmanship and finery of the stūpa, Yang writes:

> Within the precincts [of the monastery] was a nine-story pagoda built with a wooden frame. Rising nine hundred feet above the ground, it formed the base for a mast that rose another hundred feet. Together they soared one thousand feet above the ground. You could see it even at a distance of a hundred *li* from the capital. In the course of excavating for the construction of the monastery, thirty golden statues were found deep underground. The empress dowager regarded them as proof of the sincerity of her faith. As a result, she spent all the more lavishly on its construction.
>
> On the top of the mast was a golden vase inlaid with precious stones, with a capacity of twenty-five piculs. Underneath the jeweled vase were thirty tiers of golden plates. In addition, chains linked the mast with each of the four corners

of the pagoda. Golden bells, each about the size of a one-picul jar, were also suspended from the link works.

There were nine roofs, one for each story, with golden bells suspended from the corner of each one, totaling one hundred twenty in all. The pagoda had four sides, each having three doors and six windows, all painted in vermilion lacquer. Each door had five rows of gold studs. Altogether there were 5,400 studs on twenty-four panels of twelve double doors. In addition, the doors were adorned with gold ring knockers. The construction embodied the best masonry and carpentry and its design reached the limit of ingenuity. Its excellence as Buddhist architecture was almost unimaginable. Its carved pillars and gold doorknockers fascinated the eye. When the bells chimed in harmony deep in a windy night, they could be heard over ten *li* away.[8]

According to the archaeological record of the Eternal Peace Monastery, the complex was located a mere five hundred meters from the south gate of the palace, and the two buildings were the tallest structures in Luoyang.[9] Furthermore, Yang's *Record* states that certain rooms in the monastery were used to house both political prisoners and buddha images given to the Northern Wei court from foreign countries.[10] Although all that remains of the complex is the base of its gigantic and resplendent pagoda, which was said to be the tallest building in the known world,[11] excavations of the site have revealed several statuary and ornamental fragments that suggest the opulence of the décor and, perhaps, something about the Buddhists of Luoyang themselves. For example, we can determine that many of the excavated statuary heads are not those of buddhas or Buddhist figures, since they bear the hairstyles and caps of the social elite of the time and show ethnic variation.[12]

The empress dowager's Luoyang was a wonder. Not only did her own project at the Eternal Peace Monastery captivate all those who saw it up close and from afar but the entire city was filled with lesser, though still glimmering, structures. Of the rise of Buddhist infrastructure in Luoyang by the late Northern Wei, Yang boasts:

> During the Yongjia (307–313) period of the Jin dynasty, there were only forty-two Buddhist temples [in Luoyang], but when the imperial Wei received the plan to develop the residences of the Song-Luo area (i.e., by moving the capital there) sincere belief overflowed and multiplied and dharma teachings recovered and prospered. Lords, marquis, and nobles cast off their elephants and horses (as donations) just as though they were taking off their shoes. Commoners and influential families gave up their wealth and treasures as if they were just old relics. As such, the brightness accelerated, combing rows of precious pagodas side-by-side, competing to write their brilliance across the skies and vying to imitate the shadows of mountains. Golden shrines and the numinous (*ling*) platform were as high and wide as the Apang [Palaces of the Qin Dynasty (221–207 BCE)].[13]

Not only was the empress dowager's capital visually stunning; it was also lively. Yang's *Record* describes the activities that took place in these Buddhist buildings that competed with mountains, and his description is positively carnivalesque. For example, in his description of the imperially funded Nunnery of the Joyous View (Jingle si), Yang records that the nuns in residence enjoyed a splendid life as urban socialites, hosting a variety of entertainment opportunities for the people of the city. The Nunnery of the Joyous View faced directly toward the Eternal Peace Monastery, and I suspect that its name, "Joyous View," recalls its vista. The nunnery is described as a place of leisure with lush, shady gardens where the people came to enjoy a good show. The description of the shows at the nunnery reads:

> At the time of the "great fast" [six monthly fasts, *posadha*],[14] there was constant music performed by female entertainers: the sounds of their songs coiled around the beams of the roof and the sleeves of the dancers swirled around with the melodies from the instruments, bringing wondrous enchantment.
>
> As this was a nunnery, men were not able to enter. Those who were allowed to look considered it to be like arriving in paradise. After the death of Prince Wenxian, temple restrictions were more lenient and the commoners went in and out without obstruction. Thereupon, [Yuan] Yue, prince of Runan, who was the brother of Wenxian, renovated the nunnery and summoned all manner of musical performers to display their talents inside the nunnery.
>
> Strange birds and rare beasts danced in the courtyards and flew into the sky, creating an illusion the likes of which nobody had ever seen. Bizarre and heterodox arts were all arrayed: "skinning the donkey," "pulling out of the well," and planting a date seed that would instantly bear fruit that everybody could eat.[15] The ladies and gentlemen who saw the performances were utterly bewildered.[16]

The Nunnery of the Joyous View was established by a prince of the imperial house named Yuan Yi (487–520). Yuan Yi was the lover of the empress dowager after the death of Emperor Xuanwu, who was his half-brother, and he therefore came from the highest strata of the imperial elite. That he was both the lover of the empress dowager and the chief patron of the nunnery should assure us that the empress dowager knew of and sanctioned the jubilant atmosphere contained within. The story of this nunnery becomes even more fascinating after Yuan Yi's death in 520. On his death, his full brother, Yuan Yue (494–533)—whom we will meet again—is said to have changed the rules of the nunnery so that both men and women could enter its gates and behold the magical spectacle within. As he is written about in the official dynastic history of the Northern Wei, Yue stands out as a transgressive character. His official biography describes him as "queer by nature," while it also records that he undertook heterodox religious practices and engaged in homosexual relationships.[17] Such an explicit chronicle of homosexual activities among the ruling elite is extraordinarily rare in the writings of the Ru and stands out dramatically as a marker of difference in the biography of Yue. That Yue was the patron of the Nunnery of the Joyous View and that his sex life was presumably known in his own lifetime suggests that Luoyang Buddhism was not the Buddhism of texts, doctrine, meditation, and the monastic elite. Luoyang Buddhism was widely diverse and the *Record* narrates all kinds of persons and activities that enjoyed Luoyang's cultural life from inside Buddhist spaces.

In a similar explanation of the types of social activities that the nuns of Luoyang enjoyed, when discussing a eunuch-funded nunnery in the heart of the city that was constructed for high-ranking women of the court, the *Record* states that the nunnery was home to one statue of a buddha as well as two statues of bodhisattvas that were taken on procession on the seventh day of the fourth month of the year. This procession was matched in fanfare by another procession undertaken by the private temple of another of the empress dowager's courtiers. That procession is also described in carnivalesque terms: It was a party with all manner of enjoyments. The description runs:

> On the fourth day of the fourth month,[18] this statue was always taken out and pulled by *bi-xie* and lions in front and with sword swallowers, fire spitters, and galloping horses at the sides, and with unordinary things like flag-staff climbers and rope walkers. With such strange tricks and bizarre clothing in the capital city, they were unmatched in the capital. Wherever the statue stopped, spectators would encircle it like a wall. Carrying each other and jumping about, it often happened that people died.[19]

Although the commissioning of glamourous and resplendent Buddhist pleasure gardens and leisure spaces in Luoyang was a project of the wealthy, the *Record* details how these spaces functioned to cut across class and social barriers. The public of Luoyang enjoyed themselves in Buddhist monasteries that were open to them and that offered them entertainment, spectacle, celebration, and magic.

Beyond temples and their activities, one act of Buddhist patronage that the public of the city broadly engaged in was the commissioning of Buddhist statuary. Although the cost for the creation of buddha images in the Northern Wei era was exorbitant, it was still a widely popular practice that transcended class barriers. Amy McNair has conjecturally calculated the cost of creating a niche with an image and estimates that the cost of a niche of 3.1 square meters would be approximately equal to half the year's wage of a government official.[20] Thus, the Buddhist grottos in Longmen and other similar sites across the empire should only have been accessible to wealthy donors, but that was not the case. As we will explore in chapter 4, epigraphical sources contain the patronage records of collective village societies that pooled their wealth in order to build Buddhist statuary and images. Furthermore, the epigraphical record also bears witness to lone donors of lesser means who used their limited resources to build statuary. Such donors were sometimes found among the common people of pious faith. One example of such an inscription is the Zhai Man stele analyzed and translated by Dorothy Wong.[21] As to the great expense of the stele, the donor, Zhai Man, says that not only that he bankrupted his family to build a statue of the future buddha, Maitreya, but also that he had to forsake his own wife.[22]

Amy McNair understands this donor's claim to have bankrupted his family as a rhetorical device that exaggerated his piety in order to ensure that his investment in spiritual life would be returned at a high rate. McNair argues that donors participated in a religious economy of the "Karmic Gift" whereby,[23] on commissioning the image of a buddha, an intangible karmic exchange was made between the support of the image from the donors and the support of the buddha to the donors.[24] This "Karmic Gift" would therefore be a financial transaction that individuals and groups undertook in order to create positive karmic fruits for themselves, their kin, and their empire. They evidently made this financial exchange in huge numbers, as the economy of merit exchange took place in the early medieval period on a large scale.

MEDIEVAL MULTICULTURALISM

Unlike the Han empire, the Northern Wei was not ruled by Han peoples who thought of the central plains as their ancestral homeland. The rulers of the Northern Wei court traced their native lands to regions of the modern Chinese provinces of Inner Mongolia and Heilongjiang. These two areas are very different: the central plains are flat and arid; the northern regions of Heilongjiang are lushly forested with low mountains. Fed by the Yellow River, the central plains have long been settled owing to attractiveness of the land's rich soil; meeting eventually with the Mongolian grasslands, Inner Mongolia and its eastern neighbor of Heilongjiang, on the other hand, are regions of the world where horse breeding and seasonal migration have provided the means of food and mobility. As previously discussed, the peoples who settled on the central plains are known through the ethnonym of "Han," whereas the peoples who founded the Northern Wei are known through the reconstructed ethnonym of "Taghbach." The Taghbach are believed to be a subgroup of the larger Inner Asian *Serbi (Ch. Xianbei) ethnogroup.[25] These rulers from Inner Asia spoke a language related to modern Mongolian,[26] but during the latter half of the dynasty they also began speaking the language of the Han peoples from the central plains at court and, in 494, took the Han-styled name of "Yuan" as their own, making it the name of the ruling clan of the Northern Wei. Therefore, when I discuss members of the imperial clan who died prior to 494, I use the ethnonym "Taghbach" in my analysis; however, for members of the imperial clan who died after 494, I use their adopted name "Yuan."

The Northern Wei was a northern empire of the Southern and Northern Dynasties period (Nanbeichao) (420–589), a time of political and social division that is bookended by the fall of the Han in 220 and reunification by the Sui dynasts in 581 (–618). The Northern Wei was arguably the most successful of the northern polities during this time, which is demonstrated by the fact that they expanded their southern border south of the Yellow River and established their capital in Luoyang. In general, the Southern and Northern Dynasties period was characterized by dramatic transitions brought about through dual migrations. Areas south of the Yangzi River were settled by southward-moving migrants from the old Han empire in response to increased conquest of prior Han territories by Inner Asian populations.[27] The Northern Wei is considered a "conquest dynasty" of this sort in the writings of the Ru scholars because it was a collective of Inner Asian peoples ruled over by the Taghbach who moved their southern border far into the territories of the old Han dynasty and thereby spread their cultural, military, and political traditions across the central plains. Jennifer Holmgren argues that the Northern Wei's identification as a "conquest dynasty" has affected its status as a legitimate topic of historical inquiry in modern scholarship.[28] In other words, until recently, there has not been adequate scholarly interest in the study of the Northern Wei state or its court in any language because of the enduring legacy of cultural chauvinism and ethnocentrism in political and literary texts written by the Ru scholars, which have long dominated the study of Chinese history. Despite the comparative lack of secondary scholarship on the Northern Wei, Scott Pearce argues compellingly for a recognition of the empire's importance for the later development of Chinese and East Asian history by characterizing the empire as a formative example of the type of governments created by various Inner Asian populations, which would continue to overtake large swaths of the Chinese heartland for the remainder of the first two millennia.[29]

In the context of the Southern and Northern Dynasties, and as written about by the Ru, Han peoples were considered those who traced their received history through a lineage of imperial dynasties by using a compendium of texts composed in their own language. The northern dynasties were ruled over by cultural Others to the Han peoples—that is, ethnically different persons who did not compose texts in their original languages and who had largely been nomadic, horse-breeding groups unified along linguistic and familial lines. During the Han era, these groups were judged to be "primitive" and hence inferior to Han peoples owing to their lack of proximity to the imperial center.[30] In this study, the English rendering non-Han is used to refer to these groups, which, in Ru texts before the Tang are referred to by more generic terms such as hu (mounted nomads) or fan (foreigner).[31] In using the term non-Han, I again follow Abramson who argues that the term adequately expresses the outsider identity of these peoples without being burdened by the clear pejorative meanings of indigenous terms in Literary Chinese, even though those pejorative meanings were certainly in use at the time in question. Therefore, the present study employs Abramson's terms Han and non-Han to refer to the ethnic Self in historiographical and political writings of the Ru scholars and the peoples that were considered ethnic Others in these same writings. I use these terms with the caveat that they are imperfect but important. Although we know that people and families had a variety of mixed family lineages, and although we know that lineage falsification was common, we also know that these ideas of cultural insiders and cultural outsiders are a formative feature of historiography from the period, and they are important for understanding the cultural practices and attitudes evoked throughout this study.

The term *non-Han* therefore encompasses many different ethnic and cultural groups that Han peoples came in contact with and wrote about. For our purposes here, we will focus on the Taghbach. The histories and social customs of the Serbi people, from whom the Taghbach are believed to have been descended, are found in the annals of Chinese historiography that describe Han interactions with non-Han peoples. An example of such annotation is retained in the *Later History of the Han* (Hou Han shu), which tells us that the Serbi took their name from a mountain of the same name,[32] that they had large wedding ceremonies wherein they cut their hair for the one and only time in their lives,[33] and that the animals they hunted provided luxurious and warm pelts that they used for fine jackets.[34] A longer narrative of the foundation of the Taghbach is chronicled in a genealogy from the "Prefatory Annals" (Xuji) of the dynastic history of the Northern Wei, the *Book of the Wei*, which, though written in the Literary Chinese of the Ru scholars, is said to have been derived from Taghbach oral history.[35] This genealogy says that the ethnic birthplace of the Taghbach is found in modern-day Heilongjiang province in a mountainous area home to the Gaxian Cave (Gaxian dong). As Charles Holcombe notes, however, there is an inherent problem in locating the birthplace of a nomadic group. He argues that what does appear to be plausible is that by the 440s, Northern Wei Emperor Taiwu (r. 424–52) "came to believe this cave contained his family's old ancestral temple."[36] Emperor Taiwu therefore sent his court secretary, Li Chang (fl. fifth century), on a mission to examine the site. After arriving there, Li Chang decided that this cave was the home of the original Serbi clan. He therefore undertook rituals for the ancestors within the cave, and in 443 he carved an inscription in 201 Chinese characters that is still in situ today.[37] A recent archeological survey of the site records the existence of ritual structures inside the cave and therefore supports the idea that rituals were undertaken there at some early date, though we have no way of knowing if such rituals predate Emperor Taiwu's official acknowledgement of the cave as the ancestral temple of his clan.[38] The cave is still an active location for ritual today, and visitors come to circumambulate the central ritual platform while making offerings to ancient Taghbach ancestors.[39]

Returning to the Taghbach lineage preserved in the "Prefatory Annals" of the *Book of the Wei*, we read that simultaneous to the Eastern Han era the Taghbach were under the direction of the sixth of their clan patriarchs, Taghbach Tuiyin, and had begun a southern migration, settling by a large marsh in the grasslands of Inner Mongolia, where they are said to have stayed for seven generations.[40] After this, the record relates, the group was divided into eight subgroups,[41] some coming under the jurisdiction of the Eastern Han court and some establishing independent lineages.[42] Subsequently, according to the record, the remaining Taghbach subgroup succeeded in consolidating its rule and rising up as an independent political entity to eventually establish the Northern Wei in the year 386. The name of this empire hearkens back to a prior northern polity, the Kingdom of Wei (220–66), which also had its capital in Luoyang.[43] Although the history of the Taghbach is seamlessly articulated in these "Prefatory Annals," we must treat the text with skepticism given its anachronistic date, the fact that it is retained in the Literary Chinese of the Ru scholars (and not the Taghbach language), and also because it fits into the particular genre of dynastic history.[44]

First establishing a new sort of empire beyond the northern periphery of the old Han territories, the Taghbach leaders of the Northern Wei eventually made their way south to the northern reaches of the old Han territories and founded their capital city at Pingcheng. They also relocated much of their newly conquered subjects into cities. One estimate suggests that no less than fifty-eight thousand lone persons as well as one hundred thousand households were relocated to Pingcheng before the year 494.[45] This relocation of subjects went hand-in-hand with the Northern Wei dynasts' other grand project of population settlement, which they undertook in the 480s and largely in the newly conquered territories along the Yellow River plain: the establishment of an equal-field system that would see regulated amounts of agricultural land allotted, for the most part, to Han populations.[46] This system remained relatively unchanged throughout the Tang empire and was later used in Japan.[47] In sum, the story of the building of the Northern Wei empire is a story of the resettlement of large amounts of northern peoples into newly built cities in the north alongside the later redistribution of newly conquered agricultural lands to Han people in the Yellow River plains. Notably, this policy of land allocation included the distribution of land to women as well as to men.[48] It did not, however, include populations of largely non-Han peoples from the northern garrisons, and Scott Pearce argues that this failure to incorporate the northern garrisons into the economic life of the dynasty after its move to Luoyang is what would bring about the court's own downfall. In 528, militarized groups from these northern garrisons would arrive at Luoyang, sack the city, murder the empress dowager and the emperor, and bring about the fall of the Northern Wei.[49]

Although the Taghbach leaders that would become the dynasts of the Northern Wei ruled their polity as the heads of the military known in their own language as *khagan* (khan in later Mongolian usage), during the Northern Wei era they adopted the Sinitic tradition's title of "emperor." Under such Han-styled leadership, they came south to the Yellow River plains and rebuilt their capital in Luoyang with an emperor ruling from the capital instead of on the frontlines of the military as a khagan would. The move to Luoyang was symbolic but also strategic: Luoyang had long been a stronghold of Han infrastructure, statecraft, and economy.[50] Resettling the capital in Luoyang corresponded with a different kind of project developing among the ruling elite: the radical effort to remake the court from an Inner Asian polity into a type of government that more closely resembled that of the Han empire. This effort at remaking the government, its policies, and its administration reached its high point under the reign of Emperor Xiaowen, whose project of cultural and political reinvention, based on the original Chinese term *hanhua*, is often referred to as "Sinification." Xiaowen's Sinification program reached its apex in the 490s and included the adoption of a bureaucratic system modeled after the Han court, the use of the Literary Chinese for court documents, the conversion of non-Han names at court to Han ones,[51] and the employment of both Han dress and Han individuals at court.[52]

If we consider Han peoples as the ethnic Self in the writings of the Ru in Literary Chinese and the Taghbach as an example of the ethnic Other in those same writings, we see that the term *Sinification* exposes what Northern Wei historiographers sought to express about the Taghbach. Not arguing for the cultural parity of their non-Han traditions with those of the Han, they instead created a narrative that the Taghbach were holders of the very same heritage. We see this effort at cultural—perhaps, even, ethnic—invention in the opening words of the previously discussed "Prefatory Annals" from the *Book of the Wei*, which are said to chronicle the Taghbach's indigenous, oral history. The text begins as follows:[53]

> In ancient times, the Yellow Emperor[54] had twenty-five sons; those who stayed with him became the descendants of Han culture, those who went outside were scattered in the wilderness. Changyi[55] had a few sons and he conferred the northern lands on them. Within this land there was the great Mountain of the Serbi and from this they took their name. After this, for generations, they became the lords and elders who ruled over the far north, spreading out over the vast wilds while following the movements of their cattle. They used archery for hunting and their customs were pure and uncomplicated. They were accustomed to simplicity and ease and, as such, they had not developed writing. For records, they carved notches into wood and that was all, and for worldly matters both near and far, these were conferred and transferred between men. These resemble the records and registries of the court historians.[56]

This opening to the "Prefatory Annals" of the *Book of the Wei* does more than introduce the nomadic origins of the Taghbach; it also situates them within the larger framework of Chinese historiography by positing that the Taghbach people are descendants of the Yellow Emperor and that they kept records, albeit simple ones, just like their brethren in the Han regions of the empire. Tian Yuqing has analyzed the creation of this narrative as it is retained in the *Book of the Wei*. In his analysis, the received text is the culmination of an ongoing process of historiography from the time of the founding emperor of the Northern Wei, Taghbach

FIGURE 2. Burial figurine of Taghbach horseman from the Northern Wei. Piece is now held at the Musée Cernuschi in Paris, France.

FIGURE 3. Emperor Xiaowen and his procession. Originally carved in the Central Guyang Grotto in Longmen. Circa 522. Now held in the Metropolitan Museum of Art in New York.

Gui (r. 386–409), in the late fourth century, through to Wei Shou's compilation in the sixth century, which relied, in part, on Taghbach oral history though it placed that history in the service of constructing a national history.[57] Such a national history, written by elite scholars in a genre of literature strongly associated with Han culture and politics, took on the flavor of a Han history, including the narrative of the development of civilization and writing. In sum, Tian argues that the *Book of the Wei*'s version of Taghbach historiography should not be considered false; rather, he suggests that it is an outcome of the process of reinvention that the Taghbach leaders themselves embarked on during the making of the Northern Wei empire.[58] Similarly, it is also the case that the genealogy of the ancestors of the Taghbach house that is delineated in the *Book of the Wei* is matched one-for-one with the genealogy of the Han emperors.[59]

Emperor Xiaowen was the emperor who oversaw the move of the capital from Pingcheng to Luoyang in 494, and the story of his relations with his first-born son reveals that the Taghbach adoption of Han cultural norms during their migration south was not without contention. Crown Prince Yuan Xun (483–97) was born in the northern capital of Pingcheng and migrated to the southern capital of Luoyang with his father, Emperor Xiaowen, and the entire court.

Unfortunately for the father/emperor, the son/prince was not fond of Luoyang. The latter's biography in the *Book of the Wei* describes how he repeatedly tried to sneak away from Luoyang to return north but also how his father and his father's advisors prevented him from doing so. In one attempt at escape, he murdered his own advisor who wanted to stop him from fleeing. The biography also tells us that the crown prince was not interested in study (presumably in texts of the Han literary tradition) and that he chafed against the expected comportment and dress of the Han-styled official that he was supposed to be. Ultimately, the crown prince was stripped of his titles and then poisoned to death by his father's own officials at the age of fourteen. He was buried like a commoner somewhere to the south of the city.[60]

FOUNDATIONS OF BUDDHIST KINGSHIP

Beyond the Northern Wei court's official policy of Sinification, the rulers of the court in the latter half of the dynastic line also participated in cultural politics through their patronage of Buddhism. On his accession in 452, the mid-Northern Wei ruler, Emperor Wencheng (r. 452–65), is said to have proclaimed Buddhism as the state religion. The *Book of the Wei* tells us that he decreed the following:

> He who deems life and death equal sighs in admiration at [the Buddha's] penetrating insight, and he who observes the [deep] sense of his writings values his subtle understanding. [Buddhism] supports the regulations and prohibitions of kingly government, it augments the good-naturedness of the benevolent and the wise; it repels and rejects all evil, and opens one's eyes to true enlightenment. Therefore since previous dynasties none has but honoured and revered it, and likewise for our ruling house it has always been a matter of veneration.[61]

This formal declaration of the empire's support for the tradition of Buddhism illustrates how the ruling elite sought to use religion in their governance and in the legitimation of their own power. They did not, however, always or solely use Buddhism to do this. Emperor Wencheng's grandfather and predecessor, Emperor Taiwu (r. 424–52) violently suppressed Buddhists and their institutions, instead establishing Celestial Masters Daoism as his state religion.[62] Taiwu supported the use of Daoism for statecraft because it offered a radically new invention of tradition that allowed him to place himself at the center.[63] The emperor's wager was, however, unsuccessful; with Buddhism fast becoming the religion of his empire, the dynasty needed to pivot toward the adoption of this tradition in order to survive.

Wencheng's establishment of Buddhism as a state religion coincided with his imperial support for the commencement of the building of the early stratum of the Buddhist grottos at Yungang, just outside the then-Northern Wei capital of

FIGURE 4. A partial overview of the Northern Wei cliffside at Yungang showing its colossal buddha rulers. These caves are all circa 450s. Photo is author's own.

Pingcheng. Although there is debate over the precise date of the initial building of the grottos, most scholars agree on their intention. The original five grottos at Yungang were made to represent the four founding rulers of the dynasty, as well as the then-current ruler, Wencheng.[64] The original strata of grottos at Yungang were commissioned by Emperor Wencheng in consultation with the highest-ranking Buddhist monk of the empire, a man known as Tanyao (fl. 450).[65] The construction of Northern Wei emperors as forms and faces of monumental Buddha images at Yungang was a genre of imperial Buddhist practice that continued to develop throughout the dynasty. When the court moved the capital to Luoyang, they soon also funded the construction of the Buddhist grottos at Longmen.

It is arguably the case that women who held political profiles during the Northern Wei era also sought to produce images of themselves as buddhas in the monumental grottos at Yungang and Longmen. This tradition appears to have begun with a powerful empress dowager who ruled earlier than did Empress Dowager Ling. As empress to Wencheng, the woman who came to be called Empress Dowager (*huanghou*) Wenming (442–90) was regent for two emperors—the father, Emperor Xianwen (r. 465–71), and the son who ruled after him, Emperor Xiaowen (r. 471–99).[66] According to the histories of this period in the *Book of the Wei*, this empress dowager had a hand in putting to death Xianwen's birth mother, taking power as regent herself afterward. When Xianwen came of age, an intense power struggle ensued, one that saw Xianwen becoming the earliest recorded "retired emperor" in the year 471 and at the young age of seventeen. Xianwen was then murdered five years later, but by that time his eldest son, the nine-year-old Emperor Xiaowen, had already been installed on the throne for the five years following his father's early retirement. His regent was Empress Dowager Wenming who was his grandfather's empress but who was not his own grandmother. By the standards of the Northern Wei court, Emperor Xiaowen ruled for a long time, until his death in 499. Famously, he only ruled independently after the Empress Dowager Wenming's death in 490. She had ruled prior to that.

The regencies of both Empress Dowager Wenming and Empress Dowager Ling coincide with a rise in popularity of the dual image of the buddhas Śākyamuni (Ch. Shijiamouni) and Prabhūtaratna (Ch. Duobao), who are seated together in a stūpa, or reliquary, an image that references a story from the *Lotus Sūtra*, where the two buddhas meet together in a jeweled stūpa despite the Buddhological maxim that there can only be one buddha in the world at a time. Scholars refer to this image as it appears on donative inscriptions as the Śākyamuni-Prabhūtaratna (Ch. Shijia-duobao) image. In his summary of the appearance of Śākyamuni-Prabhūtaratna images in medieval times, Hou Xudong has demonstrated that the earliest images date to the 470s, that they increase dramatically in the 480s, and that they then begin to decline thereafter.[67] Significantly, such images disappear almost entirely in the 530s and beyond. The period between the 480s and the 530s, we recall, is the precise period of the reigns of Empress Dowagers Wenming and Ling.

Eugene Wang argues that we can link the early rise in Śākyamuni-Prabhūtaratna images to the reign of Empress Dowager Wenming. Focusing on the Yungang grottos during the empress dowager's regency, Wang argues that after the initial building of the first five imperial shrines—the so-called Tanyao grottos that gave form to the buddha/ruler identification—the latter stage of building at Yungang included the construction of twinned grottos. Wang believes that these twinned grottos with their buddha images can plausibly be linked to the famous *Lotus Sūtra* scene of the meeting of Śākyamuni and Prabhūtaratna.[68] He reports that of the chapels that were constructed during Empress Dowager Wenming's coreign with Emperor Xiaowen, eight of the thirteen feature twin niches with twinned buddha images. Wang argues that this twin buddha motif was specifically undertaken to give expression to the dual reign of Empress Dowager Wenming and the then-child Emperor Xiaowen. Having overseen the building of these grottos herself, Wang argues, Empress Dowager Wenming would have wanted her own regency immortalized in the faces of the buddhas at Yungang alongside those of her independent, male predecessors.[69]

In part, Wang's argument relies on evidence from Tang era sources that are more solid than what evidence we have from the Northern Wei era. Before Wu Zetian established her own direct rule as Emperor Wu Zhao, she was empress to Emperor Gaozong (r. 649–83) and is known to have exercised political influence in that role.[70] So influential was she that she and Gaozong were known as the "Two Sages." Wang believes that the "Two Sages" rule of then Empress Wu with

Emperor Gaozong is linked to a rise in images of Śākyamuni and Prabhūtaratna at Dunhuang that were commissioned during their reign.[71] Based on this, Wang claims that the Northern Wei twinned grottos at Yungang might also suggest a connection between the two rulers of Empress Dowager Wenming and Emperor Xiaowen that was articulated through the bodies of the buddhas in the same way as the original five grottos at the site were connected with other Northern Wei rulers. In sum, Wang argues that just as independent, male Northern Wei rulers were immortalized in the faces and bodies of buddhas at Yungang, so too was the regency rule of Empress Dowager Wenming. This time, however, the expression of this leadership took the form of the twinned buddha image from the *Lotus Sūtra*. Wang therefore suggests that the "Two Sages" rule of Empress Wu and Emperor Gaozong was rooted in the Northern Wei.

Wang's argument is strengthened through a deeper investigation into Northern Wei materials. Specifically, we have epigraphic evidence that both Empress Dowager Wenming's rule with Emperor Xiaowen and Empress Dowager Ling's rule with Emperor Xiaoming were referred to as the "Two Sages" during the times they lived in. As for Empress Dowager Wenming, we can consider a stele inscription that commemorates the building of the Radiant Blessings Monastery (Huifu si). The inscription is dated to 488 and dedicates the building of two, three-storied stūpas at the site to the "Two Sages" of Empress Dowager Wenming and Emperor Xiaowen.[72] Second, and for Empress Dowager Ling, we have an inscription for the renovation of an old stūpa commissioned by Yuan Yue, the prince of the Northern Wei court who was a half-brother to Emperor Xuanwu and who became patron of the Nunnery of the Joyous View after the death of his full brother, Yuan Yi, who was himself the lover of the empress dowager. The inscription is dated to 524 of and dedicates the renovation of the stūpa to the "Two Sages" of Empress Dowager Ling and Emperor Xiaoming, wishing that their reign last for ten thousand years and be unobstructed. In a Longmen grotto of a similar period, the Huangfu Gong grotto commissioned by the uncle of the empress dowager, we find a portrait of the empress dowager. Here she is presented in a royal procession that includes Emperor Xiaoming, who walks behind her. The portrait of these "Two Sages," as Yuan Yue calls them, is carved directly underneath a large-scale Śākyamuni-Prabhūtaratna image.

As such, what we potentially see in the regency governments of Northern Wei women is the expression of their rule through a similar metaphor of the buddha as ruler that we see for the reigns of male emperors of the dynastic line that that are depicted in the imperial grottos at Yungang and Longmen. From this, we also understand that this early connection between the women who ruled, the "Two Sages," and the Śākyamuni-Prabhūtaratna image constituted an interpretive framework for legitimizing regency rule in the medieval period that lasted into the reign of Emperor Wu Zhao, the only woman who would rule an empire in Chinese imperial history with the title of "emperor."

FIGURE 5. The Śākyamuni-Prabhūtaratna image in the Huangfu Gong Grotto at Longmen. Circa 527. Photo © Li Lan.

FIGURE 6. Detail of the Śākyamuni-Prabhūtaratna image. © Andrew MacIver.

BUDDHISM AS A TAGHBACH TRADITION

Although the ruling elite of the Northern Wei court adopted Buddhist forms
of statecraft alongside procedures of state inherited from the Han empire, they
also retained a connection to their own ancestral past. Sources are sparse for
the study of Taghbach lineage, but one story from the "Prefatory Annals" of the
Book of the Wei's record of Taghbach historiography is particularly illuminating

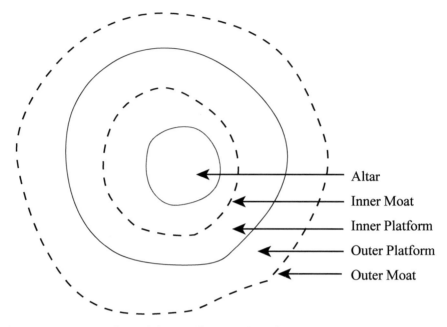

Altar
Inner Moat
Inner Platform
Outer Platform
Outer Moat

FIGURE 7. Diagram of a ritual altar used for imperial sacrifices by the Northern Wei court in Datong. © Andrew MacIver.

here—the story of two of the Taghbach's ancestors, Taghbach Jiefen (d.u.) and Taghbach Liwei (trad. r. 220–77).[73] According to the chronicle, Taghbach Jiefen was the fourteenth and last in the line of ancient founders from when the Taghbach tribe was united, and Taghbach Liwei was the pivot that took Taghbach accounts of the past from their mythological origins to more historical ones, when he founded the one Taghbach subgroup that eventually established the Northern Wei. In the preface to the *Book of the Wei*, the date of his accession was 220 and it is marked as the "first year" of Taghbach history in the sense that all subsequent rulers are dated chronologically forward from him.[74] It is no coincidence that this date also corresponds with the fall of the Han dynasty; illustrating how much of early Taghbach history was written through the historiography of the Han tradition, the choice of the year 220 as the start of Taghbach history is likely more ideological than chronological.

The story begins with Jiefen, who was leading his people south and found himself and his people dwelling in the ancestral lands of a different Inner Asian ethnogroup, the Xiongnu. The story goes:

> Emperor Shengwu had led several tens of thousands of horse riders out into the mountains and marshes and suddenly saw a bannered carriage coming on its own accord down from the heavens. He immediately went to it and saw a beautiful woman to whom he offered his support and protection and who accepted it. The emperor

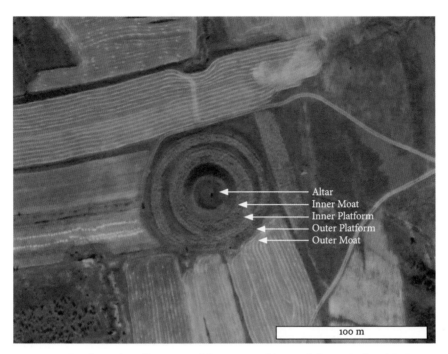

FIGURE 8. Google Earth satellite image of the remains of the ritual altar. © Andrew MacIver.

thought this was strange and so he asked her about it. She responded: "I am a celestial woman and it is our fate that we shall be a pair." And they subsequently went to the bedchamber together. At dawn, she further requested: "Come back to this same spot at this same time next year." And with those words she departed, disappearing like wind and rain. When the time came, the emperor went back to that same place and he saw her again. The celestial woman brought forth a son and gave it to the emperor, saying: "This is your son. Raise him well and care for him. The descendants will all undertake to become kings and emperors of this world." On finishing these words, she left. The son became the original ancestor[75] and therefore the people of the time made a proverb, saying: "Emperor Jiefen has no wife or in-laws; Emperor Liwei has no maternal uncle or in-laws."[76]

This story of the birth of the Taghbach's original ancestor serves to characterize the Taghbach line as divinely begotten. The strange parenthood of Liwei illustrates his celestial matronage while underscoring the idea that the Taghbach are destined to be kings of the world and to claim their sovereignty, or perhaps to reclaim it after having lost it to their Han cousins.

Establishing a celestial lineage with a central ruler accords with what else we know about the actions of the Taghbach rulers of the Northern Wei: Not only did the rulers enact the suburban sacrifices rooted in Han imperial ritual, in which the Taghbach line was authorized by the five agents' (*wuxing*) calculation that the

Taghbach leaders were ruling first under the power of earth and then under the power of water; the ruler also undertook a number of unique rituals including sacrifices for mountains and rivers in every place he journeyed to.[77] These additional rituals are rooted in Taghbach indigenous statecraft according to which the leader was considered a divine agent between this world and the next. As we saw in the above story of Jiefen and his celestial woman from the Taghbach genealogy in the *Book of the Wei*, Taghbach practices of statecraft were heavily invested in supramundane notions of sanctification. Ishimatsu Hinako characterizes the Taghbach as having practiced a form of "great hero veneration" that was complemented by the worship of various natural forces.[78] This great hero veneration arose not only from the divine origins of the ruling family but also because the Taghbach themselves had a ritual system where the leader of the tribe, and often his female companion, played the highest roles as religious officiants alongside a female priestess or shamaness-type figure.[79] These rituals proved the ruler to be in control of both this-worldly and otherworldly affairs by showing him to be a leader from both realms, and they thus accord with what we already know about Liwei from the *Book of the Wei*: He hails from celestial stock, having a Taghbach father but a divine mother.

To understand why Wencheng pivoted Taghbach notions of monarchy toward the adoption of state Buddhism, we need to appreciate just how fast the tradition of Buddhism was spreading among all sectors of society in the mid-Northern Wei period when Wencheng ruled. One way of examining this growth is to look at the record of donor inscriptions on Buddhist statuary. Hou Xudong has surveyed these kinds of inscriptions and he has observed a stunning growth of the tradition across many levels of society.[80] For example, for the sixty years between 400 and 459 Hou catalogues seventeen such inscriptions (or 0.28 per year), only two of which came from the ruling class and the rest of which came from commoners. None of them were dedicated by monastics. After this period, a rapid development in images and dedicatory inscriptions are seen. In the years 460 to 469, which coincide with Wencheng's death, the end of his rule, and the initial development of Yungang, ten such additional inscriptions are seen (or, one per year). This time, six come from commoners, two from the ruling class, one from monastics, and one of uncertain attribution. However, throughout the next sixty years, until the death of the empress dowager, Hou counts 497 such inscriptions (or 8.3 per year), with 299 from commoners, fifty-eight from the ruling class, seventy-five from monastics, and the others with mixed dedications from a variety of social classes. Based on these numbers, the practice of commissioning Buddhist art etched in stone increased by approximately 3,000 percent in the latter half of the Northern Wei. This trend continued through the Northern Qi (550–77 CE), but not as exponentially as within the period of the Northern Wei itself.

A survey of inscriptional materials of this sort only gives us one set of data by which to see the growth of the Buddhist tradition in the fifth century. Alongside

Hou's work, Wang Yongping uses textual sources to trace a similar history of the development of Buddhism during the Northern Wei era, though concentrating on the Buddhism of the imperial family.[81] In Wang's review of the historical documents, imperial patronage of Buddhist temples and monastics strongly increased under the reign of Emperor Xiaowen in the years immediately preceding and succeeding the move to Luoyang, a fact that Yong links to Empress Dowager Wenming's faith in the tradition and the political power that she held during his reign.[82] This increase in imperial patronage continued to develop through the regency of Empress Dowager Ling, reaching its high point with her own personally commissioned Buddhist building projects. In sum, primary source materials of different types from the time period in question reveal that both rulers and commoners were heavily engaged in the patronage of their new religion and that there was therefore a significant advantage to the ruler in depicting his or her own rule and reign in the imagery of Buddhism.

In his study of Emperor Wencheng, Scott Pearce argues that the mid-Northern Wei emperor's decree in support of Buddhism constitutes a "re-casting of Northern Wei as a Buddhist state, which reached its point of highest development decades later in Luoyang."[83] To interpret this move toward Buddhism undertaken by Wencheng, Pearce goes on to argue for the necessary polyvocality of the imagery of the Northern Wei ruler at the time of cultural reinvention in which he ruled. This polyvocality included both Buddhist and Taghbach idioms of rule and expressions of cultural prestige in order to appeal to the ruler's diverse polity. Extending this argument, we can ask what better method would there have been for the Taghbach in the fifth and sixth centuries to reenvision their indigenous traditions of rule by hero than by identifying the ruler with the buddha? As would have been known to audiences across the Southern and Northern Dynasties at the time, Śākyamuni Buddha was himself a prince with a divine heritage. Śākyamuni's father, King Śuddhodana, was a tribal ruler of the Śākya people in Kapilavastu. When this buddha, who was named Siddhartha, was born under miraculous circumstances, the king sought out the advice of a sage. That sage, Asita, made a prophecy that the child would become either an enlightened religious man—a buddha—or a universal monarch otherwise known as a "wheel-turning king" (Skt. cakravartin; Ch. *zhuanlun wang*), a term that will be discussed in detail below. Despite strident efforts by King Śuddhodana to have his son become the latter of the two options, Siddhartha went on to become a buddha; and yet, the mythology of his kingship never left his side and, to this day, buddhas are depicted with the marks of kingship. Textual and art historical evidence show that this story was known to audiences in the Northern Wei period.[84]

Can we imagine a circumstance whereby the Taghbach rulers of the Northern Wei court, who were eager to establish a strong ruling house, used a new and popular cultural idiom of statecraft—Buddhism and the buddha—to give expression to their own indigenous ideas of rule by divine hero? In order to

FIGURE 9. The seer Asita making a prophecy over the baby Śākyamuni Buddha. Detail from Yungang Cave 6. Photo © Yi Lidu.

employ a form of Buddhist statecraft in their governance, the Northern Wei emperors directly depicted themselves as buddhas in their monumental, imperially funded grotto sites.[85] One of the most important texts of Buddhist statecraft utilized across the entirety of East Asia is a text variously referred to in English as the *Sūtra for Humane Kings* (*Renwang jing*).[86] Charles Orzech argues that the first iteration of this text in East Asia was not itself a translation from any Indic or Central Asian language but was in fact written with the patronage of the Northern Wei court during the reign of Emperor Wencheng, when the grottos at Yungang were being carved. Whatever the origins of the text, its emergence in the mid-Northern Wei era must be understood in the context of the Northern Wei rulers' adoption of a polyvocal imagery of rulership that included not only the Taghbach-styled ruler and the Han-styled ruler but also the cakravartin. One of the central doctrinal claims that the *Sūtra for Humane Kings* makes is that the king in this material world is none other than the buddha in the transcendent world. In Orzech's interpretation, both the king and the buddha occupy the same continuum, with the king known as the cakravartin or wheel-turning king, who has the same merit but lesser insight than the buddha.[87] Although the mythology of the cakravartin came to East Asia from South Asia, it predates the life of the historical buddha, and is well-known in Indic sources from a variety of traditions; Orzech argues that the *Sūtra for Humane*

FIGURE 10. Detail of Asita making a prophecy. © Andrew MacIver.

Kings, as it is known in Literary Chinese, is a text that purposely integrates Buddhist ideals of monarchy with those of the traditional ruling elite in China as modeled after the Han empire.[88]

I agree with Orzech's interpretation of the text; however, I want to suggest that the notions of kingship invoked by it also find deep resonance with the Taghbach tradition of "great hero veneration" that saw the leader of the group conceived of as a semidivine agent and leader of the military. This person, likely known in the Serbi language as khagan, also came to be identified with the figure of the buddha. One place to look for proof of this is philology. In his explanation of the Japanese pronunciation of *hotoke* for the character 仏 (*butsu*), which means "buddha," linguist Marc Miyake conjectures that this pronunciation is a cognate with the Korean word for buddha, *puchhŏ* (부처), both stemming from a conjectural archaic Korean compound **put-ka-i*, in which **put* is a phonetic rendering of *buddha* and **ka-i* a word for ruler.[89] This term, Miyake conjectures, is ultimately analogous to the Old Turkic and written Mongolic word for "buddha," *burqan*. *Burqan*, in this instance, would literally mean "buddha khan," reflecting a shared understanding of the core defining features of the buddha legend across North Asia in the early medieval period. As such, we can say that the notion of the emergence of Buddhist forms of statecraft in East Asia has many sources and is not simply a response to Han imperial forms of statecraft. In the Northern Wei era,

Buddhism allowed for the rearticulation of the khagan as buddha, a move that also corresponded to the adoption of Buddhist notions of monarchy in developing modalities of Sinitic statecraft in the period.

WOMEN OF THE EMPIRE

There are few sources by which to embark on a general study of the lives and freedoms of Northern Wei women; however, what there is, is intriguing. One source—the "Biographies of Exemplary Women" (Lienü zhuan) from the *Book of the Wei*—offers a depiction of Northern Wei women engaging in public life that is striking because it is a depiction rarely seen in medieval historiography. It is also a depiction that counters what such texts say about the way in which gender performativity is proscribed for the ethnic Self in said texts. In her survey of these biographies, Lee Jen-der argues that Northern Wei women were active and autonomous public persons and that they were in control of their own finances. In support of her argument, Lee cites the example of a certain Ms. Feng whom, alongside many other Northern Wei women who were famed for their learning and who contributed greatly to the economies of their families or both, officials would seek out for her learned political advice.[90] Lee also cites the fact that Empress Dowager Ling practiced archery, though much to the objection of one of her Han courtiers, Cui Guang (451–523), who lectured her on the proper etiquette for a woman.[91] Cui Guang was also one of the courtiers who tried to prevent Yuan Xun, son of Emperor Xiaowen, from fleeing back to the Northern Wei's prior northern capital of Pingcheng; he was also implicated in the ultimate poisoning of that fourteen-year-old prince who refused to accept life and courtly custom in Luoyang. In the case of the empress dowager, Cui Guang rebuked her for her archery, saying:

> Confucius said: "[for the] gentleman, ambition belongs to the path [*dao*], reliance belongs to virtue [*de*], dependence belongs to compassion, and leisure belongs to the arts."[92] As for the arts, these are: ritual, music, writing, mathematics, shooting, and ruling. To clarify, the first four of these activities can be cultivated by both women and men. But as for shooting and ruling, these are matters only for men, not to be attained by women.[93]

Empress Dowager Ling did not heed the advice of Cui Guang. The independence that she displayed throughout her life may have been owing to the fact that even though she was said to be of Han descent, she was born into the culturally hybrid context of the northwest border regions at the gateway to the Hexi corridor. Such a cultural background may have allowed her to fulfill different types of gender roles than those advocated by Han scholars like Cui Guang—may have allowed her to shoot, as it were. Archeological evidence suggests that Serbi women could shoot: A recently unearthed Serbi tomb from Mongolia has revealed the skeletons of two women whose skeletal remains show repetitive stress injuries related to archery and spinal trauma associated with extensive horse-back riding, a fact that has led bioarcheologist Christine Lee to argue for the existence of gender equality in Serbi society.[94]

These shreds of evidence concerning the gender roles of women in Serbi culture resonate with what is said about the Serbi in the *Later History of the Han*. In the same section that describes the origins of the ethnonym "Taghbach," the text also records that it was the mothers of the Taghbach who held the lineage together. The text states that a man must follow his wife into her family after marriage and stay there for one or two years before the couple can strike out on their own.[95] It also states that although the Serbi people may kill their fathers and elder brothers if they are angered, they will never harm their mothers because the mother is the lineage holder.[96] Ishimatsu Hinako locates this practice of matrilineality within the context of a form of "sacred mother worship" wherein the earliest form of Taghbach religious belief seems to have been the veneration of women as mothers and matriarchs.[97] Ishimatsu's thesis regarding "sacred mother worship" is a gendered companion to her other thesis of "great hero veneration" in Taghbach society. The sources for both are intertwined in the Taghbach's own chronicle of their lineage according to which the Taghbach Serbi tribe that became the rulers of the Northern Wei traced their descent back to a human father, Jiefen, and a divine mother who granted him a child—an heir—before retreating to the heavens.

Ishimatsu's thesis on "sacred mother worship" finds possible support in the recorded existence of shamanesses (*nüwu*) among the Taghbach. According to the *Book of the Wei*, these shamanesses played important roles in early Northern Wei rituals of imperial legitimation and sanctification, which were an admixture of Taghbach and Han ritual procedures involving the shamaness as well as the emperor, his empress, and his female consorts.[98] For example, the *Book of the Wei*'s "Annals on Ritual" (Lizhi) detail the roles that shamanesses played in the state rituals of Emperor Daowu, the founding emperor of the Northern Wei. One such excerpt records a complex ritual said to be undertaken in the year 405. The record of the ritual describes the construction of the sacrificial altar, the placement of the emperor, the empress, and their courtiers, as well as the types of sacrificial animals to be offered to heaven. As to the role of the shamaness, it says:

> The shamaness held the drum and stood in front, to the east of the stage, west-facing. Seven persons of ten from the clan of the emperor were selected to hold the wine at the south of the shaman, west-facing and north of the emperor. The shamaness ascended the platform and shook the drum. The emperor paid his obeisance and the empress paid obeisance with bowed head. The hundred ministers from the interior and the exterior all paid obeisance. The ritual was finished, and again they paid obeisance. When the obeisance was over, the animals were then slaughtered. The seven persons holding the wine came from the west and sprinkled the wine on the pillars of the spirit of heaven, again paid obeisance, all seven of them doing the same. The rite finished, they returned.[99] After this, there was one sacrifice a year.[100]

This ritual is noteworthy for our study because it appears to be something like a Taghbach reinterpretation of the Han suburban sacrifice with the addition of a shamaness, or at least it was written to look that way in the *Book of the Wei*. In the accounts of imperial rituals in the *Book of the Wei* that took place after Emperor Xiaowen's implementation of his Sinification policies and his move of the court and capital to Luoyang, this role of the shamaness disappears. Although this disappearance of the shamaness from imperial ritual may suggest that the women of the clan disappeared from ritual prominence as the dynasty increasingly adopted strategies of statecraft rooted in the Han dynasty, I will argue below that the roles of women in public life were rearticulated through the merging of Taghbach, Han, and Buddhist cultural forms in the latter half of the dynasty.

The idea that Serbi women may have expressed their female gender in ways that included public performance and martial ability finds support in literature from the Han tradition beyond the *Book of the Wei*. Two tantalizing literary snippets suggest that Taghbach women may have enjoyed greater freedom of movement and personal choice than did their Han counterparts. The most enticing of these snippets comes from the observations of the southern-born Yan Zhitui (531–91), who had immigrated to the great northern city of Yecheng, the capital of the Northern Qi, and was struck by what he saw northern women doing. He attributes the behaviors of the women of Yecheng to their Taghbach origins and compares them to the women of his own cultural milieu, proclaiming:

> The customs of Ye are, however, quite different: they let the wife take charge of the family. The womenfolk are involved in disputes and lawsuits; they pay visits and receive guests; their carriages crowd the streets, and official quarters swarm with their silk dresses. They seek office for their sons or make pleas to authority on behalf of their husbands. This, I am afraid, is the legacy of Heng and Dai.[101]

Thus, according to Yan Zhitui, a member of the Ru class who wrote these observations in a record to be handed down to his family, the freedoms and powers of Taghbach women—those who enjoyed the legacy of Heng and Dai—seemed opposed to those of the women in his own cultural milieu. Yan appears surprised by the public social lives of women in the cultural context of the northern dynasties and he attributes their social freedom to the non-Han origins of the Taghbach rulers of the Northern Wei.

Yan's observations find further support from an unusual bit of information recorded in the *Book of the Southern Qi* (Nan Qi shu), which claims that Empress Dowager Wenming went out in her carriage with her court ladies and that they drove the carriage themselves without being concealed by heavy draperies, which is also a habit that Empress Dowager Ling is said to have engaged in. Most remarkably, however, in the case of Empress Dowager Wenming, the *Book of the Southern Qi* tells us that "When the Empress Dowager went out, she was accompanied by women wearing armor and riding horses to the left and right of her carriage."[102]

Although the histories of the southern dynasties cannot be taken as entirely accurate accounts of the people and cultures who lived in the polities at their northern borders, they offer striking observations from an outsider perspective and should be consulted in conjunction with other source materials wherever possible.[103] In our case, if it is in fact true that Empress Dowager Wenming had female bodyguards or cavalrywomen, then this would be a remarkable example of the autonomy of Northern Wei women in premodern times that perhaps accords with the aforementioned archeological evidence of the two women from the graveyard site in Mongolia who could evidently ride and shoot. Similarly, a further story from the *Book of the Wei* chronicles how a woman whose name is uncertain but who was empress to early Northern Wei leader, Taghbach Yiyi (fl. third century.), commanded the military in her time and was therefore considered the leader of the Taghbach alliance in the early fourth century. According to the text, such female leadership saw the Taghbach alliance being pejoratively described as a "woman's country." [104] As enticing as these accounts are, they need to be approached with caution, for though it may be true that some women did fight alongside men in the army, the army remained a male domain. Nonetheless, the inclusion of these stories in the *Book of the Wei* and the *Book of the Southern Qi* speaks to the fact that from very early times, Han culture believed Taghbach culture to have held different opinions regarding the social lives of women than it itself did.

One important criticism of the thesis that Taghbach women enjoyed public, political, and military power comes from the fact that during the mid-Northern Wei period the ruling elite are known to have enacted a policy of forcing the mother of an heir apparent to commit suicide. Expressed by the adage, "If the Son is Noble, the Mother Dies" (*zigui musi*),[105] the practice dictated that if any woman, regardless of rank, mothered an heir apparent, then the woman herself was forced to take her own life. This action was undertaken so that the natal family of the mother would have no way of interfering with the workings of the court after the birth of the designated heir and so that the mother would not be able to present challengers to the realm by mothering another child. The ideology behind this practice recalls the myth of the Taghbach ancestors Jiefen and Liwei discussed above. Not only was Jiefen an illustrious military leader who was chosen because of his ability to lead his people on their campaign to political dominance, his son, Liwei, was birthed without a mother.

The work of Cheng Ya-ju helps us to understand this practice of imperial matricide. Having surveyed the biographies of empresses in the dynasty, Cheng shows that they enjoyed abundant social power but also that their social power was not derived through their court status as "empress" (*hou*) in the same way as it was within Han-styled court structures. Instead, Cheng argues, access to political power for women in the Taghbach leadership depended on their maternal relationships to elite men, whether or not the women in question actually held the title of empress at court.[106] To express this situation of matrilineal power, Cheng argues that the early Taghbach court did not use the term *empress* in the same way as did the Han court and that a woman could be an empress but have no social power if she did not have a maternal relationship with an elite male member of the court. According to the inverse, then, the attempt to limit a woman's access to political power was also to limit her ability to be a mother. Only in this way does the policy enshrined in the maxim, "If the Son is Noble, the Mother Dies," make sense. Notably, access to this sort of maternally derived political influence for women of the court was available in roles outside that of blood mother. Regarding this matter, Scott Pearce points to the rare existence of the role of "Dowager Protectress" (*bao taihou*), an anomalous Northern Wei title that was held by the wet nurse and future dowager empress to Northern Wei Emperor Taiwu (r. 423–453), Madam Dou and, successively, by wet nurse and future dowager empress to Northern Wei Emperor Wencheng, Madam Chang.[107] In his study, Pearce argues that the basic human relationship between nursemaid and nursling facilitated these women's rise to power within the context of the increasing centralization of the Taghbach governmental system.[108] This argument dovetails with Cheng's argument that Han-styled modes of courtly title and power diminish the power of maternal kin connections at court, and that this diminishing of kinship ties conflicted with the Taghbach preference for maternal relationships—though not necessarily blood relationships—in the delineation and definition of which women could hold power.

To bring this all back to the empress dowager, she was a rare sort of woman in her court. As a northern woman, she shot arrows and participated in public life. As a woman of Han descent who, as we will see, connected herself with procedures of rule derived from the Han empire, she held the title of "empress." She also held the title of empress dowager (*huang taihou*), which identified her as regent in the type of politics styled after Han statecraft that were adopted by the Northern Wei court in the late fifth century. Furthermore, owing to her own termination of the practice of imperial matricide cited above, she was also the one and only woman to have a maternal and blood connection to the emperor for whom she was dowager while also holding the title of "empress." Her power at court was therefore doubly entrenched. She hailed from a culturally hybrid region of the empire, and the cultures that she was born into allowed for two different modalities of the articulation of female power at court. She herself tapped into a third modality: Buddhism.

A BUDDHIST MONARCH?

According to Sinitic notions of leadership, which, in the early medieval period were modeled on the Han empire, the empress dowager was regent to the monarch and not a monarch herself. However, we need not assume that notions of monarchy from the Han empire should define whom we do and do not call a monarch during the Northern Wei era. If we look at the empress dowager's actions while she was ruling, it becomes clear that she was interested in enacting a different type of monarchy—namely, that of the Buddhist monarch, the cakravartin or "wheel-turning king." In his foundational study of the early association between Buddhist images and imperial metaphors in the Chinese realm, Erik Zürcher argues that from approximately the fourth century onward, Buddhist ideas, symbols, and imagery infiltrated Han notions of dynastic and imperial legitimation.[109] He argues that dynastic legitimation during the early medieval period depended on a number of Buddhist elements, the most important of which was the merging of the notion of the emperor with that of the Buddhist monarch, or cakravartin—the archetype of which was King Aśoka (r. 288–32 BCE), the great imperial patron of Buddhism in early India's Mauryan empire (322–185 BCE). According to hagiographical legends of Aśoka, the king is said to have converted to Buddhism and repented of his violent past and political consolidation through military conquest. His conversion went along with his unwavering support of the Buddhist tradition,[110] which was shown through his fabled dispersal of the relics of Śākyamuni Buddha's body in eighty-four thousand stūpas across the known world in his time. The Aśoka legend was well known in China, attested in both the north and the south, and in art and in text, by the fifth century.[111] Recognizing the importance of the Aśokan archetype to the legitimation of the emperor in early medieval China, Zürcher identifies two cases in which the identification between the emperor and the Mauryan king were made complete: Emperor Wu (r. 502–49) of the Liang 梁 (502–56) and Emperor Wen 文 (r. 581–604) of the Sui.[112] Although Zürcher does not mention it, Emperor Wu Zhao later did the very same thing by identifying herself as a cakravartin and undertaking a campaign for the distribution of relics across her realm.[113]

Studies of cakravartin kingship in the sixth century in East Asia have focused on Emperor Wu of the Liang who in fact ruled at the same time as Empress Dowager Ling, but in a southern polity. Referred to as the "Aśoka of China,"[114] Emperor Wu is said to have convened "universal vegetarian assemblies" (zhaihui) of monastics who came together to chant texts in support of the empire.[115] Such assemblies were grand feasts open to the public, attended by foreign emissaries, and they included acts of extreme donation by the emperor himself who also gave sermons.[116] Presenting himself as a practicing Buddhist, Emperor Wu also twice undertook his own public bodhisattva ordination in which his identity as emperor was merged with that of the bodhisattva. The Book of the Wei records that this southern emperor was therefore known as "the bodhisattva emperor" (huangdi pusa).[117] Emperor Wu is famous for his interest in relics. Said to have unearthed an old relic trove from one of King Aśoka's own stūpas that was located in the Liang territory, he then reinterred the relics in stūpas across his empire in an act of imperial mimesis.[118] Emperor Wu enjoyed close and official ties with a monastery in his capital, the Brilliant Abode Monastery (Guangzhai si), which he donated his own residence in order to establish and in which he also deposited relics.[119] Those particular relics were themselves later disinterred and distributed by Emperor Wu Zhao in her own cakravartin campaign.[120]

In his recent overview of the empires from the Southern and Northern Dynasties period that took the southern capital, Jiankang, as their capital, Andrew Chittick connects Emperor Wu of the Liang's adoption of Aśoka's form of cakravartin rulership to the Jiankang region's links with South and Southeast Asia. Focusing on a different route for the transmission of Buddhism into China than that of the northern dynasties' polities, Chittick shows how the Buddhistic kingdom of Sri Lanka played a pronounced role in the transmission of Buddhism through the South China Sea and into Jiankang, where it was diffused across the southern dynasties.[121] Tracing a compelling history of the arrival of Buddhist monks, images, and texts in the Jiankang region throughout the fourth century via this southern, maritime route, Chittick shows how Buddhism became the dominant modality of dynastic legitimation and imperial ritual by the fifth century. He therefore provides a formative backstory to Emperor Wu's Buddhist practice. This backstory is interwoven at many places with references to Aśoka. As a ruler present in texts about him that were translated in the southern courts, as a predecessor with physical ties to the southern regions through the presence of his stūpas, and as a model Buddhist king or *dharmaraja* whose influence was seen and felt via physical objects that made their way through Southeast Asia and to Jiankang, Aśoka had a story that formed the backdrop for Emperor Wu's imperial Buddhism. This backdrop manifested itself not only in the Liang emperor's public Buddhism but also in a general interest in Aśokan objects in the region. As Chittick has shown, Jiankang historiography was reimagined in court-sponsored Buddhist writing to include the presence of Aśoka's personally commissioned stūpas in their region and at the sites of the capital cities of the southern kingdoms of antiquity.[122] Similarly, Chittick argues that the story of Aśoka influenced the architecture of the Jiankang region and shows evidence for the construction of Aśokan-style pillars being built there.

The north also knew of Aśoka. In her recent study of the Buddhist grottos at Yungang, Joy Lidu Yi points out that depictions of Aśoka flourished at the site in its second stage of development between the 490s and the 520s. Notably, Yi points to the rare depiction of Aśoka in these scenes: At Yungang, he is depicted in his past life, as a child offering a gift of dirt to the buddha. Yi argues that this depiction is derived not from the texts brought to and translated in the southern courts of the Jiankang region but from a text called the *Sūtra on the Wise and the Foolish* (*Xianyu jing*), which is said to have been translated by a Northern Wei monk in the mid-fifth century.[123] The circumstances involved in the creation of the *Sūtra on the Wise and the Foolish* are complicated, but it is clear that the work is connected to a monk named Tanxue (fl. 450), who is said to have been active during the Northern Wei era. According to the catalog of Sengyou (445–518), the medieval bibliographer of Buddhist texts, Tanxue and his companions journeyed to the western regions and ultimately to the Buddhistic kingdom of Khotan, where they heard the sūtra before journeying back to Turfan (then named Gaochang) and writing it down from their collective memory.[124] The sūtra is a long compilation of many stories, and it displays influences from both Sinitic and Inner Asian Buddhism; it lacks, however, a Sanskrit version. Despite the text's uncertain origin, it was popular during the Northern Wei era, as we will see in chapter 4. Further from the Northern Wei, the Aśokan story is also attested to in the "Annals on Buddhism and Daoism" in the *Book of the Wei*, where Wei Shou records that Aśoka had supernormal powers and, with the aid of the gods, built his eighty-four thousand reliquaries across the known world, including three in Northern Wei territory with one in Luoyang.[125] Finally, according to the *Record of Buddhist Monasteries in Luoyang*, the well-known retrospective on the Buddhist landscape of Luoyang after its demise, Empress Dowager Ling dispatched two monastic ambassadors to the western regions. These monks were named Songyun and Huisheng and they are said to have visited several Aśokan stūpas during their journey, most notably one built at the site of one of Śākyamuni Buddha's miraculous act of bodily sacrifice whereby he cut off his skin to be used as paper and broke off his bone to be used as a pen.[126]

The last chapter of the *Record of Buddhist Monasteries in Luoyang* contains a long account of the empress dowager's dispatch of Songyun and Huisheng to the western regions in 518, which was roughly around the same period during which the Eternal Peace Monastery was being finished. That record narrates how the empress dowager and Xiaoming were internationally promoted as great Buddhist regents in distant Buddhistic lands. At the end of their journey, Huisheng and Songyun reached Udyāna (Ch. Wuchang) in the Swat valley, where they stayed for two years under the patronage of the king while also journeying through Gandhāra (Ch. Qiantuoluo), visiting all the famous spots in the region where Śākyamuni Buddha is, according to myth, said to have visited and to have left relics during his past lives. The record of their travels contains several noteworthy stories that help us to think about the empress dowager as a cakravartin. Perhaps the most intriguing of these stories is that of the meeting of the two monks with the king of Udyāna. Regarding the king's actions at this meeting, we are told the following: "Hearing that the Empress Dowager upheld the buddha's law, he straightaway faced east, joined his hands together, and paid ritual obeisance from far off."[127] Furthermore, after asking many questions about the Northern Wei, the king is reported to have declared, "If it is like you say, it is none other than a buddha land. I desire to be reborn there."[128] After visiting the king, the two monks eventually journeyed to the famous, semimythical Queli stūpa. Rising four hundred Chinese feet above the ground and with an additional iron post of eighty-eight feet rising out of its peak, the stūpa was said to have been spontaneously self-created in a series of miraculous events. According to legend, the stūpa was prophesied by Śākyamuni Buddha himself, who said that it would be built by the Kushan king, Kaniṣka I (r. 127–44). The record tells us that when they arrived at the stūpa, Huisheng and Songyun still bore one of the hundred-foot silk banners that the empress dowager had given them with the command that they disseminate the banners across kingdoms throughout their travels. They hung the last of the empress dowager's silk banners at the top of the stūpa and they also donated their own personal slaves to act as indentured temple servants.[129]

Even though the *Record* tells the tale of their encountering relics on the journey, it does not state that the two monks returned to Luoyang with any verifiable ones; however, one might wonder if the search for relics was their original intention, given the close proximity in time of the completion of the Eternal Peace Monastery with its soaring pagoda, which was so well suited for the storing of relics for a cakravartin ruler. Whatever the intention behind the journey of the two monks, it appears to be the case that in the north—just as in the south—the ideal of the cakravartin ruler was well known by the fifth century and enacted in state ritual by the sixth century. In a 2017 study of the empress dowager's Buddhist identity, Zhou Yin enumerates how the empress dowager enacted the role of the cakravartin, perhaps modeling it after Aśoka. Zhou argues that the empress dowager constructed her pagoda at the Eternal Peace Monastery as the central masterpiece of her prefectural pagoda building project, whereby she ordered the building of five-story pagodas in every prefecture throughout the realm in an imitation of Aśoka's eighty-four thousand relic stūpas. At the same time, Zhou brings to a light a record from the *Book of the Wei* that describes how the empress dowager also commissioned "vegetarian assemblies" of monks who gathered to receive alms from her and to chant scriptures on feast days in the Buddhist calendar, presumably for the purpose of state protection. Finally, Zhou reveals how the empress dowager continued on with traditions of vegetarianism from earlier emperors and explores how her support for vegetarianism fit within her own practice of the "ten good paths" (*shi shandao*) from the *Huayan Sūtra* (Ch. Da fang guang fo huayan jing; Skt. Buddhāvataṃsaka-mahāvaipulya-sūtra). According to Zhou's research, the empress dowager invited monks to her court to lecture on the *Huayan Sūtra* and therefore reinforce her own connection with the bodhisattva ideal that is advocated within it.[130] As regards her use of sūtras for the support of her cakravartin identity, we will later see how the empress dowager patronized the translation of canonical texts that feature elite women as Buddhist teachers. We can, however, mention one here: The *Sūtra of the Woman, "Silver Countenance"* (Yinsenü jing). In that sūtra, Silver Countenance (i.e., a past-life incarnation of Śākyamuni Buddha) offers her breasts to feed a starving new mother in order to prevent the mother from eating her newborn child. After completing her act of bodily sacrifice, Silver Countenance's body is miraculously restored and then further transformed into a male body. At this point, she (now he) lies down for a rest only to be discovered by envoys from another kingdom and made into their lawful Buddhist king, or cakravartin.

As a cakravartin ruler—a type of Buddhist monarch akin to the great Buddhist patron Aśoka—Empress Dowager Ling was the most public and most prolific of Buddhist patrons in her time. According to Amy McNair in her study of the patronage of sixth-century Buddhists at the imperial Buddhist grotto site of

Longmen just to the south of the capital, Empress Dowager Ling was responsible for the patronage of the highest and largest of the Northern Wei grottos at the site— the Huoshao grotto.[131] Moreover, away from Longmen and in the city proper, the empress dowager is also said to have personally funded monasteries big and small. Her most famous project, and the one for which she is most commonly cited in historical, biographical, and political texts, was the rebuilding of the Eternal Peace Monastery. Built after a structure of the same name from the dynasty's former capital, the empress dowager's Eternal Peace Monastery was the symbolic apex of her Buddhist patronage, as well as the physical center of her Buddhist metropolis, and it conveyed that important status with stunning architecture, massive size, opulent decoration, and the empire's only nine-story pagoda. This pagoda was so famous that it was taken as the model for both the pagoda at the August Dragon Monastery (Kr. Hwangnyong-sa; Ch. Huanglong si) in Silla (trad. 57 BCE–935 CE) on the Korean peninsula and the Japanese pagoda on the site of Kudara Ōdera (Great Paekche Monastery), which was built during the Asuka era of Japan's Yamato period (538–710).[132] After its completion on the main avenue in front of the palace, the empress dowager engaged in a public display of her political power and religious patronage by climbing the pagoda alongside the child emperor Xiaoming. The two of them are said to have been the only persons allowed to climb to the top of the pagoda because the structure was so high that the vantage point gained from the top gave one a glimpse inside the palace walls.[133] According to the *Record of Buddhist Monasteries in Luoyang*, the empress dowager funded many other projects within the urban landscape of the capital, and a number of them were for her family. For her aunt, the nun who brought her to court and who was from the Hu Clan, she personally funded the building of the Nunnery of the Superintendent of the Nuns (Hutong si). This nunnery was finely crafted and beautifully resourced and it housed the most studious nuns in the capital.[134] Similarly, the empress dowager and her sister commissioned the building of a monastic complex at the site of the prior Han court's numinous platform. This complex was a mortuary complex for their deceased father and it included two majestic stūpas. The empress dowager herself provided the funds for all the monastics in residence.[135] As we have seen, the empress dowager's patronage extended beyond Luoyang. Both the *Record of Buddhist Monasteries in Luoyang* and the 13th century Buddhist historiographical collection, the *Complete Chronicle of the Buddha and the Patriarchs* (Fozu tongji), record her patronage of Buddhist missions to the western regions.[136]

The year 519 was a pivotal and fascinating year in the reigns of both Empress Dowager Ling in the north and Emperor Wu of the Liang in the south. Suggestive of a competition in the building of Buddhist infrastructure and typologies of rule between the two cakravartin rulers, 519 was the year of the completion of the Eternal Peace Monastery in Luoyang with its nine-story pagoda and it was also the year in which Liang Emperor Wu started construction on his central monastic complex, which also housed a nine-story pagoda.[137] Furthermore, 519 was the year of the Liang emperor's public taking of bodhisattva ordination, just as it was the year in which the empress dowager's court saw the translation of the *Sūtra of the Woman, "Silver Countenance."* There may also have been some textual disagreement between north and south: Although the Liang emperor merged his identity with that of a bodhisattva in a way that resonates with the ideology of the *Sūtra for Humane Kings*, he is also recorded to have rejected the use of that text in his vast vegetarian assemblies. According to Andreas Janousch, Emperor Wu's objection to the text was doctrinal in nature; however, given the apparent competition in Buddhist political legitimation between north and south, it might also be the case that the southern emperor refused to use the northern text. His refusal of the text in such court-backed monastic assemblies is striking: Used in the successor state to the Liang, the Chen (557–89), the text was also utilized in court rituals from a variety of later courts across East Asia as part of their large-scale Buddhist rites of repentance and state protection.[138]

If we look outside the Chinese mainland and to the Korean peninsula, we see that many of the strategies undertaken by Empress Dowager Ling and Emperor Wu of the Liang were also adopted by rulers in Silla as a part of their imperial Buddhism. Richard McBride has argued that much of the ideology and infrastructure of Silla's state Buddhism, including King Chinhŭng's (r. 540–76) establishment of large-scale, monastic, ritual feasts for the chanting of the *Sūtra on Humane Kings*, were based on those of the Northern Wei courts. As McBride argues, the establishment of these rituals finds historical context within the Northern Wei court's program of identifying their rulers as buddhas, both in text and in monumental art, and it came about at a time when the leaders of Silla were interested in establishing diplomatic relationships with polities on the mainland. As a nod to the cakravartin identity of the ruler of Silla, McBride notes that it was in 535 when construction began on the Promoting the Wheel of the Dharma Monastery (Hŭngnyun sa). The wheel metaphor here links up with the mythology of the cakravartin ruler. Similarly, McBride argues that "Chinhŭng embraced the imagery of the cakravartin (Kr. *chŏllun wang*) and constructed the state palladium August Dragon Monastery to combine Sinitic and Indian modes of legitimation."[139]

SOCIAL CHANGE AND THE RISE
OF THE EMPRESS DOWAGER

In the thirteen years of her reign, Empress Dowager Ling managed to construct a Buddhist Luoyang with herself as leader even though she was under house arrest for almost five of those years as a result of a coup d'état against her. Having been appointed to court at the recommendation of the highest-ranked Buddhist nun in the empire, she worked to build Buddhism into her city just as she presented herself as a Buddhist monarch. She supported monks and nuns, built majestic temples and soaring rock-cut grottos, and sponsored the activities of Buddhist translators from Inner Asia at her own Eternal Peace Monastery in the heart of the city. Her reign marks a watershed moment in the patronage of Buddhist building projects by elite women, and it had a pronounced and direct effect on the Buddhist polities that would arise across East Asia throughout the rest of the medieval period. As a leader of a multiethnic state during the time of intense cultural, religious, and political reinvention that we associate with the Southern and Northern Dynasties, the empress dowager was able to do all the things she did by connecting to social currents that would help promote a woman to a position of leadership within an urban milieu. These currents included Buddhism, its integration into both Taghbach and Han notions of imperial legitimation, and the changing roles of women in society that came about during this period of intense social change, all of which were indebted to the public status of Taghbach women, the rise of Buddhist monasticism for women, and the establishment of political roles for women both rooted in and inspired by the administration of the then-classical Han dynasty.

The empress dowager was born far from the capital and to a family of the local gentry. She has no recorded name and no recorded date of birth. She rose to become one of the most powerful politicians of her age and died having seen the completion of the tallest and most wondrous building the world had ever seen to that point. She did so by ruling directly and by controlling the court's finances. She funneled money into her projects and supported the Buddhist building projects of others. She was a Buddhist patron and a Buddhist donor. She was a Buddhist monarch who attempted to establish herself as a cakravartin in Luoyang just as did her southern contemporary, Emperor Wu of the Liang.

How did she do all of this? And why? And what did the people who knew her think about all that she had accomplished? To begin to answer those questions we must turn to the next chapter—her biography.

2

A Woman of Power,
Remembered Poorly

In this chapter, I offer a new translation of the full text of the empress dowager's biography in the *Book of the Wei* that is offered in sections supplemented by necessary historical and historiographical information aimed at helping us to immerse ourselves in the empress dowager's world.[1] Before offering the reader the translation, however, I argue that dynastic histories, in general, are not well suited to document the lives of women because the men who wrote them had restricted access to women's spaces and because they authored texts that circulated within a patriarchal court and social structure. Following the translation, I show how the representation of the empress dowager in her biography made its way into important, later texts of medieval historiography that continue to characterize her through gendered tropes that are inadequate for biographizing her in any dynamic way. In documenting the tropes that emerge from her biography, I set us up for the further chapters of this book, which use Buddhist sources to tell a different, more compelling story of the empress dowager—that is, the story of how women were able to capitalize on the invention of new social roles within the Buddhist and multiethnic urban fabric of sixth-century Luoyang.

A TEXT FROM WHOSE PERSPECTIVE?

The empress dowager's biography in the *Book of the Wei* has been the main source for reconstructing her history.[2] As a source, however, it is problematic: embedded within a historiographical tradition concerned with imperial legitimation and dynastic continuity, it records her life through the collapse of the Northern Wei. This historiographical tradition of writing dynastic histories is the cultural product of the class of elite male scholars that we have already discussed—namely, the Ru. These scholars and their texts are associated with a single yet amorphous social category in East Asia—the cultural, political, and literary tradition that is often called "Confucianism." In English, the word *Confucianism* is commonly used as a translation for the Chinese word that designates the community and traditions of these scholars, *Rujiao*. I use the term *Confucianism* more expansively. Confucianism, here, follows one of the many useful definitions of the tradition laid out by Dorothy Ko, JaHyun Kim Haboush, and Joan R. Piggott, who argue that Confucianism is an established institutional structure that "directly impinged on people's lives and behavior" in which systems of "kinship and kingship provided the concrete contexts in which such Confucian virtues as filiality and loyalty were to be realized."[3] In other words, Confucianism was more than the just the tradition of the elite male scholars that it is often identified with. It was also the tradition of those who participated in the systems of kinship and kingship that the scholars wrote about. We will see in this study, for example, how Buddhists were Confucian (and Confucians were Buddhist) and how women, too, participated in Confucian cultural institutions as agentive actors. This is not to discount the dominance and influence of the Ru scholars in the creation, definition, and standardization of Confucian institutional structures like kinship and kingship, which, are, in general, patriarchal and traditionalist; rather, this is to argue that Confucianism is a wide tradition that includes various actors and that often describes the relationship of social actors of varying gender, class, age, religion, and ability to those who hold elite forms of power, as well as the means to police it.

One form of power delineated within the Confucian tradition is literacy. If literacy is power, then the Ru scholars carry a lot of it. This power is articulated through reading and writing. As scholars who were frequently in the employ of the court, these men were able to consult the ancient records of the historical and historiographical past in order to influence policy decisions as well as to legitimate empires and monarchs. They were also able to transmit notions of social good, of right and wrong, and of family hierarchy through their reanimation of the authoritative past invoked in their composition and compilation of the official history of various dynastic lineages. As discussed in the introduction, these histories tell a version of imperial history that stresses historiographical continuity through patrilineal dynastic descent. For our purposes, here, though women feature in these dynastic histories, the genre of the text itself is generally unsuited to document them. As texts that document imperial continuity dependent on notions of kinship and kingship whereby elite and normally Han men hold both high public status and social authority, the complicated social and cultural lives of actual people—especially women and ethnic Others—are not well explored in their pages.

Women have been largely left out of such dynastic histories. Jowen Tung argues that this absence was not only known to Ru scholars while they were compiling their histories but was excused by them on the pretense that the details of women's lives were unavailable to them because they were men without access to women's spaces. On this, Tung cites a eulogy appended to the section on the "Biographies of Princesses" in the *New Tang History* (*Xin tangshu*), which laments:

> Women dwell inside their husband's houses; even for noble ladies, historians are left out and could not know their lives. In addition, after the upheavals at the reigns of Emperors Xi and Zhao, documents were destroyed, with only their birth and death dates remained; those that are lost are hence left unrecorded.[4]

Tung argues that because the Ru lacked the ability to uncover substantive information about women's lives, they instead imagined the women who feature in their texts as fables for the patriarchs, wherein shrewd wives, cunning witches, versatile courtesans, and wayward Daoist priestesses stand in for real women living at the dynamic court of the Tang as written about in the court's official dynastic history. Such a predicament can also be seen in the dynastic history of the Northern Wei where Empress Dowager Ling has been cast in similar roles throughout her brief biography. Such a caricature of a person fails to grasp the complexities of living life as a woman in a male domain and it fails also to provide a nuanced interpretation of women's activities at court and in wider society.

The texts of the Ru scholars are political texts, not anthropological texts, particularly in the sense that they represent the perspective of elite, male, and Han political and social worlds and do not describe the daily lives of those they govern who participated in a wider tradition that we can call Confucianism. Written by male members of the literati class whose familiarity with women's lives was restricted by both gender and, often, class, these texts participated in what Ko, Haboush, and Piggott further call a "Confucian discourse" in writing the lives of women. Texts of this discourse "envision a universal and undifferentiated womanhood, defined as the mutually constitutive Other of manhood,"[5] meaning that women are seen and written about in such texts only against the frame of their male relations and contemporaries. Such an optic flattens the life circumstances of real, historical women, turns them into a superficial caricature, and renders their work, their creativity, and their innovations obsolete. Furthermore, such viewing of women as the "Other" of manhood endorses a mechanism of moral judgement often at play in biographical writings about women whereby a woman who stood out on her own terms is often remembered poorly.

As we will see in the translation of her official biography below from the dynastic history of the Northern Wei, Empress Dowager Ling is just such a woman—that is, a woman of power, but poorly remembered. The story of her life that we are presented with in her biography fails to capture the complex social space between her real-life activities and the authorial choices made in writing about them. Nonetheless, the text offers a chronicle of the empress dowager's life and rule just as it has shaped further writing about her. It is therefore the place where we must begin.

THE BIOGRAPHY OF THE EMPRESS DOWAGER

In this section, I will move slowly through the biography, translating it in its entirety but doing so in sections. I have provided framing for each of the sections, as well as relevant historical information that aids our interpretation of the text. The biography is retained in two places, and in more or less the same way. The two places it can be found are: (1) the dynastic history of the Northern Wei, or the *Book of the Wei*; (2) the more expansive *History of the Northern Dynasties* (Bei shi). The *Book of the Wei* was compiled in the Northern Qi by Wei Shou, a scholar and historian who had once worked for the Northern Wei. It was presented to the Northern Qi emperor in the year 554. The *History of the Northern Dynasties* was compiled by Li Yanshou (fl. 660–65) in the Tang and therefore postdates the *Book of the Wei* by more than one hundred years. It should be the case, then, that the *Book of the Wei*'s biography of the empress dowager is the source for the *History of the Northern Dynasty*'s almost identical biography; however, the history is not that simple. The version of the *Book of the Wei* that we have today was reconstructed under the Song dynasty (960–1279) because many chapters of the original Northern Qi text had been lost. The entire section on the biographies of empresses (Huanghou zhuan) was among these lost chapters. The biography for the *Book of the Wei* was therefore mostly reconstructed from the *History of the Northern Dynasties*.[6] As such, though it may well be that the biography of the empress dowager in Wei Shou's originally compiled *Book of the Wei* was the source for the *History of the Northern Dynasties*, it is also the case that the *History of the Northern Dynasties* was used to reconstruct the *Book of the Wei* during the Song. In referring to the empress dowager's biography throughout this study, I will use the Song era text of the *Book of the Wei* with the caveat that it may not be the earliest text. I do this in order to comport with my general use of the *Book of the Wei* throughout this study and also because the two versions of the biography have only minor differences between them, a fact that will be noted. Finally, the *Book of the Wei* version is slightly longer. Since I am interested in investigating how the empress dowager was remembered, I prefer to use the fullest possible memory of her that is available to us.

A Miraculous Birth and a Nameless Girl

With the notable exception of a number of biographies of Buddhist monks and nuns, biographies of known people in Chinese historical sources commonly begin with an enumeration of the family of the person in question, often extending multiple generations backward through the patriline. Regarding this method of biography, Kate Lingley argues that "The Chinese historiographical convention of history as biography gives most premodern sources a strongly patrilineal flavor."[7] Our empress dowager is no exception. Her biography in the *Book of the Wei* begins with such a lineage, albeit a brief one. It starts as follows:

> Xuanwu's Empress Dowager Ling of the Hu clan was from Lingjing in Anding[8] and was the precious daughter of [Hu] Guozhen, the minister of education (*situ*). Her mother was from the Huangfu clan.

Although such a stock introduction to the biography of the empress dowager seems hardly noteworthy, it does allow for some investigation into her ethnic identity and social location. The Hu clan of Anding were known as a family of Han descent who lived in the ethnically and culturally diverse society of modern-day Gansu.[9] Such families were important to Northern Wei politics because they acted as cultural go-betweens. Literate in the spoken and literary languages of Han peoples and conversant in Han legal systems, they were culturally fluent in the social norms of their non-Han peers. The empress dowager's father, Hu Guozhen, held a minor title in Anding but was granted the title of the minister of education after the empress dowager became regent at the central court in Luoyang.[10] During this period, a number of other women from the Hu clan of Anding went on to marry men of the Northern Wei court, many of whom continued to play important political roles throughout the collapse of the Northern Wei and the subsequent dynasties of the Eastern Wei and Northern Qi and even into the Tang.[11] On her maternal side, the empress dowager is said to have been descended from an illustrious lineage, the Huangfu clan of Anding. This would make the empress dowager a presumed descendent of the Han general Huangfu Song (d. 195) and the scholar Huangfu Mi (215–82).[12]

Research into Buddhist materials from the fifth century shows that both the Hu clan and the Huangfu clan of Anding were Buddhist families of high repute.[13] Using Buddhist epigraphical sources, Wang Xingrui argues that the Hu and the Huangfu were the most important families for the development of Buddhism in their region in the fifth and sixth centuries. In support of this, Wang shows that the Huangfu family were major donors to a number of monastery-building projects. As for the Hu clan, not only did the eminent nun Sengzhi come from this family in the fifth century but names of certain clan members are also seen on some of the same dedicatory stele as those of the Huangfu clan, a fact that leads Wang to conclude that the families were united both through marriage and their shared commitment to Buddhist building projects in their region. What we know, then, of the empress dowager is that both of her natal families played integral roles in the development of Buddhism in her region and that her paternal aunt was an eminent nun. Furthermore, there are many points in the biography that highlight her own connection to Buddhist persons, texts, ideas, objects, and institutions. The first of these points comes in the very narrative of her birth. It says:

> On the day that the empress was born, a red glow shone all around. In the capital of Shanbei County there was one called Zhao Hu who was good at divining marks. Hu Guozhen asked him [about the glow]. Zhao Hu said: "This is an indication of the great nobility of the worthy girl: She will become the mother of heaven and earth and will give birth to the lord of heaven and earth. Do not let more than three people know this."

The empress dowager's miraculous birth, the rush to a fortune teller, and the prophecy concerning the newborn might remind us of another famous birth: the mythologized birth of the historical buddha, Śākyamuni. After his birth out of the right side of his mother's body, Śākyamuni, too, was taken to a diviner who offered a prophetic divination about his future kingship. The scene of this divination by Asita over the infant body of the buddha is depicted in Yungang Cave number six and was thus known by the Northern Wei court prior to the times of our empress dowager and the writing of her biography. On the surface, this connection seems a stretch: the story of Śākyamuni Buddha is significantly older, culturally different, and specific to a male, and we might question how widely it had circulated by the sixth century. However, one further story from the *Book of the Wei* clearly shows that the story of the birth of Śākyamuni Buddha was known at the court and was considered a model birth even for a female. That story is of a child whose name reveals her fate: Ling Ji or "Honored Concubine." The story is contained in the "Annals of Numinous Omens" (Lingzheng zhi) section of the *Book of the Wei*, and it suggests that the story of the birth of the buddha was known to Empress Dowager Ling. As the story goes:

> On the *jiwei* day of the eleventh month of the second year of the Reign of Bright Tranquility [November 30, 517] of Emperor Suzong [Xiaoming], a representative from Bingzhou[14] was sent to Qi District[15] because a person named Han Sengzhen had a daughter, Ling Ji, who had been born out of the right side of her mother's body. The empress dowager then commanded that the daughter be admitted into the women's chambers of the court.[16]

Nothing more is said of this child's miraculous birth or of her life at court. We know neither her birth name nor that of her mother. The only thing we know is that she is said to have come into to the world in a miraculous fashion—in the exact same fashion as the historical buddha did—and that this was enough for the empress dowager to bring her to court. The veracity of such a story is doubtful; however, such doubt is misplaced. What matters is that the trope of being born like a buddha appears to have been applied to at least one woman other than the empress dowager and that such a birth was seen as a reason for entrance to the court. The questions here that need to be considered include: Could a woman be born a buddha? Could she actually *be* a buddha according to the belief of the people of her time? If so, what did that mean for her political career? These questions will be addressed in chapter 4.

A Woman of the Inner Chambers

For now, a different matter of Buddhist concern awaits us in the empress dowager's biography—that of her appointment at court. Our text continues with a brief chronology of her various court positions, beginning with the account of her having been brought to court by her aunt:

> The empress [dowager]'s aunt was a nun who was particularly talented in preaching on the Way. At the beginning of [the reign] of Shizong [Emperor Xuanwu], she went to lecture in the forbidden area [of the palace]. Throughout many years, she had recited [texts] all over the place and had praised the empress [dowager]'s appearance and behavior. Shizong heard about this and therefore invited [her] to enter the inner courts as a hereditary consort bearing flowers.[17]

Emperor Xuanwu is remembered as having been an active Buddhist patron as well as a student of Buddhist texts and teachings. The final chapter of the *Book of the Wei*, the "Annals on Buddhism and Daoism" (Shilao zhi), reports that Xuanwu invited eminent monastics to court and personally lectured on Buddhist teachings while he also saw the numbers of monasteries and nunneries in the realm increase dramatically under his reign,[18] and was himself the chief patron of a particularly important one: the Jade Radiance Nunnery (Yaoguang si), which housed the women of the court. The inner, or women's, court of the Northern Wei was undergoing redefinition during the fifth and sixth centuries as the court itself adopted and modified Han-dynastic court ranks for women.[19] Pitted against each other in a patriarchal court system, the women of the inner chamber moved in and out of the Jade Radiance as it suited their livelihoods and careers. This was a necessary safeguard for court women whose very lives were dependent on their relationships with the men of the court and who therefore lived a precarious existence.[20] For example, Empress Gao, who attempted to murder the empress dowager and whom the empress dowager then had murdered, was resident in the Jade Radiance Nunnery from the commencement of Empress Dowager Ling's regency to the time of her own murder. We get a glimpse of what such precarity looked like for the women of the court in the next words of the empress dowager's biography, which tell us that:

> While in the women's chambers of the court,[21] and on account of the country's antiquarian laws, the women prayed together, with all of them wishing to give birth to a prince or a princess—not wishing to give birth to an heir to the throne. Only the empress [dowager] unwaveringly addressed the wives, saying: "How can the son of heaven be alone without a son? What reason do you have to fear the death of one person and thereby cause the imperial family to not produce eldest sons through the wife?"

This conversation is said to have happened in the inner and upper reaches of the women's area of the court and it references the previously discussed policy of the murder of the mother of the heir enshrined in the dictum, "If the Son is Noble, the Mother Dies." The biography chronicles how the empress dowager was committed to giving birth to an heir, even if it meant her death. It tells us that:

> When the empress [dowager] was pregnant with Suzong [(Emperor Xiaoming], all those in her rank became afraid on account of it and they exhorted her to concoct a plan. The empress [dowager] was firm in her intention and remained resolute. In the depths of the nights, she made a solitary vow: "If it turns out that what I am carrying is a boy and that the boy becomes the eldest son, then the child will live and I will die so as not to shirk [my responsibilities]."
>
> When Suzong was born [the empress dowager] was promoted to the position of concubine of complete loveliness [*chonghua pin*].[22] Prior to the birth, Shizong had been already bereaved by [the death of] the princes, and considering himself already quite advanced in years,[23] he placed [the boy] deep in attentive guardianship. In order to select his wet nurse, he gathered together all the suitable candidates from the illustrious families. [The child] was raised in a separate palace where neither his empress [Gao] nor the concubine of complete loveliness (Empress Dowager Ling) was able to nurture and behold him.

Even though the empress dowager is said to have bravely accepted the death that would come to her if she mothered an heir apparent, she did no such thing. In the absence of any more powerful figure than her at court who might enforce previous policies, there was nobody available to challenge the empress dowager's regency by forcing either her suicide or her murder. The policy of imperial matricide came to an end and the empress dowager lived to be a mother to an emperor as well as to become empress dowager. Pu Xuanyi has investigated the conclusion of the aforementioned policy of imperial matricide and argues that the contemporaneous construction of the Jade Radiance Nunnery was integral to the policy's demise; sheltering Empress Gao and many other court women who had experienced the loss of their court status owing to the deaths of their powerful male kin, the nunnery provided a safe haven for imperial women.[24]

BECOMING REGENT

When Xuanwu died and his son took the throne as a five-year-old child, the empress dowager seized the opportunity to exert her power and influence. The biography tells us that:

> When Suzong took the throne, the honorific of the empress was the "imperial mother" [*huang taifei*] and after that it became "empress dowager" [*huang tai-hou*]. She held court and heard governmental affairs, was called "her highness" [*dianxia*], gave orders, and handled matters. Later on, she changed her commands to

imperial edicts and the ministers as well as the chief minister called her "your majesty" [*bixia*]. She herself used the "royal we" [*zhen*].

The biography here reads as though this was an unremarkable progression of a woman's career after the death of her husband and the accession of her son. It was not. Powerful empress dowagers have long been a part of Chinese history; however, few of them have ruled directly. According to her biography, the empress dowager ruled directly and publicly:

> The empress dowager, because Suzong was young and not able to perform the ances-tral ceremonies, desired to put in use the model of the mutual offerings of the wife and the lord[25] from the *Rites of Zhou*[26] as a way for her to take the place of her son in performing the sacrifices, and so she investigated the old ceremonies. The chancellery summoned together the ritual officers and erudite [scholars] to discuss [the matter], and they considered it impossible. Yet the empress dowager wanted to use a canopy to conceal herself and oversee the matters of the three dukes,[27] and so she again asked Palace Attendant Cui Guang. Guang then found evidence in the story of Han Empress Hexi (81–121) who presented sacrifices. The empress dowager was very happy and she went on to make the initial sacrifices.[28]

This excerpt from the empress dowager's biography suggests that her rule depended on her ability to enact Han-dynastic rituals of state. Looking for precedent for her direct rule in the records of the Han court, the empress dowager's courtier Cui Guang looked to the rule of the aforementioned Empress Hexi of the Han, a woman remembered for being a virtuous and capable female ruler.[29] Similarly, Empress Dowager Ling also seems to have amplified her personal links to the Han dynasty and its cultural symbols. Not only did she build a Buddhist monastic complex at the site of the Han imperial observatory, or numinous platform, in Luoyang, but she also had her own, personally commissioned grotto at Longmen decorated with figures from Han mythology: the Queen Mother of the West and the King Father of the East are engraved on the façade of the grotto and flank the entry to the upper left and the upper right. We do not have a clear picture of what the rest of the grotto looked like, for it was destroyed by fire. Hence it is known to history as "huoshao" ("burned by fire").[30] The Huoshao grotto was the highest and largest of the Northern Wei grottos at Longmen. Amy McNair argues that it was also the most expensive. Its destruction by fire is a poignant metaphor for the empress dowager herself: As regent in control of the empire's resources at the height of the Luoyang era, the empress dowager was murdered and her city was destroyed. Although she invested in Buddhist building projects that made a nod to her identity as a Han woman during her reign, neither her religion nor her ethnicity saved her or her city. We will see later in this study how both her Buddhism and her social location allowed her male, Confucian court-iers to link her to a different, and terrible, Han ruler—her namesake, Emperor Ling (r. 168–89). We will read about this in chapter 5.

In the subsequent section of our text, the biography of the empress dowager details some of what she did at the height of her power:

> The empress dowager was intelligent by nature. Many were her talents. Since her aunt had become a nun, [the empress dowager] was entrusted to her in her youth, and [thus] had some grasp of the larger meanings of the Buddhist sūtras. [The empress dowager] personally oversaw all affairs and issued judgements in her own hand. When she visited the Hall of Dharma Dissemination in the Park of the Western Grove, she commanded her officials to shoot [arrows] and those who were unable to do so were punished. Moreover, she herself shot the needle through the hole, hitting the center. Overjoyed, she bestowed all manner of cloths and silks on everyone, in accord with their differences.
>
> In the beginning, she ordered the building of a dispute-reporting cart,[31] which was a cart for bringing disputes to court. When she was driving it, she would herself depart from the Great Sima Gate of the Cloudy Dragon, go past the palace in the northwest and then reenter at the Gate of a Thousand Autumns, having received the grievances to take to court. She also personally questioned the filial and refined as well assessed officials of the provinces and prefectures.

Here we see the empress dowager praised for her intelligence and varied talents. This praise is continued with a description of her archery and her driving, both of which stand out as remarkable abilities because of her gender. For male leaders, neither skill would be noteworthy; however, for a female leader both skills stand out as gender transgressions. We have already seen how her archery had been criticized by her Confucian advisor Cui Guang, who told her that archery, along with ruling, were not arts that a woman could (or should) cultivate. Similarly, her driving her own dispute-reporting cart, which would fall into the category of arts not fit for women, is tantamount here to ruling. For an example of a more appropriate means of transport for women, the "Annals on Ritual" section of the *Book of the Wei* contains descriptions of carts for women's use; however, these carts are all for assisting in the sacrifices at suburban temples and are to be part of the larger imperial entourage. Consider the record of the cart normally reserved for the empress or empress dowager:

> The elephant carriage: It is adorned on the left and the right with phoenixes, white horses, and transcendents preparing to take off in flight, and it is pulled by two elephants. With wings of grass and streamers like the tail of a bird, and dragon banners, flags, and standards, the adornment was just like that of the men's elephant carriage. It is used for the mother of the emperor, the empress dowager, and the empress to journey to the suburbs in order to perform their rites at the ancestral temples.[32]

Thus, when we consider that the empress dowager went out on her personally constructed cart—by herself—to collect grievances from the populace to take to court, what we should understand is that in so doing she created a means for taking on imperial tasks that were typically associated with men. Her ability to shoot, to drive, and to rule marked her as a woman that enjoyed the autonomy normally associated with male rulers in dynastic histories.

Finally, even though the empress dowager was said to be of Han ethnicity, in this last section of her biography we see her behaving in her role as regent in the same precise way as did prior khagan rulers of the Northern Wei. The text above tells us that after a particularly good shooting competition, the empress dowager was overjoyed and that "she bestowed all manner of cloths and silks on everyone, in accord with their differences." The key phrase here that clues us in to how she was behaving as a ruler is that she bestowed wealth to her courtiers "in accord with their differences." This is a characteristic practice of Northern Wei khagan, who distributed the booty from war among their soldiery "in accord with their differences," and it was one of the strategies by which the khagan amassed centralized power around them.[33] Similarly, this type of consolidation of centralized power at the frontlines has been replicated by many different polities—for example, the later Mongol empires—whose rulers distributed goods and booty to their troops. We see the practice in even the southern regimes of the period, regimes that employed such strategies in their military garrisons in order to create a system of social relationships and resource allocation.[34] What is different in the case of the empress dowager, however, is that although she is amassing her own centralized power in a way that evokes the khagan of the past and their leadership from the military frontlines, she is a different sort of ruler. Located in the opulent capital city and in control of Luoyang's comparatively much greater wealth, she is able to bestow goods in a more luxurious and, perhaps, more indulgent manner. The empress dowager did not serve on the frontlines, where goods and wealth are hard to come by, and so her bestowal of silks on her courtiers seems like an expensive gift aimed at creating support for her reign from within the capital. As such, she is behaving directly as the ruler has and should; however, since she and her court are no longer nomadic peoples serving at the frontlines of military conquest, but rather settled people serving in a wealthy and famed city, the gift is itself of a different nature. This nature perhaps befits her own personality. She is a Buddhist ruler with significant resources at her disposal; her giving away silks is therefore an act of her own religious charity born of wealth. Indulging in this act of charity also positions her as the unquestioned ruler of her realm.

Poetry and Ritual

The following section of the empress dowager's biography continues to detail further aspects of her creative use of her rule. Here the biography briefly describes an extraordinary moment in her regency—a ritual banquet at which she engaged her courtiers in a poetry contest where she and the child emperor, Xiaoming, each delivered one seven-character line of poetry. When read together, the poetry of Empress Dowager Ling alongside that of Emperor Xiaoming illuminate how the empress dowager publicly depicted her rule. The story goes as follows:

The empress dowager and Suzong [Xiaoming] went to the Park of the Flower Grove in order to fête the lords and the minsters at the Capital Pavilions for Winding Streams.[35] She commanded the princes and dukes to compose a line of seven-character verse.

The empress dowager's verse said:
  Transformations of light create things,
  [And so] embracing vital energy is righteousness.

The emperor's verse said:
  Reverencing the self is non-action,
  [And so] relying on motherly love is heroism.

The princes, dukes, and others below them were bestowed silks in accord with their differences.

When read together against the backdrop of classical notions of kingship in early Chinese literature, these two short verses provide rare commentary on the relationship between the empress dowager and her son, Emperor Xiaoming or Suzong. Two things are important to bear in mind when reading this couplet: The empress dowager was ruling independently of her son and she was doing so, in part, by having recourse to classical Han symbols and rituals. With this in mind, we can understand that her verse, though playing on gendered language of female passivity, is in praise of her own active rule; the emperor's verse, though similarly playing on gendered language of strength, is justification of his passive rule. How? Both verses play on classical literary allusions: The empress dowager quotes from the classical and now-lost commentary on the *Book of Changes* (Yijing), the "Elegant Words" (Wenyan);[36] the emperor quotes from the *Analects* (Lunyu); both of them use contrasting concepts from the *Zhuangzi*. When the empress dowager uses the phrases "transformations of light" and "creating things," she recalls the "Elegant Words" discussion of the trigram *kun* (坤), from the *Book of Changes*.[37] As a trigram, *kun* represents pure *yin* or the feminine source. Of *kun*, the "Elegant Words" say:

> *Kun* is most gentle and weak, but, when put in motion, is hard and strong; it is most still, but is able to give every definite form. By following, it obtains its [proper] lord, and pursues its regular [course]. *It contains all things in itself, and its transforming [power] is glorious* [含萬物而化光]. Yes, what docility marks the way of *Kun*! It receives the influences of heaven, and acts at the proper time.[38]

The silent quotation in the empress dowager's verse reproduces four characters from this section of the *Book of Changes* in her own seven-character creation: "Transformations of light create things/ [and so] embracing vital energy is righteousness" (化光造物含氣貞). Furthermore, the seventh character in the empress dowager's verse, *zhen* (貞), is also a common characteristic of the trigram *kun* and, as an adjective, is used to describe feminine ideals of righteousness, often of chastity.

As to the emperor's verse, his own seven-character verse (恭己無為賴慈英) includes four characters from the following section of the *Analects*, the collected sayings attributed to Confucius:

> The Master said: "Is Shun not an example of someone who ruled by means of *wuwei* [無為]? What did he do? He *made himself reverent* [恭己] and took his proper [ritual] position facing south, that is all."[39]

The effect of such quotations is radical. By referencing the trigram *kun*, the empress dowager invokes the feminine aspect of creation while simultaneously suggesting that her embrace of this ideal characterizes her as a model of feminine uprightness. Contrasting this with the emperor's verse therefore completes the political commentary. By referencing the *Analects'* discussion of the mythic ruler Shun who ruled by nonaction, the emperor is able, like Shun, to declare himself heroic, although passive in rulership. Furthermore, both verses reverse syntax in order to set two important concepts from the *Zhuangzi* against each other. When the empress dowager references the creation of things, or *zaowu*, in characters 3 and 4 of her verse, she recalls the *Zhuangzi's* creator or *zaowu zhe* (造物者),[40] which is the force in the world behind the active creation of phenomena. When the emperor echoes her by placing nonaction, or *wuwei*, in the third and fourth characters, he is recalling the text's insistence on the benefit of passive action in the phenomenal world. Finally, the two verses are well contrasted in the fifth character, the verbal unit on which my interpretation hangs: The empress dowager "contains," whereas the emperor "relies." What he is relying on, of course, is parental love, or *ci* (慈), which can also be read as a short form for one's mother, or *cimu* (慈母). Although the emperor is said to have spoken these words, he did not compose them. We see, by following the chronology of the biography, that this event would have happened between the beginning of the empress dowager's regency in 515 and the death of her father in 518. During this period, Emperor Xiaoming was between five and eight years old and therefore too young to compose such a verse himself. This was a political display orchestrated by the empress dowager and her courtiers in order to show to banquet attendees just who wielded power. The two verses justify both active rule by the empress dowager, whose virtue remains "righteous," and passive rule by the emperor, whose virtue remains "heroic."

The composition of such a verse, as well as its delivery at a ritual banquet for her courtiers, is extraordinary but not unexpected. In the next section of the biography we encounter subsequent events that the empress dowager facilitated in order to include herself in the ritual occasions of the court and thereby express her magnetism and cement her power. From taking part in burials to building pagodas, the empress dowager never missed an opportunity to position herself as a leading ritualist. For more examples, her biography records this:

When the empress dowager's father died, the hundred officials wrote a memorial requesting that he be made a posthumous duke. The empress dowager did not permit it. Then she continued on to the Eternal Peace Monastery and personally constructed a temple with a nine-story base. The monks, nuns, ladies, and gentlemen in attendance were in the several tens of thousands. When the tomb of Empress Wenzhao of the Gao Clan needed to be moved, the empress dowager did not want Suzong [Emperor Xiaoming] to preside over these matters, and thereupon she personally became the presider at the funeral. Having excavated it, it was finally brought to Peace Tumulus [*ningling*], and she personally set up the mortuary items and returned to weep in the Hall of the Great Ultimate. When the matters had been concluded, she had presided over all of them.

Later, [the empress dowager] went for an imperial visit to Mount Songgao and ascended the summit with the court ladies, the nine consorts, the princesses and lower ranks following after her, several hundred persons in all. There, she abolished all licentious sacrifices; however, the Inner Asian sky god[41] was not [included] in this list.

Later still, she went to the left (east) storehouse with princes, dukes, female attendants, lords, and lower ranks following after her—more than one hundred people. She commanded all of them to take as much silk and cotton as they could bear so that she could bestow it on them: many took more than two hundred bolts, fewer took more than one hundred bolts. Only the Changle princess took in her hand twenty bolts and then left, showing that although she was no different from anyone else, she did not put herself out [to get the silk]. The whole world praised her honesty. Of equal prestige, Li Chong, Duke of Chenliu, and [Yuan] Run King of Zhangwu—because they were carrying too much—fell to the ground: Chong injured his back; Run harmed his leg. At the time, people adopted a saying that went: "Chenliu and Zhangwu injured their backs and injured their thighs; covetous people are losers and sully our enlightened ruler."[42]

Wanting to make an imperial visit to Quekou [Longmen] and Wenshui, [the empress dowager] climbed to the summit of Chicken Head Mountain, herself shot an ivory hairpin and hit the target on her first try, and then made proclamations to both civil and military society.

Here, we learn more about the empress dowager's style of statecraft. Setting herself up as chief ritualist, she took charge of all political matters but also all matters of public ritual concern, including the moving of graves, the building of memorials, the policing of heterodox religious beliefs and groups, and the rewarding of servants through the disbursement of goods from the treasury. In sum, with all these actions we see the empress dowager ruling directly, as an emperor or a khagan would do. But she was also ruling as a Buddhist ruler and a filial daughter. Her journey back to Chicken Head Mountain is noteworthy because Chicken Head Mountain is in the region of her birth and it is home to an important Buddhist site that began to flourish in the fifth century. That site is known as the Monastery of the Hollow Rock (Shikong si) and it houses Buddhist grottos that both her Huangfu family and her Hu family were active in patronizing. Her trip there seems to suggest that, as regent and independent ruler, the empress dowager retained ties to her family and their Buddhism. The empress dowager exerted her tenuous hold on power through public ritualism—much of it, Buddhist—but although she ruled independently, she did not go unchallenged.

The Coup d'État

The next section of her biography in the *Book of the Wei* provides an example of some of these challenges, detailing a coup d'état during which the empress dowager was under house arrest before resuming her regency. According to the biography, the coup d'état was mounted by a member of the imperial family, Yuan Cha, who was the empress dowager's own brother-in-law because he was married to her sister. The conflict erupted over an affair that the empress dowager was supposedly having with yet another member of the Yuan family, Yuan Yi, the half-brother of Emperor Xuanwu, the latter of whom was the father of her son, Emperor Xiaoming.[43] According to the biography, the empress dowager forced her intimacy on Yuan Yi; however, I read this accusation as an example of the type of gendered tropes used in her life writing that will be discussed at the end of the chapter. With Yuan Yi dead, the empress dowager had lost her lover and closest advisor. The conflict also saw her lose other advisors and confidantes. The biography states that when she returned to power, she relied on the bad advice of other courtiers while showing them extreme favor. She is faulted for doing so, and yet one wonders whom she could possibly trust at this time of conflict and contestation. It appears that some of the high-ranking members of the Yuan clan were no longer supporting her; moreover, her closest Yuan family confidante was dead. The biography narrates all of this as such:

> When the empress [dowager] had grasped her ambition, she forced intimacy on Prince Yi of Qinghe [Qinghe *wang* Yi]. All under heaven detested her for being licentious and promiscuous, unrestrained and passionate. General of the Palace Guard [*lingjun jiangjun*][44] Yuan Cha, the Minister of the Domestic Service [*changqiu qing*], Liu Teng [464–523],[45] and others waited on Suzong in the Hall of Manifest Yang, held the empress dowager in the Northern Palace, and then murdered [Yuan] Yi in the restricted areas [of the palace]. After that, the followers of the Empress Dowager—the Monastic Supervisor [*doutong*] Sengjing,[46] the Guard in Personal Attendance [*beishen zuoyou*] Zhang Dongqu,[47] and several tens of others—planned to murder Cha so that they could again serve the empress dowager as she oversaw the court. The plan was not successful: Sengjing was sent into exile and corvée labor at the borders; Dongqu was murdered; and many of the members of the Hu clan were removed from office. Later on, Suzong went to the empress dowager in the Park of the Western Grove to fête the civil and military officials and ministers, and they feasted until dusk. Cha thereupon went to face the empress dowager, and explained that it was being said all around that the empress dowager had wanted to harm him and Teng. The empress dowager replied, saying, "It is not as you say." Then, in the

depths of the night, the empress dowager grabbed Suzong with her hands and took him from the hall, saying, "Mother and son have not been together for a long time. We will spend this entire night together. All the great ministers will see us out." The empress dowager and Suzong went to the little pavilion in the northeast. The General of the Left Guard Xi Kangsheng, schemed to murder Yuan Cha but it did not happen.

Liu Teng himself died and Cha then became increasingly careless. The empress dowager, together with Suzong, Gao Yang, and Wang Yong, planned to remove Yuan Cha from leading the generals. The empress dowager again oversaw the court, made a great pardon, and changed the reign title. Accordingly, the court's administration was sloppy; might and favor were not established; and the officials and guards of the realm were covetous and greedy. Cheng Yan corrupted and upset the palace apartments, and power collapsed [in the regions] between the four seas. Li Shengui and Xu Ge were both looked upon as dear servants. Within a year or two they became indispensable, and with their hands grasping the imperial ranks and with indecisive hearts, they spread depravity at court so that all in the four directions abhorred them. Civil and military all disintegrated and everything became disorderly and rebellious. The earth collapsed like rotting fish on account of it all. Sengjing then assembled together the members of the clan and, weeping, stated, "Our Majesty's mother is the model for all within the four seas, how is it proper that she neglects all of this?" The empress dowager was enraged and accordingly never summoned Sengjing.

Jennifer Holmgren has analyzed the circumstances surrounding the coup d'état and has shown that they are much more complex than suggested above. By investigating the empress dowager's favoritism at court, criticism of her rule by certain factions of the court, and the ethnic tensions embroiling the court itself, Holmgren argues that although the empress dowager relied on certain factions at court to strengthen her regency after the coup d'état, they were not factions that she created. According to Holmgren, when the empress dowager began her regency in 515, the dynasty was already in rapid decline owing to famine in the northern garrisons and the subsequently increasing political factionalism.[48] This decline, and the factionalism that ensued, is what brought down her dynasty even if she was herself the last independent ruler of it.

In the biography we see that the empress dowager had lost favor with many of her high-ranking courtiers in the years of the coup d'état and its aftermath; this claim, however, is much less certain if we look to Buddhist epigraphs and Buddhist building projects from the period. There is a notable rise in Buddhist grotto construction and donative epigraphy throughout the Zhengguang reign (520–25), which included the years of the coup d'état. This increase continues through the Xiaochang reign, which was when the empress dowager was returned to her regency with Emperor Xiaoming. Such projects were heavily invested with symbols of Buddhist monarchy and they document support for the coreign of Emperor Xiaoming and Empress Dowager Ling. In Luoyang, Crown Prince Yuan Yue, whom we have seen before was the patron of the Nunnery of the Joyous View after the death of his brother the aforementioned Yuan Yi, commissioned many projects during the Zhengguang. Two of these projects were specifically in support of Empress Dowager Ling and Emperor Xiaoming. From a stele inscription at the Northern Wei imperial burial cluster at Mount Mang, we read that he refurbished a stūpa originally commissioned by his father, Emperor Xiaowen. The inscription is complete and references Yuan Yue's contrition for his life choices, as well as his commitment to becoming a great Buddhist donor. The important part, however, comes in his dedication of merit. Using the previously discussed term for regency rule strongly associated with Empress Wu in the Tang dynasty, Yuan Yue refers to the Northern Wei Emperor Xiaoming and Empress Dowager Ling as the "Two Sages" and requests that their reign continue on "for 10,000 years without limit."[49] Also in Luoyang, and also during the Zhengguang reign when the empress dowager was under house arrest, Yuan Yue commissioned the building of a stūpa at the site of the Han-dynasty numinous platform.[50] We have already seen how the numinous platform was an important site for the empress dowager who commissioned a monastery there for her deceased father and thereby connected herself to Han-dynasty symbols and sites of imperial legitimation. Yuan Yue was full a brother to Yuan Yi, the lover of the empress dowager who died in the coup d'état against her, and half-brother to the primary husband of the empress dowager, Emperor Xuanwu. That Yuan Yue commissioned these two massive and expensive projects in support of her reign immediately following the death of Yuan Yi suggests that he was a supporter of hers and that he expressed his political support for her through the medium of Buddhist building projects.

Such patronage of the empress dowager continued over at Longmen, most notably during the few years after she resumed her regency and, according to the *Book of the Wei*, was losing the support of her courtiers. For example, Amy McNair draws our attention to a rare donor epigraph at Longmen that was commissioned by a group of nuns from a Luoyang nunnery and dedicated to the women of the imperial court, including the empress dowager.[51] This was inscribed in the year 525, just after the resumption of the empress dowager's regency with Emperor Xiaoming. In the year 527, the empress dowager's maternal uncle commissioned the building of a grotto very close to the grotto that is conjectured to have been the empress dowager's own project, the Huoshao grotto. Her uncle's grotto has a pictorial program that shows buddhas of past, present, and future, but what is truly remarkable is that, as we saw in the previous chapter, the grotto contains images of imperial processions that arguably depict Empress Dowager Ling and Emperor Xiaoming. In this case, in a Buddhist medium, the image presented is one of co-rulership: With Xiaoming following along behind her in the women's procession, it appears that support for her rule was still seen among some Buddhist donors at Longmen in the year 527.

Even in the epigraphical record, however, there is evidence of court factionalism: If the empress dowager's family and her brother-in-law, Yuan Yue, showed their support for her through Buddhist images of kingship at Longmen and in

Luoyang, other sites of donation suggest less support. For example, the earliest buddha-image grottos in Shandong province also date to the time of the Northern Wei coup d'état in Luoyang and are found at a site called the Yellow Cliff (Huang shiya).[52] Although there is a demonstrable relationship between the processes of building and donorship between Longmen and the Yellow Cliff, the few donative epigraphs at the Yellow Cliff do not appear to mention the empress dowager. In 526, when the empress dowager had resumed her regency although Emperor Xiaoming had grown into manhood and could rule on his own, an inscription cites only him as a dedicatee, not her. A similar inscription is seen in the year 527. In the year 528, another inscription cites the child emperor propped up by the empress dowager's murderer as a dedicatee, but not her. In sum, what all of this suggests is that Buddhist epigraphy documents some of the contours of political and court factionalism during the years that include the coup d'état, the resumption of the empress dowager's regency over Emperor Xiaoming, and the deaths of both of them. Some of this factionalism shows support for her and some of it does not. Such epigraphs are therefore indispensable sources for us to use in interpreting the biography. They allow us to see that the biography simply recounts the narrative of one such faction. In chapter 5, we will return to the question of whom this political faction includes and why the members of it created a narrative of lack of support for the empress dowager.

Regicide/Filicide

The second regency (525–28) of the empress dowager is characterized in her biography as one of paranoia, retaliation, and murder. This was a regency that should never have come into being in the first place because the empress dowager should have stepped down. It is difficult to pinpoint with accuracy the age at which a child emperor was thought to be able to rule in his own right during the Northern Wei period, but precedent guides us here: Emperor Xianwen was seventeen years old when Empress Dowager Wenming forced him into retirement so that she could rule behind her son. At the time of Empress Dowager Ling's second regency, Emperor Xiaoming was fifteen years old. It stands to reason, then, that he no longer required a regent. The empress dowager's second regency was therefore contested and violent. We see contestation of this second regency throughout the remainder of her biography that describes how she became increasingly reliant on new and questionable advisers because many of her confidantes had died during the coup d'état. The empress dowager did not step down and relinquish power to her son; this second regency was therefore fraught. As the biography puts it:

Considering, herself, that her own actions had been improper, the empress dowager feared that the royal family had become suspicious of her. She thereupon formed a clique with those on the inside to guard [Suzong's] eyes and ears. Of those dear to Suzong, the empress dowager brought much harm to them. [For example] there was a monk named Miduo [Skt. Maitreya] who was able to speak the language of the [Western] non-Han [peoples] and whom Suzong placed in his retinue. The empress dowager thought that he was passing down information and so, on the third day of the third month he was killed in a large alleyway in the south of the city. At that point, [the empress dowager] offered bounties to enlist outlaws to enter the palace and kill the commanders of the emperor's personal guard, as well as the Lesser Ministers for Making Loud Announcements [*honglu shaoqing*],[53] Gu Hui and Shao Da, who were both favorites of the emperor.

Suspicions and rifts frequently arose between mother and son. Zheng Yan was worried that this would be a disaster and he thereupon plotted with the empress dowager to take the daughter of the Lady of Complete Loveliness[54] from the Pan family [who was the wife of Emperor Xiaoming], and then to have the empress dowager pretend that she was a boy and then declare a pardon and change the reign name. The death of Suzong came about so rapidly that, at the time, there was a theory discussed by all that Zheng Yan and Xu Ge had planned it. The courtiers were therefore unrestrained in their indignation. The empress dowager took the baby girl from Concubine Pan and, saying that she was a prince, established her as such. After several days, seeing that people's hearts were totally at ease, she began to say that Concubine Pan had actually given birth to a girl and that there would be a further selection of the heir. Then she established the son of the prince of Lin Tao, Yuan Zhao, as heir, who was three years old. All under heaven were aghast.

According to the biography, in the last fervent years of her reign (and her life), the empress dowager formed a clique against her son, murdering his confidant, the Buddhist monk, Miduo. She then, in consultation with her courtier, Zheng Yan, planned to promote her granddaughter to the throne. At this point, though the biography does not say that she was guilty of Xiaoming's murder, it does connect Zheng Yan to that murder and go on to say that the empress dowager completed the plan they had discussed by placing her granddaughter on the throne. Chapter 4 of this book explores the reasons why they may have plotted to place a girl on the throne.

Other places in the *Book of the Wei* bear witness to the fact that the rumor about the empress dowager's hand in murdering her son had spread beyond her court. Famously, this rumor surfaces in the story of the empress dowager's own murder at the hands of the Xiongnu general Erzhu Rong (493–530). A general from the disenfranchised and impoverished northern garrisons, Erzhu Rong led an army to the gates of Luoyang after the death of Emperor Xiaoming; he is said to have done so in retaliation for Xiaoming's suspicious murder. When he arrived in Luoyang with allied forces, he murdered the empress dowager, her new child emperor, and her courtiers, he sacked the city, and he burned down the Eternal Peace Monastery. As to his apparent belief that the empress dowager had a hand in the murder of her son, he is said to have proclaimed:

> How could it be the case that when the emperor [Xiaoming] was not well, doctors were not called for immediately and that his clansmen and great ministers were not

by his side? How can this not have caused astonishment both near and far? And furthermore, [how is it that] the emperor's daughter was made crown prince and a meaningless pardon was given? Above, this is a deception of heaven and earth! Below, this is misleading of court and the common people.[55]

Although Erzhu Rong's stated doubt regarding the empress dowager and his subsequent murder of her can be interpreted in the biography as a form of noble retaliation, this interpretation is not accurate. Erzhu Rong and his collective forces from the northern garrisons had many reasons for invading Luoyang. The death of Xiaoming and the accession of his daughter were simply a pretext for the long planned military takedown of the city and the empress dowager. In his nine-volume historical overview of Northern Wei governance, Zhang Jinglong devotes much of his final volume to chronicling the precise circumstances that fueled Erzhu Rong's invasion of Luoyang. Zhang specifically argues against the veracity of Erzhu Rong's recorded statement about being invited by Emperor Xiaoming to intervene in Luoyang politics and overthrow the empress dowager by showing that, by the time of the Xiaoming's death, Erzhu Rong had already been amassing a force in the north and looking for reasons to invade the capital.[56] These reasons have much less to do with the empress dowager than they do with her predecessors: With the change of the court's location to Luoyang in 494 and the redistribution of agricultural land to Han people in the central plains, the economic heart of the empire moved southward and left the northern populations impoverished and isolated. One can also point to an early medieval clash of culture wherein the Taghbach/Yuan family that ruled the Northern Wei became a new sort of empire in the Luoyang era, with a new type of leader and a new language for administration. This Luoyang political culture was also a source of tension in the late stages of the Northern Wei itself. We must therefore read Erzhu Rong's championing of his retaliation in Luoyang as a kind of propaganda initiated on his own behalf, as well as an ideological attempt to drum up support from the countryside.

Rape and Murder

Finally, with the collapse of the northern garrisons and the arrival of Erzhu Rong and his collective forces at the gates of Luoyang, the empress dowager's life came to its end. Whether or not the empress dowager actually killed her son, Erzhu Rong appears to have capitalized on the idea of that possibility in order to justify his murder of the empress dowager and more than two thousand of her courtiers. Regarding the events surrounding her murder, the biography states:

> In the first year of the Wutai era [528], Erzhu Rong raised an army and crossed the Yellow River. The empress dowager summoned all the women from Suzong's women's chambers and commanded all of them to enter the Way [i.e., the Buddhist nunnery]. The empress dowager herself shaved her head. Rong dispatched

his mounted soldiers to escort the empress dowager and the young lord [Youzhu; Yuan Zhao, 526–28] to the south bank of the river. The empress dowager responded to Rong with copious explanations; however, Rong pulled up his jacket [for a fight] and the empress dowager and the young ruler were both drowned in the river. The empress dowager's younger sister, Mistress Pingyi [Pingyi *jun*] gathered [the bodies] and interred them in the Buddhist Monastery of the Two Lings [Shuangling si]. During the reign of Emperor Xiaowu [r. 532–35], rituals were commenced at the tomb and she was given a posthumous name.[57]

The empress dowager met her demise alongside that of her new, boy child emperor. Regarding the specifics of her murder, the Northern Song (960–1125) governmental history compiled by Sima Guang (1019–86 CE), the *Comprehensive Mirror to Aid in Government* (Zizhi tongjian), provides an expanded, although similar, summation:

> The empress dowager brought together Suzong's harem and commanded all of them to "leave home," and the empress dowager also shaved her own head. [Erzhu] Rong assembled the hundred officials and greeted them and received the imperial carriage, and in the *jihai* day, the hundred officials presented [him] the imperial seal and prepared his legal carriage and [he] brought Jingzong [Emperor Xiaozhuang] to the bridge on the Yellow River. In the *gengzi* [following] day, [Erzhu] Rong dispatched his riders to seize the empress dowager and the young lord and bring them to the south bank of the Yellow River. The empress dowager faced [Erzhu] Rong and uttered many explanations, but [Erzhu] Rong straightened his jacket [for a fight] and drowned the empress dowager and the young lord in the river.[58]

In the above telling, the empress dowager appears to have attempted to depoliticize herself by entering the Jade Radiance Nunnery as a Buddhist nun. This was a short-lived strategy of just a few days before Erzhu Rong murdered her. After her murder and the murder of her courtiers, Erzhu Rong propped up his own child emperor in an attempt to restabilize the dynasty. Furthermore, on his triumph over the empress dowager and her court, Erzhu Rong is said to have declared, "The Yuan Clan has perished; the Erzhu clan has risen!"[59]

Despite the fact that not a single one of our sources expand on it, even in the empress dowager's death, we see the presence of the Buddhist institution. On the approach of Erzhu Rong's troops, the empress dowager commanded the women of the court to enter monastic life, presumably in order to protect them by hiding them in the nunnery. The empress herself did the same.[60] Her ploy did not work. She was murdered. The fate of her court ladies is unknown, although the *Record of Buddhist Monasteries in Luoyang* records a popular joke related to the further sacking of Luoyang by Rong's nephew and successor, Erzhu Zhao (d. 533). That joke suggests the women of the nunnery were raped by his invading army: "Hurry up, you males of Luoyang!," the joke runs, "Plait your hair in the non-Han fashion, so the nuns of the Jade Radiance Nunnery will take you as their

TABLE 1. Chronology of Important Events in the Life of Empress Dowager Ling

477	Sengzhi appointed to the Northern Wei court in Pingcheng.
Late 400s	Birth of Empress Dowager Ling. No recorded birth name or date.
494	Court and capital moved from Pingcheng to Luoyang.
500s?	Sengzhi recommends Empress Dowager Ling to court.
500s?	Emperor Xuanwu appoints Empress Dowager Ling to position of imperial consort.
510	Birth of Emperor Xiaoming by Empress Dowager Ling.
510	Empress Dowager Ling promoted to senior-ranking concubine.
515	Death of Emperor Xuanwu.
515	Empress Dowager Ling begins first regency, appointed to rank of empress dowager.
517	Construction begins on the Huoshao Grotto at Longmen.
515–18	Empress Dowager hosts banquet for her politically charged poetry contest.
516	Sengzhi dies and is buried with great fanfare and the personal mourning of Emperor Xiaoming.
516	Empress Dowager Ling said to have murdered Xuanwu's Empress Gao.
518	Empress Dowager Ling sends monastic emissaries to the western regions.
519	Empress Dowager Ling's stūpa at the Eternal Peace Monastery is completed.
520–25	Coup d'état by Yuan Cha.
525	Yuan Yue dedicates the refurbishment of his father, Emperor Xiaowen's stūpa to the "Two Sages" of Empress Dowager Ling and Emperor Xiaoming.
525	Empress Dowager Ling resumes her regency.
527	Building of the Huangfu Gong Grotto with its portrait of the empress dowager.
528	Assassination of Emperor Xiaoming by poisoning.
528	Empress Dowager Ling places granddaughter on the throne for a few days.
528	Empress Dowager Ling places a different child emperor on throne.
528	Erzhu Rong drowns Empress Dowager Ling and child emperor.
528–34	Various puppet emperors propped up by Erzhu or Gao factions.
532–34	Empress Dowager Ling given honorific name, "Ling."
534	Final collapse of Northern Wei.
554	*Book of the Wei* presented to the Northern Qi court.

husbands."[61] And finally, although it seems that the ladies of the court were to find no peace in the nunnery, the empress dowager did find that peace, at least in death. Her corpse and that of the child emperor were interred in the Buddhist monastery of the Two Lings, the name of which is likely a reference to herself and the child emperor behind whom she was ruling. This monastery is not referred to in any other source and it has not been located by archeologists working in the region.[62]

LICENTIOUS FEMALE USURPER

Canonical biographies of rulers in dynastic histories are normatively constructed through the method of "blame and praise" (*baobian*), a literary strategy of impartiality employed in biographical writing from as early as the records of the rulers of the Han empire. The empress dowager's biography in the *Book of the Wei*, however, offers little in terms of praise: The text unambiguously tells us that she was licentious and that everyone detested her.[63] This depiction of her continues in later accounts of her life in Ru texts of political historiography. The following example is illustrative of the general tendency in this regard. Even though we know that the circumstances surrounding her death were woven into the collapse of the northern garrisons and the rising factionalism in the empire, the *Comprehensive Mirror to Aid in Government* borrows the narrative of the murder of her son from the *Book of the Wei* in its narrative of the invasion of Luoyang. Regarding this matter, the text sites one of Erzhu Rong's own generals, who is said to have proclaimed that:

> The empress dowager was debauched and had lost her way. Her favoritism and manipulation were such that all within the four seas are befuddled. Therefore, in order to illuminate public affairs and create justice and prosperity, we must employ our soldiers to [also] purge her court.[64]

Here we confront the idea that the empress dowager had led her realm into chaos and corruption so deep that it could only be rectified by her own political murder, a murder that occurred alongside the murders of her corrupted courtiers. This is an example of historical scapegoating. Such scapegoating was aided and abetted by the power of cultural and literary tropes about women who ruled, tropes that are seen in the *Book of the Wei* but that are also continued in later accounts of her and her rule. In the following sections, I discuss the ways in which the empress dowager was troped in biographical writing about her; I conclude by asking who made these tropes and why.

From the perspective of the Chinese historiographical tradition, the empress dowager's second regency after the coup d'état should never have happened: she should have stepped down.[65] If the biography's heavy criticism of the empress dowager hinges on the moment when she should have stepped down and handed direct rule to her son but did not, then two important historical questions emerge: Why can a woman not legitimately hold power in her own name? And what happens if she does?

As Keith McMahon has pointed out, the Chinese tradition has long held the premise, first formulated in the *Book of Documents* (Shangshu), one of five classic texts of the Confucian tradition that deals explicitly with governance, that "hens should not announce the dawn,"[66] and hence that women should not rule. Regarding the dangers of women acting as political advisers and de facto rulers, the *Book of Documents* is explicit:

> The king said: "The ancients said: 'Hens are not for the dawn.' In the case of a dawn hen, this is nothing other than the dissolution of the family.' Nowadays, the King of Shang considers his wife's speech to be of use; befuddled, he has abandoned his sacrifices and not answered for it; befuddled, he has abandoned the ways of his grandfather and his uncle. Thereupon, only those criminals who have fled in all directions are honored and esteemed, trusted and given employ, and installed as senior officials, ministers, and gentlemen. [This has] enabled tyranny over the common people and created debauchery in the towns of the Shang.[67]

The *Book of Documents* is therefore unambiguous in its declaration that rule by women results in chaos: Just as a hen cannot arrive at dawn to announce the day, neither can a woman be listened to in political matters. Rule by women is interpreted as not only a rejection of normative social roles but, more criminally, an offense against heaven. The result of such an infraction against both the material and the transcendent world is that the social order will fall to ruin because heaven's mandate (tianming) will have been lost on account of having been given to a woman. While there have been counterexamples to the maxim that a woman should not rule throughout Chinese history, McMahon has shown that the women who have been able to rule have not been remembered positively by later historiographers and historians. Relegated to the status of meddlers and usurpers, female rulers have been subject to critical judgement by dynastic historians, who have held various assumptions about women in power, such as: "Women taking part in government is the root of chaos"; and "If no distinction is made between male and female, it will be a case of two masters. If there are two masters, then all is lost."[68] The stories of female rulers told in dynastic histories portray them as incapable, power hungry, and unrestrained in their sexual desires. As McMahon argues, "If," in the opinion of Chinese historians, "women ruled, they were considered meddlers in politics. They were a sign of weakness and decline. Heaven abhorred them because rule by women was unnatural."[69]

One of the most egregious examples of this literary trope of the licentious female usurper is found in the biography of Empress Jia (256–300) of the Jin (266–420). She is said to have ruled over the emperor and she is therefore blamed for various political disasters during the period. Compiled in the Tang from earlier records, the *Book of the Jin* (Jin shu) is uncompromising in its depiction of Empress Jia. In an overview of her biography, Michael Farmer argues that the text "uses extremely pejorative language, describing her as 'jealous and power hungry,' 'a butcher,' and a 'tyrant'" and that it borrows its gendered, biased, and exaggerated language from the biography of Empress Lü of the Han (241–180 BCE) contained in Sima Qian's (145–86 BCE) Han era history of ancient China, the *Records of the Historian* (Shiji).[70] Empress Lü was the first woman in Chinese history to hold the title of "empress" (hou) and she was strongly criticized for exercising political power. Both the Jin empress and the Han empress are said to have exercised some degree of independent power at their courts and they were blamed for being cruel, murderous, and sexually promiscuous. These stories should remind us of a further collection of stories of licentious female usurpers contained in the Han era biographical collection, the *Biographies of Exemplary Women* (Lienü zhuan).[71] That text generally extols the virtues of women considered eminent from the perspective of the previously discussed "Confucian discourse" on the lives of women; however, the last chapter of the collection focuses instead on counterexamples. Titled the "Depraved and Favored,"[72] the women whose biographies are contained in this section of the text are infamous historical models of the "licentious usurper" who uses sex and debauchery to distract men of high rank, steal their power, and, inevitably, bring political instability into their realms. Perhaps the most graphic of these stories is that of the concubine of King Zhou (trad. r. 1154–1123 BCE), the last ruler of the Shang dynasty (ca. 1600 BCE–ca. 1046 BCE). The text tells us that King Zhou lost the Shang owing to the actions of his favored concubine who distracted him from his own power by building a lake of wine and by hosting parties where naked people were made to chase each other through a forest of hanging meat, and who then exerted her power in order to encourage the king to roast his dissenting lords alive. In the text's narrative, it was the king's actions, induced by the concubine, that saw the end of the Shang line. As Farmer notes in his discussion of Empress Jia, though, we have no way of knowing what the precise circumstances of the powers and reigns of elite women were in early and medieval dynasties.[73] Nonetheless, as observers of history, we should be very cautious when dealing with historical tropes—in this case, gendered ones—that serve to uphold national narratives and legitimate normative history.

This well-established trope of the "licentious female usurper" is also found in gendered criticisms of the rule of Empress Dowager Ling contained in the political narratives and courtly biographies of the *Book of the Wei*. One place of criticism of the empress dowager that occurs across the *Book of the Wei* is the description of her relationship with the aforementioned prince of the imperial house (and her brother-in-law), Yuan Yi. As we saw, her biography claims that she forced her intimacy on him. Not only that; the biography also states that her actions in this regard brought about the coup d'état that itself contributed to the final collapse of the dynasty. The coup d'état also saw the murder of Yuan Yi, who, in his own biography in the *Book of the Wei*, is lauded for the prudent caution that he gave to the difficult empress dowager while acting as her courtier. It also generally positions him as one of her victims.[74]

The most direct of the gendered criticisms made against the empress dowager center on her attempt to place a female successor to Emperor Xiaoming on the throne. Regarding this, the *Comprehensive Mirror to Aid in Government* provides a slightly more expanded discussion than does the *Book of the Wei*. The text tells us that prior to his poisoning and death, Emperor Xiaoming had called on Erzhu Rong to help him wrestle power away from his mother. In the time it took for Erzhu Rong to reach the capital, however, the emperor had been poisoned, his daughter had been put on the throne with a great pardon given, and a new child emperor had been placed on the throne after the sex of the first successor was revealed. Here, even though Erzhu Rong's gendered critique of the empress dowager is simply a pretext for his planned invasion of Luoyang, an invasion necessitated by the impoverishment of the northern garrisons after the court's move southward, it functions as a plausible pretext because it rests on gendered ideas about the failings of women who rule. Erzhu Rong's gendered critique is seen in the way in which he describes the empress dowager's attempt to put a girl on the throne and in the labeling of her granddaughter's promotion as a crime against heaven, earth, court, and polity. His gendered take on her rule, then, is consistent with the manner in which she is generally depicted in the *Book of the Wei* and its derivative texts. In such texts, the empress dowager is largely remembered through the perspective of those who stood to gain from her death. The "last-bad-ruler" trope from the *Book of the Wei* has been adopted across later political and historiographical writings. Furthermore, the "last-bad-ruler" trope in her biography dovetails with the second trope of the "licentious female usurper." These intersecting tropes, which are clearly seen in writings on the empress dowager, have made her an uncomplicated political target for those looking to explain the fall of the dynasty.

By the time of the Song, although influential encyclopedias (*leishu*) frequently contain references to Empress Dowager Ling that come from the *Book of the Wei* and the *History of the Northern Dynasties*,[75] there appears to have been an effort to purge some of the contentious and unsubstantiated details from her story, details that may speak to the bias of the presumed original text. As a notable example, we can look to the entry on Empress Dowager Ling in the voluminous and early Song era encyclopedia, the *Imperial Readings of the Taiping Era* (Taiping yulan). Much of her record there is directly copied from her biography in the *Book of the Wei*, although there are important differences. Aware, perhaps, of the many recorded biases and problematic accounts contained in the *Book of the Wei*, the compilers of the *Imperial Readings of the Taiping Era* excised sensitive and potentially libelous material from their account of the empress dowager and her life. Not included in the *Imperial Readings of the Taiping Era* is the suggestion that she was involved in her son's death. Nor is the allegation that she attempted to place a girl on the throne. Similarly, her relationships with members of the Buddhist clergy of questionable repute have been excised; notable stories of her intercourt dealings that place her in a negative light have received similar treatment. At the end of the entry, however, there is a small section which records that she was remonstrated for dressing in fine clothes and showing herself off around town when she should have been in mourning for the deceased emperor, her husband. The record of this remonstration is also included in the *Book of the Wei*, although not in the biography itself.[76]

Even though, by the time of the Song, there appears to have been some attempt to purge unsubstantiated details from historiographical writing about the life and reign of the empress dowager, this was too little, too late. As a result of her generally negative depiction in historical sources—a depiction that relies on long-standing gendered tropes to blame her for the fall of the Northern Wei—little attention has been paid to her in any kind of writing or research since the medieval period. As a female ruler who saw the collapse of her empire, and, as a ruler of a dynastic house hat was considered foreign from the perspective of Chinese historiography and therefore not a legitimate subject of historical inquiry, she is doubly silenced.

FACTIONS AND FATES

The historiographical materials of the medieval Ru scholars that mention the empress dowager silently characterize her through the gendered trope of the "licentious female usurper." This trope has facilitated the historiographical process of blaming her for the fall of the Northern Wei. To understand who would have wanted to place the blame on her, we need to understand something about the compiler of the biography itself, Wei Shou. Wei Shou was a rising scholar during the empress dowager's time. His own biography in the *Book of the Northern Qi* (Bei Qi shu) tells us that he escaped the murderous purge of the court lead by Erzhu Rong and then went on to live through the overthrow of the Northern Wei, the establishment of the Eastern Wei, and, finally, the establishment of the Northern Qi.[77] According to his biography, Wei Shou's own professional achievements mounted quickly in the tumultuous years that followed the death of Empress Dowager Ling. Under Emperor Jiemin (r. 531–32), a puppet propped up by the Erzhu faction, Wei Shou was given official titles and duties at the age of twenty-six.[78] Following Jiemin, a second puppet emperor, Xiaowu, was established by a powerful general named Gao Huan (496–547) who had raised a successful challenge against the Erzhu faction, with which he had previously cooperated in the overthrow of the empress dowager. Not himself a member of the Taghbach/Yuan clan but needing to show his allegiance to it,[79] Gao is presented in the *Book of the Wei* as a loyalist to the clan eager to reestablish its rule after the demise of Erzhu Rong. His representation as a champion of the Northern Wei in the *Book of the Wei* perhaps contradicts historical reality: His own family benefitted greatly from the empress dowager's death—so much so, in fact, that his own son later became emperor of the Northern Qi. Gao Huan's opinions on the empress dowager and her reign are made clear in his own biography in the *Book of the Northern Qi*, where he is said to have called her "licentious and rebellious."[80] Although Gao established Xiaowu as emperor after the death of Erzhu Rong, Xiaowu himself fled the capital and established the Western Wei (535–57). Gao, in turn, promoted another member of the royal family and founded the Eastern Wei. After Gao's death, his son, Gao Yang (526–99)—who was ethnically related to the Taghbach clan through his mother—went on to establish the Northern Qi as the successor to the Northern Wei.

Wei Shou compiled the *Book of the Wei*—and hence, the presumedly original biography of the empress dowager—under the direct patronage of Gao Yang, otherwise known as Northern Qi Emperor Wenxuan (r. 550–59). Unlike the writings of other dynastic histories, which were undertaken by committee, the *Book of the Wei* was compiled by a sole agent, Wei Shou, whose benefactor considered himself the direct successor of the Northern Wei after the murder of the empress dowager and the massacre of her court. The text has long been criticized for its political biases. It was even labeled a "foul history" (*huishi*) shortly after its compilation.[81] The Northern Qi bias in the text is played out significantly in the story of our empress dowager because the very men who considered themselves the true successors of the Northern Wei and who sponsored the writing of its history were none other than those who assisted in bringing down the dynasty while directly benefitting from the murder of the empress dowager. To justify their own rise to power and the eventual transition to their family's leadership of the Northern Qi, it was advantageous to depict the empress dowager as "licentious and rebellious."

Furthermore, since the biography of the empress dowager was written very shortly after her death and by men who would have known her and witnessed her at the height of her power, it is perhaps the case that they were worried about the legacy of her own political faction. After the murder of the empress dowager, Erzhu Rong led a total purge of her court. The *Comprehensive Mirror to Aid in Government* claims that more than two thousand of her supporters were murdered in this event, which is known to history as the Heyin massacre.[82] The stories about the blood that was shed in the Heyin massacre suggest that, in the eyes of her enemy, the empress dowager was so powerful that everyone close to her needed to be eliminated lest they embark on a campaign of retaliation. The people of Luoyang who witnessed the murders and dealt with the tremendous violence that affected their lives and the lives of their families were undoubtedly owed an explanation. Making the empress dowager the scapegoat for the fall of the empire was one such explanation, and this is perhaps why we see such prejudicial treatment of her in her biography.

When Erzhu Rong invaded Luoyang, he murdered the empress dowager and those who were aligned with her. The sacking of the city that ensued included the destruction by fire of her famed Eternal Peace Monastery with its nine story pagoda, as well as many other Buddhist structures she had personally sponsored. The grotto at Longmen that she had supposedly patronized was also destroyed by fire at some point and has therefore been known throughout history as the Huoshao grotto or the grotto that was "burned by fire." After Erzhu Rong drowned her in the river, her corpse was treated without ceremony. No funeral was given. Her sister gathered her body and interred it in a monastery that has not been identified in the archeological record. Empress Dowager Ling's birth name and her body are lost to history. The buildings and structures that she commissioned have long been destroyed. Her life and legacy have been erased. If women have a way of disappearing from the historical record because of the dominance of sources written by men, how much more so in the case of Empress Dowager Ling, who was forcefully and violently disappeared and whose official biography was written shortly after her murder by the very men who inherited the empire that she ruled? For these very reasons, we need a better story. The subsequent chapters of this book embark on telling that story through a wide variety of primary sources from the medieval period.

3

Brought to Court by a Nun

Until now we have been introduced to Empress Dowager Ling largely through the *Book of the Wei*. Starting with this chapter, we will begin the process of learning about her and her life through sources not created or compiled by those who benefitted from her murder. A good starting place for that process is Longmen, the imperially funded Buddhist grotto site south of the Northern Wei capital, Luoyang. Understanding the artistic program of the various caves and grottos at Longmen is difficult. The thousands of caves, grottos, and shrines show a dizzying variety of size, imagery, and motif, as well as a diversity of donors and their intentions. Arguing contrary to the work of art historians of Indian Buddhist art who have shown that some images and some inscriptions in similar Buddhist devotional sites in India were not meant to be seen by human eyes, Amy McNair believes that the images in the Longmen caves were meant to be seen. Showing that the devotional object of a shrine often sits in the shrine's very center, for example, and that shrine imagery employed at Longmen is stereotypical and therefore easily read by public audiences, McNair explores the precise visual mechanisms that made the pictorial and spatial programs at Longmen easily legible to visitors.[1] The sum effect of these caves and grottos at Longmen on the visitors who saw them must have been awe-inspiring. Offering the largest and most profuse collection of images that sixth-century people living in the central plains of China would have seen in their lives, the site was famed and acclaimed. People from all walks of life spent lavishly to have their wishes inscribed on the cliffside next to beautifully carved buddha and donor images, all of which could be viewed by the public.

As we have seen, and as we will discuss later in this chapter, it is conjectured that the empress dowager funded her own grotto at Longmen, the so-called

FIGURE 11. Depiction of the carving of the women's imperial procession in the Huangfu Gong Grotto at Longmen. The procession is placed directly under the Śākyamuni-Prabhūtaratna representation of the past buddha. Circa 527. © Li Lan.

Huoshao grotto. As the largest and highest of all Northern Wei grottos, it was definitely meant to be seen. At this juncture, however, it is instructive to refer to a different, monumentally sized grotto: the aforementioned Huangfu Gong grotto built by the uncle of the empress dowager in 527. The grotto contains a unique image of what has been identified as a royal procession that includes both Empress Dowager Ling and Emperor Xiaoming.[2] Preceded by three Buddhist nuns, two of whom are undertaking ritual worship of the buddha and one of whom is standing very close to her, the empress dowager is followed by the ladies of her entourage and then a second entourage led by the-then seventeen-year-old emperor. Built in the year before her death and that of Xiaoming, this portrait would have been known to and, assumedly, approved by the empress dowager herself. The image is one of corulership. With the two rulers united in their Buddhist worship and led by a procession of imperial nuns, there is no hint of the type of political infighting that implicated the empress dowager in the death of Emperor Xiaoming shortly after this image was made. Of course, this image is also political. The year 527 was a difficult one for the empress dowager and her supporters; having reasserted power after the coup d'état of 520–25, the years from 525 until her death were fraught with internal tension, political murder, and the realignment and reassertion of political power. It was a time when she is said to have been swayed by corrupt officials whom she favored.

For our purposes in this chapter, what is immediately interesting in this depiction of an imperial procession is the existence of Buddhist nuns as well as the apparent closeness that they are shown to have had with the empress dowager. As chronicled in her biography, the empress dowager gained appointment to court owing to the recommendation of her aunt, the eminent nun Sengzhi. Although a seemingly minor detail in the biography of the empress dowager, the power of the aunt-nun is critically important for our study of the empress dowager because it forces us to confront scholarly and traditional understandings of what Buddhist monastic women in East Asia were doing with their faith in the earliest times for which we have records attesting to their existence. In the case of the aunt, her appointment of her niece to court irrefutably chronicles how one of East Asia's earliest recorded Buddhist nuns enjoyed audience with the emperor and how she used that audience to promote members of her natal family to powerful positions at court. Precisely how the aunt came to court and exactly why she had the power and ability to support her niece's position are the subject of this chapter, because an exploration of both topics will help us to locate the empress dowager in her social and historical context. In so doing, we get a glimpse into the gendered nature of courtly life in the times of the empress dowager; this will enable us to engage the thesis that Buddhism offered women access to elite social networks to which they otherwise had no access.

In exposing the nature and power of these social networks and the individual opportunities within them, the present chapter places the aunt-nun Sengzhi in the service of a larger story of the creation of a radically new social category within early medieval society: elite monastic women. This social category arose between the third and fifth centuries of the common era but has had an incredible influence on the lives of women across East Asia until the present day. Although the Buddhist tradition is no longer the sole domain of monastic women in East Asia—Daoist women, too, have long had the opportunity to live in religious communities—between the third and fifth centuries the Buddhist tradition did provide forms of shelter, support, and community for women that were unique. In this way, Buddhist monasticism constituted an innovative social avenue for women in China that provided the space necessary to reconfigure female identities and the power to be trusted to do so. In this chapter, I explore what such opportunities looked like and what women did with them at the Northern Wei court in Luoyang, a place where female members of the Buddhist monastic community created state-funded and all-female networks of support from which they enacted new forms of virtue creation in society as chaste women a step removed from the sexual politics of the patriarchal family unit. The rise of unmarried, often autonomous, women acting in positions of social prestige and influence across the breadth of early medieval China is a fascinating and complex social history that remains largely unexplored. In this chapter, I aim to explore a piece of that history through a focus on the eminent nun, Sengzhi, and I will do so with the aim of describing the social platform by which her niece, Empress Dowager Ling, was able to rise, govern, and further support female politicians in her own court.

SITUATING SENGZHI

To begin a study of how Buddhist monasticism affected women's lives in early medieval China, we should begin with the work of Gregory Schopen, who is the world's foremost living authority on Buddhist monasticism in India. As Schopen has noted with respect to Indian Buddhism, prior to the establishment of the Buddhist community of nuns,[3] there were no "natural" or "cultural" all-women social spaces in India outside the realm of prostitution. Provocatively, Schopen notes a few of the ways in which the community of Buddhist nuns and the community of prostitutes seem to have mimicked each other in urban settings.[4] For Schopen, then, the establishment of monastic orders for women in India was more than a simple admission of individual women into monastic life. Ordination as ranking members of the Buddhist monastic organization represented a marked social change in the historical lives of women. Despite the famous hesitation of Śākyamuni Buddha on the question of female ordination,[5] the fact that women were ordained in the early Buddhist monastic community was a watershed moment for women's history, allowing women the opportunity and support to live their lives a step removed from the patriarchal family unit. This is true of India, and it also true of China.

Giving women the opportunity to depart from the traditional family structure and take up lives as unmarried, independent members of the Buddhist community, a woman's decision to identify as a Buddhist nun was a radical undertaking that necessitated a redefinition of gendered notions of work and virtue that were unavailable to women in pre-Buddhist modalities of culture and gender performance. In reference to notions of gendered work and value creation written about in the literature of the Chinese tradition, Robin Wang argues that in imperial China a woman's *dao*, or path, was to follow her male kin; by supporting their male kin's flourishing, she argues, a woman had a means of creating virtue, or *de*, for themselves. "Chinese women's social roles as daughter, wife, and mother," Wang states, "are the embodiment of their *dao*."[6] This means that, for a woman, *de*, or virtue, is only created in relation to a male *dao*. In her argument, Wang offers a sympathetic interpretation of a Chinese heuristic known as the "three followings" (*sancong*), which, in its origin, was a descriptive model for mourning rites first recommended in the Confucian Classic from times prior to the Han dynasty, the *Book of Etiquette and Ceremony* (Yili). The text here recommends that, in terms of funerary rites, "Women have the rule of the three followings and do not have a unique path. Therefore, a young woman should follow her father; if she is married then she should follow her husband; if her husband has died, she should follow her son."[7] Although this maxim is intended to establish mourning and funerary rites that indicate within which family lineage a woman should be buried and who should mourn her, the idea of "following" has been extended to suggest that a woman's life is defined by her role as daughter, wife, and mother. It was through these roles, Wang argues, that a woman was able to create virtue for herself and garner public standing.

The canons of early and early medieval Chinese literature archive the biographies of many such eminent women, women noted for their strength and foresight in family matters. For example, the *Biographies of Exemplary Women* contains the biography of the mother of Mencius (Meng mu, 372–289 BCE), who is arguably the most famous mother in the history of China. As an example of her fame in Confucian cultures across East Asia, she is featured on a board game for women that is housed in the Korean National Museum and that is thought to have been created by Queen Inhyeon (1667–1710) of the Joseon dynastic house (1392–1897). In playing the game, a female player ascends through various levels of virtue in a snakes-and-ladders-style format in order to attain the status of eminent women of old. Featured prominently among these women is the mother of Mencius.[8] As her own biography tells us, the mother of Mencius was widowed and yet raised her son to be one of history's most celebrated philosophers. Having chosen a suitable location for their lodging in which her son could appreciate both ritual and learning, having slashed her own weaving in order to impress on him the importance of making progress in his own studies, and having educated him in the matters of proper relations with his wife and in-laws, she has been known throughout East Asian history as a model mother. She is famous for having raised a peerless son without the need for a male partner; however, her biography in the *Biographies of Exemplary Women* also includes a number of instructions for women and their partners that she relays to her famous son so that he can relate to and respect his new wife. She tells her son:

> The rites for a wife require that she purify the five grains, strain the wine, care for her father-in-law and mother-in-law, and sew clothing, and that is all. Thus, she takes care of the inner quarters but has no ambitions beyond that sphere. The *Book of Changes* says, "She prepares the food within but pursues nothing beyond that." The *Odes* says, "She has no transgressions and no authority to decide,/ Wine and food are her only concerns," to explain how a woman does not usurp authority but practices the Way of the Three Obediences. Therefore, according to the rites, when she is young she obeys her parents, when she marries she obeys her husband, and when her husband dies she obeys her son.[9]

These notions of the gendered nature of work and personal freedom that the mother of Mencius here explicates in no way amount to a universal deprecation of women, though they do work to heavily invest women in the family unit. Arguing for the importance of women within the patriarchal family order, Mark Edward Lewis reminds us of the sixth-century family manual, the *Family Instructions of the Yan Clan* (Yanshi jiaxun), where the aforementioned Yan Zhitui argues that, "In forbidding the violence of children, the injunctions of a teacher or a friend are not as good as the commands of a nurse or a maid. In stopping the quarrels of ordinary people, the teachings of Yao and Shun are not as good as the instructions of a widowed [mother] or wife."[10] As Yan makes clear in his manual, women should be entrusted with power and authority in the domestic sphere. As mothers, women earned rites of mourning from their sons, a public act of filial closeness between mother and son that was popularized at the highest levels of society from approximately the second through the fifth centuries.[11] The women whose biographies are included for veneration in the *Biographies of Exemplary Women* are all filial women; as mothers, wives, and daughters, they find their *de* through supporting the thriving of their male kin. Even in the "Depraved and Favored" chapter of this text, all the women biographized are women connected with men.[12]

Despite such female modeling in the classical canons of Chinese literature, Lisa Raphals has argued against any notions of the timeless oppression of women in China by showing that women have long been influential within Chinese political and literary worlds.[13] There are countless stories of eminent and socially prestigious Chinese women throughout all the eras of Chinese history. Crucially, however, until the arrival of Buddhism in China, the ideal woman of the Han literary, philosophical, and historiographical traditions created social virtue and wielded social influence through her location as a holder of family identity: wife, mother, daughter. To explain this gendered dynamic of filial location, Ko, Haboush, and Piggott argue that although women of differing age and class (and, I would add, ethnicity) related to gendered ideas about the home and the family in different ways, nonetheless such an importance on gender roles within the family unit constituted a Confucian discourse that ran through East Asian history, which defined women as the "Other" of manhood.[14]

Indeed, a single, never-married woman living from her own means is one we rarely encounter in the many stories of virtuous women that have come down to us from our earliest sources on women's lives in the Chinese literary tradition. The mother of Mencius is an eminent example of the type of virtuous life that an honorable widow might lead, but hers was also a life unavailable to most women in imperial times for whom marriage helped to create financial security. This tying of a woman's virtue to their fulfilment of gendered family roles is not only true of the tradition we commonly term "Confucianism" in modern, English-language studies. Although women have long had space to act in roles of religious leadership within Daoist communities, the early Daoist tradition does not have a lineage of unmarried women who draw virtue from outside the family structure. The early tradition's women are wives and mothers.[15] For example, although the second-century Celestial Masters community certainly made space for Daoist priestesses in their liturgies and treated them as the equals of their male members, they were women partnered with men.[16] Relatedly, although Robert Campany has pointed out that women have reached high levels of prestige and attainment within the lineage of Daoist transcendents,[17] it is also the case that the women we have stories of are wives who often trump their husband's abilities,[18] revealing thereby an unusual display of high-level attainment because, normatively, women do not surpass men in such matters.

One example of an eminent and unmarried woman in the pre-Buddhist literary tradition is Ge Hong's (283–343) "Hairy Woman" (maonü), who is memorialized in the text of Ge that carries his own sobriquet, the *Master Who Embraces Simplicity* (*Baopuzi*). The Hairy Woman wanders the mountains in a half-human, half-animal state, a sign of the type of religious transformation that Ge advocates.[19] In the same text, Ge offers other sorts of commentary on female religious activity for nonimmortal women, and disapproves of women being in Buddhist spaces. The earliest reference I have seen within the Chinese literary tradition to groups of women associated with Buddhist temples is found in Ge's text, where he offers testimony on what he feels are changing gender dynamics in his time. He laments that:

> The common women of our times have stopped working at sericulture, have abandoned their work at making cap strings [worn on ceremonial robes], and have discontinued [weaving from] hemp. Rather, they go out to dance in the cities; they abandon their cooking and like to mingle with others. They pay visits on each other and go to see relatives. They grasp their torches under the stars (i.e., late at night) and continue to roam about. They take many servants with them, [thus appearing conspicuous]. The glamour [of their equipages] fills the roads. [They are accompanied by] maidservants and menservants, guards, and soldiers, in a mass as at a marketplace. On the road they laugh and joke—a deplorable situation!
>
> Some lodge at others' houses for the night. Some return under the cover of darkness. They entertain and amuse themselves at Buddhist temples and observe men fishing and hunting. They climb heights and enjoy themselves on riverbanks. They leave their districts for parties and funerals. When riding in carriages, they open the curtains and circle about all over town. Cups and goblets are filled and poured, and strings and songs come forth while they are on the road. They think that such conduct is lofty, and so gradually what is wrong becomes customary, and the opportunity [for illicit relationships] arises. There is nothing which they are unwilling to do. This is the cause of lasciviousness in our time.[20]

With regard to Ge's opinions on the bad behavior of the women of his time, what has yet to be commented on is the brief but important connection that Ge makes between Buddhism and women's behavior. Although it is well known that men often enjoyed parties and picnics in Buddhist monasteries and temples,[21] Ge's description of women doing the same is our earliest record of such events. In his voice we hear anxiety about women abandoning domestic life and household crafts to engage in modes of leisure that place them in the public eye. Notably, Buddhist temples provided a social space in which women could behave in much the same way as men, and this did not sit well with Ge.

Ge Hong belonged to a markedly different society from that of, for example, the Hu clan of Anding whence our empress dowager hailed. Living in the southern regions of the old Han empire near to the Yangze River, the perceived type of gender expression and transgression that he wrote about is drawn from the long-standing ideas about the connection of women to family and home that we have discussed. Although we do not have a similar literary record from the peoples at the northern reaches of the Han empire or from the northern dynasties, we might assume, based on our previous discussion of Taghbach notions of gender, that women in Inner Asian cultural traditions had a different relationship with Buddhism than women of the southern regions did. Such an assumption finds little in the way of contemporaneous documentation; however, Diego Loukota has recently translated a number of documents from the ancient Silk Road city of Niya, which sat on the southern rim of the Tarim Basin, that do suggest that Buddhist women were public actors in society and that they were ordained as nuns earlier than women of the southern courts and cultural areas were.[22] In his documents, which date to the third century, Loukota has uncovered proof of women not only holding the title of "nun" but also of these nuns owning and selling slaves as well as acting as witnesses in legal cases. This extraordinary find does suggest that women in the Buddhist centers of the northwest regions of the Han empire and beyond may have carried the title of "nun" significantly earlier than southern women did and that they engaged in public life. The documents that Loukota has translated, however, are preserved in Gāndhārī and they speak for a quite different historical situation than that of our Northern Wei women. For Empress Dowager Ling and her aunt, the nun Sengzhi, it appears that they were Han Chinese women living in a multiethnic and multicultural milieu at the gate of the Hexi corridor to the western regions. Hence, their stories display both a marked ability to engage in social and political life alongside their own engagement with Han cultural, religious, and political traditions.

The most well-known text of the Chinese literary tradition that discusses early nuns and their works in the Southern and Northern Dynasties period, the *Lives of the Nuns* (T. no. 2063: Biqiuni zhuan), includes some discussion of early Buddhist nuns from Inner Asia who made their way into the reaches of the Han territory and it perhaps captures the predicament of our Northern Wei women and their hybrid cultural lives. The *Lives of the Nuns* is a biographical collection of the earliest monastic Buddhist women known to the Chinese Buddhist tradition and it is attributed to a monk called Shi Baochang (trad. d. 518) who was active in the sixth century, but in the southern dynasty of the Liang. Scholars have objected to this attribution, arguing that the text was likely composed during the Tang.[23] Whatever the date of the text, Brett Hinsch argues that the collection is less aimed at documenting an accurate historical chronicle about early Buddhist women and their lives than it is meant as an ideological text of Chinese Buddhism that works to "construct new female identities specifically designed to resolve conflicts between Buddhism and Confucian family values."[24] Hinsch further contends that these stories do not so much provide biographies of early nuns as they provide evidence of the negotiation between Confucian and Buddhist notions of gendered virtue creation that become important in the medieval period and that is often expressed as the confrontation between filial piety and renunciation.[25] Hinsch argues that the author of the *Lives of the Nuns* took the aforementioned *Biographies of Eminent Women* as a template for his text and "manipulated his stories of exemplary women within a traditional genre to construct Buddhist female ideals appropriate to Chinese culture,"[26] thereby positioning the nuns as Confucian exemplars who, when the occasion to be become Buddhists arose, brought their Confucianism to their practice of Buddhism and vice versa.

Furthermore, in the *Lives of the Nuns*, these Confucian family values were also thought to have been important in the lives of non-Han women, such as in this famous biography of a fourth-century Sogdian nun, An Lingshou. It says:

> When she was young, Lingshou was intelligent and fond of study. Her speech was clear and beautiful; her nature modest and unassuming. Taking no pleasure in worldly affairs, she was at ease in secluded quiet. She delighted in the Buddhist teachings and did not wish for her parents to arrange her betrothal.
>
> Her father said, "You ought to marry. How can you be so unfilial?"
>
> Lingshou said, "My mind is concentrated on the work of religion, and my thought dwells exclusively on spiritual matters. Neither blame nor praise moves me; purity and uprightness are sufficient in themselves. Why must I submit thrice [to father, husband, and son], before I am considered a woman of propriety?"
>
> Her father said: "You only want to benefit one person—yourself. How can you help your father and your mother at the same time?"
>
> Lingshou said, "I am setting myself to cultivate the Way exactly because I want to free all living beings from suffering. How much more, then, do I want to free my two parents?"[27]

This brief story illustrates the conflict between Buddhist and what we might call Confucian perspectives on the social and religious roles of women. However, since this story is placed in the service of biographizing a non-Han woman whose father served a dynastic house of peoples from the Jie ethnic group (one such group from the so-called "five barbarians," or what are called *wuhu* in Han writings), we can read the story of An Lingshou through the additional lens of the development of particularly Han Chinese cultural forms of Buddhism at a time when the non-Han peoples of the north were physically and culturally moving farther south. Sengzhi is also part of this story, which will be further discussed below.

Although the aforementioned sources from Niya suggest that Buddhist nuns may have been present in the northern border areas of the Han empire as early as the third century, the Chinese literary tradition recognizes that the commencement of the full lineage of nuns took place only in the fifth century and only after the Liu-Song (420–79) court in the south had supported the Buddhist monastic community in its struggle to introduce canonical ordination for Buddhist women in China. From the point of view of Buddhist law, the legal ordination of a nun requires both a full set of monastic laws to be ordained under and a quorum of already-ordained women to be present at the ordination. Such standards were hard to come by in early medieval times, when there were no legally ordained nuns present, perhaps particularly so in the south, and when monastic law codes, or *vinayas*, were still being translated into the Chinese language.[28] As such, ordinations for nuns were performed without full legal authorization until the year 433, when, with the support of the Liu-Song court, the first legal ordination was undertaken with a group of Sinhalese nuns.[29] The other significant factor that supported this first legal ordination of Buddhist nuns was the arrival of the *Dharmaguptaka-vinaya* and its translation into Chinese by the monk Guṇavarman (Qiunabamo, 367–431). The story of Guṇavarman's role in advocating for and facilitating the ordination of women in the Liu-Song dynasty is told in the account of his life in the *Biographies of Eminent Monks* (Gaoseng zhuan).[30] Since the time of this first ordination of Chinese women into the Dharmaguptaka lineage, countless women have taken up the opportunity to live as legally ordained, Buddhist nuns in this tradition. In today's world, it is the Dharmaguptaka lineage of nuns that has been transmitted continuously without fracture, despite the unbroken transmission of other traditions for monks.[31]

What is true of monastic women, north and south, is that a woman's status as a Buddhist nun placed her outside of her natal family or her husband's family, which allowed her to work and create virtue in a space that was different from the family unit. This did not mean that a woman severed herself from her family completely. We have seen how Sengzhi promoted her own niece, the empress dowager, to court. What it did mean, however, is that she was able to identify herself outside the family unit and was removed from the sexual and reproductive politics of marriage and motherhood. Such an opportunity for social value creation through chastity and all-female community seems to have been particularly attractive to widows, since they, too, were divorced from the family unit owing to the deaths of their husbands and they therefore experienced estrangement within the patrilocal family. Such a precarious position as widowhood—that of involuntarily being removed from the social prestige of the family unit—was creatively leveraged by becoming a Buddhist nun.[32] Similarly, throughout the biographies contained in the *Lives of the Nuns*, we see a number of women using entrance to the Buddhist community as an alternate and sometimes complementary path to social virtue than what was offered by dominant and gendered familial structures in pre-Buddhist China. For example, the text contains stories relating Buddhist monasticism for women to themes of rape resistance with the threat of death,[33] marriage resistance by almost fasting to death,[34] and using entrance to the community of nuns as a cause for divorce and a means to escape a bad husband.[35]

A woman's involvement in Buddhist monasticism accords with what Lo Yuet Keung argues is a shift toward sexual abstinence for women in medieval China, a shift that saw a redefinition of female virtue from the ideal of sexual procreation to the ideal of pure chastity.[36] An illustrative example of Lo's argument is seen in the following story of a nameless Buddhist nun from the *Records of the Hidden and Visible Realms* (You ming lu), an early collection of "tales of the strange" (*zhiguai*) literature authored by Liu Yiqing (403–44). As the story goes, the Jin dynasty general Huan Wen (312–73)[37] was considering raising a rebellion against the emperor and usurping the throne, at least until a Buddhist nun came around to teach him the folly of his ways. As the story puts it:

> Huan Wen harbored the mind of a usurper. At that time, a Buddhist nun came from afar. It was in the summer, during the fifth month [of the year]. The nun was bathing in another room. Wen spied on her stealthily and saw the naked nun cut her belly with a knife and take out her five internal organs (the viscera) first, and next she severed her two legs, head, and hands as well. After a long while she finished bathing. Wen asked her, "Previously I saw you. How could you mutilate yourself like that?" The nun replied, "When you become the Son of Heaven, you should also be like that." Wen felt disconsolate.[38]

Although the idea of women acting as ad hoc political advisors to powerful men is not a new idea in the history of Chinese writing on women,[39] what is new in this story is the way in which the message is delivered. The medium of delivery is further clarified in another version of this same tale from a similar and perhaps contemporaneous text, the *Sequel to in Search of the Spirits* (Soushen houji).[40] This second text tells us that the nun in question took Wen as a benefactor and that he was so appreciative of her learning and talents that he allowed her to lodge within the inner gates of his home.[41] Despite Wen's respect for the woman, he was also curious about what she did in the shower. This curiosity turned him into a voyeur instead of a benevolent benefactor. His peeping at the nun—a reference to his sexual curiosity, which was akin to his questionable political ambition—is turned on its head when the nameless nun in question dismembers her own body, showing it to be both grotesque and impermanent. By mutilating her body in an act of self-sacrifice symbolizing the self-sacrifice of an emperor, the nun shames Wen and puts an end to both his sexual curiosity and his political machinations. Her actions are strongly reminiscent of the type of bodily mutilation and dismemberment explored by Liz Wilson in her pioneering work on disfigurement and disgust within early Indian Buddhist hagiographies and the depiction of her actions is perhaps modeled after the story of the nun Subhā, who, according to the foundational Indian text, the *Songs of the Sisters* (*Therīgāthā*), is said to have plucked out her eyes to prevent the sexual advances of a pursuing man.[42]

The nameless nun described in the story of the usurper Huan Wen draws on an entirely different repertoire of eminence in order to gain prominence in society than did the women whose lives are recorded in the *Biographies of Eminent Women*. Through the grotesque dismantling of her physical form, she displays her independence and self-reliance, her ability to choose when and how she lives, her advanced learning shown through magical arts, and her inversion of normative sexuality. In Lo's words, she manifests the idea of pure chastity over the ideal of sexual procreation. This shift to pure chastity represents a new way of being a woman that we see arising in various historical sources from early medieval China. It is this new type of womanhood that supported Sengzhi's rise and power at court.

WHO WAS SENGZHI?

We know of Sengzhi only through her entombed biography, which is the earliest dated biography that we have for a Buddhist nun for all of East Asia.[43] Sengzhi died in the year 516 and the biography is also dated to that year. Although the *Lives of the Nuns* collects the stories of nuns who are said to have lived before Sengzhi, that text is not dated and it is likely from the Tang era. We have also seen, above, how that text describes the behavior of Buddhist nuns in a way that encodes female virtues associated with the Confucian tradition. Sengzhi's biography is different. Not only is it our earliest, dated biography; it was also written in the year of her death and presumably by people who knew her, who witnessed her work at court, and who may even have attended the funeral described in the text. The biography thus offers critically different data than does the *Lives of the Nuns*. The data offered includes a chronicle of her life working for the imperial family and rare terminology attesting to the practice of Buddhism in her time, as well as to her own practice of that religion. It tells us which ranks she held at court and where she lived as a nun. And yet the biography is no simple eye witness. As we saw in the introduction to this study, commemorative biographical accounts of a person's life etched into stone and entombed with them in their death are a common genre of elite writing in the medieval period that, by the time of the Northern Wei, had become stylized and fixed in form.[44] They are a genre of literature strongly associated with elite male authorship and they do not offer the deceased's version of their own life. Nonetheless, as discussed in the introduction to the present book, they are incredibly rare sources regarding the lives of women in history that offer data nowhere else available in the Chinese Literary tradition. In the case of Sengzhi, her biography offers the earliest such data available for a Buddhist nun in East Asia.

In wanting to bring these critically understudied entombed biographies of elite women from the Northern Wei era to my study of the rise of political and Buddhist women in the medieval period, I have adopted a tripartite method for critically reading them. First, I do not read these texts as unproblematic historical fact; while offering data that is important and unique, I endeavor to place these texts in their historical context by reading them with and against other sources of information, such as dynastic histories, Buddhist texts, and art historical remains. Second, even though I handle these sources with critical awareness of their limitations, I insist that the information they provide is substantially different from the information about the lives of women offered in other source materials and that we have no compelling reason to be suspicious about the sort of information revealed by names, ranks, and dates in the biographies since, in all the cases studied here, they were written by contemporaries of the deceased. Third, given the rise in popularity of Buddhism in the early medieval period, I am particularly attentive to the ways in which Buddhist ideas and institutions shape what constitutes the type of virtue, rank, and prestige that is an integral aspect of the composition of these entombed biographies and I argue throughout that since Buddhism was a tradition generally open to women in the medieval period, it actually facilitated the mechanisms by which women could be praised for their individual merit outside the patrilineal family.

The epigraphical record of the Northern Wei has thus far yielded four different entombed biographies for Buddhist nuns, including that of Sengzhi.[45] All four of these were commissioned by the Northern Wei court during the regency of Empress Dowager Ling and are from tombs at the imperial burial cluster at Mount Mang. These biographies are incredibly rare, early sources and we will survey all of them in this chapter. The information offered documents how monastic women in this period began to fill the types of political roles that normally earned one their own entombed biography and elite-level mortuary rites—these roles were normally held by men.[46]

In the case of Sengzhi, she is remembered and praised in her entombed biography for holding positions in both civil and religious administrations. Like her niece the empress dowager, Sengzhi was a woman from the non-Han regions of the northern boundaries of the old Han empire. Her social location within the hybrid culture at the gateway to the western regions may have given her access to social freedoms not offered to the women in the heartlands of the Han. Drawing social prestige and influence from her status as a nun, as well as her position as advisor to the emperor, Sengzhi's entombed biography details her life in both domains. In so doing, her entombed biography is a rare source that contradicts what we know about the lives of early Buddhist nuns in China from the aforementioned *Lives of the Nuns*. Specifically, if the purpose of the *Lives of the Nuns* is to show that Buddhist practice was an avenue for women to enact Confucian notions of virtuous gender roles, then it is no surprise that political nuns like Sengzhi are not included in that collection. The exclusion of nuns with political portfolios from the collection is not only a historical inaccuracy, it is also an irony because it was only with the support of the Liu-Song court that women in East Asia achieved

FIGURE 12. Photo of rubbing of the entombed biography of the nun Shi Sengzhi. Circa 516. Photo reproduced from Zhao and Zhao, *Heluo Muke Shiling*, 20.

canonical ordination as legally recognized Buddhist nuns. The earliest biographies of Buddhist nuns collected in the *Lives of the Nuns* are of women who practiced Buddhism during the Jin dynasty, the southern dynasty prior to the Liu-Song. Although many of the biographies of the women of the Jin cannot avoid a discussion of those women's relations with the court, the collection minimizes such political connections as a means of extolling the women for their extraworldly religious commitments. For example, the *Lives of the Nuns* contains the biography of the nun Huixu (431–99),[47] who was frequently asked to visit the Jin palace and for whom a royal monastic lodging was built nearby. Although Huixu was connected to and may have been dependent on the court, her biography in the *Lives of the Nuns* stresses how she sought to avoid any courtly entanglements or positions. According to the text, she staged a hunger strike in order to enforce her rejection of the court and its politics, and the text claims that the court went into decline as a result of her withdrawal. Although, by the seventh century, we have examples of Buddhist monastic women creating and working within practice communities outside the capital city and the court that ruled it—the most preeminent of these being the medieval community of nuns at Baoshan studied by Wendi Adamek[48]— in the Northern Wei we have no such evidence at all. Instead, what we have is plenty of evidence that early nuns of the fifth and sixth centuries worked in tandem with the court and populated both the court and the nunnery.

Sengzhi's story preserved in her entombed biography is therefore of critical importance. As the earliest dated biography of a Buddhist nun in East Asia that we currently have, it provides a markedly different chronicle from what we are accustomed to seeing in the *Lives of the Nuns*, and it therefore challenges past scholarship, which has strongly relied on that text. For example, we see the effect of the source on the area of study in the work of Chikusa Masaaki, one of the few scholars to have studied the lives of the Buddhist women of the Jin dynasty like Huixu. Chikusa details the relationships between courtly life and religious life in these early biographies, but characterizes the women's joint religious/political undertakings as a "corruption" of the Buddhist faith.[49] In the story of Sengzhi, her joint religious and political undertakings were in no way considered a corruption of her faith by her contemporaries, patrons, and benefactors. On the contrary, her ability to hold rank in both religious and political domains was seen as a sign of her strength and eminence.

AN EMINENT BUDDHIST AT COURT

Sengzhi's entombed biography describes both her personal virtue as well as her accomplished practice of Buddhism. It says the following:[50]

> The aunt of the empress dowager who venerated the teachings,[51] [Sengzhi] was endowed with the true vitality of the three capabilities[52] and embraced the refined energy of the seven governances.[53] Her knowledge of the Way grew forth from innate knowledge and her spiritual demeanor came forth from her heaven-sent nature. Clean of all falsity and pure on the inside, she studied and taught the arcane gate. She left home at seventeen and her practice of the precepts was clear and pure. When she reached the age of twenty, her moral virtue was rich and profound. By abiding in concentration, she had arrived at the six supernormal powers[54] and so could serenely recite many [sūtras] after hearing them one time. She chanted more than twenty scrolls of sūtras, including the *Nirvāṇa Sūtra*,[55] the *Lotus Sūtra*,[56] the *Śrīmālā Sūtra*,[57] and thus, the great assembly recommended that she lecture on the sūtras. With a single exposition in the Dharma-master's elegant prosody, those who admired her righteousness [amassed] like clouds; with a fleeting chant in her

marvelous voice, those who took refuge in the Way were [thick] like a forest. Thus, she could shake the Yellow and the Wei Rivers with her voice, and reach both the Qi and the Liang Mountains with her virtue.

The account of Sengzhi's Buddhism above is rare among the entombed biographies of other monastic women of the Northern Wei because it indicates that her virtue was associated with her Buddhist practice more so than with her elite status. Of the four entombed biographies of nuns from the Northern Wei imperial burial site of Mount Mang that are currently available for study, two are for women who share monastic names beginning with the word *compassion* (*ci*), Ciyi and Ciqing. Their shared religious name is perhaps because they were sister nuns at the imperially funded Jade Radiance Nunnery. We have met Ciyi before: otherwise known as Empress Gao, she was the empress to Xuanwu who attempted to murder Empress Dowager Ling; however, the latter pushed her to the nunnery and eventually had her murdered there. This story is recounted in Empress Gao's official biography in the *Book of the Wei* and it implicates the empress dowager in her murder.[58] As for Ciqing, and according to her entombed biography, her entrance into monasticism happened while at court. According to the text, she was the wife of a leader of a rebellion that was quashed by the Northern Wei.[59] As a result, she was brought into the female ranks of the court as a slave, yet she quickly ascended to the high position of royal governess. In this role she cared for the young emperors of the dynasty, notably Emperor Xiaoming who considered her like a mother and ordered her state funeral after weeping at her bedside. Her ascent from court slave to imperial mother was made possible through her renunciation. Allowing her to reconfigure her public virtue from "rebel wife" to "chaste matron," her association with the Buddhist monastic institution was a pivotal and strategic turn that placed her in a position removed from the sexual politics of court life and her rebel in-laws. For both Ciqing and Ciyi, then, their entrance into monastic life was necessitated by their location at court: Ciyi was forced into the nunnery by Empress Dowager Ling, while Ciqing appears to have chosen monastic life as a means of renouncing her rebel family and converting her public virtue to that of pure chastity. The final entombed biography that we have is for a princess of the imperial clan, who is identified as a "nun" (Skt. *bhikṣuṇī* ; Ch. *biqiuni*) but not in the way we might expect. Instead, her title contains a unique appellation—*biqiu* "*yuan*" *ni*. We should understand that this title means "Nun of the Yuan family," with "Yuan" being the name of the royal family. However, that the Yuan family name is inserted into the monastic title of *biqiuni* in a way that obfuscates the underlying Sanskrit title of *bhikṣuṇī* suggests that those who gave her the title did not actually understand what it meant.[60] Such confusions might further suggest that the princess was not a normal sort of Buddhist nun at all, and indeed, her biography does not mention that she ever "left home" or practiced the Buddhist precepts. On the contrary, as a princess, she was made to marry twice for reasons of family alliance despite her desire to live a contemplative life. Reading her entombed biography reveals that her life as a "nun" seems to have been a self-styled one embarked on after the death of her second husband. In this role, she lived at home serving her family with great care while also studying Buddhist texts. She died in old age on her way to a hermitage. In the case of this princess, her title matches her actions: self-styled renunciation without the authority of a monastic community to which a nun would normally belong.

Unlike those of the three other elite Buddhist nuns from Empress Dowager Ling's court, Sengzhi's title on her entombed biography—dharma master (*fashi*)— bears witness to the fact that she was a higher-status Buddhist than they were. While in modern usage the epithet "dharma master" is common in Buddhist monastic communities, it was rare in the context of the Northern Wei. In her study of the rock-cut grottos at Yungang, Joy Lidu Yi argues that dharma masters were important community leaders and preachers of the dharma within the Yungang grottos and that their dharma lectures were attended by members of the Buddhist laity who also undertook rituals, such as offerings and circumambulation.[61] Yi also argues that the content of these dharma masters' lectures were linked to scenes from Buddhist scriptures that were carved into the grotto wall. As such, dharma masters were entrusted with the power to both officiate at rituals and interpret Buddhist teachings for large audiences. As far as I am aware, Sengzhi's biography is the earliest example we have of a woman having had the title of "dharma master" in all of East Asia, a title that was also rare in her time. I know of no other earlier women who held the title, though, as we will see below, two of her own disciples did hold the title after her.

Her status as a dharma master unites her with one other eminent Buddhist at the Northern Wei court: the Northern Wei Dharma Master named Sengling, the Great Superintendent of the Śramaṇas Who Clarifies Profundities (*Da* Wei *gu zhaoxuan shamen datong* Sengling *fashi*). According to his entombed biography, also from Mount Mang, Sengling died in the year 535 at the age of eighty-one. His biography tells of his own Buddhist practice and reveals that, upon ordination, he "deposited his heart in the clan of *Shi*,"[62] *Shi* being the first character of the trans- literated name of Śākyamuni Buddha in Chinese (Shijiamouni). This is notewor- thy because it suggests that ordination for elite Buddhists in the period included taking the name of the buddha as their new family name. Sengzhi also bears the family name of *Shi* as a monastic name. This may be evidence of her own canonical ordination. Similarly, her biography specifically says that she "left home" and that her practice of the precepts was "clear and pure"—important markers of Buddhist monastic affiliation that are not mentioned in the other entombed biographies of Mount Mang. Although there are scattered records of Buddhist nuns in epigraphi- cal sources from many geographical areas throughout the latter half of the North- ern Wei, there is no record of any sort of formal ordination for them. As such, we have no idea what affiliation these nuns belonged to and if they would have been legally recognized nuns from the perspective of *vinaya*, or Buddhist monastic law. In fact, in the case of Ciqing and Ciyi, there is no reason to think that they were legally ordained at all, or even that they were committed practitioners of Buddhism. Their status as nuns seems to be derived from the fact that they lived in the Jade Radiance Nunnery because of the loss of their male kin. For the princess nun from the Yuan family, her status as a nun appears to be self-professed, just as her title *biqiuyuanni* displays a fundamental misunderstanding of the Sanskrit word for "nun" and hence brings into question whether or not she was legally ordained. Sengzhi is different: her monastic name, her status as an eminent Buddhist, and the monastic position she held, all suggest that she was unlike her peers at the Northern Wei court and may have been legally ordained.

I believe that Sengzhi was ordained as a legally recognized nun in the *Dharmaguptaka* lineage being popularized at the southern courts during her life. As we have seen, it was the court of the Liu-Song that finally established legal, canonical ordination for women. The same court also sponsored the translation activities of the monk Guṇabhadra (Qiunabatuo; 394–468) who translated the above-mentioned *Śrīmālā Sūtra*, which Sengzhi is said to have been fond of preaching. Sengzhi's entombed biography includes the earliest epigraphical attestation to the text that we have for all of East Asia. Bearing in mind that the text was translated in the Liu-Song and known in the Buddhist worlds approximately ten years prior to Sengzhi's recorded date of renunciation and that the Liu-Song, also, seems to have been the only court in all of East Asia then sponsoring canonical ordination for Buddhist women, it might be possible to place Sengzhi and her ordination in the Liu-Song.[63] If this is true, it would suggest that her ordination was lawful according to canonical Buddhist law and that she held a status among Northern Wei society that demarcated her as a virtuoso practitioner of the Buddhist faith worthy of the titles she held.[64]

NUNS' WORK, WOMEN'S WORK

Outside of her status as a dharma master, Sengzhi also held a second important title that identified her as a court servant who helped to administer the Buddhist faith in the empire, perhaps mostly in the capital city. She was the Northern Wei superintendent of the nuns (*biqiuni tong*). Like her status as a dharma master, her status as "superintendent of the nuns" aligns with similar Northern Wei naming practices for monastic men, though Sengzhi is evidently the first woman to hold the title of "superintendent." Tsukamoto Zenryū's foundational work on Northern Wei monastic superintendents is still relevant here. In his study of the revival of Buddhism under its severe suppression by Northern Wei Emperor Taiwu, Tsukamoto sees the establishment of monastic superintendents as a part of the empire's need to police the growth of Buddhism from within the court itself. Such superintendents, then, were used by the court to disseminate and enforce the court's restrictive policies to monastic communities across the empire. Richard McBride has shown how this system of imperial monastic superintendents was also employed in the Korean kingdom of Silla, based on Northern Wei precedents.[65] Sengzhi's role as the "superintendent of the nuns" was a court-appointed role that identified her as the senior administrative monastic woman of the empire.

Although her entombed biography does not say when and why she received the title of superintendent of the nuns, it might make sense that this title indicates the original role that she was called to serve by Empress Dowager Wenming. Famously, the Northern Wei court under the reign of Emperor Wencheng established political oversight over the affairs of the Buddhist monastic community. Wencheng formalized the roles of the court-appointed overseers of monastic communities across the empire that were called superintendents and who were tasked with both propagating and policing the monastic community on behalf of the laws, decrees, and policies of the court. The appointment of such superintendents reflects both the anxieties and the hopes of the court: Hoping to capitalize on the social power of Buddhism in legitimating its rule and holding on to its power, the court was also deeply anxious about harnessing and growing a Buddhist tradition that it could control. The job of the superintendent was therefore not an easy one. Throughout the latter half of the dynasty, various Northern Wei leaders supported the spread and building of Buddhist ritual, devotional, and monastic structures, just as they enforced limits on the building of such structures among the populace. The superintendents supported the court in transmitting and enforcing these restrictions. Shi Sengzhi was such a superintendent, and she is the only female member of the monastic community that I am aware of as having held any titles during the rules of Wencheng and Wenming and, hence, during the founding eras of such positions at the court.

The first Buddhist superintendent in East Asian Buddhist history was engaged by the court of the Northern Wei. He was a monk named Faguo (fl. fifth century) and he is famous for having directed the Buddhist community to bow to the emperor by arguing that the Northern Wei emperor was a living buddha.[66] Faguo served the court of Emperor Wencheng's grandfather, Emperor Mingyuan (r. 409–23), who attempted to bestow the imperial title of "duke" on Faguo because of the monk's helpful service to the empire. Faguo declined but did accept the position of "religious superintendent" (*daoren tong*) and publicly declared Emperor Mingyuan to be the tathāgata, a buddha.[67] Faguo was not the only monk to enjoy such a title. During the reign of Emperor Wencheng, the monk Tanyao was given the newly constructed title of the "superintendent of the śramaṇas" (*shamen tong*)[68] and is himself said to have been the force behind the initial strata of building at Yungang, effectively giving form to the buddha-ruler identification made by his predecessor, Faguo. The *Book of the Wei* records that at some point in the mid-460s:

Tanyao stated to the emperor that west of the capital city, at the Wuzhou fortress, [one could] chisel out stone walls in the rock and open up five rock chambers and in every one of them, by carving [the rock] away, erect a statue of the Buddha. [In the event], the largest [statue] was seventy feet high, smaller ones sixty feet, and once they had been as exquisitely and monumentally adorned, they were the wonder of the world.[69]

The establishment of such court-monastic appointments under the Northern Wei speaks to the desire that both institutions had to establish a mutually beneficial relationship that would support the stability of the court and the patronage of the Buddhist community.[70] As an integral part of this relationship, Wencheng resurrected the monastic "superintendent" role that his grandfather, Emperor Mingyuan, had granted to the monk, Faguo, with Wencheng himself granting the title to Tanyao after the suppression of Buddhism undertaken by his immediate predecessor, Emperor Taiwu. Although the story of Tanyao is very well known, and although both of the stories of Tanyao and Faguo are recounted in the "Annals on Buddhism and Daoism," what is much less known is that Sengzhi also served in this role.

Sengzhi's position at court may also have been made possible by Emperor Wencheng's reorganization of the women's inner court. According to the *Book of the Wei*, prior to Wencheng's reign, ranks for women at the Northern Wei court were increased in both number and diversity. The text tells us that in the early stages of the Taghbach dynasty, the rulers used their own processes to bring women to court and title them and that, as a result, the ranks of women in the inner court swelled to the extent that the court was "saturated" in women.[71] It makes sense to think that, in an era as turbulent as the Northern Wei dynasty, when emperors, generals, dukes, and other men of the court often lived much shorter lives than their womenfolk, and also when the emperor himself had an inner chamber populated by large numbers of women placed there for political reasons, women were actually a more common feature of court life than were men. Their numbers were certainly greater. The early rulers of the Northern Wei kept a "mobile court," as they were constantly moving back and forth between the capital and the frontier, going where military matters required them to be.[72] This befitted their role as khagans and leaders of the military. As such, they left their empresses and concubines at home in the court of the capital, where the women were amassed together in the inner chambers. The *Book of the Wei* suggests that the inner chambers were poorly organized prior to the reign of Emperor Wencheng and that he oversaw the standardization of ranks for women, both employing the classical Han-dynastic canons of ritual in order to do so and aligning his newly established female ranks with those of the men in his court.[73] Regarding this, the *Book of the Wei* tells us:

Gaozong changed the order of the inner chambers: The ladies of clear etiquette of the left and right were established relative to the minster of war, the three ladies

FIGURE 13. Burial figure of a female official from the Northern Wei court.
Circa early sixth century. Excavated from Mount Mang. Piece now held
in the Royal Ontario Museum in Toronto, Canada.

relative to the three dukes, the three concubines relative to the three ministers, the
six concubines relative to the six ministers, the mother of the realm relative to
the ordinary grand master, and the palace women relative to the gentleman of the
Yuan family. After arranging the women's posts, [Gaozong] employed the classics for
internal issues: the inner officer was established relative to the director and servant
of the secretariat; the three common bureaus of the acting officer, the great overseer, and the women's attendant were relative to the second rank; the overseer, the
women's secretary, the talented women, the women's historian, the female sages,
the scribes, the scribal ladies, and the lesser female scribes of the five bureaus were
established relative to the third rank; the central lady of talent, the provisioner, the
ladies of talent, the respectable palace envoys were established as relative to the fourth
rank; and the spring clothier, the female libationer, the banqueteuse, the restaurateuse,
the menial service and the female slaves were established relative to the fifth rank.[74]

Although we cannot know to what extent such ranks were fully implemented, they were modeled after the ranks of male courtiers. These ranks were also known outside the Northern Wei, in the writings produced by other early medieval courts. The dynastic history of the Liu-Song, the *Book of the Song* (Song shu), describes the complex court ranks for women of the Northern Wei in its delineation of court ranks for women from the Han through the Liu-Song.[75] Critical for our understanding of Sengzhi is the fact that these court ranks for women were purposefully aligned with the ranks of the regular male bureaucracy of the court. This might be why we see Sengzhi brought to court by the very people that promoted, protected, and listened to Tanyao: Sengzhi was Tanyao's counterpart in a reorganization and realignment of ranks for women undertaken by the same court that brought her there.

Sengzhi was appointed to court during this time of the reinvention of roles for women courtiers, but she was appointed directly by Empress Dowager Wenming in 477. Empress Dowager Wenming was regent for two emperors: the father and the son, Emperors Xianwen and Xiaowen. When Xianwen died, he left behind no shortage of children from the many consorts of the court. One of those children, the then-nine-year-old child Emperor Xiaowen, who was installed on the throne in early childhood and whose regent, again, was Empress Dowager Wenming, had already been on the throne for five years by the time of his retired father's death. In 477, then, having finally rid herself of the father, the empress dowager was in full control of the son. Together, they ushered in a new era that would last beyond the death of the empress dowager in 490 until the death of the emperor in 499. To support this stability and cement her control over the nine-year-old child emperor, his siblings, and the many women now amassed at the inner court, Empress Dowager Wenming may have needed help in the form of a governess. It is possible that she found that help in Sengzhi.

Shayne Clarke has shown that although Buddhist nuns in India did indeed care for their own children in the nunnery, the caring for another's child—a child of the laity—was prohibited by monastic law.[76] Such law appears to have not been followed (or perhaps even known) in early medieval China, where we have evidence of nuns as caregivers of the royal elite. Most notably, and later than the Northern Wei, is the story of a divine Buddhist nun (*shenni*), who raised Emperor Wen (r. 581–604) of the Sui.[77] According to the story, the divine nun had requested that she be able to care for the young emperor because she recognized his outstanding caliber and did not consider him fit for secular life. Her actions were so noteworthy that they were taken as cause for the erection of relic stūpas across the realm in an act that Chen Jinhua associates with the rule of the Indian Buddhist King, Aśoka.[78] In the case of the Northern Wei, we have direct proof that such a situation existed in the case of the nun Ciqing, whose story we read above. According to Ciqing's entombed biography from Mount Mang, after being taken as a rebel slave and then rehabilitating her identity through becoming a Buddhist nun, Ciqing was given the task of caring for the imperial young during their childhood. The biography records that on her death bed, Emperor Xiaoming himself—then fourteen years old and only four years away from his own murder—came personally to her bedside, wept, and declared that she had been with him since the day of his birth, guiding and protecting him.[79] Here we should remember that Xiaoming was taken away from both his mother, Empress Gao, and his stepmother, Empress Dowager Ling, as a means to safeguard his life and ensure dynastic succession through the patriline. Evidently, it was a nun that was tasked with the incredibly important job of keeping the young emperor alive. The biography further relates that Xiaoming posthumously granted Ciqing the title of "superintendent of the nuns," the exact title that Sengzhi held in her life, though she herself had already passed away. Even though she was granted the title of "superintendent" only after her death, Ciqing held the aforementioned title of "lady of clear etiquette" when she was still alive. We cannot be certain as to what the duties of the "lady of clear etiquette" were, but we do know that this title was among the highest of court ranks for women, second only to that of the empress.[80] In the story of Ciqing, then, we have direct and contemporaneous evidence for the existence of nuns as royal caregivers bearing the title of "superintendent of the nuns." It makes sense to consider Sengzhi's own appointment in that light, and we have corroborating evidence for such a consideration in her entombed biography. In the account of her death, the entombed biography tells us that Sengzhi died at the Nunnery of the Le'an Princess (*Le'an gongzhu si*). The Le'an Princess was an orphaned daughter of Emperor Xianwen and the sibling of the child emperor, Xiaowen. If Sengzhi was playing the role of imperial caregiver, the Le'an Princess would likely have been placed under her care as a child. Perhaps, then, in her old age, the care that Sengzhi may have placed on the princess was reciprocated: Sengzhi lived her last days in the princess's nunnery after having been her contemporary and her caregiver for almost forty years.

As chaste matrons a step removed from the politics of sexual procreation, Buddhist nuns would have been useful in medieval courts as caregivers of young emperors and administrators of the female ranks of the inner chambers. We see many aspects of this caregiving role in Sengzhi's entombed biography. From her primary relationship with Emperor Xiaowen, to her position as overseer of the inner chambers of the court, her role as superintendent of the nuns saw her caring for a number of people who were not in fact nuns, and she fulfilled this role from the time of Empress Dowager Wenming until the time of Empress Dowager Ling, whom she herself brought to court owing to her influence over Emperor Xuanwu. As to the roles Sengzhi played at court, her entombed biography goes on to relate that:[81]

Empress Dowager Wenming was in the imperial city[82] determined to transcend worldly custom. Greatly admiring [Sengzhi's] mastery and venerating her manner and intent, she consequently commanded the postal carriage to immediately and officially summon Sengzhi. When [Sengzhi] arrived at the capital, she was venerated with extraordinary protocols.

Gaozu, Emperor Xiaowen, whose path brought abundance to heaven and earth, and whose brilliance exceeded the sun and the moon, poured all of his sincerity into his receptions [with Sengzhi] [such that] the matter transcended the ordinary principle of human relationships.

Shizong, Emperor Xuanwu entrusted his heart to the three treasures, bestowed more and more favors on her, and led her into the women's quarters to instruct the six palaces.[83]

Sengzhi enjoyed a long tenure at court. According to the biography, she was appointed in 477 while dying in 516 after thirty-nine years of service. She served the two empress dowagers who bookended her career as well as the emperors they ruled behind: Xiaowen and Xiaoming. She also served at the court during the reign of Emperor Xuanwu, who was the son of Xiaowen and the father of Xiaoming. Sengzhi's long court service would also have seen the move of the capital from Datong to Luoyang, the decision to employ a majority of Han Chinese bureaucrats at court and officially adopt their language as the language of the court, the building of the Buddhist grottos at Yungang and Longmen, and the rise of an extremely powerful and influential Buddhist monastic community that served the court she was such an integral part of.

Sengzhi's titles and dates show us that the proliferation of female court ranks supported by various Northern Wei courts extended also to the administration of the Buddhist monastic organization. Interested in having bureaucratic control over the institution of Buddhism, Northern Wei leaders installed a monastic bureaucracy that worked to implement the court's policies in the wider monastic community. They were also engaged in the proliferation of ranks for women, possibly because of the relatively high social position that Taghbach and Serbi women reputedly held. In building their Buddhist empire, the Northern Wei leaders included female monastic courtiers within its structure to act as organizers of the inner court and caretakers of the royal children. A woman like Sengzhi was a good fit. Said to be from a literate Han family at the gateway to the Hexi corridor and possibly in possession of a more verifiable ordination status and an elite practice of Buddhism than other women of her time and place, Sengzhi became a fixture at court and the favorite religious teacher of Emperor Xuanwu, whose personal audience she enjoyed. Within the confluence of religion, politics, and gender that the Northern Wei court is known for, Sengzhi saw herself installed as the first ever superintendent of the nuns, serving and influencing an incredibly powerful northern court for most of her life. These facts have received little scholarly attention to date.[84]

NETWORKS OF WOMEN

Unlike that of her male counterparts, Sengzhi's work as superintendent of the nuns may not have been enacted in the public eye. We have no records of her involvement in public statecraft that can compare with Faguo's declaration of the Northern Wei emperor as the Buddha nor with Tanyao's involvement in giving form to this buddha/ruler identification by having it carved into the cliffside at Yungang.

What we do know is that Sengzhi was active at court and as an administrator of the inner court, presiding over the affairs of the women of the inner court and caring for their children. We know this because Emperor Xuanwu appointed her to be in charge of the inner chambers of the court, regulating and supervising the deposed and widowed women who found themselves under her guidance as new members of her Buddhist monastic community. Her entombed biography further tells us something about what this work looked like. It continues as follows:[85]

> Empress Feng of Xiaowen and Empress Gao of Xuanwu[86] and more than twenty wives and concubines—even Madam Xie, the wife of the former General of the Carriages and Horses and the Minister of Works, Wang Su[87] who was herself the daughter of the Great minster of the Glowing Blessing of the Office of Fasting of the Right and the Secretariat of the History Section, [Xie] Zhuang [d.u.] who came from Jinling,[88] sought refuge in the seclusion of the imperial palace.[89] Considering the way of the dharma master to crown the universe, and her virtue to be commensurate with the creation of things, [the women] therefore cast aside their extravagant customs, clothed their bosoms in the gate of the teaching, and all became disciples of the dharma master. From all of these nuns so cloaked in their integrity, those who rose up in rank and those who took the high seat were too many to record.

The above story of the court women who became Sengzhi's disciples reveals the gendered nature of her work as the superintendent of the nuns at the Northern Wei court in Luoyang: She served the court by providing its women with refuge after the deaths or estrangement of their imperial husbands. For example, as to the three women identified by name as her disciples, Empresses Feng and Gao were the two most eminent in the nunnery, both widowed, and Madam Xie was a southerner who had traveled on her own to the Northern Wei capital in Luoyang in order to publicly shame her own husband who had abandoned her for both a position at the Northern Wei court and a princess from the imperial house.[90] Widowhood and abandonment for women of the court were dangerous matters: More than losing their spouses, they also lost their own social standing. In a patriarchal and patrilocal setting, a woman's own social standing relied on that of their husband. A loss of husband was therefore tantamount to a loss of one's own privilege, livelihood, and, in cases like that of Empress Gao, even life. What Sengzhi offered to the widowed and deposed women of the court was Buddhism. By taking these women of the court on as members of the monastic community, Sengzhi shepherded them through the pitfalls of widowhood, offering them invaluable social and institutional support in their most vulnerable state by bringing them under her care, often housing them at the Jade Radiance Nunnery, which the *Record of Buddhist Monasteries in Luoyang* notes was specifically for the use of court ladies-turned-nuns.[91] In providing the women of the court with an alternate means to create social prestige than the court itself was able to do—a means that was necessarily a step removed from family life—Sengzhi enabled the women of the court to construct a new virtue of pure chastity, even leading them in worship and devotion through her status as a "dharma master." This virtue allowed them to negotiate the social conundrum of being a woman without a man in a society that, historically, has not made similar space for such women. As a poignant depiction of the value of Sengzhi's work, Empress Dowager Wenming—the very woman who appointed Sengzhi at court—is said to have attempted suicide by throwing herself on the funeral pyre used to burn her deceased husband's possessions and was pulled off by her female courtiers.[92,93] She appointed Sengzhi to court twelve years after this apparent attempted suicide, when she had become the de facto monarch of the dynasty. Her appointment of Sengzhi helped to guarantee that the very same female courtiers that pulled her off of the fire would not meet the fire themselves—metaphorically or otherwise.

We must not deny the gendered nature of Sengzhi's work, and we also cannot underestimate its value. Her work saw the creation of long-lasting institutional ties between the court and the nunnery. These ties become increasingly entrenched and important throughout the medieval period, particularly during the Tang era. Sengzhi's contributions to the development of Buddhism in East Asia have gone unrecognized in studies of both Chinese Buddhism and the history of the Chinese court; however, they did not go unrecognized in her time. In recognition of her almost forty years of dedicated service to the women of the court, she was honored at her death with an elaborate state funeral, which was well attended by the women of the court who mourned her vigorously. One of the standard features of an entombed biography is a discussion of the funeral and mourning rites established for the deceased, and in the case of Sengzhi the text extols her deep connection to the imperial house by starting with the personal mourning of Emperor Xiaoming. The biography tells us:[94]

> The emperor was overcome with grief and the clergy and the laity were bound together in mourning. Then, on the twenty-fourth day of the month, a *xinmao* day [March 12, 516 CE], they buried her north of Luoyang on the south slope of Mount Mang. Her great disciples, the *Bhikṣuṇīs*, Metropolitan *Weinas*,[95] and Dharma Masters, Senghe and Daohe, mourning the long-dimming of [her] numinous shadow and yearning for the eternal cover of [her] divine authority, wailed [for her] until they lost their voices, and ceremonially spoke about [her] fragrant merit.

Sengzhi's burial is recorded as having been a well-attended, elite event that included the personal mourning of Emperor Xiaoming and the attendance of the female monastic community. Noteworthy is the fact that two other eminent nuns, Senghe and Daohe, attended the funeral and appear to have led the mourning. We know nothing else about these women other than this brief mention in Sengzhi's entombed biography, but we can understand from their titles that they were eminent Buddhist nuns in the service of the empire who were Sengzhi's subordinates. The two women both hold the title of metropolitan *weina* (*duweina*).[96] *Weina* is a monastic title often translated as "comptroller." Those who held the title were in charge of a number of monastic affairs—from the daily running of the nunnery or monastery to the implementation of the court's directives meant for the monastic community. We can find descriptions of the duties of the weina in many places across the "Annals on Buddhism and Daoism." The picture of the weina that appears is one of a court-enforced, often-but-not-always-monastic individual working within a network of regulatory officials. In the "Annals on Buddhism and Daoism," we see that the Northern Wei court used weinas to transmit their edicts to the monastic community. For example, the weinas were in charge of making sure that the court's restrictions on the numbers of monastics to be ordained in every region were adhered to and that, similarly, the restraints on the building of new monasteries were as well.[97] Furthermore, the text records that weinas were also in charge of certifying and handing out monastic travel permits.[98] The job of the weina was thus an important administrative position in the Northern Wei that facilitated the court's official oversight over the monastic body. Senghe and Daohe's title was not simply weina. Instead, they are listed as the "metropolitan weina," which I take to mean the head monastic organizers of an urban center, though it is possible that this title was simply an honorific signifying the head weina of a particular community.

What we therefore have in this record of Sengzhi's funeral is the attendance of her immediate subordinates. Sengzhi was the superintendent of the nuns and her disciples Senghe and Daohe were in her employ as administrators of the state/monastic complex. It is no surprise, then, that they attended her funeral and led the mourning. There are many other mentions of female weinas listed as patrons in the records of donor inscriptions from the time period; however, this record of Sengzhi's funeral is the only source I know of in which we see the female metropolitan weina at work, venerating their superior and leading the mourning at her funeral. The image of two metropolitan weina nuns working alongside their superintendent is strongly reminiscent of the donor image of the empress dowager's procession from the Huangfu Gong grotto wherein there is a depiction of two nuns completing a ritual and a third nun standing closer to the empress dowager. Gu Yanfang suggests that the third nun could actually be the aunt of the empress dowager[99]—Sengzhi—however, she would have passed away approximately ten years prior to the building of the grotto. The image might suggest that the empress dowager had appointed a new superintendent to take her place, though we have no other evidence of that. In any case, the image of a nun close to the empress dowager and two other nuns completing ritual is strongly reminiscent of the scene at Sengzhi's funeral recounted in her entombed biography. The mortuary veneration of Sengzhi by her disciples is beautifully captured in the final words of her eulogy:[100]

> [In order to] cultivate and disseminate her Way in the world.
> The fragrance of flowers fills all four directions,

and the nirvana carriage[101] is high and lofty.
Both monastic and lay are overcome with melancholy:
Brahma-sounds enter the clouds,
As do mournful and sour dirges.
Her disciples weep and wail as they take part in the procession,
calling themselves poor orphans and lonely rejects.

Here we see Sengzhi memorialized and remembered by the very women of the Northern Wei court who staffed the newly-created court ranks for women surveyed above and who, at various times in their lives, relied on the Buddhist monastic community to help them negotiate between and retire from those ranks. When we consider the almost forty years that Sengzhi spent in the service of the Northern Wei court, we must highlight the fact that she was appointed to her position by an empress dowager and later died in her position under the patronage of a different empress dowager, one who supported her state funeral and the writing of the very words from which we know anything about her life. It was powerful women who bookended Sengzhi's career, one who likely brought her in as a caregiver of the inner chambers and another, her own niece, whom she brought in, likely because of her close relationship with the emperor. The fact of Sengzhi's intertwined court, monastic, and filial responsibilities nuances, complexifies, and problematizes what we know about how women in patriarchal court and family systems created opportunities for themselves and for others. In the Northern Wei, as in many other times and places, women of the court were often famous for their infighting. Sharing the same physical space and competing for the same males to rely on and link their lives and careers to, court women have long been guilty of perpetuating the very same systems of oppression of which they were victims in order to gain a higher standing within those very systems. One need only think of the infighting between Empress Dowager Ling and Emperor Xuanwu's empress from the Gao Clan. At the death of Xuanwu, both women attempted to have the other assassinated, and Empress Dowager Ling succeeded. That success, however, came at an unlikely juncture: Empress Gao was murdered while in the imperial nunnery, a fact that suggests that the empress dowager still feared the power that her competitor held, even from the nunnery. Sengzhi's story provides us with a different portrait of the women of the court. With her, we see all-female networks functioning to increase the social opportunities afforded to women of the court and doing so through refuge in the institution of the Buddhist monastery. That Empress Gao attended Sengzhi's funeral and then was murdered by the empress dowager shortly afterward suggests that Sengzhi's safeguarding of the nuns in her care may have diminished after her death.

As representatives of a newly emerging means of creating social virtue for women in the early medieval period, celibate Buddhist women like Sengzhi were able to facilitate the lives and careers of women of the court without becoming embroiled in the sexual politics of the court. This ability was owing to the fact that women like Sengzhi and her contemporaries manifested the virtue of pure chastity, which set them one step apart from the traditional family system that a saw a woman's public social power largely authorized by her connection to male members of her family. For a woman like Sengzhi, her social power was validated through her identity as an eminent and learned woman of pure virtue: she was chaste; she had no children; she did not depend on the career of her husband; and she was new to the elite political worlds of early medieval China. From this new social role, Sengzhi was able to work for most of her life at the Northern Wei court. As a woman of new virtue, Sengzhi was an ideal candidate for facilitating the lives of women who were, by the nature of the patriarchal court and family, necessarily situated in deep conflict with and pitted against each other with their lives depending on their own success with the men of the court.

WORK, PAYMENT, AND THE MATRILINE

Sengzhi was at the vanguard of new forms of womanhood that were on the rise in society during her lifetime. Her work is a historical testimony to changing notions of gender and family in the early medieval period and to the tenacity by which women worked to bring them about. Her work was also not unpaid. Just as she was the benefactor of the empress dowager in her childhood, so too was the empress dowager Sengzhi's benefactor in the latter's advanced age. Having used her influence to bring the empress dowager to court, Empress Dowager Ling used her power to publicly repay Sengzhi. The *Record of Buddhist Monasteries in Luoyang* provides a description of the Nunnery of the Superintendent of the Nuns that the empress dowager had built for Sengzhi. It says:

> Nunnery of the Superintendent of the Hu Clan: Under the direction of her aunt, the empress dowager had it established. [Her aunt] had entered the Way and become a nun and she dwelled in the nunnery, which was a bit further than one *li* south of the Eternal Peace Monastery. [It had] a jeweled pagoda of five stories which was crowned in gold surrounded by cavernous rooms whose doors all faced it and opened onto it. With vermillion beams and unadorned walls, it was extremely beautiful. [In] this nunnery were all the nuns who were famed for their virtue within the imperial capital and who excelled at enlightened teaching and whose work was discussion and argumentation. [These nuns] often went to the palace to lecture the empress dowager on the dharma. The expense for caring for these monastics and their disciples was beyond compare.[102]

From this description we see that Sengzhi presided over a community of elite and learned nuns that were regularly granted entrance into the palace in order to teach and that this community was funded by the empress dowager, even though its expenses were "beyond compare." As we will see in subsequent chapters, the empress dowager was the most prolific patron of Buddhist building projects in Luoyang and her frequent commissioning of large Buddhist structures such as the Eternal Peace Monastery was a result of her desire to show to the populace and to the court that she controlled the imperial purse. Amy McNair argues that one of the ways that she did this is through the commissioning of the Huoshao grotto at Longmen, which, she further argues, was commissioned in 517 as a mortuary grotto for the empress dowager's deceased mother who passed away in 502.[103] In full agreement with McNair's careful argument for how this grotto may have been sponsored by the empress dowager, I suggest that perhaps it was not built as a mortuary grotto for her mother. Perhaps it was built as a mortuary grotto for her aunt, Sengzhi, just as it contains a scene strikingly reminiscent of that described in the record of Sengzhi's funeral.

As McNair describes, the Huoshao grotto was likely a private grotto for the empress dowager on which work was started in or around 517.[104] It also appears to have been a mortuary grotto or a commemorative grotto for the dead because its dramatic façade contains a non-Buddhist image of the Han-dynasty mortuary deities—namely, the Queen Mother of the West and the King Father of the East. With these images in mind, McNair argues that the grotto must have been meant for a person of Han descent such as someone from the empress dowager's family. The empress dowager's mother is certainly a viable candidate for dedicatee because the empress dowager did bestow many posthumous honors on her in the years after she took power. Sengzhi, however, might be a more viable candidate. Having been the empress dowager's patron and having had that patronage publicly reciprocated in a resplendent nunnery dedicated to her, the empress dowager publicly celebrated her closeness with her aunt in her capital city. Unlike her mother, who died in 502, Sengzhi died in 516, thus making the temporal connection more immediate. Furthermore, it might make sense that the Huoshao grotto was established to represent her father's line, that of the Hu clan, and not her mother's line, that of the Huangfu clan. As McNair has shown, a later inscription in the grotto does connect the grotto to the empress dowager; however, that connection is made through the Hu line and not the Huangfu line. Finally, in simple terms of religious affiliation, would it not make sense for the largest of the Northern Wei grottos at the Buddhist site of Longmen to be dedicated to the most famous Buddhist woman of the time, one who had died a few months before and who had shepherded the empress dowager to her high political office?

I believe that the Huoshao grotto was built for Sengzhi after her death, but even if it was built for the empress dowager's mother, one thing we can take from its very existence is the striking observation that with this grotto we see how communities of women began to make their presence known by having carvings in stone dedicated to their memory. They did this in a Buddhist medium. Using the example of a different Northern Wei shrine at Longmen, Kate Lingley argues that it is with such acts of Buddhist donorship that we can begin to see and thus make

FIGURE 14. Detail of the façade of the Huoshao grotto at Longmen showing the Queen Mother of the West and the King Father of the East to the upper left and right of the cave entrance. Circa 517. Photo © Li Lan.

matrilineal relations, and that we have no other sources by which to reconstruct such connections because women's names are often not recorded in other modes of writing from the medieval period.[105] This is true of both Sengzhi and Empress Dowager Ling. Both women began their lives as "nameless" daughters from the Hu clan of Anding, and yet both women ended their lives with important imperial titles made possible by both women's connections to Buddhist monasticism. Furthermore, both women's titles are carved in stone because of their high status, even if we will never know their birth names. In sum, the study of the Buddhist profile of the nun Sengzhi is much more than what it seems. By utilizing Buddhist sources in order to provide additional support for the study of women's history, this chapter has chronicled how the rise of the aunt, who earned her fame through the Buddhist notion of pure chastity, fostered the accession of the niece, who used her power to repay her aunt and thereby document, in stone, the all-female relationships of the Hu clan of Anding. These relationships were female, Buddhist, and imperial, and they form the context of the rise of Empress Dowager Ling.

4

A Girl on the Throne

The *Book of the Wei*'s narrative of the empress dowager placing her granddaughter on the throne offers no plausible explanation as to why she may have done it. As we saw in chapter 2, the biography of the empress dowager tells us that she and her advisor, a man who was reputed to be her lover, had undertaken the plot as an act of political expediency that would assist the empress dowager in extending her regency. However, as we also saw in chapter 2, the *Book of the Wei* and the *Comprehensive Mirror to Aid in Government* record that placing a girl on the throne was not at all politically expedient: Erzhu Rong is remembered to have used the act as a pretext for his invasion of Luoyang and his ultimate murder of the empress dowager and her court. Moreover, if placing a girl on the throne was simply an act of succession supported by her advisors because of the lack of more suitable heirs, how is that those in the empress dowager's circle so quickly found another male heir from the royal clan to take the throne when their original plan had failed? The accession and inauguration of a new emperor is perhaps the most scrutinized of political acts. It is doubtful that the empress dowager and her courtiers took such a cavalier attitude toward this important event in their rule that they propped up any child that was close to them regardless of past precedent and regardless of the child's gender. Why, then, did they do it?

In this chapter, I reconsider the story of the granddaughter-as-emperor and I do so in order to bring both non-Han and Buddhist notions of gender, its construction, and its performance into our historical understanding of the granddaughter on the throne. By using donative epigraphy evidencing the life of female administrators in the empire, the entombed biographies of elite women who worked at the Northern Wei court in the service of the empress dowager, Buddhist sūtras that were either translated or popularized with the patronage of the Northern Wei court during its latter stages, as well as an analysis of key Buddhist ideas of monarchy that were quickly becoming popular in the medieval period, this chapter will argue that the imperial Buddhism of the Northern Wei court in Luoyang was staffed by women at many levels, that the Buddhist organization provided an avenue for women to enact such powerful political roles, and that Buddhist sūtras, as well as popular Buddhist imagery in the period, may have provided a doctrinal basis and historical model for elite Buddhist womanhood in the service of the court, maybe even of the emperor. Furthermore, this analysis of the lives of women at court derived from Buddhist sources will also be shown to have a deep and complementary resonance with a type of gender performance that may have been known to the Taghbach people who ruled the Northern Wei and who, I will argue, knew the social category of "honorary men." Finally, and most provocatively, this chapter will explore the idea that when the empress dowager placed a girl on the throne, she did so herself as a Buddhist regent familiar with the idea that Buddhist notions of rule might support the notion of female rulership in her realm.

It is impossible to go back in time and ask the empress dowager why she saw fit to place her granddaughter on the throne; however, in this chapter I provide carefully researched and historically responsible conjectural answers that make more sense than does a Confucian perspective gleaned from dynastic histories written by Ru scholars working in the service of the court but with little access to women's spaces within it. The answer suggested here is multivalent: Peeling back the many layers of gender, its performance, and its interpretation that surround the story of the nameless granddaughter on the throne in a multiethnic, Buddhist Luoyang, I argue that the placement of a girl on the throne may not have been as reckless as it seems and that, in fact, it makes sense in a variety of ways that a Ru scholar like Wei Shou may have been either unfamiliar with or unwilling to write about.

WOMEN AS ORGANIZERS

We begin this chapter by returning to the person of the weina, whom we first were introduced to in the story of Sengzhi's funeral in the previous chapter. The inscriptional record attests to the existence of weina working in Buddhist communities across the empire during the Northern Wei. Women serving as weina are commonly attested in such materials. For example, we can cite a donor epigraph from the reign of the empress dowager that records several women acting as weina in the commissioning of twenty-four buddha images. The inscription comes not from Luoyang, but from further afield at the previously discussed Yellow Cliff site in Shandong province, and it bears witness to the religious lives of women as enacted in a Buddhist community in the sixth century. Shandong had a variety of political fates during the Southern and Northern Dynasties period, with different polities ruling the peninsula. By the Luoyang period of Northern Wei rule, the peninsula and its surrounding areas were under Northern Wei jurisdiction; research on the Yellow Cliff site shows that the individual donors had strong connections to the central court in Luoyang, just as the artwork at the site is similar in style to the Northern Wei art at Longmen.[1] Luoyang Buddhism was both a model and an impetus for projects at the Shandong site, even though it was more than five hundred kilometers from the capital. For our purposes, the inscription that we will consider from the Yellow Cliff reads:

> On the twenty-ninth day of the seventh month of the fourth year of the Zhengguan era (August 25, 523), a dharma collective of brothers and sisters reverently commissioned a stone grotto with twenty-four figures. Everyone who undertook the completion of this [has made a] record of their names enumerated here.
>
> Shi Fushou and Xinqu.
>
> The weina presider, Liu Ainü; the weina presider Mu [missing character] ji; Jia [missing character]; Liu Faxiang; Wang Baoji; Liu A'Xiang; Liu A'Si; Liu Shengyu; Hu A'zi; Wang Lijiang; [missing] ting Fuji; Jia A'Fei; Liu Taoji; Wang Zu; Sun Jingzi; Zhao Feijiang; Zhang Shengjie; Zhang Hanren; [missing] Jiangnü; [missing] Guzi; Xu Qingnü; the weina presider, Zhang Niunü; the weina presider Huting Moxiang; Bai Qijiang; Shi Taonü, Zhao Yijiang; Zhang Daonü.[2]

This inscription describes the building of a niche undertaken by a group of mainly women working together with two monks, Shi Fushou and (Shi) Xinqu. It is difficult to say with absolute certainty which genders the donors belong to: The majority of the personal names listed are either common names for women in the time period (as in the name *a* 阿) or feature semantic elements that identify them as women, such as *nü* (女), or girl, or words like *ji* (姬), *fei* (妃), *jiang* (姜), which all refer to the titles of concubines or courtesans, or finally the name *xiang* (香), or "fragrant." I have never encountered an example of a man taking on such names in other inscriptions.

This rock-cut inscription shows that women and men collaborated on projects, that women had adequate financial autonomy to be able to take the lead in expensive projects of this type, and that there seems to have been no restriction against women acting as weina within a group of women presided over by male members of the monastic community. Even more noteworthy in this inscription is the fact that unlike the metropolitan weina that we met in the record of Sengzhi's funeral, here there is no indication that the weina belonged to the monastic order. This observation on their nonmonastic status accords with Kate Lingley's work on Eastern Wei inscriptions at the Gaomiao cave temple in Shanxi where we also see community organizers in donative inscriptions holding the title of weina but not holding monastic titles.[3] In sum, from such inscriptions we see that women in the Northern Wei were able to organize among themselves, spend money by themselves, and have their ability to do these things carved in stone for posterity.

To further our analysis of how women were involved in public Buddhist donor-ship and administration during the Northern Wei we can look to another donative inscription from the Yellow Cliff site that also features nonmonastic women in the role of weina. Notably, the site contains a donative inscription for an image of Mai-treya commissioned by a religious society that was composed of thirty-five mem-bers and that existed for the benefit of the emperor and the imperial clan.[4] It says:

> In the second year of the Xiaochang reign in the ninth month which had its new moon on a *dingyou* day and on the eighth day, a *jiachen* day [September 29, 526], a dharma collective for the emperor and imperial clan [composed of] thirty-five people commissioned the building of one image of Maitreya. Universally, [this is] on behalf of all sentient beings in the dharma realm, the three existences, and [those from the] four benevolences who wish to meet Maitreya.
>
> Metropolitan weina and monk Jingzhi, metropolitan weina Yang Luzi, metro-politan weina Jia Daoshun, metropolitan weina Zhao Funian, the monk Daoyun, the monk Hong [missing], Feng Daoxiang, Deng Gongbo, Zhang Huiyin, Zhang Huangsi, Zhang Shesheng, Ma Sengzhi, Huang Wailong, Liu Huan, Liu Shinu, Chen Yide, Wang Nansheng.
>
> Weina Liu Amunü, weina Zhao Shengjiang, Cui Lingzi, Yu Xiaoji, Bai Sheji, Zhao Anji, Xue Nansheng, Zhang Jinzi, Wang Sisheng, Zhang Nüzhu, Liu Zhai, Liu [miss-ing], Guo Nan, Ximen Qingjiang, Zhao Yingnan, Jia'E, Zhang Waizi, Yuan Sanying, Zhang Shengjiang, Wang Fuji, Zhao Gounan, Zhao Shengzi, Liu Mingsheng, Zhao Taonü, Zhao Zuxi.

In the list of names on the inscription, the members are grouped together by gen-der, with males listed before females. Similarly, within each gender grouping, the names of the weina are listed at the top of each gendered group so that the inscrip-tion follows in this manner: male weina; male members of the dharma collective; female weina; female members of the dharma collective. As to the male group-ing, there are four metropolitan weina, one of whom appears to be a Buddhist monk. Following this are the names of two monks and eleven men. After the men are listed, the inscription lists the women, beginning with the weina, of whom there are two, neither of whom appear to be nuns. There are no nuns listed on this inscription, but there are the names of twenty-one women.

These inscriptions and hundreds more like them were produced by locally orga-nized religious collectives during the medieval period. Such collectives—called, as in the case of the above-mentioned examples, a *fayi* or otherwise an *yiyi*—became an important part of religious and social organization in the north of China begin-ning around the fifth century. Such collectives often came together to support the building of statuary or to undertake social service work, such as the building of bridges.[5] Notably, these dharma collectives include the participation of women in many roles and they reflect the ambitious support for Buddhism across the medieval empires from both women and men who went along with expansive building projects in Buddhist art and infrastructure.[6] In Hou Xudong's magisterial treatment of the development of widespread belief in Buddhism among grassroots groups in the medieval period, he uses inscriptional material to argue that village-based practices of Buddhism were deeply connected with new religious ideas revealed through miraculous stories by charismatic teachers. Hou argues that a local and dynamic context was responsible for the spread of Buddhism in early medieval China to a much larger extent than was the politicized Buddhism of the court and the elite.[7] In short, Hou argues for a "bottom-up" interpretation that sees the spread of Buddhism flourishing at the local level first, and then creating a mimetic movement at the level of statecraft and the court.

Thus, the establishment of Buddhist communities on top of preexisting social organizations throughout the heartland of traditional Han China signifies two important changes: (1) the large-scale patronage of Buddhism on top of pre-Buddhist modalities of social and religious organization; (2) the participation of women in these communities at a variety of levels.[8] In the most recent study of such societies, Hao Chunwen describes the development of such women's groups from the Northern dynasties through to the Song dynasty and provides detailed and fascinating data on the types of roles that women held within them. However, Hao cautions that such inscriptions cannot tell us much about women's freedoms with respect to their social status because all the women in question were elite women in their local contexts.[9] Nonetheless, what we can see is that such village devotional groups were instrumental to the spread of Buddhism in early medieval East Asia and that women were important and agentive actors in these associations. In short, Buddhism in the sixth century was—to no small extant—female.

One striking aspect of donor inscriptions from this period are the semantic meanings of the names themselves. Here, I will focus on trying to make sense of gendered names. In the inscription above, we see female donors whose names translate into English as something like "Male Birth" (Nansheng 男生), "Man" (Nan 男), "Welcoming Man[hood]" (Yingnan 迎男), and "Evoking Male[ness]" (Gounan 勾男). These names are similar to those listed on another inscription for the commissioning of an image of Śākyamuni Buddha in 504 CE by the eminent Gao clan of Dangmo,[10] which lists two women whose names evoke manhood or male birth.[11] The donor inscription lists the first of them as "A Servant of the Buddha called Xing Nansheng who is the wife of Gao Mai, a Gentlemen of Pure Faith" wherein the characters for her name "Nansheng" mean "male birth," like in the name above. Moreover, "Male Birth" is the wife of a "gentleman of pure faith," a term common in inscriptions that signified a person's status as a lay Buddhist.[12] The second of these names is similar: "A Servant of the Buddha called Ni Dainan who is the wife of Gao Xiang, a Gentlemen of Pure Faith," wherein the characters for her personal name Dainan (殆男) translate to something like "Almost a Man."

All the names of these women are puzzling; however, there are a few points of clarification that may help us make sense of them. The first and foremost point is that the names certainly have semantic intent, which we saw above in how the names of women often feature words identifying them as women. In the case of men, the names are also semantically meaningful. For example, the above inscription lists men named "Community Born" (Shesheng 社生), "Difficult Birth" (Nansheng 難生), "Suitably Virtuous" (Yide 宜德), "Foreign Dragon" (Wailong 外龍), and "Financial Benefit" (Huiyin 惠銀). A straightforward survey of such names suggests that they have semantic meaning and are unlike the types of phonetic transcriptions of Taghbach names seen on inscriptions like Emperor Wencheng's "Stele of the Southern Progress."[13] These names are not typical Han Chinese names; rather, the names speak to the nan-Han identities of their namesakes.[14] This is also true of the women's names that evoke maleness or manhood. Although it is possible to interpret names such as "Man" and "Evoking a Man" through the lens of Confucian discourse and therefore see them as indicative of wishes for husbands and male children, I believe that they are to be understood differently. In what follows, I argue that these rare names for women that evoke or suggest maleness or male birth on Northern Wei inscriptions are better understood within the notions of gender and its performance that were known to the Taghbach, which were defined positionally within the family unit and may have allowed women to act as men in certain situations.

WOMEN AS COURTIERS

The epigraphical record so far contains the entombed biographies of two women who held the title of "woman secretary" (nü shangshu) at the court of the Northern Wei. Although the authoritative Dictionary of Official Titles in Imperial China states that the establishment of the woman secretary came about in the Tang dynasty,[15] we have already seen in the previous chapter's discussion of expanded court ranks for women under Emperor Wencheng that the Northern Wei included the woman secretary at the rank of third grade. As for the position itself, the Dictionary of Official Titles in Imperial China tells us that the secretary was the highest administrative position in the court during the time period in question, being in charge of all six of the major bureaus of administrative procedure, and that the person who held the role was required to take examinations in order to show their literacy and ability. The woman secretary was even in charge of arranging the emperor's own meetings with the women of his inner court as well as keeping those women properly administered.[16] This description accords with the description of the two women secretaries from the Northern Wei that we know of, particularly in that we know that the women's court was also divided into six bureaus like that of the male court. Both Northern Wei women secretaries for whom we have entombed biographies have honorary names that evoke social maleness. Their names are "Saṃgha Man" (Sengnan 僧男; Saṃgha is the term for the Buddhist monastic community) and "Welcoming Man[hood]" (Yingnan). In the case of "Saṃgha man" we do not know her birth name and she is consistently referred to only as "Man" in her entombed biography. "Welcoming Man[hood]'s" birth name was said to have been "Girl" (Nülang 女郎), but she was given the name "Welcoming Man[hood]" as an honorific perhaps befitting her role as woman secretary.

In the case of our two women secretaries from the empress dowager's court who both have honorary names that evoke their proximity to maleness and the male gender, we can narrow the hypothesis of social maleness for women within forms of gender organization known to the Taghbach even further: I postulate that in certain cases women who had no fathers became the social men in their families. To elaborate on this argument, I begin by offering a full translation of the entombed biography of "Saṃgha Man." It reads:

> The woman secretary[17] was from the Wang clan and her honorary name was "Saṃgha Man." She was from Yanyang in Anding. She was the grandchild of Governor Gong from Anding and the child of Governor Na from Shangluo. The earth blossoms [in the regions of the] Jing River and Long Mountain[18] and [those who oversee it] are led by illustrious descendants of noble clans. On account of his bravado and machismo, "Man's" father broke the law, led his cavalrymen into criminality, and was therefore punished. All alone, "Man," along with her mother, was left helpless and endured suffering and by herself she entered the palace. At that time, she was six years old.[19] Because her intelligence and talents were splendid and bright, she was selected to fill [the role of] student. With a wise nature and an agile perception, she daily chanted one thousand words. She listened to the explanation of ancient texts with comprehension, fully grasping the meaning after only hearing them one time. She was promoted through the palace administration, ascending to [the rank] of woman secretary of the third grade. Able to record and explain the female court, she brought about an established order and was able to assume a manly [qian] heart. Because she disseminated brilliance by employing the scarlet pipes,[20] she was conferred the second grade. Heaven did not repay her goodness, wiping out this fine sage at the age of sixty-eight. She reached her end in the Jinyong palace of the great Wei.[21] Upon taking into account that "Man" had already been presented with the second [grade] and that she continued [as a] virtuous elder [to be] hardworking, she was again promoted and conferred [the rank] of first grade. She was bestowed with a casket of the type used by the imperial family[22] as well as a sleeping carriage.[23] The expenses for her funeral were all gathered together from collective donations and she was interred at long last at the north of Peace Tumulus. Through a compromise of abundance and frugality and in complete accord with ritual protocols, [we] carve this stone and engrave her name [so as to be] handed down to future descendants! On the twentieth yimao day in the ninth month, under the xingqi asterism,[24] in the second year of the Zhengguang reign of the great Wei (November 5, 521).

If we compare the details of Saṃgha Man's entombed biography to those in the entombed biography of Welcoming Man[hood], significant similarities emerge.[25] In both cases, the girls had absent fathers. In the case of Saṃgha Man, her father was a criminal who was put to death for his crimes. In the case of Welcoming Man[hood], her father appears to have lost his life in the service of his prefecture.

After his death, mother and child joined the menial service of the palace because life was too difficult for them in the countryside to remain there independently. Like Saṃgha Man, Welcoming Man[hood] was noted as a youth for her intelligence and was chosen as a palace student at the age of eleven. When she was fifteen, she was brought into imperial service at the level of woman secretary, where she was responsible for ordering the inner chambers. Both women died while staying at the palace in Jinyong, just north of Luoyang, which had been a substitute palace throughout the dynasty and which had housed out of favor royals in the early medieval period in general. Their presence at that palace may have occurred owing to the coup d'état during which they both died, though there is nothing to suggest that their deaths were brought about by state violence. For Welcoming Man[hood], the entombed biography tells us that she became ill and died, though the precise date of her death was not remembered. She was buried in Luoyang with much mourning from the women of the court. Her death contrasts with Saṃgha Man's in certain ways because we have been told that Saṃgha Man's funeral was incredibly expensive and that she was posthumously rewarded the rank of first grade. Saṃgha Man's entombed biography also does not provide a cause of death, ambiguously saying that "Heaven did not repay her goodness" and she was "wiped out at the age of sixty-eight." The record therefore might suggest malicious intent behind her death, but it is impossible to say one way or another. Unlike Welcoming Man[hood], Saṃgha Man was promoted to the rank of first grade after her death, and the reasons for this are also left ambiguous.

For both women, we have a situation wherein two young girls without fathers and without any known brothers took on political roles at court that had long been the prerogative of males. It was the Northern Wei's alignment of male and female courtly titles that allowed them the opportunity to do so. Their appointments therefore coincided with that of Sengzhi: Sengzhi was brought to the palace in 477 and was already an eminent nun; Welcoming Man[hood] was given the title of Woman Secretary in 480, and Saṃgha Man was brought to court in 459 as a six-year-old child and would have therefore reached maturity and appointment in the same general timeframe as the other two women. As a group, these three women were all unmarried, autonomous, and gender-ambiguous women in professional positions. Sengzhi's gender identity was simultaneously female and ambiguous: As a nun, we have seen how she was desexualized through the virtue of pure chastity and therefore entrusted to work closely with the emperor, never fearing that she would bear his children. As women secretaries, both Saṃgha Man and Welcoming Man[hood] were clearly women, though they held positions in the women's area of the court that were aligned with the positions that men held in the outer court, and they were known by honorific names, suggesting their proximity to the male gender. They also, like Sengzhi, were given positions that placed them in direct proximity to the emperor, perhaps a role allowed by their gender ambiguity. Unlike Sengzhi, whose gender ambiguity was made possible through her status as an eminent nun, the gender ambiguity displayed by both Saṃgha Man and Welcoming Man[hood] was linked to their social existence as women without men who served the court in a traditionally male role.

WOMEN AS MEN

Beyond the shared nature of their work and their male-sounding names, a striking similarity exists between Saṃgha Man and Welcoming Man[hood]: They were both women neither of whom had fathers nor brothers. Their lives and their work therefore find resonance with the life of the most famous Taghbach woman of the Northern Wei who is believed to have ever lived: Hua Mulan. Mulan is fabled to have been a Northern Wei woman who dressed as a man in order to join the military in lieu of her incapacitated father. The story about her therefore assumes that she had no brothers to take on this work for her. The extant text of her story that we can read today dates to the Song dynasty, although the earliest version of the story is said to have been compiled in the sixth century from Northern Wei precedents, likely in the Serbi language.[26] In his excellent study of the Mulan story, Chen Sanping argues that although when read in Chinese the name "Mulan" is an obviously feminine name calling to mind a fragrant flower,[27] its meaning in the Taghbach language is entirely different and also masculine: "Unicorn."[28] Altaic peoples, including the Serbi, are well known for their worship of animals from the Cervidae family, such as deer and elk; Chen argues that the Taghbach's own particular obsession with the unicorn falls within this Altaic Cervid worship.[29] As such, the name "Mulan" would suggest masculinity and martial prowess. Just like the names and family situations of Saṃgha Man and Welcoming Man[hood], Mulan acted as a male in society, taking on traditionally male work and being given a masculine name.

The precise biographical similarities between Mulan and our two other women who served the Northern Wei court under masculine names leads us to a fascinating historical question: Did the Taghbach organize their understanding of gender differently from how we in the modern West do and differently from how the Han populations in their polity did as well? In other words, did they know a form of gender that was tied less to physical sex than to social and family location? And if so, does this also account for the names of women on Northern Wei inscriptions that evoke proximity to maleness?

If the Taghbach had such a practice in their cultural repertoire, we do not need to assume that it was unique to them. Within the context of early medieval China, other ethnic and cultural groups from the Inner Asian Steppe did not have forms of written language, and we therefore have few sources by which to understand their gender regimes. In the case of the Taghbach, however, they adopted Literary Chinese as a written language during the Northern Wei dynasty and employed Ru scholars at court who wrote dynastic histories and entombed biographies.

The common people, too, used this language to compose donor inscriptions on Buddhist art. In sum, we know more about the Taghbach from this early period than we know about other contemporaneous steppe peoples. That we see noteworthy forms of gender expression in the sources that the Taghbach left behind during the Northern Wei does not mean that such gender expression was practiced only by them, but it does mean that we only know about it through them. In an effort to explain what I see in the sources regarding gender performance in the period, I adopt the concept of social or honorary maleness to categorize women who, in their lack of male kin, behave as men in society and take on male names and male work.

Social or honorary maleness is a typified form of gender expression practiced in diverse cultures around the world. In their 2015 study of global preference for male children, Christophe Z. Guilmoto and James Tovey point to the ongoing practice of traditions of social maleness in the world today, arguing that:

> Sex permutations are a possibility in some regions, with biological daughters treated socially as boys in response to the lack of a son. Traces of this practice can be found in the temporary pre-puberty transformation of the gender of *bacha posh* (girls "dressed as boys") in Afghanistan and in the permanent conversion of "sworn virgins" (*virgjinesha, burrnesha*, or *zavetovana devojka*) into men in Montenegro, Albania, and Kosovo.[30]

This is not to suggest that Taghbach culture shares any form of continuity with the cultures of Afghanistan or Albania, or that those cultures share any continuity with each other, but it is to suggest that gender can operate in nonbinary modalities for divergent social reasons and in different cultural contexts. This, I believe, was true of the Taghbach. Whether it is derived from their specific cultural repertoire or shared among other steppe peoples is a question I cannot yet answer; however, I am inclined to accept the latter explanation, given the fact that Saṃgha Man herself, like the empress dowager, hailed from Anding in modern-day Gansu, which was an area of the world more commonly associated with the Xiongnu.

My hypothesis that Taghbach notions of social gender were positional within the family and not permanently tied to biological sex requires a wide survey through diverse materials because we do not have texts written in the indigenous Taghbach language that might describe gender on its own terms, independent from how Ru scholars understood gender to operate in Taghbach society. We therefore begin in a very different place: modern and contemporary ethnography and anthropology. In her study of the anthropological character of the shaman, Silvia Tomášková reviews early twentieth-century scholarship on the shamans of North Asia. She concludes that gender was a fluid category for shamans in the indigenous cultures of the area, and argues that it was only early anthropologists who began to fix the shamanic form onto the male body, thus obfuscating the ways in which gender had operated in the past. Although she acknowledges that prehistoric notions of gender are largely obscured in modernity, she challenges us to "attempt to 'image the unimaginable' rather than only mirror the most recent arrangements and 'see only that which we deem comprehensible.'"[31] Inspired by her study, we can revisit the gendered norms of Taghbach society not with the question of how they were different from those of the Confucians who wrote about them in the Chinese language but with the question of how they were articulated within their own indigenous ways of knowing. To further this line of inquiry, Joel Bourland uses Queer Theory to approach the topic of gender fluidity among the Chukchi people of Siberia whose shamans of both sexes are known to have changed their social gender and undertaken homosexual marriages.[32] Bourland argues that such creative uses of gender "see through arbitrary paths" and emerge as "creative 'play'" within a given cultural context.[33] It is precisely this sort of gender flexibility that I see in the medieval sources on the Taghbach, wherein a woman can be a social man with a male name doing men's work but also still be a woman and mother children.

In a recent ethnographic study of the Evenki people, a hunter-gatherer ethnogroup from Siberia, Tatiana Safanova and István Sántha have recorded the cultural establishment of "tomboys," whom they refer to in Russian as *patsanka*. From the perspective of contemporary public policy in the People's Republic of China, the Evenki are considered one of the country's official ethnic minority groups and are also considered to be the long-distance cultural or blood descendants of the Taghbach, or both.[34] Based on Safanova and Sántha's research in the Baikal region of Siberia, which is approximately one thousand kilometers west of the Gaxian Cave and contains early Serbi tombs even though the region is more commonly associated with the Xiongnu,[35] they describe the life of one such woman they have named "Nadia." According to Safanova and Sántha, Nadia embraces the Evenki tradition of *manakan*, or "personal freedom." Employed as a park ranger on horseback, she is extolled in her culture for her general independence. Her independence, however, genders her male and allows her to participate in traditionally male-demarcated rituals of the Evenki people and to live her life in men's spaces even though she has mothered a child. The ethnographers argue that it is her status as an unmarried woman that facilitates her ability to transgress binary gender lines in both formal and informal ways. This further allows the authors to argue that binary gender among the Evenki is related to the act of marriage more so than it is to biological sex, because it is within the boundaries of marriage that the division of family labor takes on a binary mode with attendant, gender-specific specialization.[36] Finally, Safanova and Sántha argue that Nadia's identity within her culture is not bound to a specific gender "role" but is, rather, defined through her own autonomy:[37] As an unmarried woman by choice, she need not conform to the binary gender of male and female and is therefore a biological woman but is known in her community by her male nickname "Volodia,"[38] spends her leisure hours among men, and is also allowed to share their ritual space. It is also interesting to note that Nadia/Volodia's role within their culture is also not bound to their identity as an Evenki person, for both the male and female names that they take are Slavic in origin. This dynamic of cultural fluidity might further remind us of the Taghbach rulers and their Sinicized name, Yuan.

Although Nadia/Volodia was by no means a Northern Wei person, their cultural location within Tungusic hunter-gatherer society once again calls to mind the famous story of Mulan. Hua Mulan is similar to Nadia/Volodia in that she is said to have embraced her own autonomy as an unmarried woman with an incapacitated father and a masculine name while being proficient at horseback riding and granted access to social spaces normally demarcated as male. The Disney versions of the Mulan story known in the West today construct her narrative through the Confucian optic of filial duty within the patriarchal family system and they therefore stress the gender transgression of being a woman in a man's job. This version of the story is sourced in texts written in Literary Chinese that long post-date the Northern Wei. In such stories, the Confucian framing makes Mulan's gender transgression both shocking and meaningful and it finds context in the Han literary tradition with the emergence of Chinese tales of heroic filiality wherein we see women taking on men's filial obligations in situations where they lack male kin. Keith Knapp has pointed out how, for daughters in the medieval period, heroic acts of filiality that even included suicide became the mechanism by which women were able to fulfill the male role of filial duty and thereby be considered exemplary, and he refers to a subset of these filial daughters who take on the male role of seeking revenge for crimes against their family as "surrogate sons" who remain women but who act as men would do for a short time and take personal vengeance or lead troops in retaliatory battle.[39] Scholars of early medieval Chinese history have pointed out many places in the texts of the Han tradition wherein women have taken on violent roles in order to avenge wrongs committed against their family members.[40] Such an extreme act of filial piety as abandoning one's typified gender performance and putting oneself in physical danger is seen by the biographical tradition as favorable. In these stories, the gender transgression is clear: The women are exemplary because they have done something normally unthinkable for a woman to do and all for the cause of maintaining their family honor. These stories from the Han tradition date back as early as the Eastern Han and they provide the interpretive context by which the Mulan story has long been read within the Chinese literary tradition.

There is a different interpretation of the Mulan story that we should consider. I believe that if Mulan was in fact a Northern Wei woman, she would not have had to hide her gender, nor would her actions have been seen by her contemporaries as transgressive as much as they were heroic. Within Taghbach articulations of gender, Mulan may have been seen as particularly brave for living up to the difficult family situation that would lead a woman to act as a man in place of her deceased male relatives; that she did so while securing a successful military defeat would have stressed her bravery. We know of many cases in the annals of Taghbach history where women fought in the military as women, and although they did not wear "men's clothes," they did wear military clothing. I would assume that, just as in the Mulan story, they would put on their regular clothing after returning from battle. In a horse-riding, hunter-gatherer society such as the Taghbach, women likely did wear clothing that to Han culture seemed masculine. They likely wore pants.[41] What I am suggesting, here, is that participation in the military would not have been what made the Mulan story remarkable in Taghbach cultural norms, for women did participate in the military. That Mulan did so as a surrogate for her father and with great success is what makes the story remarkable. As an honorary man, she lived up to tremendous life challenges, and she succeeded. This is precisely the case of our two women secretaries who were named Saṃgha Man and Welcoming Man[hood]. In their entombed biographies, they are extolled for their work, work that was normally thought of as exclusive to men. Importantly, their stories are different from those of the surrogate sons of the Han tradition; not women seeking vengeance through violent or militaristic means, these honorary men have a wider repertoire of cultural practice available to them on account of the deaths of their male kin. Again, it is also likely true that such cultural practices were shared across steppe peoples and can still be seen in the world today. In the early medieval period, we can really only see it through the example of the Taghbach and the Northern Wei.

Although it might seem extraordinary, it might be true that the Taghbach identified certain categories of biological women as social men. If they did, this would offer a new interpretation of the Mulan story while also shedding light on gender-ambiguous naming practices and the establishment of court positions for women who held such names. Furthermore, such an understanding of Taghbach forms of gender expression allow us to understand the story of Mulan, if she ever existed, in ways that are potentially more resonant with how she knew herself. Finally, there is one more daughter whose story makes sense within the context of the possibility of honorary men in Taghbach culture: The granddaughter of Empress Dowager Ling. Fatherless, brotherless, and of mixed Han and Taghbach descent, the granddaughter was placed on the throne in lieu of a male heir. Read alongside the stories of Saṃgha Man, Welcoming Man[hood], and possibly, also, Mulan, the granddaughter's story begins to make more sense.

This potential context of honorary men within forms of gender organization known to the Taghbach that may have seen women known and acting as men in the situation of absent fathers and brothers and doing so at the court of Empress Dowager Ling is augmented by the Taghbach's own experimentation with monarchy. Until the time of Emperor Xiaowen—the emperor who moved the court to Luoyang in 494—the monarchs had all been leaders of the military. Following Taghbach notions of the monarch as khagan, military leadership was integral to the political legitimacy of the leader. However, from Xuanwu forward—or, in other words, throughout the Luoyang period—the association of the monarch with military leadership was displaced in favor of a more Sinitic model of the emperor being at an arm's reach from the military. This meant, practically speaking, that the emperors in the Luoyang period were ruling from the capital and not from the frontlines. As Anne Broadbridge has argued in her study of the roles of women in the later Mongol empire, with the military led by the khan himself, women supported the empire by building, maintaining, and servicing the nomadic camps while also engaging in trade and diplomatic relations.[42] A similar situation is seen in the Northern Wei: as khagans, the Northern Wei rulers led the military and therefore ruled far away from the capital, leaving women in the capital to support the empire in other ways. However, as the Northern Wei rulers in the Luoyang era were no longer khagans by definition and practice, power became concentrated in the court of the capital, which was a space that was arguably much more female in population and where women were accustomed to holding powerful roles. In sum, the reinvention of monarchy in the Luoyang period brought the monarch back home to the women's arena where women, in the absence of men, had become accustomed to living as men. Maybe they were even thought of as fit to serve as the leaders of men.

WOMEN AS BUDDHAS

Before embarking on the ultimate question of the granddaughter on the throne, we must first consider another vector of gender expression active at the Northern Wei court: Buddhist canonical depictions of elite women and their bodies alongside the frequent depictions of elite Buddhist womanhood within the context of statecraft. As we have seen, Sengzhi was credited with chanting the *Śrīmālā Sūtra* while in the service of the Northern Wei court. The *Śrīmālā Sūtra* was first translated during the Liu-Song dynasty some ten years before Sengzhi was potentially ordained there; as we saw, Sengzhi's entombed biography includes the earliest epigraphical attestation to the text yet found. The narrative of the *Śrīmālā Sūtra* describes the actions of Queen Śrīmālā, who is said to have been the queen of Ayodhya, in India, as well as the daughter of the buddha's great benefactor, King Prasenajit. In the sūtra, Queen Śrīmālā teaches profound lessons on emptiness, forms, perception, and the path of Buddhist practice that align with the framework of other "Lion's Roar" sūtras.[43] Her teachings inspire both women and men of the court to convert to Buddhism. The rarity of the *Śrīmālā Sūtra* comes not from the teaching but from the teacher. Preached by a woman whose command of the Buddhist teachings is equal in quality to that of a buddha's own teaching, the sūtra begs the question of the spiritual readiness of women according to Buddhist texts.

Buddhist canonical depictions of a woman's spiritual potential constituted an important and unstable question within the development of East Asian forms of Buddhism because many texts conflict with each other regarding the eschatological vision for the female body contained in Buddhist teaching.[44] The spiritual potential of women is thought to be denied in what is East Asia's most popular Buddhist text that Sengzhi also preached at the Northern Wei court—the *Lotus Sūtra*. Famously, the *Lotus Sūtra* contains the story of the daughter of the dragon king, who, when faced with male, monastic disbelief over her spiritual development, changes her body in to that of a male one and then goes on to complete all of the actions of attaining buddhahood.[45] Her act of sexual transformation or "turning away from the female form" (*zhuannü*) has been the subject of much theological and scholarly discussion because the story is ambiguous concerning the question of whether she changes her body because she must do so on the path to buddhahood or whether she does so as a sign of her buddhahood already attained.[46] On this topic, the *Śrīmālā Sūtra* is not particularly helpful; although Śrīmālā constantly preaches the universality of the true body of a buddha, she also states that "independence" is a condition of one's ability to achieve it.[47] Such a condition might seem opaque, and yet it appears again in a popular medieval text on the topic of sexual transformation, the *Sūtra on Turning Away from the Female Form* (Zhuan nüshen jing),[48] wherein a woman's lack of independence or inability to be self-sovereign (*bude zizai*) is cited as the precise reason why a woman must leave behind her female body if she would like to attain the highest levels of spiritual achievement.[49]

Buddhist textual discourse on the female body and its readiness for buddhahood was known at Empress Dowager Ling's court, and not just from the famous *Lotus* and *Śrīmālā Sūtras*. In general, the Northern Wei is not known for its patronage of Buddhist textual translation in the ways in which the Northern Liang and the southern courts were; however, Emperor Xuanwu and Empress Dowager Ling were both patrons of Buddhist texts and their translation. When we survey the textual materials that are recorded to have been translated by monastic translators supported by Xuanwu and Ling, a curious observation arises: Three of the texts are explicitly about women's bodies and their potential for Buddhahood, and they all feature settings attached to courtly life. These three texts were translated by the Northern Wei's best-known translators, all of whom worked for the Northern Wei court in Luoyang. First, the *Sūtra of the Woman, "Silver Countenance"* is recorded as having been translated by Buddhaśanta (Ch. Fotuoshanduo; fl. fifth century) who is said to have been placed in the palace in Luoyang in 508 CE to translate Buddhist texts with his colleague, Bodhiruci (Ch. Putiliuzhi; d. 527), who was himself later ordered to continue his translation activities at the imperially funded Eternal Peace Monastery after its completion.[50] One of the texts that Bodhiruci may conceivably have translated while working for the Northern Wei is the *Sūtra on the Prophecy of Kṣemavati* (Chamopodi shouji jing). Bodhiruci did not live to see the destruction of the capital and the Eternal Peace Monastery; however, his colleague Buddhaśanta is said to have gone from Luoyang's White Horse Temple (Baima si)[51] to the Eastern Wei capital of Yecheng where he continued to translate texts.[52] Finally, a third translator, Gautama Prajñāruci (Ch. Qutan Boreliuzhi; ca. sixth century), came to the Northern

Wei in 516. At some point before the fall of the sacking of Luoyang he translated the *Sūtra of Vimalī* (Dewugounü jing). After Luoyang's fall, he also relocated to Yecheng, where he and Buddhaśanta worked together.[53] Buddhaśanta's *Sūtra of the Woman, "Silver Countenance"*, Bodhiruci's *Sūtra on the Prophecy of Kṣemavatī*, and Gautama Prajñāruci's *Sūtra of Vimalī* all deal with the question of the readiness of women for buddhahood and they all include episodes of female-to-male sexual transformation along the path to attaining it.

The *Sūtra of the Woman, "Silver Countenance"* is a past-life story of Śākyamuni Buddha from when he was a woman. As the story goes, he-then-she was out begging for alms and stopped by a house where a new mother was starving to the point that she was about to eat her newborn baby. Faced with this horrific scene, Silver Countenance then asks for a knife from the woman and proceeds to cut off her own breasts to feed to the starving new mother.[54] Her breasts are subsequently and magically restored after she swears to the villagers that there was no vexation in her heart when she offered them in the first place. Indra then appears disguised as an old brahmin to ask her the same question. She declares that she will take on a male body if it is true that she harbored no vexation in her heart when she sliced off her breasts. She then takes on a male body. After all this, she-turned-he takes a rest under a tree where they are discovered by envoys from another kingdom and made their king. Ultimately, after a series of births and deaths, Silver Countenance is born as Māṇava, who sacrifices his body to a hungry tigress in a well-known story of Śākyamuni Buddha's past lives.

The *Sūtra of Vimalī* tells the story of its namesake, Vimalī, who is the daughter of King Prasenajit, who is also the father of Queen Śrīmālā. In the sūtra, Vimalī goes out for a walk and her parents insist that she be accompanied by five hundred brahmins to protect her from wayward Buddhist teachers. As she is walking, she comes across just such a group of Buddhists, declares her adherence to and understanding of the buddha's teaching, and then engages a series of the buddha's major disciples in doctrinal conversation. The back-and-forth between them all eventually lands on the question of why and how Vimalī can be so learned in Buddhist teaching while also retaining a female body. In order to prove to the disciples that physical sex is not a barrier to Buddhist practice, she spontaneously changes her sex into that of a man and the earth quakes in six different ways like it does at the birth of a buddha. All the brahmins in her entourage convert to Buddhism as does King Prasenajit himself. King Prasenajit is said to have been the ruler of the kingdom of Kosala, a kingdom in the Gangetic plain in the north of the Indian subcontinent that existed from the seventh century to the fifth century before the Common Era. The kingdom of Kosala was integral for the development of early Buddhism in India because King Prasenajit sponsored the construction of foundational Buddhist monasteries.[55]

Neither the *Sūtra of Vimalī* nor the *Sūtra of the Woman, "Silver Countenance"* were new translations under the Northern Wei: Both are recorded as having been previously translated during the Western Jin dynasty although the *Sūtra of the Woman, "Silver Countenance"* bore the earlier title of the *Sūtra of the Transformations of the Three Prior Ages* (Qianshi sanzhuan jing) and the *Sūtra of Vimalī* was known by its earlier name, the *Sūtra of the Girl Vimaladattā* (Ligou shinü jing). In both cases, the translations have few notable differences between them, and yet it is important to note that the texts share strong resonances with many other texts from the early medieval courts that discuss the female body and its possibility for buddhahood in remarkably similar ways.[56] These texts were all translated between the third and seventh centuries. Together they typify the form of elite Buddhist womanhood enacted by Sengzhi and many others at the Northern Wei court—a sort of Buddhist womanhood inflected by gender ambiguity, proximity to manhood, and elite status.

We see this type of womanhood on display in Saṃgha Man's entombed biography. Although she is not explicitly identified as a Buddhist or a nun, her very name evokes the Buddhist monastic institution. Moreover, the description of her character employs stereotypically Buddhist language like "wise nature" (*huixing*) and "agile awareness" (*minwu*), which are qualities commonly associated with buddhahood or with the development of Buddhist ideals of good character. Moreover, as we have already seen, the ability to chant texts is a Buddhist skill par excellence and, just like in Sengzhi's entombed biography where she is said to have chanted many sūtras after only hearing them one time, so too is Saṃgha Man remembered as having chanted so many words and studied the texts so diligently that she could clearly retain them after only hearing them once. In a manner that is even more similar to Sengzhi, Saṃgha Man is responsible for organizing and regulating the ranks of women filling the inner court and doing so with a "manly" heart, which is another character trait that we might associate with Buddhist practices of monasticism for women as well as with their attendant gender ambiguity.

The Northern Wei translators not only replicated and amplified such teachings on elite Buddhist womanhood already known in early medieval China; they also acted as innovators in textual translation. For example, as we have seen, Bodhiruci translated the *Sūtra on the Prophecy of Kṣemavati* for the first time during the Northern Wei. Centering on the question of the readiness of women and their bodies for buddhahood, the *Sūtra on the Prophecy of Kṣemavati* features similar conversations on the relationship of physical sex to spiritual progress as they relate to the female protagonist Kṣemavati, who is the wife of another famous Indian Buddhist king, Bimbisāra.[57] According to the text, the buddha and his retinue arrive at Bimbisāra's palace to beg for food and are instead greeted by his wife, Kṣemavati, who is covered in shining jewels from head to toe. The buddha asks Kṣemavati about her jewels and she responds to him by saying that like a tree that has had good seeds planted, she too, in prior lifetimes, had planted the seeds of the teaching so that she could now be enjoyed in a beautiful form.

Following this argument, she then goes on to acknowledge the necessity of sexual transformation on the path to buddhahood. She says, in verse:

> In deeds of my body, speech, mind,
> I have cultivated the practice of all kinds of goodness,
> Vowing to achieve great bodhi,
> I have sought out the buddha's wisdom and cultivation of merit.
> I will abandon my female form
> And attain the superb male body.
> Having attained the male body,
> The next step is to attain the buddha body.
> Having attained superb bodhi,
> I will turn the unsurpassed wheel of the teaching,
> I will bind up the prison of life and death,
> And extinguish and liberate all living creatures.[58]

This text reinforces the idea that imperial and elite women were featured in Buddhist textual materials known to the Northern Wei court and that they were seen as eminent teachers on bodies and buddhahood. They were also queens and princess who advocated for the act of female-to-male sexual transformation along the path to buddhahood.

So far as I have seen, the earliest mentions of the ideal of female-to-male transformation as a religious practice surface in the context of early medieval Chinese Buddhism, particularly in the northern dynasties. For example, Chikusa Masaaki argues that the textual desire to achieve a man's body manifested socially in Buddhist women committing acts of deadly self-immolation more often than their male counterparts in the early medieval period.[59] In the case of the Northern Wei, Amy McNair has summarized sixth-century donative inscriptions by women from Longmen in which the donors lament their female forms and transfer the merit generated from their donation to others like them who are bound by the "three followings"[60]—women. Similarly, Chen Ruifeng has recently uncovered the colophon on a collection of copied Buddhist texts from Dunhuang that contains the wishes of the donor, a Buddhist nun named Jianhui. In this colophon, Jianhui expresses her desire to be reborn as a man. Although Jianhui's colophon is dated to 536, and although this date falls under the Western Wei's control of Dunhuang, it stands to reason that Jianhui was a nun there prior to the demise of the Northern Wei some two years before when the Northern Wei controlled Dunhuang. Jianhui commissioned the writing of seven different sūtras, with two copies of the *Lotus Sūtra*, and states (in Chen's translation): "By the little merit, [I aspire] to become male after leaving this female body, and for the multitudinous beings in the realm of reality to become buddhas at the same time."[61]

In his work, Chen Ruifeng asks the question of whether Buddhists in the early medieval period understood the meaning of the texts they patronized. He does this by probing the possible connection between the personal colophons that feature on sponsored manuscript copies of texts from Dunhuang and the actual content of the texts themselves. Chen's conclusion is that, in general, there is a strong concordance between the religious aspirations of a text's patron and the contents and teachings contained in the texts themselves.[62] This might seem like a natural conclusion; however, the textual situation in medieval China is complicated by questions of translation, literacy, and market saturation that make Chen's study both important and helpful. In our case, what his study suggests is that elite women of the court in Northern Wei Luoyang lived in a Buddhist milieu in which they were familiar with the ideal of female-to-male sexual transformation particularly linked to elite women of the court who were the princesses and queens of Buddhist antiquity. Again, whether such a history is true or not misses the point. The teachings on female bodies seen in the texts of Northern Wei Buddhism supported the rise of the Buddhist ideal of female-to-male sexual transformation among elite women and went alongside new practices of self-immolation, lamenting the female body, and vowing to become men.

By the late Northern Wei, Buddhism was a religion that was flourishing in every village, town, and city. At all levels of society, from the court in the capital to the villages and towns in the countryside, Buddhism had become established as the religion of men and women, north and south. In the case of the Northern Wei, by the time of Empress Dowager Ling, art historical, textual, and material sources tell us that people understood many aspects of their new religion, including the contents of Buddhist texts, the structure of the monastic organization, and the methods of devotion that would come to affect the Buddhist practice of East Asia much more broadly. One of the things that they likely understood—because they would have had multiple layers of exposure to the concept—is that Buddhist texts of their period featured women as high-level teachers who were often princesses and queens. These female protagonists frequently took on male bodies or advocated doing so as a sign of their spiritual readiness. At the level of elite Buddhist womanhood, the women in these sūtras provided a canonical basis for the type of womanhood that Buddhist women at court then modeled. Women like Sengzhi, Saṃgha Man, and the many weina we have met through this study exemplify the close connection between political and public women, Buddhist teaching, and gender ambiguity that we see in Buddhist texts commonly known from this period.

The gender ambiguity present in elite forms of Buddhist womanhood during the Northern Wei does not adequately explain why the empress dowager placed her granddaughter on the throne; if these women saw themselves as close to manhood as a condition of buddhahood, how does this explain placing a girl in a typically male role? The answer lies in a different but related Buddhist devotional figure, the bodhisattva. Buddhas are not the only objects worthy of reverence in the Buddhist tradition. The buddhas to be, or beings on the path to buddhahood otherwise known as bodhisattvas, were widely popular as devotional figures in early medieval China and many sūtras translated in the period were specifically linked to the worship and popularization of them and their cults. According to influential Buddhist texts of the period, buddhas must be in male bodies. However, this is not the case for bodhisattvas. Bodhisattvas can and do appear in female bodies, and they do in the sūtra material cited above. For our purposes, we need to ask an important question: If women of the court and the administration of Buddhism modeled themselves after high-level Buddhist queens in sūtra literature who enjoyed a certain bodily and gender ambiguity that comes from Buddhist doctrine but who also resonated with the gender ambiguity of both monasticism and honorary maleness seen in the sixth century, is it possible that women as emperors could have modeled themselves after bodhisattvas, who do indeed appear in female bodies within canonical Buddhist scripture?

Maitreya in Stone

The future buddha, Maitreya, is arguably the most popular bodhisattva of the sixth century. Images of Maitreya across the period are commonly linked to a schema of the buddhas of the three ages wherein Maitreya is depicted as the next buddha to come. This interpretation of the buddhas of the three ages is seen in Northern Wei grottos, such as the Huangfu Grotto at Longmen,[63] which was commissioned by the uncle of the empress dowager, as well as the Binyang Grotto, which Amy McNair argues was commissioned by Emperor Xuanwu himself.[64] In both grottos, Maitreya is the buddha of the future; Śākyamuni is seen as the buddha of the present; and Prabhūtaratna is the buddha of the past (depicted in his Śākyamuni-Prabhūtaratna image discussed in chapter 1). A beautifully clear articulation of this formula is found on an early Northern Wei stele from the Buddhist cliff and cave site of Maiji shan, also in Gansu province. In this instance, even though Maitreya is the buddha of the future, he is the central image on the stele. Maitreya's central position on this rare and early stele from Maiji shan suggests his centrality as a devotional figure of significant importance in the sixth century.[65] At Dunhuang, the monastic city along the Silk Roads famed for its Buddhist grottos that contain art and texts, the few Northern Wei grottos that were built there feature Maitreya as an image of devotion: both of the major devotional grottos at Dunhuang that date to the late Northern Wei (numbers 257 and 254) prominently feature Maitreya.[66]

Such images that center Maitreya inaugurate a particular understanding of political leadership that had wide resonance across East Asia in medieval times: A Buddhist interpretation of political legitimation in which the leader was connected with one figure in particular—the bodhisattva and future buddha, Maitreya. According to Buddhist cosmology, Maitreya's appearance in the world will usher in a new era of peace and prosperity that will bring an end to the dark ages we are currently living under. This message found wide appeal across East

FIGURE 15. Rubbing of #10 image stele from cave 133 at Maiji shan grottos in Gansu, China. Steles shows the three buddha paradigm, with Maitreya at center. Circa mid-sixth century. Stele in situ. Rubbing is from the author's collection.

Asia and the type of millenarian political orientation that it invoked continued to develop throughout the medieval period. April Hughes has conclusively demonstrated how, beginning with Northern Wei rebellions against the court, Maitreya-based millenarianism became an integral component of the reigns and rules of Emperor Wen of the Sui and Emperor Wu Zhao herself.[67] Richard McBride has also shown how such Maitreya-based political ideology was replicated on the Korean peninsula where Kungye (d. 918), the founder of what is known as the Later Koguryŏ period (901–18), declared that he, too, was none other than Maitreya reborn.[68] McBride links Kungye's use of Maitreya ideology to the reign of Emperor Wu Zhao, arguing that he modeled himself, in part, on her. Such Maitreya-based imagining of the ruler is not unique to East Asia: The ancient Silk Road Buddhistic kingdom of Khotan also saw many of their semimythical, ancient kings identified with the bodhisattva and future buddha Maitreya.[69]

Within the context of the Northern Wei, we see the bodhisattva Maitreya identified with the emperor as early as the 490s, just after the move of the capital city to Luoyang. Chapter 1 of this study offered a brief overview of Emperor Wencheng's program of imperial Buddhism in Pingcheng and argued that the buddha was identified with the Northern Wei ruler during that time. This identification of the ruler with the buddha took on two visible manifestations: (1) the building of the imperial grottos at Yungang where the buddha/ruler identification was given monumental form; (2) the appearance of the previously discussed *Sūtra for Humane Kings*, a text that argues the ruler is the manifestation of the buddha in this world. In the Luoyang era, this matching of the buddhas with the rulers continued on with one notable difference—a new generation of princes and emperors. Amy McNair argues that within Longmen's Guyang grotto, a cluster of seven shrines was originally constructed to represent the six past rulers of the dynasty as well as the current ruler, Xiaowen. She further argues that these seven buddha rulers were represented in a Central Asian style of monastic dress, which would mark them as prior, foreign, and consistent in style with the depiction of the buddha rulers at Yungang. However, McNair also points to an eighth shrine within the grotto, which was completed at a slightly later date and in which, she argues, the buddha image is represented in a Han style of monastic dress. McNair argues that this image was made to represent the heir apparent, Emperor Xuanwu, in the guise of a Han-styled future buddha, Maitreya. This is an argument that she can connect with external evidence: In 492, McNair tells us, "a Maitreya image was made for the 'Temple of the Seven Wei Emperors'" in Dingxian, Hebei province, therefore adding an eighth emperor to the temple, which was imaged as the future buddha, Maitreya.[70] McNair suggests that the move to a Han style in the depiction of Emperor Xuanwu as Maitreya is linked to its later date when the Northern Wei had formally adopted policies of Sinification. More specifically, the move from depicting the ruler as a foreign king represented in a buddha of the past to a Han-styled emperor in a buddha of the future also marks the change in the form of leadership undertaken in the Luoyang period. As discussed previously, Emperor Xuanwu was the emperor who reinvented Northern Wei forms of monarchy by breaking away from Taghbach understandings of the leader as khagan; acting as the pivot to a more Sinitic notion of monarchy, Xuanwu abandoned the notion of the monarch as khagan and head of the military and embraced the notion of the emperor as head of state in the capital city.

But if we look at the images in Buddhist sites that were not commissioned to inaugurate Xuanwu's reign, we see that the image of Maitreya as emperor is not specifically and only connected to Xuanwu, but also—and often—to his son, Emperor Xiaoming. A poignant example of this is found in the region of the world from which the empress dowager hailed. At a lesser-known Buddhist grotto site in the empress dowager's region of Gansu—the aforementioned Monastery of the Hollow Rock at Chicken Head Mountain that the empress dowager visited when Emperor Xiaoming was a young child—the regional inspector (*cishi*) of the area, a Taghbach courtier named Xi Kangsheng (467–521), commissioned the building of a grotto with the seven past buddhas as well as a cross-legged Maitreya representing the buddha of the future.[71] The site was built in the year 510—the year of the birth of Emperor Xiaoming. I do not think it is a coincidence that the grotto with its image of Maitreya and the seven past buddha-emperors was commissioned by the regional inspector of the empress dowager's ancestral land in the very year in which the empress dowager birthed the only heir apparent. I believe that, just like his father, Xiaoming was emblematized as the future buddha Maitreya. His father was born in 489 but only named heir apparent in 493, the precise year in which Amy McNair argues that the Guyang grotto was planned and the year after the Temple of the Seven Wei Emperors added its own Maitreya figure. That a similar image of Maitreya with the seven past emperors was built in the empress dowager's homeland and by the court-appointed regional inspector suggests that the motif of the seven past rulers, plus the heir apparent as the future buddha, came to be a more generalized way to express, in Buddhist terms, the commemoration of the birth or appointment of an heir apparent. It was also a way to celebrate that new ruler's reign and legitimate that new ruler's power. Furthermore, for Xiaoming, we see how his reign continued to be connected to the bodhisattva Maitreya at the Yellow Cliff site in Shandong. Above, we surveyed a donor inscription of a dharma collective of thirty-five people who commissioned the building of an image of Maitreya and said of themselves that they were supporters of Emperor Xiaoming. They commissioned this image in the year 526—just after the empress dowager had resumed her regency after the coup d'état and when the question of whether or not Emperor Xiaoming was old enough to be ruling directly was presenting ever-increasing challenges.

A deeper study of the caves that Xi Kangsheng commissioned in the year of Emperor Xiaoming's birth once again finds connection with the work of contemporary scholar April Hughes. Working on the rise of millenarian Buddhist religion at the various courts of medieval China, Hughes has shown that a Buddhist text that appears to have been written in China with no Indic analog and that positions the bodhisattva Maitreya in a millenarian and salvific role was integral to the identification of Emperor Wu Zhao as a birth of Maitreya in a female form.[72] The text that Hughes has studied in-depth is known as the *Sūtra Expounded for the Bodhisattva Samantabhadra on Attesting Illumination* (Puxian pusa shuo zhengming jing). The origins of this text are unknown; however, historian of Chinese art Patricia Karetzky argues that the text provided the narrative behind the visual program at Hollow Rock Monastery at Chicken Head Mountain that was commissioned by Xi Kangsheng. In a short article thoroughly illustrated with rare and high-quality photographs of the inside of the cave, Karetzky interprets the perplexing visual program as a direct rendering of a particular scene from the sūtra that includes seven buddha images with attendant bodhisattvas, the independent image of the bodhisattva Samantabhadra on his elephant mount, the presence of asuras, and two independent images of the bodhisattva Maitreya. Karetzky argues that such a unique collection of Buddhist deities can only express a particular narrative within the *Sūtra Expounded for the Bodhisattva Samantabhadra on Attesting Illumination* wherein Samantabhadra seeks an efficacious method for combatting the decline of the buddha's law in the world, recommends worshipping the seven buddhas of the past, and beseeches Maitreya to speak on the topic of the coming of the next buddha himself. At Samantabhadra's urging, Maitreya tells of a future in which the world is burned to the ground by an asura who is holding seven suns, and that only after this destruction will he himself finally descend. As such, the presence of this visual program at the caves commissioned in the year of the birth of Emperor Xiaoming and in the ancestral land of his mother, Empress Dowager Ling, suggests very strongly that Maitreya-based millenarianism was alive and well at the court of the Northern Wei and that Emperor Xiaoming, like his father, was seen as a millenarian ruler connected to the bodhisattva Maitreya.

Maitreya in Prophecy

Although Maitreya is typically cast in a male figure, East Asian traditions of lore and worship that center on the figure of Maitreya are not always and exclusively tied to maleness. Studying a Buddhist text that is listed in numerous medieval catalogs as the *Sūtra on Maitreya Taking a Female Form* (Mile wei nüshen jing)—even though that text can no longer be found in the modern Buddhist canon—Tang Jia has located the text in other medieval compendia and has shown how, in this story, Maitreya takes a female body on his own path toward buddhahood. Tang locates this story within a Mahāyānic trope of advanced female bodhisattvas that features in many texts in early medieval China, which advocate for the buddhahood of women. Tang also connects this form of Maitreya to the popular worship of Maitreya by women in the early medieval period.[73] Within this cluster of texts that come to associate Maitreya with women, Tang cites the *Sūtra of the Rain of Jewels*

(Baoyun jing) that was presented to Emperor Wu Zhao and that she used as part of her campaign to have herself identified as the rebirth of Maitreya in a female form.

In her quest to be interpreted as the reincarnation of Maitreya in her time and therefore a cakravartin ruler of her empire, Emperor Wu Zhao and her supporters found support in a Buddhist text called the *Great Cloud Sūtra* (Dayun jing).[74] In the *Great Cloud Sūtra*, the buddha praises the wisdom and understanding of a heavenly woman named Pure Radiance (Jingguang) who has appeared in his assembly and engaged him in a conversation about the appearance of past kings and rulers in the world, of which he was once one. The buddha praises her by saying:

> Heavenly woman! At that time there was a queen, and you are none other than her. From a different buddha, you once suddenly heard the *Nirvana Sūtra* and from that karmic cause have now attained this heavenly body which is suitable for leaving our world. [When you] again hear the deep teaching, you will cast off this heavenly form and take on a female body and will be the king of a country and attain one quarter of the realm of the cakravartin. Attaining great autonomy, receiving and upholding the five precepts, and serving as *upāsikā*, you will teach and convert all those who belong to the cities and villages and settlements, men and women great and small. Receiving and upholding the five precepts, defending the true dharma, bending and destroying the external ways of all of the heterodox dissenters, at that time you will be a true bodhisattva and will manifest in a female body for the sake of converting sentient beings.[75]

Emperor Wu Zhao's court writers composed a commentary on this Buddhist text that claimed she was the rebirth of the bodhisattva in question, none other than Maitreya.[76] As a bodhisattva ruler in a female form, Wu Zhao brought the prophecy of the *Great Cloud Sūtra* to life and she did so by positioning herself as Maitreya. But was she the first to do so?

Sources for the study of both Buddhist manuscripts and women's lives are comparatively much less available and much less studied for the Northern dynasties than they are for the Tang. Unlike in the case of Emperor Wu Zhao, we have no manuscript fragments that show us directly how the *Great Cloud Sūtra* may have been understood by Northern Wei courtiers or by Empress Dowager Ling. What we do have, however, are two textual colophons from Dunhuang attesting to the fact that the text was known by at least one member of the imperial house that worked for the empress dowager's court. For a study of these colophons, we return to the work of Chen Ruifeng, particularly to his survey of the various colophons for textual copying that were commissioned by Yuan Rong (d. 545). A fourth-generation grandson of the Northern Wei emperor Mingyuan (r. 409–23), Yuan Rong was sent by the central court to serve as the regional inspector of Guazhou in 525 and he served in that role until his death in 542. Guazhou prefecture included Dunhuang, and Rong Xinjiang has commented on Yuan Rong's influence in the region, particularly showing how Yuan Rong consolidated power among the elite and patronized the copying of Buddhist texts and the construction of a large Buddhist grotto, Mogao grotto number 285.[77] In a style reminiscent of the empress dowager's Huoshao grotto, Mogao grotto 285 also combines Han-Chinese deities with Buddhist motifs. Yuan Rong was both a political and a religious force in the Dunhuang area, which, given its peripheral location, spared him much of the violent disaster that befell the central court in Luoyang between 528 and 534. In short, he lived while others died. While he lived, he regularly commissioned the copying of sūtras. In the colophons to his copies, we find mention of the *Great Cloud Sūtra*.

Although Yuan Rong lived far from Luoyang, we see his support for the Northern Wei emperor and the crumbling imperial line manifesting in increasingly urgent ways throughout the colophons to sūtra copies that he commissioned at Dunhuang. Unlike many other Taghbach courtiers, Yuan Rong continued to hold his title after the death of the empress dowager and was even granted a new title which he used on his colophons. That title, Prince of Dongyang (*dongyang wang*), was granted to him by Emperor Xiaozhuang, who was the first emperor propped up by the Erzhu faction and who eventually murdered Erzhu Rong in his attempt to assert his own power.[78] Yuan Rong commissioned copies of the *Sūtra for Humane Kings* in both the years 530 and 531. In 530, when Yuan Rong twice commissioned the text, the ruling regent was Emperor Xiaozhuang. After Xiaozhuang's murder of Erzhu Rong, the latter's clansmen murdered Xiaozhuang in retaliation and briefly propped up a new emperor, Yuan Ye (r. 530–31). During Yuan Ye's very short reign, Yuan Rong again commissioned the copying of the *Sūtra for Humane Kings*. The aspirations that he declares on this colophon are that his family all be safe and awakened and that they all be returned to the capital city, which was also near the site of the Heyin massacre that saw the deaths of many members of their clan who had served at the court of the empress dowager.[79] Finally, in 532, Yuan Rong again commissioned the further copying of Buddhist texts, which included the *Sūtra for Humane Kings* and several other items. This time, however, the puppet in question was Emperor Jiemin. Jiemin attempted to assert his own power away from the Erzhus to reestablish the legitimate imperial line; however, he was murdered when Gao Huan rose to prop up his own emperor. In the colophon dated to the reign of Jiemin, Yuan Rong states that he had sent his son to the capital to renew the family's imperial commitments. He also expresses his personal happiness that the "Son of Heaven has been restored" because, as he states, "since heaven and earth have been abnormally barren, the royal way has been obstructed."[80] In this colophon dedicated to the restoration of the Taghbach imperial line, Yuan Rong states that he commissioned the sūtra copies so that the Northern Wei's current "era be endless" and so that the "lineage of the emperor not be broken off."[81]

Yuan Rong's dated colophons display how a member of the Taghbach imperial family used Buddhist textual copying to support the reigns of three Taghbach puppet emperors and, by extension, to support his own authority as a member of the imperial family. For the most part, Yuan Rong frequently commissioned a text that contains the most forceful argument that we have for the identification of the ruler with the buddha, the *Sūtra for Humane Kings*. And yet, after his commissioning of texts in support of the renewal of the Taghbach line under Emperor Jiemin, he commissioned a different corpus of sūtras, many of which were popular in his time. Among those texts, one stands out for its rare, early epigraphical attestation: the *Great Cloud Sūtra*.[82] Similarly, in another of his colophons from 533, the *Great Cloud Sūtra* is again listed as one of the texts that he had commissioned.[83] In keeping with Yuan Rong's pattern of patronage, this group of texts was commissioned during the reign of the last of the Northern Wei's emperors, Emperor Xiaowu, who had been propped up by Gao Huan but who had also attempted to break free of his power, an act that led to the final demise of the Northern Wei.

Until now, historical records of the existence the *Great Cloud Sūtra* have strongly been linked to the Tang because of Emperor Wu Zhao's claim that she was the fulfillment of the text's prophecy of a female ruler as the Bodhisattva Maitreya. With Yuan Rong's colophons, however, we can place the sūtra within the textual and social context of other popular Buddhist sūtras in the sixth century. Chen Ruifeng has carefully analyzed all those sūtras in his study; in brief, they contain many of the sūtras we have already discussed in this study such as the *Lotus* and the *Nirvana* but also other texts that were popular in the Northern Wei such as the *Sūtra on the Wise and the Foolish* and the *Vimalakīrti-nirdeśa Sūtra* (Weimojie suoshuo jing). What this suggests is that Yuan Rong knew about the *Great Cloud Sūtra* and thought it appropriate to have copied it on two separate occasions, along with other well-known texts from his era and that were circulating in his milieu. With Yuan Rong, then, we can place the *Great Cloud Sūtra* in the striking context of a Northern Wei courtier and member of the Taghbach royal house who worked for the empress dowager and then commissioned the copying of Buddhist sūtras for four out of the five emperors that came in the six years between her death and the end of the dynasty.

Is the fact that the *Great Cloud Sūtra* was known by at least one of the empress dowager's courtiers and commissioned alongside other popular texts of the age enough to link it to the empress dowager herself? Specifically, can we postulate that the empress dowager may have known about the text and that it informed her own Buddhist practice? Michael Radich has shown that the two different Chinese versions of the text of the *Great Cloud Sūtra* that we have today are both strongly linked to the translator Dharmakṣema, with one of them most certainly being his own translation and the other bearing a striking resemblance to that one in terminology and phrasing.[84] Dharmakṣema was active in the mid-fifth century when the great translation bureau at Guzang was under the jurisdiction and sponsorship of the Northern Liang. The empress dowager was born in the late fifth century between Chang'an and Guzang. As we have already seen, both her matrilineal and patrilineal family were local gentry and known Buddhist patrons. Her aunt, the nun Sengzhi, was so esteemed for her Buddhist practice that she was called to work at the Northern Wei court. What we can say, then, is that the empress dowager's family were known supporters of the Buddhist tradition from Gansu who lived at the gate of the Hexi corridor and would have been immersed in the Buddhist texts, ideas, persons, and objects being transmitted through their region from Guzang. Dharmakṣema was a famous monk in his time, widely known across the north. So renowned was he that Emperor Taiwu attempted to steal him from the Northern Liang ruler, Juqu Mengxun (r. 401–433), who then killed the monk instead of handing him over to the enemy.[85] We therefore have every reason to think that the texts he translated circulated widely through the northern dynasties where they became known by the Northern Wei's regional inspector and likely also by the empress dowager's famous family of eminent Buddhists and Buddhist patrons.

THE NAMELESS GRANDDAUGHTER AS MONARCH

Let us return once again to the rare names for women from this time period, names that evoke social maleness. Particularly, the names from the Gao clan in Dangmo present unique opportunities for historical interpretation. To remind us, the names of the two women in question can be translated into English as "Male Birth" and "Almost a Man." Both women are identified in the inscription as wives of men from the Gao family who hold the title "Gentlemen of Pure Faith." This title identifies the women's husbands as lay Buddhist practitioners, and I believe that the names of their wives identify them in the same way; in the case of the Gao family inscription, these names for women that evoke social maleness seem to be dharma names. As dharma names, they suggest Buddhist affiliation and knowledge of Buddhist teachings in ways that resonate with the dharma names of members of the monastic community also seen in the period.[86] They also resonate with the names of the two women secretaries who were given their names as honorifics. In the case of the women secretaries, though there is some connection to Buddhism in their stories, what is more striking is their status as "honorary men" in their families. What we have, then, are two groups of two different kinds of women sharing similar names. In the case of the women of the Gao clan, I find it unlikely that they were considered honorary men because their husbands were eminent men in their society, and because it would be too suspicious a coincidence that they would both hold such names related to family circumstances prior to marrying into the Gao family, unless they were sisters. Yet, in the case of the women secretaries, I think it likely that their names evoke honorary male status, given their family situations, their gender ambiguity, and their work at court. In the case of the Gao women, the honorary nature of these dharma names identifies them with popular currents of Buddhist thought in their day; whereas, for the women secretaries, their honorary names evoke a different type of gender expression linked to diverse forms of gender organization known to the Taghbach in the sixth century.

These divergent ways of understanding the names of women in the late Northern Wei, when women served at court and Buddhism was the religion of the land, are not at odds with each other. Rather, both forms of naming belong to the cultural matrix of the Northern Wei, wherein the intersection of Taghbach or Inner Asian ways of knowing, Han Chinese ways of governing, and Buddhist ways of worshipping supported women's lives in entirely new ways. As we saw in the previous chapter, women leveraged their belonging in the Buddhist monastic institution to create safety, space, and opportunity. So, too, did they with other forms of Buddhist identity and practice. As donors, as weina, as women secretaries, as empresses and empress dowagers, and perhaps even as the emperor, Buddhist-affiliated women in the late Northern Wei enjoyed both social fluidity and social protection through Buddhist ideas and institutions. In the dynamic context of hybrid Buddhist/Taghbach/Han forms of faith, gender expression, and work, women in the sixth century created opportunities out of intersection.

Returning to the central problem of the unnamed granddaughter on the throne, we can ask a final question: Did this dynamic cultural context of women in Buddhist texts, Buddhist deities as monarchs, Taghbach honorary men, and the reinvention of the Taghbach leader from khagan to emperor result in a baby girl becoming the Northern Wei monarch for a few days? Although the Han-styled emperor is male, and although Buddhist women of the Han-styled court in Luoyang adopted a form of gender ambiguity linked to both monasticism and honorary maleness that was modeled on canonical Buddhist literature known to them, it is also true that the granddaughter in question could arguably have been seen as an honorary male in Taghbach culture at a time when Buddhist texts also supported the idea that Maitreya could be reborn in a female body and when, simultaneously, Maitreya was linked to the identity of the heir apparent as well as to the emperor who was her deceased father. Unlike in the Tang where we have historical sources documenting how Emperor Wu Zhao capitalized on this context of the gendered reinvention of the monarch through Buddhism, we do not have similar sources for the Northern Wei. What we can say, simply, is that all the same pieces that allowed Emperor Wu Zhao to identify herself as a female monarch—including the *Great Cloud Sūtra*—were also in play at the time Empress Dowager Ling placed her granddaughter on the throne. Additionally, during the Northern Wei, women known as honorary men already worked for the court in the capital of Luoyang. I believe that we should consider the nameless granddaughter as a similar sort of honorary man, one who fulfilled a prophecy of a Buddhist monarch in a female body just as she took on her father's identity as the Bodhisattva Maitreya in an act of honorary maleness.

5

No Salvation in Buddhism

If, as I have argued above, Empress Dowager Ling had all the same resources in play as Emperor Wu Zhao of the Tang did; if, that is, she had a bodhisattva emperor ruling over a Buddhist populace after having taken control of the court and its ritual and staffed the court with women, why did it not work as well for her as it did for her Tang successor? Why was she not able to rule unchallenged? Why has she been forgotten while Emperor Wu Zhao has been celebrated?

The simplest answer to these questions is that Empress Dowager Ling was a weak ruler. Although I believe that she provided a model for direct rule by Buddhist women that was later fulfilled by Emperor Wu Zhao at the end of the seventh century, she did not herself enjoy the support that the latter ruler did. Empress Dowager Ling took power at a deeply divisive point in Northern Wei history when internecine war and political rebellion were brewing on all sides. When Erzhu Rong drowned the empress dowager in the river in Luoyang, and when his army murdered her courtiers and destroyed her city, he did so in large part owing to the culmination of many years of resentment by the military men of the impoverished northern garrisons against their rulers who had moved south and abandoned them economically and culturally. His murder of the empress dowager was therefore not a personally motivated assassination, though he is said to have taken particular glee in destroying her hallmark projects and violently purging the court of any of her supporters.

I believe that this simple answer of long-brewing political instability is the correct answer as to why the empress dowager was not more successful; however, this is not the entirety of the answer provided in the *Book of the Wei*. As we have seen in that text, Erzhu Rong is remembered as having invaded the capital on the pretext of avenging the empress dowager's murder of her son and placing her granddaughter on the throne. Because I have argued that the placement of the granddaughter on the throne was a political act legitimized through Buddhist notions of kingship known throughout the Northern Wei, in this chapter I further argue that the empress dowager's murder and subsequent legacy were innately and inextricably tied to her own practice of Buddhism in her time. That Erzhu Rong and his armies—many of whom, like the Gao Clan of Gao Huan were public patrons of Buddhism—did not hesitate to murder the empress dowager and destroy the Buddhist city she had created speaks to the fact that, for them, Luoyang was no Pure Land and the emperor was no bodhisattva.

To explore the reasons why the empress dowager's assassination included a total destruction of the Buddhist landscape of the capital that she had helped create, we must examine how her Buddhism was viewed by those who sought to challenge her power. Buddhism was incredibly popular across all sectors of the society of the northern dynasties, but not everybody practiced Buddhism in the same way. Until now, we have examined the type of Buddhism used by the court in the legitimation of the court's own power. This type of Buddhism was heavily regulated by individuals who held court-monastic appointments, just as it was ideologically formed around the idea of the Northern Wei emperor as the buddha. We have seen how the empress dowager continued this type of Buddhist practice in her reign; however, what we have not yet seen is how she also aligned herself with Buddhist elements in her population that were seen as unstable, indulgent, and heterodox by her own advisors. As a woman born without a recorded name in the far reaches of the empire, Empress Dowager Ling came to the central court in Luoyang with her own practice of Buddhism. As I will explore here, her Buddhism was closely aligned with the common Buddhism of her polity and her home territory, and it was a Buddhism that made her courtiers uncomfortable. I argue that the empress dowager's reign was emblematic of a Buddhism that the court found difficult to control, just as it found her difficult to control. In the end, I show that even though her murder was the result of long-bubbling tensions in the empire, her legacy, as told in the Ru histories compiled under the direction of her immediate successors, suggests that they did not approve of her Buddhism and saw it as partial justification for her overthrow.

A TRADITION UNDER SUSPICION

Although they used Buddhism to express their vision of kingship, the rulers of the Northern Wei court, as well as their political advisors, viewed the Buddhist tradition with deep suspicion and ambivalence. This is true even though many of these advisors were themselves Buddhist patrons. To understand why this was the case, we move beyond Luoyang and its urban Buddhism full to the brim with opulent temples and donative sites and out to the countryside where we see a different type of Buddhist movement frequently arising throughout the Northern Wei: Buddhist rebellion. The Northern Wei saw, from its beginning to its end, continual and violent political uprisings articulated along ethnic and cultural lines. What is less known is that such ethnically aligned, anticourt factions were often aligned with Buddhist ideology and infrastructure. For example, Liu Shu-fen has explored the ethnic boundaries that backed the Buddhist-supported Gaiwu Rebellion of 445, when Buddhist monasteries were accused of being storehouses for weapons to be used in the fight against government forces. In her work on the rebellion, Liu begins by making the connection between the Lushui branch of the Xiongnu peoples, their competition with the Northern Wei, and their Buddhist faith. The Lushui branch of the Xiongnu ruled over the Northern Liang, which the Northern Wei conquered in the year 439. The Lushui were fervent Buddhists as well as political opponents and, while in power, had sponsored large-scale translation projects, which included the support of two of China's most eminent translators of early Buddhist texts: Kumārajīva and Dharmakṣema. When the Northern Wei fought to take the Northern Liang, Buddhist monks took up arms against the Taghbach in solidarity with the Lushui.[1] Liu Shu-fen argues that although the Taghbach took the Northern Liang in 439, the Lushui continued to hold power over many parts of the country, particularly the trade routes leading from central to western China, and that because of this they were able to quickly take Chang'an during the Gaiwu Rebellion, apparently storing arms in monasteries along the way. It was the discovery of these stockpiles of weapons that is said to have spurred a widespread suppression of Buddhism under the early Northern Wei leader, Emperor Taiwu. The Gaiwu Rebellion first erupted in Xingcheng and spread widely across the old Northern Liang territory and even beyond. It was a serious threat to the Northern Wei, who vigorously suppressed it.

The Gaiwu Rebellion was not the only such Buddhist-supported rebellion during the Northern Wei. No less than ten antigovernmental rebellions arose in the Northern Wei, many of which utilized Buddhist ideas in the articulation of their aims.[2] Such rebellions were typically millenarian in orientation and depicted the overthrow of the government as a way of bringing about a new and Buddhist world order backed by a saintlike figure. Buddhism was popular among northern groups living in an increasingly Sinicizing cultural milieu because the tradition was understood by non-Han peoples as precisely "foreign" and therefore theirs. They celebrated northern, non-Han Buddhist teachers like the miracle-working, eminent monk Fotucheng (232–348) as their leaders and they joined the Buddhist community in great numbers at that time, seeing the tradition as simultaneously religiously powerful and as something that belonged to them as northerners.[3] David Ownby has traced a useful history of millenarian rebellions in China from the Eastern Han period through to the creation of Buddhist texts and messianic figures, such as the Bodhisattva Prince Moonlight (Yueguang Tongzi), who appeared throughout the entire Six Dynasties period.[4] He argues that although millenarian rebellion in China was not new with Buddhism, Buddhism brought a new and powerful medium of expression for it, particularly in the northern dynasties.[5] Furthermore, and from a sociological angle, these rebellions often erupted among the commoners, suggesting that the common form of Buddhism was different than that of the educated elite, particularly in the Northern Wei.

Such rebellions continued to gain intensity throughout the latter half of the Northern Wei with four Buddhist-inflected millenarian rebellions happening between the years of 509 and 515 and with all of them being led by Buddhist monks.[6] Finally, in the year 515—the very year of the death of Xuanwu and the rise of the empress dowager—the largest and most violent of these rebellions occurred against the court and it took more than two years to fully quash. This rebellion, the so-called "Mahāyāna Rebellion" is discussed in the *Book of the Wei*, which tells us that the rebellion was led by a monk named Faqing who was also called "Mahāyāna." Faqing, along with his assistant, Li Guipo, who also held the titles the bodhisattva of the ten bhūmis (Skt. *daśabhūmibodhisattva*, Ch. *shizhu pusa*), the prince who pacifies Han (*ding Han wang*), and the director of the army for combating māra (*pingmo junsi*), led a rebellion in which members of their army were awarded the first stage of *bhūmi* upon murdering an enemy and were thus given the title *ekabhūmibodhisattva* or the "bodhisattva of the first *bhūmi*" (*yizhu pusa*).[7] Their apparent goal was to bring about a messianic Buddhist revolution and overthrow the Northern Wei. It took the government three months and an army of one hundred thousand to quell the rebels,[8] only to have them resurface briefly in 517.

Although the Mahāyāna Rebellion was quashed in the year 517, the region where it had taken place retained both a connection to Buddhism and to the challenge of imperial power. The rebellion took place in modern-day Hebei province, in the region of Jizhou. At the final collapse of the Northern Wei, the general and then kingmaker Gao Huan moved the capital away from Luoyang and established the Eastern Wei dynasty with its capital at Yecheng. Yecheng is also in Hebei province, in a region to the south of Jizhou. After his death, his son took the throne as Northern Qi Emperor Wenxuan and also ruled in Yecheng. During this Eastern Wei and Northern Qi transition an additional and fantastic set of imperial Buddhist caves was carved, this time just outside the capital of Yecheng. These caves are collectively called the "Mountain of Echoing Halls" (Xiangtang shan). The north cave of the site has long been considered to be Gao Huan's own mausoleum. The Jizhou and Yecheng regions of Hebei therefore retained their connection to Buddhism as well as their status as alternate regions for the exercise of political power throughout the empress dowager's reign, and they emerged as the center of power of the Northern Qi court and its own Buddhism.

GOVERNMENTAL SUPPRESSION

The previously discussed Gaiwu Rebellion happened under the rule of early Northern Wei Emperor Taiwu, who was Emperor Wencheng's grandfather, and during a time in which the Northern Wei was aggressively expanding its territory while ruling from Pingcheng. From the perspective of Taiwu's court, which sought control of the Northern Liang territories where the Gaiwu Rebellion had been raised, the recognition that enemy arms had been stored in monasteries during the rebellion was cause for the violent suppression of Buddhists and their institutions. This court-backed suppression included the sacking of monasteries and the forced laicization of monks. Such tactics were encouraged by Taiwu's adviser, Cui Hao (381–450),[9] who was a supporter of the Daoist tradition of the Celestial Masters under the leadership of Kou Qianzhi (365–448),[10] who successfully engaged Emperor Taiwu in supporting his tradition over and above Buddhism. Taiwu's sponsorship of the Celestial Masters sect, which was then under the leadership of Kou Qianzhi, is detailed in the Daoism section of the "Annals on Buddhism and Daoism" in the *Book of the Wei*. In the text, Wei Shou tells us that Kou was given the title of Celestial Master via a revelation from a high-ranking Daoist god, the Supreme Lord Lao (Taishang Laojun), and that, furthermore, in a second revelation, Kou was given new registers for himself and his disciples. In his recent overview of the Celestial Masters tradition in this period, Terry Kleeman notes that the registers were for the purpose of supporting Emperor Taiwu's Daoist-styled reign—that of the Perfected Lord of Great Peace (*taiping zhenjun*, 440–51).[11] While in his position as religious adviser, Kou is said to have used Daoist arts to advise the emperor on military matters, and he attempted to invest the emperor himself with magical powers through the creation of various elixirs of immortality.[12] Notably, although he patronized Daoism and violently suppressed Buddhism, Emperor Taiwu was also interested in harnessing the magical powers of the Buddhist tradition: He was the ruler who had tried to steal the Northern Liang's infamous monastic thaumaturge, the magic-wielding Dharmakṣema, who was then murdered by the Northern Liang leader.

What the "Treatise on Buddhism and Daoism" does not tell us, however, is that other than the emperor's own fascination with the arts of immortality, he also likely chose to patronize Kou and his Celestial Masters tradition because that tradition then represented a form of religious orthodoxy at a time when religious cults of many forms were mushrooming across the empire and creating violent rebellions. The Celestial Masters, under Kou's leadership, represented a tradition charged with the task of "purifying and reforming the Taoist Religion."[13] In particular, these Celestial Masters advocated an innovative and hybridized form of the religion that included the use of Buddhist morality as a means to combat the heterodox practices of other communities that were deemed licentious by society's elite. They also used Confucian ritual and etiquette to restrain the actions of those groups by creating a law code not unlike Buddhist monastic law.[14] Thus, as a way of aligning with a religious orthodoxy and establishing a powerful government, Emperor Taiwu elevated Celestial Masters Daoism to the level of state religion and used it to challenge other nonorthodox religions, including Buddhism.

Following on the heels of this violent suppression of Buddhists and their institutions, the reign of Wencheng, Taiwu's grandson as well as his successor, saw the official installation of Buddhism as the state religion, a political gesture that we can understand as a move toward solidarity that brought the tradition of Buddhism to the heart of the court and sought to ease bubbling tensions across the empire. As we saw in chapter 3, Wencheng created Tanyao as the "superintendent of the śramaṇas," thus establishing an innovative religio-political bureaucracy that continued to develop throughout the Northern Wei in which the weinas served as court-monastic go-betweens who kept tabs on monastic activities. This religio-political bureaucracy that Wencheng created worked to police the spread of Buddhists and their activities from the inside. We see the perceived necessity of such insider policing in a memorial made to the court of Empress Dowager Wenming and Emperor Xiaowen by one of their courtiers, Lu Yuan (fl. fifth century) when the court was still located in the northern capital of Pingcheng.[15] Against the backdrop of Buddhist unrest across the empire, and on the heels of the Gaiwu Rebellion, Lu Yuan links popular Buddhism in the countryside to the revolt of the Yellow Turbans (*huangjin*) during the Han—a massive peasant rebellion that sought to overturn the ruling house and establish a new religio-political order. Famously, this rebellion contributed to the eventual fall of the Han empire.[16] In part, Lu Yuan's memorial reads:

> Your slave has also heard, what is generally known, that among the common people in the eastern regions since many years there is a virtual competition in establishing vegetarian societies [*zhaihui*]. [Their leaders] falsely claim to be nobles to agitate and delude [their followers]. Obviously, they use their position among the populace to arouse feelings against the ruling dynasty. Their ambitions are boundless and beyond compare. In my ignorant view it would be appropriate to punish them as soon as possible to stop these activities and to execute their leaders. Otherwise, I fear, they may become a disaster such as the Yellow Turbans and the Red Eyebrows. If we tolerate the small seedlings and do not cut them as soon as they appear or chop them with an axe when they have grown up, we may face a mass of criminals.[17]

Although this memorial was presented slightly after the death of Wencheng, it describes a rise in Buddhist activity during his time that continued to vex the court. Starting with Wencheng, the central court attempted to control the tradition by co-option instead of by suppression. As we have already seen, Wencheng initiated the early strata of monumental buddha/ruler images at Yungang. This building project was furthered under the regencies of Empress Dowager Wenming, who may also have had her regency government depicted in those grottos in the paired images of Śākyamuni and Prabhūtaratna from the *Lotus Sūtra*. Through their unprecedented patronage, the rulers merged themselves with the buddhas, engaging in a tactic that allowed them authority over the religion. Emperor Wencheng was even able to secure the reverence and obedience of the monastic community, ensuring that they bow to him.[18] Similarly, in carrying on Wencheng's tradition of patronage, in 477 then-ten-year-old Emperor Xiaowen commissioned the building of the Repaying Virtue Monastery (Baode si). This commissioning was for the purpose of repaying the "support" of his regent, Empress Dowager Wenming. Built just outside the northern capital of Pingcheng, the Repaying Virtue Monastery was built over the top of the site of the imperial hawkery and therefore also brought an end to the popular but "un-Buddhist" practice of hawking by the imperial elite. As a result, all the birds of prey within the area were released. This story is recorded in Empress Dowager Wenming's biography in the *Book of the Wei*, where it says:

> In the first year of the Chengming Era [477], the empress dowager was respectfully called Great and August Empress Dowager [*taihuang taihou*] and again heard court and presided over government. By nature, the empress dowager was wise and cunning. When she came to the palace, she had but crude knowledge of letters and numbers and yet she ascended to the most venerable of ranks, scrutinizing and settling all the myriad affairs.
>
> Gaozu therefore made an edict, saying: "Because I was the only one, I inherited this illustrious lineage as a child [and so] relied on [her] compassion and understanding to pacify the four seas. Desiring the virtue of recompense and in accord with complete enlightenment,[19] all of the birds of prey and other injurious sorts of animals should be released to the mountains and forests, and we should use this spot to start building a numinous pagoda for the empress dowager." Thereupon, the class of hawkers was ceased, and the area was used the area for the Buddhist Monastery of Repaying Virtue.[20]

In this story from the *Book of the Wei* we see Empress Dowager Wenming's leadership style through the child emperors that she controlled. When the edict was issued, it was in the name of Emperor Xiaowen, then ten years old, in the first year of his reign, and under the influence of the empress dowager. As such, this was truly the story of Empress Dowager Wencheng using Emperor Xiaowen as a legitimate and public mechanism for employing her own policies: his edict served her reign. As a means of legitimating her second and contested regency, the empress dowager built a Buddhist monastery over the imperial hawkery, thus championing Buddhism over the traditional hunting of both the Han and the Taghbach.[21] In turn, she established herself as a Buddhist leader who controlled the court/monastic bureaucracy and caused it to work in her favor. We see this strategy at many points in her rule, including in the following edict from Xiaowen's accession in 471, in which the two rulers are depicted as the "father and mother of the people." The edict reads thus:

> In order to raise and establish felicitous merit, people in- and outside [of the saṃgha] have stūpas and temples made and erected which, however high and wide, conspicuous and spacious, share the one aim to illuminate and exalt the Supreme Doctrine. Ignorant knaves, however, each trying to outstrip the other and competing over poverty and wealth, spend their entire property and holdings to make sure [their] edifices maintain [a certain] height and width, indeed they would go so far as to kill to reach their goal. If only they were capable of sincere intent, even piling up some clay and heaping up some sand their measure of merit would be incorruptible. They want to establish the [kind of] factor that causes merit, unaware of the retribution [that comes of] harming life. We, father and mother for Our people, make it Our duty to cherish and nurture them. From now on, [such building projects] shall all and one be stopped.[22]

The above edict characterizes the ambivalent relationship that the Northern Wei had with Buddhism under the reigns of Wencheng, Wenming, Xianwen, and Xiaowen: On the one hand, the government consistently supported their own Buddhist building projects; on the other hand, they forbade the building projects of nonelite Buddhist patrons under the guise of protecting the populace from both financial bankruptcy and moral corruption. We should interpret this ambivalent approach of patronizing and policing as a continuation of the state suppression of Buddhism by Taiwu, though by different means. Under all these leaders, including Xuanwu, a long series of edicts was issued by the court. In some cases, these edicts gave support to the monastic community by allowing them forms of funding, including slaves and land, as well as access to social and political prestige. In many other cases, the edicts worked to delimit the unrestrained spread of Buddhism among the nonmonastic elite by forcing the weina to inspect the caliber of monastics and enforce limits on their numbers. Such restrictions on the building of monasteries and the staffing of them with court-allocated numbers of monastic residents speaks to the real-life situation of the Northern Wei court in its agricultural policy. Having established an equal-field system that included the allocation of agricultural land to largely Han populations in the central plains, the court also established a system of taxation that necessitated an active agricultural tax base to support the empire.[23]

In sum, throughout the fifth and early sixth centuries, the government of the Northern Wei was heavily invested in both supporting and regulating the monastic community as a means of controlling the spread of Buddhism in the realm. They did so to curtail rebellion and delimit the social power of the religion, which continued to spread rapidly across all regions of the empire. In creating their imperial form of Buddhism, they sought to manage the religion of the empire by defining its terms of practice, placing it under their purview, and forming it into a system that ultimately supported governmental stability.

THE BUDDHISM OF THE EMPRESS DOWAGER

Empress Dowager Ling was a different sort of ruler than those who came before her. Her patronage of Buddhist building projects far exceeded that of her imperial predecessors, perhaps surpassing the sum of four million medieval cash coins.[24] She spent extravagantly on Buddhist building projects, just as she was known to have audience with a diversity of patrons to Buddhist projects and members of the monastic order alike. She was also steeped in Buddhism from birth. With her parents being notable Buddhist patrons in the region of her birth and her aunt and personal benefactor being the court's most celebrated Buddhist nun, the empress dowager came to court deeply familiar with the practice of Buddhism and she continued that practice with one significant difference: wealth. As an independently ruling regent of a powerful empire located in the economically powerful heartlands of the central plains, the empress dowager enjoyed tremendous financial advantage, and she used that advantage to spend lavishly on Buddhist structures. In this section of the chapter, we begin by surveying the empress dowager's massive expenditures on Buddhist building projects before moving on to interrogate the precise type of Buddhism the empress dowager seems to have practiced in her time. Was her Buddhism more closely aligned with the court and its careful policing? Or was it more closely aligned with her populace in the carnivalesque Buddhism of the capital?

The empress dowager had a penchant for building tall things: Her pagoda at the Eternal Peace Monastery was the tallest building in the known world; her grotto at Longmen was the tallest and highest on the cliff face of all the Northern Wei grottos.[25] But these were not her only projects. Although the Eternal Peace Monastery was situated outside the palace gates, its sister complex, the Jade Radiance Nunnery, was the only Buddhist building constructed within the palace walls. Its construction was commissioned by Emperor Xuanwu. The *Record* locates the Jade Radiance just north of the palace, between the northwest corner of the palace, the palatial gardens to the east, and a fortress built in the northwest corner of the city wall.[26] This proximity between court and nunnery was owing to the fact that the nunnery was home to the most elite women of the realm who still enjoyed close ties to the court and may have needed the court's protection. Of the nunnery's inhabitants, Yang says:

> Imperial consorts from the "Pepper Chamber" studied the path there, as did the ladies of the court who dwelled there together with them. Likewise, there were maidens of reputable clans whose disposition was to cherish this place of practice and so they shaved their heads, bade farewell to their families and came with proper

deportment to this nunnery. Rejecting their rare and beautiful ornaments and wearing the clothes for cultivating the path, they surrendered their hearts to the eight truths[27] and entrusted themselves to the one[28] vehicle.[29]

Not only was the empress dowager connected to the Jade Radiance through the women of her court, but she was also a patron of it: She personally funded the construction of the nunnery's majestic pagoda,[30] which was similar to the famed golden pagoda at the Eternal Peace Monastery. A brief description of the pagoda and the nunnery is found in the *Record*:

> There was a five-story pagoda that rose fifty *zhang* from the ground. Its "immortal's palm"[31] crested into the sky and its bells were hung on the clouds. The brilliance of its workmanship matched with the beauty of the Eternal Peace Monastery. Of the lecture halls and the nun's quarters, there was over five hundred rooms. Elegantly scattered, they were all connected, as their doors and windows shared a passage on which there were rare trees and fragrant grasses that could not be expressed in words.[32]

Furthermore, beyond the court's own Jade Radiance Nunnery and Eternal Peace Monastery, the *Record* tells us that the empress dowager built yet another pagoda in a monastery to the south of the city, the Bright View Monastery (Jingming si), which, like the Jade Radiance, had also been established by Emperor Xuanwu. Regarding this project, the *Record* says that the pagoda was seven stories and that the ornamentation and gold work were equal to that of the nine-story pagoda at the Eternal Peace.[33] It seems also that the empress dowager's populace understood her penchant for pagoda building: For example, we have seen how her supporter and brother-in-law, Yuan Yue, commissioned two pagoda building projects in her honor. One of his projects was to rebuild a pagoda built by his father, Emperor Xiaowen, in which he dedicated the merit to the "Two Sages" of Empress Dowager Ling and the child Emperor Xiaoming. The other of his projects—building a pagoda at the site of the numinous platform—was also an act of imperial mimicry of the empress dowager and in support of her.

We must linger a little longer on the story of the numinous platform. I believe that this was a special place for the empress dowager and it may also be the place where her body was interred. The numinous platform was located just outside the south edge of the city walls of the capital proper and slightly to the east of the city's central avenue, and there the empress dowager engaged in a cooperative building project with her younger sister, the Mistress of Pingyi (Pingyi jun, d. 557), in commemoration of their deceased father, Hu Guozhen. The two sisters each built a separate complex, each with its own five-story pagoda. The *Record* tells us that the site was collectively referred to as the Monastery of the Two Women (Shuangnü si) by the people of the time on account of its patronage by the two sisters.[34] Yang's *Record* also tells us that this monastery was the only one given a dedicated eunuch attendant who would organize the donations and supplies offered for the great feasts in the liturgical calendar. The eunuch and the supplies came from the empress dowager, who personally sent them for the care of the monks who dwelled in and maintained what was effectively her own patrilineal clan's family shrine.

As stated in the *Record*, the Monastery of the Two Women was built at the location of the numinous platform, which, as we discussed, was the imperial observatory of the Eastern Han court. This location for the selection of her father's mortuary temple aligns with what we already know about the empress dowager's pattern of patronage from Longmen. As we have seen, the empress dowager was the patron of the Huoshao grotto that features rare images of the Han dynasty gods, the Queen Mother of the West and the King Father of the East. Whereas Amy McNair has argued that the grotto was built for the veneration of the empress dowager's deceased mother, I argue that it was built for Sengzhi, the aunt/nun. Regardless of whether it was built for mother or aunt, it is a Buddhist grotto for the commemoration of the deceased members of the empress dowager's family and it features Han dynastic imagery that serves as a display of the family's own known status as belonging to the Han ethnicity. Unlike the Huoshao grotto, which we do not know much about, it appears that the Monastery of the Two Sisters was commonly associated with the then-classical Eastern Han numinous platform, and we are certain that it played a role as a family shrine built for the empress dowager's father. But could this in fact be none other than the Monastery of the Two Lings, where she herself was buried? Although archeological excavation has largely located and confirmed the existence of the Northern Wei Buddhist structures built at the numinous platform and described in the *Record*,[35] the Monastery of the Two Lings—which is not in the *Record* as such—has not been found. If we recall from chapter 2, the *Comprehensive Mirror to Aid in Government* states that the empress dowager was brought to the bridge over the river that led into Luoyang and then drowned there. Furthermore, her own biography in the *Book of the Wei* states that her body and that of the emperor were brought to the Monastery of the Two Lings by her sister, Mistress of Pingyi, and interred there. The Mistress of Pingyi was the copatron of the Monastery of the Two Women, which is, in fact, located just on the bank of the river where the empress dowager would have been drowned. It makes sense to think that the sister brought the corpses to her own, personally funded monastery that already served as a family shrine. In fact, where else could she have brought them, since we have no other record of her patronizing or commissioning other Buddhist structures? Furthermore, it could be the case that the name Monastery of the Two Lings is a contraction of a compounded name for the complex, a name that includes the "two sisters" and the "numinous platform," such that the Monastery of the Two Sisters at the Numinous Platform would have been abbreviated as the "Monastery of the Two Lings." As an abbreviation, however, the "two Lings" could also refer to either the empress dowager and the emperor or the empress dowager and her father. Given that archeological surveys of Northern Wei Luoyang have provided no evidence of the existence of a separate Monastery of the Two Lings and that Yang does not describe it in his record, it perhaps stands to reason that the Monastery of the Two Women became known as the Monastery of the Two Lings in the times after the death of the empress dowager, when the associations between the complex and the numinous platform as well as the empress dowager herself became more apparent.

The *Record of Buddhist Monasteries in Luoyang* catalogs and eulogizes the most splendid Buddhist architecture of the Northern Wei capital, and the presence of the empress dowager is woven through almost every story. Either directly connected to her or her policies or indirectly connected to her through her own eunuchs and courtiers, the resplendent monasteries of Luoyang were built and rebuilt with her oversight, her permission, and, often, her money. Her patterns of donation and patronage accord with her participation in Buddhist life in her city: Inviting nuns to lecture her at court, convening large-scale Buddhist feasts at court, and, along with her courtiers and eunuchs, personally funding carnivalesque and spectacular monasteries and nunneries, the empress dowager provided the pulse of her very Buddhist city. Sima Guang expresses a similar sentiment in his *Comprehensive Mirror to Aid in Government*, saying:

> The empress dowager loved the buddha. Her court erected monasteries without end. She commanded all the prefectures to each build a five-story pagoda. So that the resources of the common people did not run low, the lords, aristocracy, eunuchs, and imperial guards were to each build a monastery in Luoyang that was both tall and beautiful. The empress dowager established numerous vegetarian assemblies, provided the monastics resources for tens of thousands of plans, granted rewards everywhere and without limit. There was not an expense that she did not pay and still she did not give as much as the common people.[36]

Here, the *Comprehensive Mirror* tells us that although the empress dowager spent untold riches in support of the Buddhist tradition, her populace spent more. In such a way do we see her own alignment with the Buddhist followers in her city. As a political figure, she spent like them and established herself as the single largest donor and patron.

Not only did the empress dowager build pagodas but she was also sympathetic to Buddhist causes in general. Two notable examples of her sympathy toward Buddhist causes can be found in the *Book of the Wei*. In the first instance, during her reign, a child was born in the countryside and was propped up as the aforementioned messianic Prince Moonlight to inspire political rebellion. Even though this child was a direct threat to the sovereignty of the ruler, the empress dowager did not give him the death penalty, and instead argued that the boy was a victim of those around him and did not identify himself as Prince Moonlight even if others did.[37] Similarly, the *Book of the Wei* records that the empress dowager personally patronized a magic-wielding Buddhist monk who claimed that he could heal the sick.[38] She did so contrary to the wishes of her courtiers and in a movement away from the Northern Wei court's practice of controlling and policing such magic makers before they had the opportunity to sow discord among the populace.

The *Comprehensive Mirror to Aid in Government* retains a telling anecdote that expresses the delicate situation that the empress dowager found herself in with respect to the Buddhism of her court and the Buddhism of her polity, and that also shows whose side she may have been on.[39] The anecdote relates that one of her own minor courtiers spoke harshly against Buddhism, arguing that a teaching that causes one to stop having children constitutes the worst sort of crime against filiality and is nothing other than a "teaching of ghosts" (*guijiao*). This criticism of Buddhism is said to have been reported to the empress dowager by one of her monastic superintendents, who argued that this labeling of Buddhism as a "teaching of ghosts" constituted a slander of Śākyamuni Buddha. As a result, the empress dowager then questioned her courtier on his meaning. In response, the courtier artfully explained how he had not meant any slander. He argued that since "heaven is called spirit, earth is called gods, and humans are called ghosts," and that since Śākyamuni Buddha went out into the world of humans, he is therefore called a ghost. He also cites the classical Confucian text, the *Book of Ritual*, to argue that in the case of the ancient sacrifices to heaven, the ritual was organized such that "on the bright side, there is ritual and music; on the dark side there is ghosts and spirits."[40] He then uses this logic to explain that Śākyamuni's teaching is "dark" because it is directed to humans, who are ghosts, in contrast to the Confucian worship of heaven and the ancestors, which is "bright," but that the two traditions are two sides of a complementarity. At the end of the debate, the empress dowager fined her own courtier one *liang* of gold, thereby siding with her monastic superintendent in his opinion that this was slander. This story highlights the religious tensions in the empress dowager's court while also showing that she was the arbiter of religious truth in her time. Notably, the *Comprehensive Mirror to Aid in Government* goes on to say that even though the empress dowager thought that her own courtier's words were fair, she could not disagree with her monastic superintendent. I read this interpretation of the events through the optic of a later Confucian discourse that wants to side with the Confucians at court during this time of turmoil, even if the empress dowager herself was more aligned with Buddhism—a tradition that she spared no expense in espousing as her own.

What kind of Buddhism was the empress dowager aligned with? Why did she build so many pagodas in her glimmering capital and why did she entertain questionable Buddhist elements in her populace? I want to argue that the answer to these questions is more historically murky than is the easy answer of political expediency. Although we have certainly seen how the empress dowager benefitted politically from her association with Buddhist monastics, texts, and ideas, I also think we should consider how the empress dowager saw herself in relation to the

Buddhist tradition. In other words, did she practice Buddhism herself? And, if so, what variety of Buddhism was it?

The empress dowager had a unique relationship with the Buddhism of the people in her polity because her own Buddhism was much like the Buddhism of her people—perhaps she was just like them. Perhaps the empress dowager herself had a religious practice that carried the flavor of the localized forms of Buddhist practice seen throughout the empire that were so often at odds with the Buddhism of the court. Brought to the central court in Luoyang from a region near the edge of the empire that was associated with the Lushui Xiongnu-led Gaiwu Rebellion, the empress dowager hailed from a family of known Buddhist patrons from the local gentry. She is said to have been the favorite of her aunt, the famous nun Sengzhi, who had her appointed to court on account of her precociousness. Once at court, she was quickly promoted to high-ranking concubinage by Emperor Xuanwu, who was himself known to have a great interest in Buddhist texts and ideas. Perhaps he was interested in her because she came to Luoyang deeply familiar with the Buddhist practice of her region, just as his own private Buddhist teacher, the aunt-nun Sengzhi, had been. If the empress dowager did indeed faithfully practice a form of Buddhism brought to the court and capital by families like hers who hailed from the western, Buddhist, and conceivably Xiongnu regions of the old Han territories, it might also stand to reason that the empress dowager was herself faithful to the religion. Her expenditures on Buddhist building projects may have seemed to her an imperial investment in the economy of merit exchange that she participated in, just as did countless thousands of others around the empire and in her capital city. If we accept the idea that the empress dowager practiced her faith in public and did so by behaving much like the people in her capital who funded Buddhist spaces, persons, art, and architecture, then we can see the empress dowager less as a politically expedient usurper who carelessly supported unstable Buddhist elements that challenged the court and more as a Buddhist ruler of a Buddhist population that practiced her tradition in a similar fashion to that of the people from her city and polity. Adding this consideration of the empress dowager's personal faith to our understanding of why she was such a prolific Buddhist patron helps us to make sense of the historical situation, for it is the case that Buddhism—as a political force—was not powerful enough to save her from the economically driven, militarized collapse of her dynasty.

BUDDHISM AGAINST BUDDHISM

Buddhist rebellions that constantly erupted in the Northern Wei—and that perhaps resonated with the empress dowager's own Buddhism—were similar in political orientation to the imperial Buddhism of the Northern Wei court. Both forms of Buddhist practice and ideology held the millenarian belief in the imminent descent of the Bodhisattva Maitreya, a mainstream idea in the Buddhism of the period that provided the rationale for both the legitimation of imperial authority as well as the challenge to that very authority.[41] Similarly, in the previous chapter of this book we have seen how Maitreya worship was behind imperial support for the Northern Wei emperors Xuanwu and Xiaoming. As I argued in the previous chapter, such an ideology also explained why the empress dowager placed her granddaughter on the throne. Yet, just as many political groups experimented with millenarian monarchy, some members of the imperial court who worked in the service of this type of Buddhist practice did not always agree with it. Scared of the power of Buddhist belief to create challenges to their own power, the Buddhists of the court spoke against the Buddhism of the people. As we will see here, the empress dowager's own courtiers openly criticized her for patronizing a form of Buddhism that made them nervous.

To understand why they were so nervous, we should start by acknowledging just how fast Buddhism was growing in the late fifth and early sixth centuries. According to Tang Yongtong, before the move of the capital to Luoyang, there were approximately one hundred monasteries in the old capital of Pingcheng, which housed some two thousand monastic residents. There were also 6,476 monasteries in the lands under control of the Northern Wei, which housed some 77,258 monastic residents. However, by the reign of the empress dowager, these already substantial numbers had swelled to such a degree that Luoyang itself had 1,376 monasteries, with the empire in general housing approximately thirty thousand monasteries. Altogether, there were more than two million members of the monastic community accounted for.[42] The *Book of the Wei* provides corroborating evidence for the popularity of extra-imperial Buddhist building projects in Luoyang in the form of a lengthy memorial presented to Empress Dowager Ling by Yuan Cheng,[43] a powerful member of the Taghbach royal elite who accompanied the move of the capital from Pingcheng to Luoyang. He made his memorial to her soon before his death in the year 519. Instead of celebrating the lavish wealth and prosperity of Buddhist spaces in the capital, Yuan Cheng presented an alternate description of the Buddhist situation in the city, characterizing it as corrupt, defiled, and potentially dangerous. In part, his memorial criticizes the unrestrained building projects of the commoners, characterizing them as an inappropriate way of practicing their religion:[44]

> Delicate and subtle are the marks of learning: someone of shallow discernment will not recognize them; spacious and still is the gate to [Buddhist] mysteries: how could a few short sentences ever get to the bottom of them? Nonetheless, a pure life away from the dust [of the ordinary world], that is what the adepts of the Way make their priority; the causes for [the accumulation of] merit being as obscure as they are profound, they ought not to set store by a retirement in the midst of splendour. If they are capable of sincere belief, even children piling up sand can surpass [the merit gained by building] a ritual space; even the frugal spread of [the Buddha's patron] Chuntuo is worth presenting [to the Buddha attaining nirvāṇa]

between the twin [śāla] trees. Why should we allow their depredations, with which they finance the construction of [Buddhist as well as Taoist] temples? Such [behaviour] may be a case of "many people trusting to luck," but it does not serve the well-being of the State.[45]

Perhaps because Empress Dowager Ling was deeply involved in the Buddhist tradition, the logic of Cheng's argument is entirely Buddhist: If enlightenment is profound and obscure, how can it be quantified financially through merit donation? To make his case, Prince Cheng relies on Buddhist precedent and cites the story of King Aśoka's past-life childhood gift of piled sand to Śākyamuni Buddha. Cheng argues that if Aśoka was able to reap the great karmic reward of rebirth as a king from this humble gift of dirt, then it makes no sense that the monks of his day expect large donations of wealth from the struggling populace in order to facilitate the merit exchange. Similarly, Cheng argues that if Cunda (Ch. Chuntuo), the devotee who provided Śākyamuni Buddha with his last meal that ultimately killed him, still reaped karmic reward, then how could it be that the populace needed to bankrupt themselves and bring instability to the empire in order to gain their share of Buddhist "luck"?

After making his Buddhist arguments, Cheng's memorial states that the monks of his time had become wealthy landowners because the populace wanted their share of Buddhist "luck" and that such a situation was spelling disaster for the empire. He continues:

And yet Saṃgha temples of today are everywhere. Whether they stand packed one next to the other in the city centre, or whether linked in rows they spill over into butchers' stalls and wineshops, or again whether three or five young monks join together to form a temple of their own, the chanting of hymns and the cries of the butchers resound in chorus up the eaves; [Buddha] statues and stūpas stand wreathed around by the rank smell of meat, spirituality is drowned amid lustful craving, genuine and bogus live jumbled together and come and go in perfect riot. But by long usage none of the authorities finds fault with this, and they don't bother that the Saṃgha Bureau acts contrary to the Ordinance. Is it not a scandal, though, how true practice [of the Buddhist precepts] is being polluted, how observant monks are being defiled, how [fragrant] orchid and [noisome] reeds are put in the same vessel?[46]

The picture painted here is of a Luoyang so full of monasteries and stūpas—funded by the populace and not the government—that the line of demarcation between sacred and profane could no longer be drawn. Prince Cheng describes Buddhist monks inheriting the karmic gift from the populace as "the dregs of Buddhism, the 'rats under the altar' at the heart of the Doctrine, whom their own internal precepts do not condone and who—by our royal canons—we ought to expel" and who "encroach on the small people and rob them, occupying [their] fields and homes on a large scale."[47]

Prince Cheng's memorial went on to implore the empress dowager to enforce more vigorously the court's already established laws for governing the building of new monasteries and the ordination of new monastic candidates, he argued that the Buddhism of their time was not like it was in the time of her predecessors. Buddhism, Prince Cheng argued, flourished far more during the empress dowager's reign than it did in Xiaowen's time, just as it was far more corrupt than it was in Xuanwu's. Prince Cheng argued that the monastic members of Empress Dowager Ling's polity required the heavy hand of government lest they rise to rebellion like they did before under the monk Faxiu.[48] Such government intervention, Prince Cheng insisted, should have included the destruction of illegal monasteries and images, the forced resettlement of monasteries to the countryside, and the forced amalgamation of small monasteries into larger ones of at least fifty monastic members.[49] In his memorial, Prince Cheng argued that such policies would work to reestablish order in Luoyang and set right what he saw as a deplorable reality on the streets of the city: the ownership of land and buildings by the monastic community and the attendant intermixing of sacred and profane such that buddha images were cloaked in the stench of the meat market and the common people were the victims of greedy and corrupt Buddhist monks.

Although Prince Cheng's memorial is said to have been approved by the empress dowager's court, Wei Shou states that it did no good because it was not enforced. Nearing the end of his record of the Buddhist tradition in his "Treatise on Buddhism and Daoism" in the *Book of the Wei*, Wei Shou states that wealthy courtiers were increasingly turning their homes into Buddhist monasteries and temples in the latter stages of the dynasty with no intervention by the government, one consequence of which was that wealthy individuals were being ordained as monks in order to avoid conscription to the army. Although Wei Shou states in his text that Empress Dowager Ling issued a number of commands aimed at controlling the spread of Buddhism among her polity and the prevalence of false, tax-evading monks,[50] he also laments that the empress dowager did not enforce her commands. Immediately following his record of the empress dowager's commands in his text, Wei Shou states that "At the time, the laws and prohibitions were lax and loose and it proved impossible to rectify and adjust them."[51] For Wei Shou, this was, at least "for men of judgement, reason indeed to sigh in desperation."[52]

As further recorded by Wei Shou, the empress dowager was warned about the possibility of a Buddhist rebellion by her own courtiers. Reiterating the above-stated warning of the potential dangers of Buddhism and its practitioners, which likened them to the infamous revolt of the Yellow Turbans, Yuan Yi directly compares Empress Dowager Ling to the Han ruler who is blamed for the Yellow Turban uprising. This story is found in Yuan Yi's own biography in the *Book of the Wei*, which states that:

There was a śramaṇa named Huilian who spoke spells over people's drinking water and was able to cure their illness. Of the sick who went to him, there were a thousand a day. The empress dowager commanded that he be given clothing and food and because the power of his service was particularly favorable, he was sent to the south side of the west of the city to administer the healing of the commoners.

[Yuan] Yi brought a memorial of admonition: The ministers hear that the law is submerged [by] bewildering schemes that ritual has been cut off [by] licentious taboos. In all cases, therefore the ruler [must] remain orthodox and dispel heterodoxy! In ancient times at the end of the Han, there was one called Zhang Jue [d. 184] who used such arts to bewilder his contemporaries. In considering these actions against those of today, they are no different. On account [of them] [Zhang] was able to deceive and seduce the people and bring about the disasters of the Yellow Turbans wherein all the world was mud and ashes[53] for a period of ten years on account of following [Zhang] Jue. In the past and as in now, evil needs to be walled up so that it cannot ascend to the bright hall, squander the five benefits and bring a death sentence to the young."[54]

In his memorial presented in response to the empress dowager's patronage of a magic-making Buddhist monk, Yuan Yi links the empress dowager directly to the emperor who ruled the Eastern Han at the time of the Yellow Turban revolt: that emperor is the only other emperor in all of Chinese history to also have the posthumous name of "Ling"—that is, Han Emperor Ling (r. 168–89), who also ruled from Luoyang.[55] Yuan Yi compares the empress dowager to Han Emperor Ling by suggesting that her sympathy for a particular magic-wielding monk would lead to the downfall of her kingdom in the same way as did the Han Emperor's sympathy for Zhang Jue, the leader of the Yellow Turbans.[56]

Wei Shou's desperate sighs over the state of Buddhism in the late Northern Wei that he says are shared with other "men of judgement" or, in other words, Ru scholars in the service of the court, center on the Zhengguan reign of Emperor Xiaoming, the son of the empress dowager behind whom she was ruling. The five years of this reign coincide with the aforementioned coup d'état, when Yuan Cha was regent behind the emperor and Empress Dowager Ling was removed from power. After 525, the empress dowager reestablished her regency but the empire continued its decline into chaos and disorder until the eventual murder of Emperor Xiaoming in 528 and the supposedly retaliatory murder of the empress dowager a few months later. This period of murderous dynastic transition was a symptom of a larger disease: the collapse of the dynasty's northern garrisons, many of which were economically, culturally, and politically impoverished because the court had moved the capital to Luoyang, which saw the relocation of their soldiers to the interior.[57] This, in turn, was disastrous for the stability of the empire, whose rulers had decided to exhaust their resources on building a new capital while impoverishing their own military. As such, internecine war brought to the gates of an unfortified Luoyang in the year 528 induced the final collapse of the empire in the year 534. According to Wei Shou, this time of increasing violence saw commoners taking refuge in Buddhist monasteries instead of heading to the front lines to fight for the empire. Implicitly, the empress dowager is behind this critique because the collapse of the dynastic house is laid at her feet and because, as we saw above, she is criticized in the *Book of the Wei* for failing to enact limits on how many Buddhist monasteries could be built and on how many persons were permitted to populate them as monks and nuns.

Wei Shou depicts the empress dowager as a person who helped to destroy the purity of the Buddhist faith by encouraging masses of unfaithful and illegitimate monastics to fill the monasteries and taint the reputation of the buddha. This interpretation of the empress dowager's support of Buddhism during her reign is telling regarding Wei Shou's own predicament with respect to Buddhism. Although it has been argued that Wei Shou was himself a Buddhist because his childhood name was "Buddha Helper" (*fozhu*),[58] he was also a literatus and a courtier. If he ascribed to the Buddhist faith at all,[59] the version of Buddhism he paid homage to was likely not of the same variety that the empress dowager encouraged, which was a Buddhism of the masses that left policymakers afraid of its power and critical of what they saw as its failings and indulgences. Wei Shou's insider critique of the empress dowager's Buddhism was also influenced by the role that he played at the court of the Northern Qi, whose rulers were also notable patrons of Buddhist art and institution. Therefore, in crafting his political critique of the empress dowager, Wei Shou needed to be careful not to criticize Buddhism, per se. He needed only to criticize the empress dowager and her support of a Buddhist tradition that he characterized as prone to violence and uprising and one that defiled the buddhas and their teachings through its connection to urban life, rebellion, and avoidance of conscription to the army. This criticism comes not only from the writings of Wei Shou but through his record of memorials brought to her in which she is directly compared to Han Emperor Ling and in which the Buddhism she patronized is compared to the revolt of the Yellow Turbans.

These Buddhism-contra-Buddhism arguments that we see in the *Book of the Wei* are important because they have longevity across the medieval world and point to a larger tension that develops between what we might call Ru Buddhism— or the Buddhism of the literate elite—and the Buddhism of lay followers. Later historiographical texts of the Ru tradition under different dynasties largely reiterate the words of the *Book of the Wei* in their descriptions of Buddhism in Luoyang in the sixth century before its collapse. For example, the *Comprehensive Mirror to Aid in Government* contains an abbreviated but still lengthy version of Prince Cheng's memorial to the empress dowager where he argues that she has let Buddhism become totally defiled by refusing to police the Buddhist community and enforce the boundaries between what he considered to be sacred and profane.[60]

Such a critique of the empress dowager was not only adopted by Sima Guang in his *Comprehensive Mirror to Aid in Government*, but also by later Buddhist historiographers as well. For example, in the Tang era compilation, *The Expanded Collection for the Proclamation and Clarification of Buddhism* (Guang hongming ji), the eminent monk Daoxuan (596–667) records both the story of the empress dowager's funding of the Eternal Peace Monastery and the memorial against her support of such funding quoted in the above selection from the *Comprehensive Mirror to Aid in Government*, which is derived from the *Book of the Wei*. Notably, Daoxuan does not challenge the characterization of the Buddhist monks of the empress dowager's time as "the Dregs of the Śākya Clan." Instead, he provides additional commentary on why they were known as such. Citing the memorial of Yuan Yi, Daoxuan reiterates that these "dregs of the Śākya Clan and altar rats of the gate of the teaching did not abide by their own internal laws and considered it appropriate to discard imperial rules."[61] He further explains that when the Northern Wei fell into terminal violence that, "those courtiers who had died further cast their families into the monastery."[62] Daoxuan's account of the state of Buddhism in the late Northern Wei is clearly based on Wei Shou's analysis from the *Book of the Wei*. What we see, then, is that Wei Shou's criticisms of the empress dowager and her practice of Buddhism were known among elite Buddhist monastics in the Tang. This represents both a marked and a rapid shift within the development of elite forms of Buddhist monasticism in China that saw the incorporation of a Ru worldview into the leadership of the Buddhist monastic community.

Furthermore, in another Tang era historiographical account of the tradition of Buddhism, the *North Mountain Record* (Beishan lü), the elite monk Shenqing (d. 820) describes the Buddhism of the empress dowager at length. Arguing that the destruction of her Eternal Peace Monastery and pagoda by Erzhu Rong was deserved because its benefactor stood as an affront against heaven and empire as a female ruler, he explains that:

> Northern Wei Empress Dowager Ling commissioned a stūpa for which she exhausted the resources of millions on millions. Its peak towered like a mountain, appearing to create and transform. People truly cherished it; Heaven, it seems, rejected it. Therefore, the court underwent catastrophe.
>
> With smoke and scarlet flames on all nine stories, steam and ash enveloped it completely. Was this not a metaphor for how [she] had gone against the will of Heaven? The masters said, "Now, in order to be virtuous, things must accord with their limits. To forget one's limits is evil. Acting on behalf of virtue is the criterion for permanence; acting on behalf of evil is the criterion for loss." Madame Hu is evil! This is therefore a transgression of harmony. How can it be that the banality of gods and ghosts has surpassed the power of men?[63]

In his *Record*, Shenqing tells us that the empress dowager transgressed the natural order of things and, as such, that her pagoda burned to the ground as a result of heaven's retribution and divine reordering. The text continues by explaining what the precise transgressions of the empress dowager were. Shenqing criticizes the empress dowager's extravagances by relating the story of the two Zhang brothers of the later Zhao (319–50), who each erected a fantastic pagoda. Instead of being praised, their pagodas earned the scorn of the aforementioned great northern patriarch, Fotucheng, whom Shenqing records admonished the brothers as follows:

> Buddhist works abide in clear purity and are without desire; compassion and pity should be taken as their core. Almsgivers expound and uphold this great law. [By contrast,] greedy misers never stop. They will hunt without limit and accumulate things without end. In fair measure, they receive punishment in this world. How can they have the hope of meritorious retribution?[64]

Implicit in Shenqing's use of Fotucheng's remembered chastisement of the Zhang brothers who built resplendent stūpas while transgressing basic Buddhist teachings on desirelessness and renunciation is a critique of the empress dowager who had done the same. The empress dowager's huge expenditure of resources on the building of the Eternal Peace Monastery was, according to Shenqing, a crime against both heaven and buddha. This sentiment furthermore agrees with a discussion of the monastery in the *Book of the Zhou* (Zhou shu), which records that:

> At the time when Empress Dowager Ling held court, she reduced the salaries of her court servants by ten percent and built the Eternal Peace Monastery and commanded outstanding ceremony for it.[65]

Further in his treatment of the empress dowager and her transgressions, Shenqing relays a gendered criticism of the empress dowager's rule and of the reasons heaven felt it necessary to intervene. Referencing the passage on hens from the *Book of Documents* cited in chapter 1, Shenqing argues that the empress dowager's position as a female ruler was a transgression against heaven and that it therefore deserved the retribution it received. In providing more context for heaven's righteous action in destroying the empress dowager's Eternal Peace Monastery, Shenqing explains that:

> Therefore, when considering those who are good, we must use the good to arrive at the good and we cannot use the not-good to arrive at the good. The *Book of Documents* says: "Hens are not for the dawn. In the case of a dawn hen, this is nothing other than the dissolution of the family." How reckless that Empress Hu has subverted the Yuan family![66]

What we see in these examples of Tang era Buddhist historiographical writing is that elite Buddhist authors from the Tang were thinking about their tradition through the *Book of the Wei*. However, even though he was writing about Empress Dowager Ling, Shenqing, at least, was not necessarily thinking about the Northern Wei when he crafted his criticism. What is more likely is that he was thinking about his own society in the Tang. The Tang empire, of course, saw the rise of the one and only woman to directly rule China under the title of emperor, or *di*. That woman, Wu Zetian, or Emperor Wu Zhao, has been discussed many times in this book because it is a well-established fact that she, too, legitimated her reign through the use of both Buddhist and Han-dynastic symbols of monarchy. One of her most famous projects was the construction of her own majestic complex of buildings in Luoyang that contained the towering bright hall (*mingtang*). A structure of this same name was an important part of the state ritual palladium in the Han empire; therefore, Emperor Wu Zhao's construction of it placed her at the center of traditional Han notions of monarchy as it was the architectural center of her religio-political landscape. However, much of the symbolism employed on the decoration of the bright hall was Buddhist in nature; the structure was therefore also deeply interwoven into her own project of state Buddhism.[67] Like Empress Dowager Ling, Emperor Wu Zhao is blamed for bankrupting her populace to fund such a large-scale and expensive project.[68] Even more like Empress Dowager Ling, Emperor Wu Zhao's state palladium with the bright hall was ill-fated: First destroyed by wind, it was rebuilt only to be destroyed by fire, all within a span of five years.[69] As such, we might be best served by reading Shenqing's detailed and gendered criticism of the empress dowager's pagoda at the Eternal Peace Monastery as a critique of Emperor Wu Zhao. The descriptions of the fires that struck the hearts of their imperial and Buddhist building projects became, in the Tang, a sort of Buddhist trope by which to criticize the rule of a female regent.

Both Empress Dowager Ling and Emperor Wu Zhao participated in modalities of statecraft that we can call Confucian; however, they did so as Buddhists. For Empress Dowager Ling, it is clear that although she was said to be of Han ethnicity and although she advocated the usage Confucian virtues of filial piety that were symbolically rooted in the Han empire, she was not a Ru scholar. For our purposes, we can think about her practice of both Buddhism and Confucianism distinctly not from the perspective of the elite male class of authors and text masters known as the Ru. Although she worked with Ru scholars at court, she was not one of them; her cultural location as both peripheral and female prevented her from being so. In this chapter, I hope to have shown that her Buddhism was also not the same Buddhism as patronized by the Ru. Even though she participated in a world and court structured along Confucian lines, her practice of Buddhism allowed her to push those lines and even transgress them. She was aided in this task by the public cultural lives of Serbi women in Luoyang whose own gender performance included taking on tasks normally demarcated as male in Confucian culture. This distinctly non-Ru, non-Han, and Buddho-Confucian world that the empress dowager was located in is not something discussed by Ru scholars and is therefore not seen in either Confucian or Buddhist historiographical writings throughout the medieval period. I do not believe that this kind of writing about the empress dowager's cultural world and practice of Buddhism was intentionally done; rather, I think that her world was a world that the Ru scholars of her time and later simply did not participate in, and it was one that they struggled to adequately write about.

THE NAME THAT CAPTURED A REIGN

The ambiguity that surrounds the empress dowager and her cultural practice that is seen in the above discussion of her Buddhism is emblematized by her name "ling." *Ling* is a tricky word to translate into English. Graphically, the character 靈 is composed of a shaman (巫), three mouths (口), and rain (雨). We might therefore interpret the basic meaning of the word as "shaman praying for rain." Metaphorically, however, the word is interpreted to signify the supernormal efficacy of particular individuals, forces, and objects in the material world that inspire impact and effect from the spiritual world. In English translation, *ling* is often rendered as "numinous"; however, its usage in medieval Literary Chinese is more expansive, and it can refer to ghosts or spirits or to the magical or spiritual properties associated with material things or natural elements. When applied to a person, the word might be understood as describing a supernormal or an extraordinary element in their personality. Here, we will attempt to understand the word *ling* in the context of sixth-century Luoyang, and we will do so in order to understand more about how the empress dowager was remembered by those who knew her.[70]

In Buddhist usage during the times in which she lived, the word *ling* would have signified a desirable spiritual association or benevolent supernormal efficacy. For example, the *Record of Buddhist Monasteries in Luoyang* notes the existence of the Numinous Response Monastery (Lingying si) and the Numinous Awakening Monastery (Lingjue si). In a more straightforward connection to imperial life, the aforementioned stele from the year 499 on the Radiant Blessings Monastery that refers to Empress Dowager Wenming and Emperor Xiaowen as the "Two Sages" also states that the "numinous monastery" was built for the veneration of the emperor.[71] Read as such, then, the *ling* in the empress dowager's posthumous name strongly associates her with the Buddhist religion practiced in Luoyang and it retains a positive connotation of divine inspiration and efficacy.

Despite the positive Buddhist associations of the word *ling* in the empress dowager's time, another interpretation of the name also exists. This interpretation is negative in tone and linked with the Confucian history of imperial naming. As mentioned above, the only other regent in Chinese history to hold the posthumous name of "Ling" is the aforementioned Han Emperor Ling. Like the empress dowager, the Han emperor also saw the destruction and collapse of his empire. In both cases, the rulers are said to have shown problematic favoritism and to have ignored unstable elements in their polities.[72] They were also both criticized by their courtiers for their excessive expenditures that were said to bankrupt the populace.[73] For the Han emperor, this was particularly disastrous because he ruled over the peasant uprising of the Yellow Turbans that was partly responsible for the fall of the Han, which is often remembered as China's greatest empire. Unlike in the case of the Northern Wei empress dowager, in the case of the Han emperor, historical sources give us clear guidance for how to interpret his posthumous name. His biography in the *Book of the Later Han* directly says that he was under the influence of dishonorable court servants and therefore ignored his duties in favor of wine, women, and merriment.[74] For this reason, the biography tells us, "did Han Emperor Ling become *ling*."[75] Although there are no other regents who share the posthumous name "Ling," there is one official from the Northern Wei who was posthumously called "Ling." In this case, the name is articulated in the exact same way as the idea of "becoming Ling" as expressed in the biography of Han Emperor Ling above.[76] This official, Gao You (d. 499), has a biography in the *Book of the Wei*,[77] which clearly states what *ling* means and why the official was called by this name. Although Gao You had been an effective policymaker early on in his career, he came under the influence of Liu Chang (436–97), the ninth son of Emperor Wen (r. 424–53) of the Liu Song, whom Northern Wei Emperor Xiaowen had granted the title of "King of Song" (*songwang*) after the collapse of the Liu Song. Liu Chang bestowed riches and concubines on Gao You, which evidently swayed the latter from his duties. Upon Liu Chang's death, Gao You was promoted to the office of director of the imperial clan (*zongzheng*); however, in this position he ignored the commands of the central court. He was then dismissed from his post, exiled for three years, and demoted to his original rank. At his death in 499, Emperor Xiaowen made an edict according to which, "Not taking orders from one's superiors is called '*ling*;' he shall posthumously be called 'Ling.'"[78] In such a case, then, *ling* can designate a person who is unrestrained by established hierarchy and therefore insubordinate. Given the otherworldly associations of the term, such insubordination could be understood as having being coerced by unknown—even supernormal—causes.

As we have seen, the empress dowager's courtiers disagreed with her unrestrained support for popular Buddhism and unfavorably compared her to Han Emperor Ling, who was besieged by the uprising of the Yellow Turbans. At the same time, the name "Ling" seemed to be one that the empress dowager endorsed through her patronage of the Monastery of the Two Women at the site of the Numinous Platform. As a Buddhist name, "Ling" would have carried a beneficent valency. To further investigate how such an ambivalent name was heard and received in the empress dowager's time, it is useful to think about who it was precisely that gave the name to her. The empress dowager's biography states that her name was given under the reign of the last of the puppet emperors of the Northern Wei, Emperor Xiaowu. Xiaowu's own biography in the *Book of the Wei* states that he granted her the posthumous name and that he also saw that her remains were buried after almost four years in an undisclosed location said to be the Monastery of the Two Lings.[79] As we will see, Emperor Xiaowu inherited a mixed dynastic legacy that befits the granting of the ambiguous name of "Ling" on the Empress Dowager.

A puppet emperor and the last of the dynasty, Emperor Xiaowu was a legitimate Taghbach heir. Otherwise known as Yuan Xiu (510–35), he was a grandson of Emperor Xiaowen and the nephew of Emperor Xuanwu. He was born in the same year as Emperor Xiaoming, the empress dowager's son and coruler. Emperor Xiaowu is even less well loved than the empress dowager in the *Book of the Wei*, so much so that he is consistently referred to by the pejorative expression, "the Emperor Who Fled" (*chudi*). The use of this pejorative is owing to the fact that although Xiaowu was originally propped up by Gao Huan and had married one of Gao Huan's daughters, he eventually broke free from Gao Huan and fled the capital to attempt to establish the Western Wei. Even though he broke free from Gao Huan, however, he was murdered by his collaborators in the process. Gao Huan, as we have seen, went on to establish the Eastern Wei and his son was the first emperor of the Northern Qi, under whose auspices the *Book of the Wei* was written. Xiaowu's biography in the *Book of the Wei* tells of a man who loved war, murdered any other claimants to the Northern Wei throne, and was disloyal to his supporter, Gao Huan. Gao Huan, of course, was the winner to emerge from the collapse of the Northern Wei, and the *Book of the Wei* narrates the fall of the empire from the perspective of the winners who established the Northern Qi—namely, his family. This is why Emperor Xiaowu is referred to as "the Emperor Who Fled."

Before he fled, the emperor reigned with the backing of Gao Huan. His accession came on the heels of a bloody five-year internecine war, which saw Luoyang invaded by a collective force that included the Erzhu clan and the Gao clan, the empress dowager murdered by Erzhu Rong, the subsequent establishment of two successive puppet emperors supported by the Erzhu faction, the ultimate murder of Erzhu Rong by Emperor Xiaozhuang, the rise of the Gao Clan, and Gao Huan's support for Emperor Xiaowu's accession. As such, by the time of Xiaowu, although the empress dowager had been the enemy of the Erzhus, the Erzhus were now the enemy of the Gaos. Did it stand to reason, therefore, that the enemy of the enemy was the friend? In Xiaowu's accession edict, we see both explicit and implicit support for the empress dowager in the context of the slaughter of the Taghbach line by the Erzhu faction. Xiaowu's accession edict begins with a summary of the decline of the ruling house, saying:

> Prosperity and decline have been passed down; the rise and the fall are mutually constitutive. The dark sky hides nothing and the clever numen [*ling*] is unable to command. The line of the great Wei has dried up. Virtue has trickled away from the world and the nine garments [of rulership] are bound up in prison, putting aside the light of the three luminaries [of the sun, moon, and stars]. Moreover, Heaven's calamities have befallen and set in motion much hardship. Ritual and music have collapsed and decrees and regulations have fallen by the wayside. The illustrious Zhou ancestors have been cut off [from us] because of armed bandits; the venerable imperial shrine has become thick straw. The barbarians of the Jie seized the

opportunity and were reckless in their dark tyranny, killing the sovereign and harming the princes and gutting the territory inside the seas. Competing with [each other] in their intentions to bite and swallow, the heart of their intoxication and gluttony cannot be understood. There has never been anything like this ever [recorded] in scripts and writings![80]

From these opening words of his accession edict, it is evident that Emperor Xiaowu and Gao Huan behind him positioned themselves at what they hoped would be a turning point in Northern Wei history. The edict argues that there had never been recorded such a violent pillage as that of the "dark tyranny" of the barbarians of Jie. The barbarians of Jie are here a reference to the Erzhu. The Jie are one of the non-Han groups commonly included in the so-called "Five Barbarian" groups in Han Chinese writings, and the Erzhu arguably hail from their ethnicity or past political alliances, or both.[81] In the beginning of his edict, therefore, we see Emperor Xiaowu's attempt to both blame the Erzhu for the destruction of the Northern Wei line and position himself as a legitimate, Yuan-family heir capable of renewing it. Most notably, in this depiction of the state of the rule of the empire we see multiple references to the empress dowager. The opening sentence of the edict reads: "The dark sky hides nothing and the clever numen [*ling*] is unable to command." The use of the word *numen* in this sentence implies a reference to the empress dowager, who was herself given the name "Ling" by this same government. Similarly, the edict laments the loss of rule in terms of the loss of Han-dynastic modalities of imperial legitimation. Given that the empress dowager was the only Northern Wei ruler of Han descent, and given that she emphasized this descent by including Han era gods and structures in the commemoration of her own deceased family members at both the Huoshao grotto and the Monastery of the Two Women at the Numinous Platform, we can read the edict as a statement that the rule of the empress dowager had been cut off by the rebellion of the Erzhu, who had pillaged the empire and harmed the people with an intensity never before seen. Furthermore, the usage of "dark sky" above might also refer to the Erzhu, with the explanation being that the Erzhu can no longer hide and that their crimes are now brought under scrutiny and have been avenged. In this way, then, the reference to the empress dowager is again positive. As a ruler of spiritual efficacy associated with Han dynastic modalities of rule and reign located specifically at the numinous platform, she was seen in a sympathetic light by those who gave her the name, even if this sympathy was simply because of their shared enemies, and even if those who gave her the name also had a hand in her death.

The empress dowager and her posthumous name both stand out in history for their rarity. If we contrast Empress Dowager Ling's posthumous name with that of the other infamous ruling woman from the Northern Wei, Empress Dowager Wenming, the strangeness of Empress Dowager Ling's name becomes even more clear. Empress Dowager Wenming's posthumous name means "Civilized and

Illuminated" and it matches that of her partner, Emperor Wencheng, "Civilized and Accomplished." Although she was a powerful empress dowager, Wenming enacted her regency government as normally conceived of in an imperial system of patriarchal descent—indirectly and in a manner that was dependent on the regent. Her posthumous name therefore suggests her partnership with Emperor Wencheng and her generally positive posthumous reputation, even though she was a woman who effectively seized power by forcing the emperor into retirement. What is strikingly different between the two women is how they vested their power: Wenming remained behind the scenes and her posthumous name suggests a maintenance in the gendered order of rulership; Ling, on the other hand, ruled directly and her posthumous name is not connected to that of any male rulers. This lack of a male reference in her posthumous name makes her name even more meaningful because it indicates her independent rule.

In sum, the empress dowager's posthumous name, "Ling," is a remarkably apt summation of her reign. As a unique name not connected to names of men in the imperial line, it signals her difference as an independent female ruler. As a religious name denoting supernormal efficacy that was both associated with Han court's imperial legitimation and popular in the Buddhist worlds of Luoyang, "Ling" was a name invoked by the empress dowager herself, in her lifetime. Yet, as a double entendre, "Ling" also resonated with her courtier's fears that she had been dangerously subverted by Buddhist forces that they deemed unstable to the empire in a manner similar to the Yellow Turbans of the Han dynasty. Her name therefore also links her forever to the Han emperor whose name and whose numinous platform in Luoyang she shared. The divergent meanings invoked by the name "Ling" also help us to appreciate the very character of Northern Wei Luoyang under the rule of the empress dowager: diverse, energetic, unstable, and creative, the city that knew the empress dowager as their cakravartin was one of deep ambiguity and precarity but also one of excitement and, possibly, supernormal efficacy.

DESTRUCTION/REINVENTION

Thinking through the Northern Wei court's various political spectacles in the latter half of the dynasty, Scott Pearce invokes Clifford Geertz's theory of the theater state in order to make sense of some of the chaos and power plays that are attested to in historical sources documenting Luoyang politics. What I find particularly useful in this framing is Pearce's insightful characterization of the fall of the empire under the empress dowager. Using the metaphor of theater, Pearce argues that the political spectacle so carefully orchestrated and leveraged by the empress dowager in her city failed to capture the sympathies of the armed men who came to her city gates and "who care[d] neither for the spectacle nor the principles of its organization."[82] Nonetheless, although she failed to convince the armed men from the northern garrisons of her particular form of Buddhist kingship enacted in the public eye, her theater is one that we need to pay attention to because it was precisely this theater that Emperor Wu Zhao was more successful at in the implementation of her own accession and reign. With her active patronage of Buddhism as a crucial component of her political theater, Empress Dowager Ling showed herself both pious and generous and placed herself at the center of her vibrant Buddhist capital in order to gain the support of its people—an important undertaking for a female ruler. Such political theater, however, was a choice, and the choice did not always play out in her favor. By aligning herself with popular Buddhism, she alienated some of her own courtiers who, according to Wei Shou at least, wished that she would have enacted more stringent policing of the tradition to ensure control over Buddhists, and they came to compare her with the infamous Han emperor whose name she shares. Her courtiers were wrong in their estimation: it was not Buddhists who would overthrow the court. Instead, a collection of disenfranchised, largely non-Han groups from the impoverished northern garrisons murdered the empress dowager, proving that neither her bejeweled Buddhist capital nor her role as ritualist and dramaturge could outlast economic collapse.

The prophecy of the future birth of Maitreya says that he will arrive on this earth to usher in a time of great peace and prosperity. The late Northern Wei capital knew a handful of potential Maitreya rulers, and the rapid and dramatic construction of the jeweled capital city that they oversaw must have felt like the dawning of a new age. The new age never materialized: The city was burned, the Buddhist structures were destroyed, the court and its ruler were murdered, and the population was dispersed. The dream of a new buddha age proved fleeting and the world was shown to be impermanent, just as Buddhist teaching says that it is. Luoyang's history of rise and decline are an apt metaphor for the Buddhist idea of creation, which sees our world and all beings in it subject to death and rebirth because of the causal powers of ignorance, delusion, and greed. The city's cycles of destruction and rebuilding have long been decadent and illustrious and then dark and violent. With the story of the empress dowager that I have told throughout this book, we see the Northern Wei cycle completed in a mere forty years in which the city was built, prospered, destroyed, and abandoned. The empress dowager's attempt to establish herself and her granddaughter as Buddhist monarchs that might withstand the pending collapse of the dynastic line was unsuccessful and Luoyang fell, once again, to the destruction that it had seen with other dynastic fates, particularly with the fall of the Eastern Han. Like Empress Dowager Ling, Han Emperor Ling is considered the last independent ruler of his dynasty. For both rulers centered in Luoyang with its central avenue and numinous platform, their deaths brought about the final collapses of their weakened dynasties and thus threw Luoyang into decline.

In a Buddhist sense, the decline of Luoyang brought about by the deaths of the two rulers named "Ling" paved the way for the city's rebirth. After the fall of the Eastern Han, Luoyang rose again in the Northern Wei when Empress Dowager Ling built her majestic Eternal Peace Monastery. And it rose again in the Tang when Wu Zhao built her bright hall and ruled her own dynasty with the gendered male title of di, or emperor. In this story, Buddhism has not provided salvation— nor was it meant to—but it has provided opportunity. With each rebuilding of the city, Buddhist structures, institutions, and ideas were rearticulated and revived. The opportunities that a Buddhist Luoyang in all its various cultural sources and tensions created were many, and they affected people's lives in myriad ways. With this book, my interest has been to draw out for analysis the affect that this tremendous city and all its cultural practices and opportunities had on the lives of elite, Buddhist women in the early medieval period, particularly during the sixth century. These opportunities were manifold: As administrators, nuns, politicians, regents, rulers, and maybe even monarchs, Buddhist women were at the core of Northern Wei Luoyang. The story of these new opportunities for women witnessed in the Northern Wei chronicles the radical reinvention of tradition in the sixth century just as it indexes the main social currents that allowed for such reinvention.

Conclusion

The Northern Wei court's choice to adopt Han-Chinese names, language, and court procedures after a century of their own established rule in the northern reaches of the old Han empire integrated the north of China into the culture and politics of the central plains in a new way. As a result, the Northern Wei's sphere of influence extended both geographically and temporally beyond itself and throughout the various administrations and polities in later China and across East Asia. The immediate effects of the Northern Wei's prominence in the region were seen in Silla Korea, in Yamato and Nara Japan, and, later, in Tang China. According to Herman Ooms, the early courts of Japan were well aware of the power and prestige of the Northern Wei and held certain fascination for them. As a result, they adopted the Northern Wei's legal codes and Yamato archaeological sites contain Northern Wei mirrors. Furthermore, several important names and phrases were adopted from the Northern Wei and integrated into Japanese parlance. For example, Ooms argues that the Yamato pronunciation for Pingcheng, the northern capital of the Northern Wei, was in fact Heijō (Nara).[1] As for the Kingdom of Silla, Northern Wei motifs show up in the ornamentation of Silla objects;[2] moreover, unique glasswork bowls developed in the early Northern Wei capital of Pingcheng have been found in Silla tombs,[3] while the famed wooden pagoda at Silla's August Dragon Monastery and state palladium was modeled after the empress dowager's stūpa at the Eternal Peace Monastery in Luoyang. Furthermore, the Silla court employed monastic overseers and sponsored Buddhist ceremonies for state protection in the same way that the Northern Wei did.[4]

It is an attestation to the longevity of the Northern Wei outside East Asia that the Uyghur equivalent for the word "Taghbach," to take one example, was generally used in Uyghur-language sources to refer to China itself centuries after the demise of the Northern Wei.[5] In this same vein, the Byzantine historian The-ophylact Simocatta (fl. 630), who lived approximately one hundred years after the fall of the Northern Wei, records in his *Historiae* that what is now recognized as China was then called Taugust, as was the capital city and the ruling class—a name that almost certainly means Taghbach.[6] Similarly, the founding house of the non-Han Western Xia dynasty (1038–1227) legitimated their own reign and power in much the same way as did the rulers of the Northern Wei, also taking the name of Taghbach as the name of the Tangut ruling family.[7]

The Northern Wei's importance across medieval East Asian history is too large of a topic to broach in any depth here; however, in this conclusion to the study of the life and times of Empress Dowager Ling, it does make sense to wrap things up by asking what the impact of the empress dowager's life, work, and court may have had on the larger question of women's history in East Asia. I would particu-larly like to conclude by tracing a trajectory of the emergence of rule by Buddhist women in East Asia that finds its earliest recorded attestation in the Northern Wei.

WHERE CAN WE SEE THE EMPRESS DOWAGER'S LEGACY?

The arguments and sources presented throughout this study have told the story of how the nameless girl from the Hu clan of Anding relied on Buddhists, Bud-dhist institutions, and Buddhist ideas, as well as unique ideas about gender and its performance that were known to the Taghbach people who founded the Northern Wei in order to become one of the most powerful politicians of her day. This story has been cobbled together from a diverse mixture of historical sources that docu-ment a more generalized change in the lives of women in the medieval period that we can tie to the empress dowager. Sleuthing across this broad array of primary sources, I have constructed a world that I believe explains the empress dowager's rise, rule, and demise. The approach I have used to do this is one that I have termed "Buddhist feminist historiography." This approach seeks to prioritize both women in social history and Buddhist sources that document them as a method of histo-riographical interruption, clarification, and revision.

In proposing my theory about the emergence of Buddhist monarchy for women, which finds its earliest attested iteration in the Northern Wei and which was a social movement relying on the cultural norms of the Taghbach people alongside Buddhist ideas about women and their social roles, I am aware that much of this story has been told before. Empress Wu or Wu Zetian or Emperor Wu Zhao began her independent rule in 690 of the Common Era, precisely 175 years after Empress Dowager Ling began her regency. We know from many sources that Emperor Wu Zhao used Buddhism to legitimate her reign, but what is in all likelihood the most compelling of these sources is a commentary on the *Great Cloud Sūtra*, which was

commissioned by Emperor Wu Zhao on her accession in 690 and which identified her as the fulfillment of that sūtra's prophecy regarding the female cakravartin
about which we read in chapter 4.[8] This commentary was integral to her usurpa-
tion of the Tang and her rule over her own polity, the Zhou (690–705).[9] Similarly,
in 693, a translation of a text called the *Sūtra of Raining Jewels* (Baoyu jing) was
presented to her with the addition of an apocryphal section that once again explicitly identified Emperor Wu Zhao as the fulfillment of the prophecy and positioned
her as a bodhisattva.[10] In this way, then, Emperor Wu Zhao was the inheritor of
a Northern Wei tradition of identifying a female ruler directly with buddhas and
bodhisattvas.[11] Furthermore, in shaping her identity as a cakravartin, she also
embarked on a nation-uniting scheme of venerating relics across the land in the
same way her famous Indian predecessor, Aśoka,[12] as well as Empress Dowager
Ling and Emperor Wu of the Liang, did.

Although Emperor Wu Zhao engaged in a relic campaign in the same way that
Emperor Wu of the Liang did, also positioning herself as a bodhisattva in a similar
manner, she did so as a woman. This is an important difference that needs to be
considered within the larger questions of how and why Buddhist notions of monarchy swept across East Asia in the medieval period. I believe that we can only
explain this difference by putting Emperor Wu Zhao's story directly into a trajectory of social change in the lives of women that we see so clearly documented in
the Northern Wei sources I have referred to in this study. Emperor Wu Zhao is the
most commented on woman in Chinese history. We have no shortage of studies
that document and describe the ways in which she connected her rule to Buddhism that resonate with other rulers—normally thought of as Emperor Wu of the
Liang and Emperor Wen of the Sui—before and after her. In her story, what is less
recognized is that she explicitly connected her rule to the Northern Wei. Emperor
Wu Zhao had strong connections with the Northern Wei. Her ancestors in her
father's line held official positions in the courts of both the Northern Wei and the
Northern Qi. Her great-great-great-grandfather was a certain Wu Keji who was a
high-ranking official under the Northern Wei; she herself posthumously bestowed
on him the title of the Duke of Lu (Luguo gong). His son Wu Juchang was a general
under the Northern Qi, and Empress Wu bestowed on him the rank of Great Officer (*taiwei*).[13] As to the Emperor's connections to Northern Wei women, we have
already seen how she adopted the "Two Sage" model of corulership that developed
in the Northern Wei and how this model of rulership contributed to a rise in imagery of the Two-Buddha scene from the *Lotus Sūtra* during both of their reigns. We
have also seen how Empress Dowager Ling, too, may have been known through
this type of paradigm, in her case evoked in the name of the monastery where her
body and the body of the emperor were interred, the Monastery of the Two Lings.
This image of corulership is evoked in the image of the Two-Buddha scene in the
Huangfu Gong grotto, which is located directly above the image of her, Xiaoming,
and both of their entourages.

In terms of more concrete patterns of rulership, we must pay attention to the connection between the statecraft of Empress Dowager Ling and Empress Wu/Emperor Wu Zhao. As empress, Wu completed the *feng* and *shan* imperial sacrifices alongside Emperor Gaozong, and she did so in an interpretation that stressed the female role.[14] Similarly, in chapter 2, we saw how Empress Dowager Ling commanded her courtier, Cui Guang, to scour the classical canons of ritual to find a way to be able to enact the ancient rites alongside the emperor. Cui Guang found such precedent in the reign of Han Empress Hexi, and the empress dowager went on to perform rites of imperial legitimation with Emperor Xiaoming. Furthermore, both Empress Dowager Ling and Emperor Wu Zhao employed female politicians at their courts,[15] and we have dated evidence for these female politicians through their entombed biographies.[16] Both these women knew Luoyang as their capitals while Luoyang had also been the capital of the Eastern Han, and both rulers made use of Eastern Han ruling structures in their cities while they also both built infrastructure that connected their city to the Han city. Both their flagship structures of state administration in Luoyang were burned to the ground shortly after their completion. In sum, both of these ruling women relied on Han dynastic symbols and structures to help legitimate their contested reigns even though those very structures did not leave ideological space for the accession of women to seats of direct power.

To augment the lack of support for women rulers in the Han traditions they both inherited and innovated, they also utilized then-popular Buddhist modalities of rulership. They both built central stūpas with prefectural stūpa connections in order to establish themselves as Buddhist rulers. In Emperor Wu Zhao's case, these pagodas were all named after the *Great Cloud Sūtra* and hence invoked its prophecy of a female cakravartin;[17] however, in Empress Dowager Ling's case, these prefectural pagodas were built in imitation of her great Eternal Peace Monastery with its soaring pagoda. In both cases, therefore, the female regents had pagodas built that directly related to their own leadership as Buddhist rulers. Similarly, both regents worked closely with members of the monastic elite in order to facilitate their projects of imperial Buddhism. For Emperor Wu Zhao, one of her closest monastic servants was a monk named Fazang (643–712), who, sources say, lectured the emperor on the *Avataṃsaka Sūtra*, translated sūtras, dispelled invaders through the use of esoteric Buddhist rituals, and facilitated the emperor's personal veneration of the relic at the Dharma Gate Monastery (Famen si) in Luoyang.[18] Another thing that Fazang did was to compose the biography of a monk named Lingbian (d.u.),[19] who Fazang says worked in the service of Empress Dowager Ling. In analyzing this biography, however, Zhang Wenliang has argued that Fazang largely fabricated the biography and did so to promote the evolving Huayan tradition in his time.[20] There is no record of Lingbian in either the *Book of the Wei* or the *Record of Buddhist Monasteries in Luoyang*. That it was important for Fazang to link his own Buddhist tradition to that of Empress Dowager

Ling—even if it was a false or imagined connection—speaks to his desire, from the perspective of the Tang, to commemorate and publicize the Northern Wei's program of courtly Buddhism. In other words, even if Fazang's biography of Lingbian is fiction, the very fact that he wrote it suggests that the power of Empress Dowager Ling's Buddhist court was present in the cultural memory of the Tang and Emperor Wu Zhao's immediate monastic servants.

In his study of the textual precedents that helped Emperor Wu Zhao secure and legitimate her own rule, Antonino Forte is careful to show that the *Great Cloud Sūtra* was in circulation prior to the reign of the female emperor and that it was only the commentary to the text that was written to specifically legitimate her reign. Forte undertakes this analysis in order to counter what later histories of the Tang would have us believe—namely, that Empress Wu actually authored the *Great Cloud Sūtra*.[21] Forte's study is of tremendous importance for the field of Tang studies; however, in his time, he would not have known of Northern Wei courtier Yuan Rong's colophons. In chapter 4 we saw that Yuan Rong twice commissioned the copying of the *Great Cloud Sūtra* in the violent times after the death of the empress dowager and did so to publicly show his support of the various emperors backed by competing militarized factions at the end of the dynasty. Importantly, he commissioned the text alongside other well-known Northern Wei Buddhist texts, and therefore placed the *Great Cloud Sūtra* in the context of a collection of then-popular Buddhist texts. If we consider the *Great Cloud Sūtra* in the further context of the other texts, such as the *Sūtra on the Woman, "Silver Countenance"* and the *Śrīmālā Sūtra*, which we know were patronized by Empress Dowager Ling, we begin to see how Buddhist texts about political women and women as rulers and cakravartins were well known in the Northern Wei. These, I believe, are part of the legacy of the dynasty that resurfaced in the Tang under the reign of Emperor Wu Zhao. Just like in the *Sūtra of the Woman "Silver Countenance,"* where Silver Countenance has reached transformative religious attainment in her female body prior to being made a cakravartin, the queen in the *Great Cloud Sūtra* has not yet changed her sex, though she is prophesized to do so. Just like Silver Countenance, the queen in the *Great Cloud Sūtra* has reached full spiritual attainment in her female body. That spiritual attainment allows her to rule as a Buddhist ruler who will, in her next life, electively change her sex as a final act on the path to buddhahood. Both texts were known in the Northern Wei and promoted the political prominence of Buddhist women. As a mini corpus, they existed in the reigns of both Empress Dowager Ling and Emperor Wu Zhao. The support that both these women gave to such textual production and proliferation in their time created a certain continuity between them, with the Northern Wei providing the backdrop for the Tang.

In his study of the diverse cultural and religious sources that Emperor Wu Zhao employed to secure her rule, N. Harry Rothschild argues that this woman who ruled had a lesser-known predecessor: Queen Seondeok (r. 632–47), the first woman ruler of the Kingdom of Silla in Korea. Postulating that Queen Seondeok was the prototype for Emperor Wu Zhao, Rothschild points out that she may have been seen as a descendent of the Śākya clan of the Buddha and therefore was vested in Buddhist foundational mythology in the same way as Emperor Wu Zhao was. In support of this argument, Rothschild cites an account from the Buddhist chronicle of Three Kingdoms Korea, the *Omitted Events of the Three Kingdoms Period* (Samguk Yusa), where, in his translation, the Bodhisattva Mañjuśri appeared to a Sillan pilgrim at Mount Wutai (Wutai shan) and told him, "As your nation's sovereign is a member of India's Kshatriya class, she already received a prophecy from the Buddha."[22] Such a statement signals a prophecy of future Buddhahood like that seen above in the *Sūtra of Kṣemavati* and suggests the common association between elite women, buddhahood, and rule that was en vogue between the fifth and seventh centuries of the Common Era. Although we know less about Queen Seondeok than we do about her Chinese counterparts, it seems plausible that she also may have been a prototype for Emperor Wu Zhao. The latter certainly knew of the former, who had sent many emissaries to the Tang.[23]

What Rothschild does not consider, however, is that Queen Seondeok herself had a likely prototype: Empress Dowager Ling. In his study of the development of the Buddhist tradition in Silla, Richard McBride reveals several ways that Buddhism in Silla was intimately connected to Northern Wei Buddhism; notably, the shared Buddhist practice of Empress Dowager Ling and Queen Seondeok is foundational in this history. Empress Dowager Ling's signature project across the Buddhist landscape of the resplendent city of Luoyang was the Eternal Peace Monastery with its soaring, golden, nine-storied pagoda. This pagoda was so resplendent and so famed across the Buddhist world that it was rebuilt in Silla in the compounds of the August Dragon Monastery, which functioned as the state's signature Buddhist monastery in the same way the Eternal Peace Monastery did. Although, as we have seen, the project of rebuilding the pagoda was initiated by Silla King Chinhŭng, it was completed under Queen Seondeok. Furthermore, both Richard McBride and Sem Vermeersch have discussed the adoption of the Northern Wei's court-governed ecclesiastical administration in Silla, as well as Silla's employment of monastic superintendents and managers across its polity as court/monastic go-betweens and police.[24] As we have seen, this system came to its maturity under Empress Dowager Ling, though it has earlier roots in the Pingcheng era of the Northern Wei.

With Queen Seondeok as the intermediary between Empress Dowager Ling and Emperor Wu Zhao, what we see is the development of the strong connection between Buddhism and women regents that is first seen in the Northern Wei but that became popular across East Asia from the fifth to seventh centuries. This connection is made only stronger when we look to Japan's Yamato period, known for its own women regents with connections to Buddhism. Although difficult to pin down historically, Empress Suiko (r. 592–628)[25] is remembered as having been the first in a successive line of women rulers, just as she worked diligently to support Buddhism in her realm. Empress Suiko was known to lecture on Buddhist texts, and she legally recognized Buddhism as an official religion in Yamato. Furthermore, and rather famously, Empress Suiko's courtier, the semi-mythical Prince Shōtoku (574–622) is said to have written a commentary on the *Śrīmālā Sūtra* while serving at her court.[26] As we have seen, the earliest epigraphical attestation to the *Śrīmālā Sūtra*—a text that ties together women, Buddhism, and statecraft—is found in the entombed biography of Empress Dowager Ling's aunt, the nun Sengzhi. According to the entombed biography, Sengzhi was famed for chanting the text and was brought to the Northern Wei court on account of that fame. Although Suiko provides a compelling comparison with Empress Dowager Ling, a second Buddhist woman who ruled Japan makes for an even more compelling one, and one for which historians have more certain sources. That woman was known as Empress Kōken in her first reign (749–58) and Empress Shōtoku in her second (764–70). Like Empress Dowager Ling, Empress Kōken/Shōtoku was a ruler deeply invested in Buddhist activities whose reigns were interrupted by coup d'état. Indicating an even more fundamental similarity, the two rulers are also said to have had licentious sexual relationships, to have been inappropriately close to destabilizing Buddhist monks, and to have patronized propitiatory Buddhist magic. They were both inheritors of a family tradition of Buddhist patronage and they both personally promoted the production of Buddhist texts.[27]

PROPOSING A FEMINIST PERIODIZATION

Even though we have no direct, single source from the empress dowager's time wherein she explicitly states that she has positioned herself as a cakravartin ruler and her granddaughter as a bodhisattva emperor, when we look across East Asia to the ruling Buddhist women that came after the empress dowager, we see how comparable structures in the rules of other women across East Asia have allowed them to do similar things. Taken together, Empress Dowager Ling, Empresses Suiko and Kōken/Shōtoku, Queen Seondeok, and Emperor Wu Zhao belong to a historical era in which women who were Buddhist and who had some connection with religious and gender-based forms of culture from north Asia, largely via the Northern Wei, had success as politicians. This is particularly interesting given that this time period also coincides with the wide adoption and adaptation of Sinitic imperial structures rooted in the Han dynasty across the region. These structures never made space for women to rule; however, when the structures themselves began to adapt to the strong presence of Buddhists, their ideas, and their institutions, they became a form of imperial Buddhism that seems to have made space for women, especially when those women were already accustomed to living the sorts of public and even martial lives that the women of the Taghbach cultural milieu lived. Herman Ooms has discussed this rare collection of East Asian female rulers in the seventh century, but he does not discuss their Buddhist patronage, which I believe is integral to their stories.[28] As powerful rulers in their empires, these female regents helped to facilitate the adoption and adaptation of the Sinitic imperial system, including legal and penal codes, imperial rituals, and the adoption of Literary Sinitic as an official language with its associated names and ranks, yet they did so as nominally Buddhist women. Looked at somewhat differently, we can say that all their realms—Northern Wei and Tang China, Yamato/Nara Japan, and Silla Korea—adopted a form of imperial Buddhism that was both open to and encouraged by women in positions of power and that I believe was connected to the type of imperial Buddhism that we see under the Northern Wei where women with public lives were able to capitalize on the growth of Buddhism in the region in unique ways that were indebted to the cultural heritage of the Inner Asian peoples and polities that settled in East Asia during this period. This imperial Buddhism is noted for its strong patronage of the Buddha as a religio-political figurehead, but it is also known for its use of traditionally Han-Chinese modes and strategies of rule, the Sinitic calendar, and a form of Literary Chinese that we should refer to here as Literary Sinitic because of its use outside China proper. Finally, this form of Buddhism at court appears to have been a conflux of ideas and practices in which women were able to climb to high positions as politicians. Their ability to do so was affected both by a Buddhist institution that made space for women of rank and by Buddhist ideas about women as religious practitioners and political powerbrokers.

When we look backward from Empress Kōken/Shōtoku to Emperor Wu Zhao to Queen Seondeok to Empress Suiko to Empress Dowager Ling, we see a historical era in which women patrons of Buddhism became supreme rulers of their polities. Although the Northern Wei is the earliest attested instantiation of Buddhist rulers who were women with connections to Inner Asian and steppe cultures, the era in which these women came into their own cannot be adequately characterized as a neat historical line from the Northern Wei to the other relevant places in medieval East Asia. A better way to think about this would be to say that the early medieval era was a time involving the reinvention of tradition along many vectors whereby women and their societies inherited a complex and intersecting web of methods and models for enacting gender, politics, and religion. We see clearly in the Northern Wei how this allowed for the rise of Empress Dowager Ling. Even though she may have been somebody that other women across East Asia had known about it, these same women were tasked with reinventing their own traditions through the sources available to them and in the times in which they lived.

With a final statement on these sources available for the reinvention of tradition in the medieval period, I make my last argument: Historians of East Asia would be well served by engaging with new, and feminist, modalities of periodization that characterize points of cultural change in the lives of historical persons who tradition-ally have not controlled the writing of historical and historiographical documents—in this case, women. Normative periodization of China's medieval period adopts imperial narratives that are androcentric and ethnocentric. Therefore, the period of the Southern and Northern Dynasties is often characterized as one of "division" and "brokenness." This indicates a China that was lost between the famous empires of the Han and the Tang. A sort of dark age, the period we call the "early medieval" in Chinese periodization unavoidably calls to mind social unrest and the lack of centralized power. In his overview of the period, Mark Edward Lewis points out that this period has been relegated to a secondary status in Chinese historiographical materials, which "prefer to focus on times of unity and political power."[29] In that same overview, Lewis leads his reader away from the idea of the second-class status of this era by showing how the internationalism, multiculturalism, and migration that characterized the period contributed to the rebuilding of historically prominent traditions of art, culture, religion, military, and politics that would continue to develop in the area of the world that we now call China.

In thinking with Lewis on this topic, I want to bring the question of women into our understanding of this era and suggest that a feminist periodization would find, in the Southern and Northern Dynasties period, a high point for the development of diversified social roles for women. This was a period involving the disintegration of classical modes of authority, including the basic modality of social authority enforced in the patriarchal family and governmental structure. With new ways of enacting gendered authority for women that arrived in the central plains with both Buddhism and the influence of Inner Asian gender paradigms from the migratory peoples of the steppe, women suddenly found themselves with tremendous and innovative social opportunities that were inherently hybrid and creative, given the lack of centralized and classical structures of social authority. We have seen how this all came together in the Northern Wei in the mid-sixth century in order for one woman and her court to change the course of history in her time. Based on this study, I would like to argue that adopting a wider feminist periodization that sees this era as a unique period in the social history of women would allow further case studies to be revealed and also to ask the historically pressing question of what happened to women's social and political autonomy *after* the mid-Tang when government again became centralized and dominant social structures like the court and the Buddhist institution became recodified in ways that were androcentric, and, I would argue, patriarchal.

ON THE FAILURE OF GREAT MEN
AND THEIR HISTORIES

I close this book with the same question I started it with: Why is Empress Dowager Ling not better known? Here, though, I flip the question: Why has it taken so much effort for us to know something about her? This book has been filled with an occasionally overwhelming amount of historical detail that I have brought together in order to tell the story of one woman and her world. I have done this research and written this book because I believe that it tells an historically important story that has not been told: the story of the rise of Buddhist women as regents in East Asia's medieval period. Why does no single historical source tell this story in the same way that they so easily tell us about men who ruled? An instructive counterexample here is Emperor Wu of the Liang whom we first met in chapter 1. Although Emperor Wu lived and ruled at the same time as Empress Dowager Ling did, his practices of Buddhist kingship have been well described in the very same historical sources that have remained relatively silent on the topic of Empress Dowager Ling.

The Ru scholars who wrote the official histories in medieval China were serious historians who were tasked with the complicated job of compiling and composing histories that they considered to have veracity but also documented political continuity. In my opinion, these great men failed in some areas. In constructing their own texts through a methodology that prioritized "great men," these medieval scholars failed to create narratives that in any meaningful way described the contributions that women and cultural outsiders made to the development of political institutions in their time. Such a failure has important consequences for the ways in which they also chronicled and characterized other great men in their times. For instance, how much more interesting is it to think about Emperor Wu of the Liang as a ruler whose practice of Buddhist kingship was in conversation and, at the same time, likely competition with the Buddhist ruler to the north of him, Empress Dowager Ling? If we leave her out of the story, his own story becomes less accurate, less meaningful. Even larger than that, if we leave Empress Dowager Ling out of the story of Buddhist kingship in East Asia, then the whole story of the Southern and Northern Dynasties itself loses veracity: The similarities between these two rulers are suggestive of a shared cultural, political, and religious nexus north and south that was not limited by human borders and the military defense of them.

Ru scholars who wrote the histories of medieval dynasties adopted the schema of heaven's ordering and the emperor's arbitration of it as the foundational source of imperial legitimation and continuity in their writing about the past. They wrote their histories within an ideological framework of political order that is andro- and ethnocentric, bureaucratic, and concerned with documenting kingship and kinship. They did so even while they themselves lived within complex social systems that challenged the very ideas that framed their own writing. Empress Dowager Ling is fascinating because she is one such challenge, and it is clear to me that the Ru scholars who wrote about her were largely unequipped to do so within the tradition of dynastic continuity and imperial legitimation that they were familiar with. In writing the life of the empress dowager across the medieval period, such scholars characterized her as a "hen who announced the dawn" and who therefore brought chaos to the world instead of order. They troped her as a licentious usurper and showed little attempt to understand the social worlds in which she lived as a woman from the edges of the empire who came to a central position of power because her family's connections to the Buddhist tradition and because of the opportunities afforded to women within Taghbach gender organization—another topic that the Ru were ill-equipped to document. Instead of engaging with her story in its multivalent historical reality, historiographers who wrote about the empress dowager reiterated the idea that "all under heaven detested her" and that "all under heaven were aghast" at the methods that she used to hold on to power. These same men also compared her to Han Emperor Ling, whose name she shares, thereby associating her with supernormal sources that were fundamentally outside heaven's ordering and therefore prone to chaos and collapse.

I believe that the empress dowager conceived of herself differently. As a ruler who invested herself in symbols and modalities of imperial legitimation from the then classical Han empire, she would have been familiar with the idea of the ruler as arbiter of heaven's mandate. She would have also been aware of the fact that, as a woman who ruled directly over a dynasty founded by ethnic Others from the Han whose political philosophy she was articulating, and as a public Buddhist serving an institution that we might call Confucian, she was ill fit for the job of emperor as it was conventionally understood in her time. She appears to have taken seriously her role as ruler of all "under heaven" just as she reinvented it. Utilizing the Eastern Han's imperial observatory, or numinous platform, she also renovated the space by making it into her own, personally endowed, Buddhist mortuary temple for her deceased father. In so doing, she not only paid homage to her classical inheritance but she also showed herself as an innovator in her time who capitalized on diverse social structures that allowed her to play an integral role in the reinvention of kingship in this period.

The empress dowager cultivated an identity of supernormal efficacy rooted in Buddhism as a part of her strategy of rulership and also, perhaps, because she herself practiced Buddhism. She did so in the cultural context of the non-Han northern dynasties that made space for women to take leadership roles in society. In so doing, the men who criticized her used her invocation of supernormal efficacy, or *ling*, against her and connected her with the much-maligned Han ruler whose name she shares. I would suggest, on the other hand, that the empress dowager's efficacy as a supernormal ruler connected with the Buddhist tradition far outlasted her rule and far outlived the lives of those who failed to write about her in an accurate way. Empress Dowager Ling was a woman at the vanguard of the emergence of Buddhist kingship in the medieval period. Although she was not ultimately successful in her bid to rule her polity independently as a Buddhist monarch with longevity, she nonetheless provided a model for later women who were. That we do not find her story in normative historical and historiographical sources is not her failure; rather, it is the failure of the men who wrote about her and who employed a strategy of "great men" history in their own writing. In writing this present book, I hope not to have merely shown that great women like the empress dowager simply existed; instead, I hope to have argued that we can only tell meaningful and accurate historical stories about them by seeking to overturn the very methodologies that wrote them out of history in the first place.

NOTES

INTRODUCTION

1. *WS* 13.337. The empress dowager's biography in the *Book of the Wei* runs from pages 337 to 340. All translations from her biography are my own; however, I have consulted Holmgren's translation throughout (see Holmgren, "Empress Dowager Ling," 160–70).

2. Xuanwu's biography in the *Book of the Wei* can be found here: *WS* 8.191–92.

3. We know of Sengzhi primarily through her entombed biography, *The Muzhiming of the Wei Superintendent of the Bhikṣuṇīs, the Dharma Master, Shi Sengzhi,* which is published in Zhao and Zhao, *Heluo muke shiling,* 20.

4. Hu Guozhen has a biography in the *Book of the Wei*. See *WS* 92.1833–36.

5. Xiaoming's biography in the *Book of the Wei* can be found here: *WS* 9.221–23.

6. Empress Gao came from the Korean kingdom of Koguryŏ (37–668) and is known both through her biography in the *Book of the Wei* (*WS* 13.336–37) and her entombed biography, *Tomb Memorial of Gao Ying, Empress to Shizong,* which is found in Zhao, *Han Wei Nanbei chao mu zhi hui bian,* 1.12 (transcription), 1.35 (image).

7. For more on this event, see Balkwill, "When Renunciation Is Good Politics," 241–43.

8. In general, I follow Yuri Pines's categorization of the Chinese monarch as a sacrosanct individual both empowered by ritual and sometimes cut off from power by the governmental apparatus, the outline of which is invested in the literature and history of Han peoples (*The Everlasting Empire,* 44–75). The Northern Wei was something of an experiment in monarchy in that the role of the emperor was being redefined and differently legitimated through non-Han cultural practices, just as, under his direct imperial policy, sweeping reforms aimed at adopting Han political culture were enacted. All this happened alongside the formal adoption of Buddhism as the state religion. In keeping with Pines's discussion of the powers of the emperor within the imperial institution, I argue that the presence of female rulers (as well as the popular reaction to them) indicates the changing nature of the

monarch himself/herself in the Northern Wei period and perhaps also that the governing apparatus remained concerned with tempering or augmenting the power of the ruler.

9. Just outside modern-day Luoyang, Mount Mang houses the tombs of royals from many dynasties, the most famous of which might be Northern Wei Emperor Xuanwu, who ruled the dynasty after its move to Luoyang, who was an avid Buddhist, and who took Empress Dowager Ling as his concubine. The empress dowager's body, however, is not interred at Mount Mang, owing to the violent nature of her death and the collapse of government brought about by it.

10. A recent volume has addressed the political profiles of several Northern Wei women although it largely compiles and reiterates information available in dynastic histories without challenging those narratives. For this, see Song, *Beiwei nüzhu lun*, 221–44. Similarly, a new master's thesis provides a summary overview of the empress dowager's Buddhist practice. See Wang, "Beiwei nüzhu he Fojiao—yi Ling taihou Hu shi wei zhongxin." As I indicated above, Jennifer Holmgren has also translated the empress dowager's biography. Her translation provides a critical, political analysis of the empress dowager's situation at court. See Holmgren, "Empress Dowager Ling of the Northern Wei," 123–59.

11. The issue of what to call this language is contested. Some scholars prefer the term *Literary Sinitic* because that term is useful for referring to the written language of many non-Han peoples from across East Asia (from medieval times to the present), peoples who have adopted and adapted parts of the language in their own written scripts. However, because "Chinese" is itself a language, of which these texts provide examples in written classical form, I prefer to use the term *Literary Chinese*. When speaking about the individual characters that form the Chinese script, I prefer to describe them as "Sinitic characters" rather than Chinese ones in recognition of the fact that many polities outside China have used them in their own written languages. When referring to polities that have never been part of China per se but that have used the written form of the language to compose their own documents, I do adopt the term *Literary Sinitic*. In the case of the Northern Wei, since it is clear that they were ambitiously and purposely taking on Han modalities of culture and writing, I use the term *Literary Chinese* so as to not obfuscate the cultural policies of that dynasty.

12. Abramson, *Ethnic Identity in Tang China*, 2.

13. For a study of the forms that *muzhiming* took in their development throughout medieval China, including a discussion of their genre conventions and limitations, see Davis, *Entombed Epigraphy*, 25–32.

14. On the topic of how the impetus to rank and appraise intersects with women's history in the genre of entombed biographies, see Pang, "Eminent Nuns and/or/as Virtuous Women," 77–96. See also the work of Yao Ping referred to in the bibliography.

15. The standard form of epigraphs for elite women of the Northern Wei usually traces a woman's virtue through her male kin, a long-standing tradition that highlights the patrilineal nature of tradition Chinese society. In her work on Han dynasty stele inscriptions, Patricia Ebrey has shown that, in early times, women were not mentioned on the tombs of their husbands at all. See Ebrey, "Later Han Stone Inscriptions," 333.

16. The most up-to-date social analysis of the function of *muzhiming* is found in Jessey Choo's recent monograph, *Inscribing Death*. See, in particular, pages 3–8, where the author discusses the limits of the Ru tradition with respect to the ritual project of social memory.

This discussion sets the course for her own analysis of how *muzhiming* adapt to changing circumstances of death. In the medieval period, one aspect of death culture that is radically new is Buddhism, and Choo expertly shows how Buddhist ideas of memory and belonging became part of a culture of remembrance during this period.

17. See Traill, ed., *The Works of Thomas Carlyle in Thirty Volumes*, 5:29.

18. Morgan, "Theorising Feminist History," 399.

1. LUOYANG REBORN

1. Wang, Cao, and Han, "The Mingtang Site at Pingcheng," 251–57.

2. On the topic of Zoroastrian grave goods in Sogdian tombs of a slightly later date, see Lerner, "Aspects of Assimilation." For an archaeological overview of the types of persons represented in the statuary in Luoyang's Buddhist temple/state palladium, see Zhongguo she hui ke xue yuan kao gu yan jiu suo, *Beiwei Luoyang Yong Ning si*, 57ff.

3. Lourme, *Yang Xuanzhi*, ix.

4. Lourme, *Yang Xuanzhi*, ix.

5. Notation on the empress dowager's pagoda is common in historical sources on the empress dowager and it continues through the medieval period. For a brief but interesting record, see the thirteenth-century Buddhist historiographical compendium, the *Complete Chronicle of the Buddha and the Patriarchs* (*T* no. 2035, 355c10–13).

6. Dien, *Six Dynasties Civilization*, 72.

7. *LYQLJ*: *T* no. 2092, 1000b19–21.

8. *LYQLJ*: *T* no. 2092, 1000a1–14. Trans. McNair, *Donors of Longmen*, 63.

9. Zhongguo she hui ke xue yuan kao gu yan jiu suo, *Beiwei Luoyang Yong Ning si*, 6.

10. *LYQLJ*: *T* no. 2092, 1000a20–21.

11. Tang, *Han, Wei, liang Jin nanbeichao Fojiao shi*, 441. This pagoda is further discussed in Steinhardt, *Chinese Architecture*, 199–202.

12. Zhongguo shehui kexue yuan kaogu yanjiu suo, *Beiwei Luoyang Yong Ning si*, 57ff.

13. *LYQLJ*: *T* no. 2092, 0999a11–16. Translation adapted from Wang, *A Record of Buddhist Monasteries*, 5–6.

14. During a *poṣadha* feast, lay people take vows and the *Prātimokṣa-sūtra* is recited.

15. How to precisely understand the first two of these magic tricks remains unclear. Wang reads the four characters 剝驢投井 in question as one trick described as such: "dismember an ass and throw the cut-up parts into a well, only to have the mutilated animal quickly regenerate its maimed parts" (*Record of Buddhist Monasteries*, 52). However, the *Book of the Sui* provides some potential context. Describing a fête undertaken inside the empress's chambers during the Northern Qi, the *Book of the Sui* recounts that the party had included an array of magical practices all called the "one hundred games" (*Sui shu* 39.15.380). The list makes clear that the skinned donkey in question constitutes a different magical act from that of pulling something out of a well, and yet a further one from the seed and the fruit also mentioned in our text. In chronicling this party, the *Book of the Sui* uses *ba* (拔) as a variant for the *tou* (投) in our text, rendering the trick: "pulling it out a well." Moreover, a Dunhuang text entitled the *Sūtra on the Nature of the Buddha, the Ocean-store of Wisdom and Salvation, and which Shatters the Marks of the Heart* (Foxing haizang zhihui jietuo poxin xiang jing) also uses this variant in its description of the eight kinds of

heterodox acts rejected by the Buddha (*T* no. 2885, 1399a06). What, precisely, such magic tricks entailed is unknown, but it seems clear that they belonged to a popular retinue of magical arts known in the sixth century and, possibly, connected to the parties of women.

16. *LYQLJ*: *T* no. 2092, 1003b08–16. Translation adapted from Wang, *A Record of Buddhist Monasteries*, 51–52.

17. *WS* 22.593

18. This marks preparatory celebrations for Śākyamuni Buddha's birthday.

19. *LYQLJ*: *T* no. 2092, 1002c17–20. Translation adapted from Wang, *A Record of Buddhist Monasteries*, 46.

20. McNair, *Donors of Longmen*, 59.

21. Wong, *Chinese Steles*, 98.

22. Wong, *Chinese Steles*, 98.

23. McNair, *Donors of Longmen*, 31ff.

24. The notions of karma, rebirth, and karmic exchange were features of Buddhism that were the most popular in the medieval period, as they allowed for Buddhist believers to still express their filial piety toward their deceased parents by giving them a way of helping them to achieve a better rebirth after their death. For book-length studies of this issue by two leading scholars in the field, see Bokenkamp, *Ancestors and Anxiety*; Teiser, *The Ghost Festival in Medieval China*.

25. Owing to the fact that these languages did not have a written form, both "Serbi" and "Taghbach" are reconstructions of what may have been the indigenous pronunciation of these ethnonyms.

26. Debate continues over precisely what language the Serbi Taghbach spoke, with some concluding that it likely belonged to the Altaic family. For a good review of this debate, see Tseng, *The Making of the Tuoba Northern Wei*, 11–12. More recently, Andrew Shimunek has conjectured that it is a "proto-Serbi-Mongolic" language related to modern Mongolian because of the common ancestor (*Languages of the Ancient Southern Mongolia and North China*, 13). Finally, Juha Janhunen characterizes the Taghbach language as "para-Mongolic," which is a form of language "collaterally related" to "proto-Mongolic," though spoken by a variety of steppe peoples from diverse ethnic backgrounds (*The Mongolic Languages*, 391, 405–6).

27. Lewis, *China Between Empires*, 1.

28. Jennifer Holmgren has complicated the term *conquest* within the context of labeling certain regimes in China as "conquest dynasties" and has shown how the label works as a delegitimating pejorative in Chinese historiography and how this, in turn, has affected the modern state of scholarship on such polities ("Northern Wei as a Conquest Dynasty," 8–11). She further argues that this was particularly exacerbated by the influence of historical inquiry from the late Qing dynasty (1636–1911) through the early Republican era (1912–49) when anti-foreigner sentiment was high (Holmgren, "Northern Wei as a Conquest Dynasty," 2).

29. Pearce, *Northern Wei*, 300–301.

30. Di Cosmo, "Han Frontiers," 202.

31. Abramson, *Ethnic Identity in Tang China*, 3.

32. On the topic of toponyms and naming, see Nina Duthie "The Nature of the *Hu*," 27. Duthie translates the relevant section from the *Book of the Later Han* and retains the Sinified pronunciation of the term "Serbi," which is "Xianbei."

33. The Serbi were described as identical to another non-Han group called the Wuhuan except that they cut their hair: Wang, *Wei, Jin, nanbeichao shi*, 476.

34. This description is found in "Biographies of the Wuhuan and the Serbi" (Wuhuan xianbei liezhuan): *HHS* 90.2985.

35. This early history of the Taghbach is said to be from the "Annals of Dai." See Jennifer Holmgren, *Annals of Tai*; Nina Duthie, "Origins, Ancestors, and Imperial Authority," 66–100.

36. Charles Holcombe, "The Xianbei in Chinese History," 16.

37. This story is recounted in two places in the *Book of the Wei*. First, it is told in some detail, including the measurements of the Gaxian Cave, in the section of the *Book of the Wei* titled "Biographies of the Wuluohou" (Wuluohou zhuan) (*WS* 100.2224). It is also mentioned again in the "Annals on Ritual" (Lizhi) (*WS* 108.2738).

38. The archaeological remains of the site have recently been surveyed and it appears that rituals may indeed have been undertaken in the grotto. On this, see Liu and Ni, "Gaxian dong yizhi," 53–61.

39. I visited the grotto in summer of 2018 and saw local tourists undertaking ritual circumambulation of, and making offerings to, the remains of the ritual platform that still remain in the cave, which was explicitly identified ancestral home of the Taghbach people in tourist literature at the site.

40. Wang, *Wei, Jin, nanbeichao shi*, 475.

41. This origin story for the Taghbach has undeniable overlap with the origin story of the Khitan, who also came from mountains and who saw their tribe divide into eight subgroups. See Twitchett and Franke, *Cambridge History of China*, 52.

42. Psarras, "Han and Xiongnu," 59–60.

43. Wang, *Wei, Jin, nanbeichao shi*, 477.

44. For a recent and much expanded description and analysis of the development of the Taghbach and their ascension to political power, Scott Pearce's *Northern Wei (386–534): A New Form of Empire in East Asia* provides a detailed reconstruction based on an outstanding variety of primary and secondary source materials.

45. Tseng, *The Making of the Tuoba Northern Wei*, 37–38.

46. For a thorough analysis of how this system worked, including extensive annotation to relevant passages from the *Book of the Wei*, see Lin, *Beiwei Juntian Zhidu Zhi Yanjiu*.

47. For a study of this equal-field system and its impact on later China, see Xiong. "The Land-Tenure System of Tang China," 328–90. Of particular interest for this study is the influence of the cultural background of the Taghbach in the establishment of the system: Hori, *Kindensei no kenkyū*, 96–150. For the possible implementation of the Northern Wei system in Japan, see Wang, *Wei, Jin, nanbeichao shi*, 501.

48. Hori, *Kindensei no kenkyū*, 168–74.

49. Pearce, *Northern Wei*, 283ff.

50. On the cultural reasons behind the move, see Wang, *Wei, Jin, nanbeichao shi*, 506. For economic reasons, see Sun, *Tuobashi de Hanhua ji qita*, 47ff.

51. A complete listing of these names changes is available in *WS* 113.3006–14.

52. For a full monograph study of the policies of the Northern Wei that have been considered "*hanhua*," see Sun, *Tuobashi de Hanhua ji qita*.

53. Holmgren has also analyzed this passage of the *Book of the Wei* from the perspective of the historical movement of the Serbi group. See Holmgren, *Annals of Tai*, 51. My translation differs only slightly from Holmgren's.

54. The Yellow Emperor is one of the early, mythical rulers of China who is supposed to have aided the development of agriculture in China as well as made great strides toward the development of Chinese court structures and language.

55. Changyi is said to have been the youngest son of the Yellow Emperor.

56. *WS* 1.1.

57. Tian, *Tuoba shitan xiudingben*, 210–31.

58. Tian, *Tuoba shitan*, 231.

59. Boodberg, "The Language of the T'o-Pa Wei," 179.

60. The Crown Prince's biography is found at *WS* 32.528–29.

61. *WS*: 114.3035–36. This translation is from Declercq, "Wei Shu, Chapter 114," 80–81. A different version of the translation, which has also been consulted and which includes substantial historical annotation, is available in Hurvitz, "Wei Shou. Treatise on Buddhism and Taoism," 69–70.

62. This era of the elevation of Daoism and the persecution of Buddhism in Northern Wei history will be discussed in chapter 5. The most up-to-date and comprehensive survey of the rise of the Celestial Masters is found in: Kleeman, *Celestial Masters*.

63. Pearce, "A King's Two Bodies," 100–101.

64. In her recent study of the Yungang grottos, Lidu Yi provides a thorough review of scholarship on the topic of the dating of the five Tanyao grottos and ultimately argues for the year 460 CE as the beginning of construction and as late as 489 for completion (*Yungang*, 59–64), which would mean that the initial building was undertaken by Emperor Wencheng and the later building by Empress Dowager Wenming. However, in his review of the book, Scott Pearce reaffirms the fact that the dating for the grottos and the motivations behind their construction remain theoretical, since there is no inscriptional data at the site in question (review of *Yungang*, 111). For an earlier foundational work on the topic, see Soper, "Imperial Grotto-Chapels of the Northern Dynasties," 241–70.

65. The five early grotto shrines, built around 460 CE, are the so-called "Tanyao group," named after the monk who was in charge of the administration of the monastic community in the mid-fifth century. For a review of scholarship on the buddha-ruler identification with the Northern Wei rulers, see Tseng, *Making of the Tuoba Northern Wei*, 53. However, for a foundational work on the topic, see Soper, "Imperial Grotto-Chapels," 241–70. The precise dating of the Tanyao group of caves is contested but is generally agreed to between the early to mid-460s. Caswell argues that the majority of the early building happened between 461 and 467 (*Written and Unwritten*, 20). Mair, however, puts the date slightly later between 465 and 467 (review of *Written and Unwritten*, 349) with the difference being that Emperor Wencheng died in 465. Thus, Mair's later date would place the building of the grottos squarely in the regency reign of Wencheng's empress after his own death.

66. Also commonly known by her family name Feng, Empress Dowager Wenming will be discussed in many places throughout this book. Like Empress Dowager Ling, Empress Dowager Wenming ruled unchallenged, though not independently. She was also a public Buddhist and, further like our empress dowager, may have been of Han ethnicity. Her biography is preserved in the "Biographies of Empresses" section of the *Book of the Wei* (*WS* 13.328–31).

67. Hou, *Fotuo Xiangyou*, 122–24.

68. Watson, *The Lotus Sutra*, 170ff.

69. Wang, *Shaping the Lotus Sutra*, 6–10.

70. The *feng* and *shan* sacrifices are important rituals of imperial legitimation that connect the emperor to heaven and make him sovereign. The rituals were performed as early as the Han dynasty, and we are fortunate to have a record of those rites translated into English (see Bokenkamp, "Record of the *Feng* and *Shan* Sacrifices," 251–60). For an overview of Empress Wu and Emperor Gaozong's performance of the sacrifices, see Rothschild, *Emperor Wu Zhao*, 115–18 and 260n44.

71. Wang, *Shaping the Lotus Sutra*, 141.

72. I am indebted to Gil Raz for bringing this stele to my attention. The transcription of the inscription is available on the CBETA database: *I* no. 1: *Duke of Dangchang stele for Radiant Blessings Monastery* (Dangchang gong huifu si bei). The reference to the "Two Sages" can be found here: no. 1, 3b10–11.

73. Boodberg has shown this chronology to be more mythological than it is historical by exposing how it has been created to match the chronology of Chinese emperors with Taghbach Liwei being the eighty-second emperor after the legendary Emperor Shun ("The Language of the T'o-Pa Wei," 179).

74. In the lineage of Taghbach leaders provided in the preface to the *Book of the Wei*, the fourteen ancestors of the Taghbach are listed with names and titles but no dates. When the list arrives at Taghbach Jiefen we are offered the story about the celestial woman and then, without any explanation, the text begins a dating system at Taghbach Liwei and dates him as the first year. Subsequent leaders are then dated with successive years so that the next leader is dated at "year 29." This invention of history is a salient feature of the *Book of the Wei* in that the text represents the Northern Wei as the fruition of a turning point in history, which includes a shift toward religion, particularly Buddhism.

75. Although he is actually the fifth ancestor, his story signals a pivot in Taghbach history placing him as the first ancestor and he is literally called *shizu*, or the first ancestor.

76. WS 1.2

77. Chen, "State Religious Ceremonies," 108. In this article, the author provides a lengthy and detailed explanation of the rituals that the Northern Wei undertook and shows that they both took Han rituals seriously while bringing their own innovation to the ritual schedule. For specific reference to how the Northern Wei understood these ceremonies, see 67ff.

78. Hinako, *Beiwei Fojiao zaoxiang yanjiu*, 13.

79. Tseng, *The Making of the Tuoba Northern Wei*, 23.

80. All the statistics in this paragraph come from Hou, *Fotuo xiangyou*, 97.

81. Wang, *Qianluo yuanwei*, 41–63.

82. Wang, *Qianluo yuanwei*, 44.

83. Pearce, "The King's Two Bodies," 101–13.

84. All the *Āgama* material, which contains life stories of the Śākyamuni Buddha, was known in China, having been translated into Literary Chinese by the time of the Northern Wei. Also, the famous Indian poem of the life of the Śākyamuni Buddha, depicting popular scenes of his birth and royal upbringing, the *Buddhacarita* (Fo suoxing zan), had been translated into Chinese by the end of the fourth century. This translation is attributed to the well-known, magic-wielding translator at the court of the Northern Liang,

Dharmakṣema, or Tan Wuchen though there is cause to doubt this attribution. In a similar vein, another Indian life of the Śākyamuni Buddha, the *Lalitavistara* (Puyaojing) was translated into Chinese in the early fourth century. The translator was Dharmarakṣa, or Zhu Fahu (d. 316). As for art, in Yungang Cave 41 there is a depiction of Asita making his prophecy over the young Siddhartha Gautama who would live to choose the religious life over the courtly one and become Śākyamuni Buddha. We can find further corroborating evidence for this at Maiji shan. Although this site was on the fringes of the Northern Wei territory, a few Northern Wei works remain there intact. One such eminent example of the Śākyamuni Buddha's life story depicted in imagery is seen on a Northern Wei stele at the site (see Chen, "Maiji shan 133 Ku," 75–105). In one panel of the stele, the Indian king, Aśoka, known as a cakravartin for his promotion of Buddhism, is depicted as a past life incarnation of Aśoka and is a child, giving a gift of dirt to Śākyamuni Buddha.

85. For a definition and characteristics of what I call Buddhist statecraft, see Balkwill and Benn, "Introduction," 3–15.

86. There are two different versions of this text. One is attributed to the famous Tang dynasty translator and esoteric master, Amoghavajra (Bukong, 705–74). His version is titled the *Prajñāpāramitā Scripture for Humane Kings to Protect Their States* (Renwang huguo bore boluomiduo jing). The earlier text, on which the Tang text is based, is of unknown authorship and is titled *Prajñāpāramitā Scripture for Humane Kings, Spoken by the Buddha* (Foshuo renwang bore boluomi jing).

87. Orzech, *Politics and Transcendent Wisdom*, 63, 121.

88. Orzech, "Metaphor, Translation, and the Construction of Kingship," 63.

89. These observations are drawn from Miyake's ongoing Asian philology blog: Miyake, "'Buddha Khan in Korea and Japan."

90. Lee, "The Life of Women in the Six Dynasties," 53. Here, Lee cites the introduction to the "Biographies of Eminent Women" in the *Book of the Wei* (WS 92.1978).

91. Lee, "The Life of Women in the Six Dynasties," 53; citing: WS 67.1492.

92. Here, the *Book of the Wei* is citing from the *Analects* (Lunyu. Shuer 6).

93. WS 67.1492.

94. Personal Communication. Jan. 18, 2021.

95. *HHS* 90.2979

96. *HHS* 90.2979.

97. For more on this, see Ishimatsu, *Beiwei Fojiao zaoxiang yanjiu*, 14.

98. These rituals are arguably from the north Asia steppe tradition. See Kang, *Cong xijiao dao nanjia*, 167–69; Tseng, "The Making of the Tuoba Northern Wei," 24.

99. WS 108.2736.

100. WS 10.2736–37.

101. This is a famous passage cited in much of the secondary literature. The translation adopted here is from Tian and Kroll, *Family Instructions for the Yan Clan*, 45.

102. *Nan Qi shu* 57.986

103. Pearce, "Nurses, Nurslings" 298.

104. Pearce, *Northern Wei*, 79. These references to the "women's country" in primary source texts also come from Pearce's study: WS 1.10; ZZTJ 91.2891; BS 13.491

105. The origins of this practice are hotly contested, but I agree with Scott Pearce and Tian Yuqing who argue that the practice is not necessarily a long-standing Taghbach

practice, but instead one instituted by Emperor Daowu with respect to his situation of declaring an heir, and that later Taghbach rulers use this practice to legitimate their own rules for a variety of reasons. For more on this, see Scott Pearce, "Nurses, Nurslings," 290; Tian, *Tuoba shitan*, 1–49. For an overview of the differing opinions on the origins of this practice among the Taghbach, see Golavachev, "Matricide among the Tuoba-Xianbei," 1–42. See also Pearce's response to Golavachev: Pearce, "A Response," 139–44.

106. Cheng, "Hanzhi yu hufeng," 35.

107. Cheng, "Hanzhi yu hufeng," 15ff. Scott Pearce, "Nurses, Nurslings," 291ff.

108. Pearce, "Nurses, Nurslings," 309.

109. Zürcher, "Buddhism in a Pre-Modern Bureaucratic Empire," 406.

110. Although Buddhist mythologies of Aśoka stress his identity as a Buddhist, non-Buddhist sources suggest that he was an ecumenical ruler who tolerated a number of religions without personally ascribing to any. On the differences between the Aśoka of history and the Aśoka of mythology, see Strong, *The Legend of King Aśoka*, esp. chapter 1.

111. A survey of the transmission of Buddhist textual material on the life and mythology of Aśoka is available in: Loukota Sanclemente, "The Goods That Cannot Be Stolen," 85–90. Loukota shows that differing textual traditions were seen in China as early as the fourth century and he also explores their Indic sources. For art historical evidence of the Aśokan story in early medieval China, at Yungang, see Yi, *Yungang*, 152–53.

112. Zürcher, "Buddhism in a Pre-Modern Bureaucratic Empire," 406.

113. For a detailed study of Wu Zetian's political usage of relics, see Chen, "Śarīra and Scepter," 33–150.

114. Janousch, "The Aśoka of China," 255–95.

115. For an overview of these assemblies, see De Rauw, "The Political Use of Buddhism," 127–29.

116. Chittick, *The Jiankang Empire*, 304.

117. WS 98.2187. See also Chittick, *The Jiankang Empire*, 296.

118. Faure, "Les Cloches de La Terre," 34–35.

119. Chen, "Śarīra and Scepter," 54.

120. Chen, "Śarīra and Scepter," 49.

121. Chittick, *The Jiankang Empire*, chapter 10, esp. pages 274–82.

122. Chittick, *The Jiankang Empire*, 292.

123. The story of Aśoka's gift of dirt to the buddha runs from *T* no. 202: 368c05–369a19.

124. Victor Mair has translated Seng You's introduction to the text and has also studied the complicated origins of the text and possible textual precedents of the text. See "Linguistic and Textual Antecedents," 1–95.

125. WS 114.3028.

126. *LYQLJ: T* no. 2092, 1020b11–14.

127. *LYQLJ: T* no. 2092, 1020a09–1020a10.

128. *LYQLJ: T* no. 2092, 1020a16–1020a17.

129. *LYQLJ: T* no. 2092, 1021a25–1021c12.

130. Zhou, "Beiwei ling tai hou," 26.

131. Amy McNair argues that the empress dowager was the patron of Longmen's Huoshao grotto, the only Northern Wei grotto to exceed the size of Emperor Xuanwu's and is also the highest of the Northern Wei grottos at the site. See *Donors of Longmen*, 65.

132. Carriere, *Silla Korea and the Silk Roads*, 94. For an expanded discussion of this, see McBride, "King Chinhŭng," 58.

133. *LYQLJ: T* no. 2092, p1000b16.

134. My translation of this title supplies an additional interpretation. Wang translates the title of the nunnery as that of "The Chief of the Hu Clan" (see *A Record of Buddhist Monasteries*, 21). This translation makes the dedication ambiguous because who, exactly, is the chief of the clan? Given that this was a nunnery for the most studious and serious nuns in Luoyang, I believe that here the word *tong* in the title designates not the "chief" of the clan but is instead an abbreviation for the title that Sengzhi held, "Superintendent of the Nuns" (*biqiuni tong*). This will be discussed further in chapter 3.

135. *LYQLJ: T* no. 2092, 1010c19–21.

136. *T* no. 2035, 315a5.

137. Chittick, *The Jiankang Empire*, 305.

138. On the use of the *Sūtra* by the Chen dynasty rulers, see Chittick, *The Jiankang Empire*, 319. For the use of the *Sūtra* in later East Asia, see McBride, "King Chinhŭng," 50–58; Bryson, "Images of Humane Kings," 87–118.

139. McBride, "King Chinhŭng," 50.

2. A WOMAN OF POWER, REMEMBERED POORLY

1. Although I refer to Holmgren's translation throughout, the new translation of the biography of the empress dowager offered here is different. Using both secular and Buddhist sources, and making inferences regarding the practice of Buddhism at the empress dowager's court, this translation and study reveals how the empress dowager's rise and rule was intimately connected with and supported by the practice of Buddhism as it was then known to her and her society.

2. Scholars of medieval Chinese Buddhism have paid limited attention to the empress dowager's patronage. For example, she is briefly discussed in both Tang Yongtong's authoritative history of early medieval Buddhism (*Han, Wei, liang Jin*, 441–49) and Tsukamoto Zenryū's foundational study (*Shina Bukkyō shi*, see p. 226 for a description of her patronage in Luoyang; pp. 402–4 for Longmen; p. 492 for Buddhist activities during her regency; p. 554 on sending monks to the Western Regions). In more recent studies, both Xia ("Beichao huanghou yu Fojiao," 65–73) and Chen (*Xingbie, xinkou, quanli*, 109–42) discuss the wide popularity of Buddhism among Northern Wei empresses, in general, but they do not offer an explanation of why these women found Buddhism so compelling. The most interesting study of recent years is a short but noteworthy article that deals with how the empress dowager established herself as a cakravartin. See Zhou, "Beiwei Ling tai hou."

3. Ko, Haboush, and Piggott, *Women and Confucian Cultures*, 5.

4. Tung, *Fables for the Patriarchs*, 51.

5. Ko, Haboush, and Piggott, *Women and Confucian Cultures*, 2.

6. Li, "*Weishu yuanliu kao*," 371.

7. Lingley, "Lady Yuchi in the First Person," 25.

8. Lingjing is in modern-day Zhenyuan county in Gansu province. Not far from modern day Xi'an, Anding was an administrative unit in Liangzhou, which was the region of

present-day Ningxia and Gansu. See Declercq, *Writing Against the State*, 161. Liangzhou was an important center for the development of Buddhism in early medieval China.

9. Holmgren, "Empress Dowager Ling," 156.

10. *WS* 83.1833–36.

11. Holmgren has sketched out a useful diagram of this intermarriage through the Northern Qi ("Empress Dowager Ling," 126). For the Tang, we can point to epitaphs of the Hu clan from Tang dynasty courtiers. See Yang and Du, "*Luoyang chutu*," 54–61.

12. The official biography for Huangfu Song is found in *HHS* 101.61. The official biography for Huangfu Mi is found in *Jin shu* 51.21. Declercq provides an informative overview of the Anding Huangfus in his study of Huangfu Mi (*Writing Against the State*, 159–205, in particular 161–70).

13. Wang, *Longdong beichao Fojiao yanjiu*.

14. Bingzhou was an administrative prefecture that occupied almost the entirety of modern Shanxi and had its center in Taiyuan district.

15. Qi province is in modern day Shanxi, in the Fenhe River valley.

16. *WS* 112.2915–16.

17. The Chinese here reads, *chenghua shifu*, which seems to be a general term for a woman appointed as an official lady of the court during the time period. Hucker is unclear as to the meaning of *Cheng-hua* (Hucker, *Dictionary of Official Titles*, s.v. "cheng-hua"); however, the *Hanyu da cidian* takes it to be simply an indication of the imperium. As to *shifu*, Hucker consistently takes this as "hereditary consort," which makes sense here as a general term. As we will see later in the biography, the empress is soon given more specific titles as her prominence at court grows.

18. *WS* 114.3042.

19. For an in-depth analysis of the establishment and renovation of the roles and titles in the inner court throughout the Northern Wei, see Miao, *Beiwei houguan zhidu yanjiu*.

20. For a study of the lives of court women viz-a-viz their relationship with the Jade Radiance nunnery, see Balkwill, "When Renunciation is Good Politics."

21. Lit. "Pepper Chamber" (*jiaofang*). According to Hucker, this is an indirect reference to the wife of the emperor, one of which, as legend goes, was delighted by pepper-wood paneling in her bed chamber (*Dictionary of Official Titles in Imperial China*, s.v. "jiaofang").

22. According to Hucker, this is the official title of a second rank court concubine, also of the group of nine concubines (*Dictionary of Official Titles in Imperial China*, s.v. "chonghua").

23. "Quite advanced" in age, here, means that he was twenty-seven years old and had failed to father an heir to the throne. He died aged thirty-two.

24. Pu, "*Ziguimusi de xiemu*," 33.

25. Ch. *furen yu jun jiaoxian zhi yi*. Empress Dowager Hexi's biography gives us insight into what this means. It tells us that she took responsibility for rituals of the court by undertaking them together with the child emperor, and that this was referred to as "mutual offering" (*jiaoxian*) in bringing together protocols for court women with those of the emperor (*HHS* 10.425). The *Classic of Rites* (Liji) also provides an early description of what this ritual looked like, labels it explicitly as a ritual of the "lord and his wife" (*jun yu furen*), and details extensive animal blood sacrifices that were integral to the ritual (Liji. Liyun. 8).

26. The origins of the *Rites of Zhou* are debated, though in modern scholarship it is most often said to be a text from the Warring States (476–221 BCE). The text chronicles political bureaucracy and defines the roles of state servants and bureaucrats from antiquity.

27. The "three dukes" (*sangong*) refers to the three top administrative aids of the emperor. Though their precise titles have changed throughout imperial history, they have been a mainstay of the court since classical antiquity. According to Hucker, they were of the highest rank during the Northern Wei (*Dictionary of Official Titles in Imperial China*, s.v. "sangong"). The fact that, here, Empress Dowager Ling overtakes their lead indicates that she has completely taken over the rule of her son and was the de facto ruling monarch of her time.

28. According to the *Comprehensive Mirror for Aid in Government* (*Zizhi tongjian*), the southern sacrifices were performed in 516 CE, the year in which Suzong took the throne as a six-year-old child (*ZZTJ* 148.70). Presumably, then, they were done by the empress dowager.

29. Empress Dowager Hexi's biography is found in: *HHS* 10.418–30.

30. McNair, *Donors of Longmen*, 66.

31. This cart appears to be a formal name of a particular type of cart that Emperor Xuanwu also used. Here, she has her own built so that she can gather disputes just as he did. For Xuanwu's use of the cart, see, for example, *WS* 8.212–14.

32. *WS* 108.2812.

33. I owe this insight to Scott Pearce who, in private conversation, pointed out to me that "in accord with their differences" (*geyoucha*) is a phrase attested to in many places in the *Book of the Wei* and often refers to the division of plundered wealth and goods gained from military conquest. Pearce also finds it noteworthy that the empress dowager was taking on this role with all her new wealth.

34. Andrew Chittick has written on similar practices in the military garrisons of the Jiankang regimes in the south. See *Patronage and Community in Medieval China*, 7–10. As for later and similar practices among the Mongol empires, see de Raschewiltz, *The Secret History of the Mongols*, 1.76.

35. The "winding streams" (*qushui*) party is part of a purification festival held on the third day of the third month in the Chinese lunisolar calendar (*Hanyu da cidian*, s.v.). Popularized by the fourth-century poet and calligrapher, Wang Xizhi (303–61). As described in his *Preface to the Orchid Pavilion*, the party involved "floating wine cups down a floating stream, composing verses, and contemplating nature and the cosmos" (Schwartz, "Revisiting the Scene of the Party," 277). The first of these celebrations, which was hosted by Wang Xizhi, took place in 353 and became an integral part of the festival throughout East Asian history, and is often depicted in painting. Here, Empress Dowager Ling is playing the role of Wang Xizhi, and, in so doing, displaying her Han-affiliated cultural awareness and fluency.

36. Although traditionally attributed to Confucius, as part of the "Ten Wings" Commentary, the "Elegant Words" are retained only in discussion of the first two of the trigrams and prove to be much older than the rest of the "Ten Wings."

37. Liu Ts'un-Yan argues that the passage "transformation of light" reveals that the empress dowager practiced the Zoroastrian religion because it suggests the worship of fire (*Selected Papers*, 16). However, I disagree with this interpretation as there is nothing more by way of corroborating evidence to suggest that the empress dowager practiced Zoroastrianism. Although this is not the place to thoroughly explore the possibility of

Zoroastrian practice in the Northern Wei, a summary statement is warranted: Zoroastrian practices may have been part of the cultural milieu of Northern China in the empress dowager's day and verifiably Zoroastrian tomb elements have emerged from Sogdian tombs in China of a slightly later date (Lerner, "Aspects of Assimilation," 18); however, Northern Wei sources provide no reason to conclude that either the religion or the god of the Taghbach house or the empress dowager was Zoroastrian.

38. Legge, *The I Ching*, 418–19.

39. Slingerland, *Confucius*, 44.

40. *Zhuangzi. Neipian. Dazong shi* 5.

41. I have chosen to translate the Chinese text here (*Hu tianshen*) as "Inner Asian sky god" because, although *hu* is often translated as "barbarian" or "foreigner," it more specifically references non-Han people from various regions across Inner Asia, more specifically those peoples who commonly rode on horseback. Furthermore, the "sky god" or *Tengri* is common across the religious traditions of ancient Altaic cultures that hail from the Western regions. My translation provides an alternative to what is found in the authoritative *Grand Dictionary of the Chinese Language*, which defines the *Hu tianshen* as a god of the Zoroastrian religion; however, the attestation it gives for its translation is the very text we are reading, the empress dowager's biography. Again, I find the theory that the empress dowager was Zoroastrian untenable. There is no specific mention of fire worship in any place in the *Book of the Wei*. There is, though, a mention of the worship of a god of heaven, both in the case of our text's mention of the *Hu Tianshen* and in a number of other discussions, including that of a shamanic ritual practice engaged in by the emperor and a shamaness in the early years of the dynasty, a practice whereby the deity presiding over the ritual is also a *tianshen* (*WS* 13.2735–37). This ritual does not include fire worship and there is therefore no reason to conclude that it is Zoroastrian. This reference to the *Hu Tianshen* is the second of the three events in the life of the empress dowager that Liu Ts'un-yan takes as further proof of her practice of Zoroastrianism, but again, though the suggestion is compelling, I find it unconvincing. By contrast, my translation of "Inner Asian sky god" suggests that the empress dowager is forbidding sacrifices but allowing the Taghbach their god. Such religious accommodation makes sense in the context of the society and politics of her time, whereas a religious accommodation for Zoroastrianism does not.

42. This portion of the text is not found in the *History of the Northern Dynasties* version of the biography, but only in the *Book of the Wei*. The reasons why are discussed in chapter 4.

43. A recent study of mortuary biographies of these two half-brothers briefly discusses the nature of their disagreements and the court factions that separated them (see Su, "*Yuan Yi, Yuan Cha muzhi*," 111–15).

44. Although Yuan Cha does not have a biography in the *Book of the Wei*, his entombed biography has been excavated and is available in a critical edition (Zhao, *Han, Wei, nanbeichao muzhi huibian*, 181–83). A more distant relative of the imperial clan, Yuan Cha came to hold one of the highest levels of office during the reign of the empress dowager, perhaps because he was married to her sister. Cha managed to take hold of Xiaoming under the pretense that the empress dowager's lover, Yuan Yi, was plotting to overthrow him.

45. According to Hucker, the office of the domestic service was a eunuch-staffed office (*Dictionary of Official Titles*, s.v. "changqiu si"), and it seems that Liu Teng was the head of the office, and so, a eunuch. His biography is available in *WS* 94.2027–29

46. The title of *doutong* is similar to *weina* in that it designates a court-*saṃgha* bureaucratic appointment. According to the biography of Hu Guozhen, the empress dowager's father, Sengjing was also his son, making Sengjing the brother of the empress dowager (*WS* 83.1836).

47. According to Hucker, this position was specifically demarcated for the guard of an heir apparent (*Dictionary of Official Titles*, s.v. "beishen zuoyou").

48. Holmgren, "Empress Dowager Ling," 138–45.

49. The inscription is held at the Luoyang Ancient Art Museum. My translation is based on a publication of the image of the rubbing: *Inscription for the Refurbishment of an Old Stūpa by the Prince of Runan (Runan wang xiuzhi guta ming)* (Tan, *Zhongguo gudai beizhi*).

50. *LYQLJ: T* no. 2092, 1010c21–1011a02.

51. McNair, *Donors of Longmen*, 72–73.

52. A recent overview of the site has substantially documented the art and epigraphy seen there and made further research possible. The inscriptions that I cite in the paragraph are all found in that study. See Wang and Tsai, eds., *Shandong Province*, 11–26, 155–201.

53. These were high-ranking officials at court in charge of receiving tribute.

54. This is the same rank that the empress dowager herself once held. For more information, see note 22 above.

55. *ZZTJ* 152.19. A similar memorial was first recorded in Erzhu Rong's biography in the *Book of the Wei* (*WS* 74.1643–44).

56. Zhang, *Beiwei Zhengzhi Shi*, 9. 425.

57. The *Book of the Wei* version of the biography does not specify the name given. The *History of the Northern Dynasties*, however, specifies that it was "Ling" (*BS* 13.505).

58. *ZZTJ* 152.24.

59. *BS* 48.1754.

60. This is according to the thirteenth-century *Complete Chronicle of the Buddha and the Patriarchs* (*T* no. 2035, 356a02).

61. Translation from Wang, *A Record of Buddhist Monasteries*, 49.

62. Private correspondence with Li Lan, formerly of the Longmen Research Academy.

63. *WS* 13.340.

64. *ZZTJ* 152.25.

65. Jennifer Holmgren, "Empress Dowager Ling," 124–38.

66. Keith, "Women Rulers in Imperial China," 186.

67. *Shang shu*. Zhou shu. Mu shi. 2

68. McMahon, "Women Rulers in Imperial China," 186, translating from the *Records of the Three Kingdoms*, or *Sanguo zhi*.

69. McMahon, "Women Rulers in Imperial China," 186, translating from the *Hanfeizi*.

70. Farmer, "Jia Nanfeng," 303.

71. This collection was composed in the Western Han (206 BCE–24 CE) by the scholar Liu Xiang (79 BCE–8 CE) to act as a moral textbook for instructing young women in models of womanly virtue. As such, it is a valuable document revealing gendered notions of virtuous behavior from the annals of early China. The text is available in English translation: Kinney, *Exemplary Women of Early China*.

72. Kinney, *Exemplary Women of Early China*, 135–56.

73. Farmer, "Jia Nanfeng," 302–3.

74. *WS* 22.591–92.

75. Both Zheng Qiao's (1104–62) *Comprehensive Records* (*Tongzhi*) as well as the volu-minous *Prime Tortoise of the Record Bureau* (*Cefu Yuangui*) include numerous derivative references to her across a number of sections and topics.

76. This section is taken from the biography of the Prince of Rencheng (Rencheng Wang), which begins with Taghbach Yun (446–81), who held the title, and ends with his grandson, Taghbach Cheng (467–519), who also held the title. Taghbach Cheng made many memorials to the court of Empress Dowager Ling and, it seems, they were often at odds with each other, as the section on her improper mourning suggests (*WS* 19.483). These memorials will be discussed in chapter 6.

77. Wei Shou has a biography in the *Book of the Northern Qi* (*Bei Qi shu* 37.483–95)

78. *Bei Qi shu* 37.483.

79. By studying the genealogies of the Gao clan in the *Book of the Wei* and the *Book of the Northern Qi*, Jennifer Holmgren classifies the Gao clan as belonging to the cultur-ally hybrid society of the north where, although they may have had partial Taghbach or other ancestry, they were probably more culturally similar to Han people, from whom they also had descendants. Holmgren also points out that in the charged racial atmosphere at the end of the dynasty, it was likely that Gao Huan and his descendants were pressured to declare their allegiance to the Xianbei and the Taghbach ruling house (Holmgren, "Family, Marriage and Political Power in Sixth Century China: A Study of the Kao Family of the Northern Ch'i, c. 520–550," 11).

80. *Bei Qi shu* 1.3.

81. Klein, "Wei Shu," 368. This argument about the "foul" and biased nature of the *Book of the Wei* is further corroborated here. See Chaussande, "Être historien dans la Chine Classique," 241–54.

82. *ZZTJ* 152.25.

3. BROUGHT TO COURT BY A NUN

1. McNair, "Ways of Reading and Writing," 186–205, esp. 189.

2. For the identification of this image and a description of the grotto, see Gu, "*Huangfu gong*," 84–91.

3. *Bhikṣuṇī* (Ch. *biqiuni*) is the Sanskrit term used to denote an ordained Buddhist nun. I have not used the term throughout this book to discuss the lives of Buddhist women for the simple fact that the ordination status of many of these women cannot be verified, as we will see below. Thus, because of the many problems with the understanding of ordination, I have chosen simply to call these women "nuns" and to examine their potential status within the community on a case-by-case basis, though this convention has the drawback of not capturing the cultural allure and mystique of the Sanskrit word transliterated into Chinese and used that way in Chinese sources.

4. Schopen, "On Emptying Chamber Pots," 248.

5. The *Cullavagga* of the Pali Vinaya records the story of the ordination of the first Buddhist nun, Mahāpajāpatī, the Buddha's aunt, in which the Buddha initially refuses to allow women into the community, and, when convinced to do so, creates the eight additional "heavy" rules for nuns. For a recent study of the possibilities and legalities

involved in the ordination of Buddhist nuns in the Theravada tradition, see Anālayo, "Women's Renunciation in Early Buddhism," 65–98.

6. Wang, ed. *Images of Women*, xii.

7. *Yili* 30.359.1.

8. Beverly Foulks-McGuire has discussed the prevalence of games of this type in East Asia. See "Playing with Karma," 4–28. The games that she discusses are not specific to women as some of them take the becoming of a buddha or the gaining of official titles as their goal.

9. Kinney, *Exemplary Women*, 19–20.

10. Translation from Lewis, "Writing the World," 34–35.

11. Lewis, "Mothers and Sons in Early Imperial China," 246.

12. This is from Kinney's translation of the title of the last chapter of the main body of the text, which is instructively contrasted with the names of the other chapters, "The Maternal Models," "The Worthy and Enlightened," "The Sympathetic and Wise," "The Chaste and Compliant," The Principled and Righteous," and "The Accomplished Rhetoricians."

13. Raphals, *Sharing the Light*, 1–4.

14. Ko, Haboush, and Piggott, *Women and Confucian Cultures*, 2.

15. There were eminent women in Daoist traditions prior to the Tang, when Daoist renunciation for women became common place; however, they were married women. For example, the woman/deity responsible for the Shangqing revelations, Wei Huacun (252–334), was a wife and mother. See Despeux and Kohn, *Women in Daoism*, 17.

16. For more on the roles of women in the Celestial Masters, see Despeux and Kohn, *Women and Daoism*, 10–13.

17. This is also true of Huangfu Mi's *Biographies of Eminent Gentlemen* (Gaoshi zhuan), a formative pre-Buddhist collection of biographies of Chinese men, which includes men living a hermetic life. This is in contrast to the *Biographies of Exemplary Women*, which does not include such eremitic tales for the lives of women. As discussed previously, Empress Dowager Ling is herself a descendant of Huangfu Mi.

18. Campany, *Making Transcendents*, 197–98.

19. *Baopuzi neipian*: 11. 207. Campany also discusses Ge Hong's Hairy Woman and shows that there are at least two biographies of her in early materials, one that suggests that she became a transcendent and one that suggests she did not (Campany, *Making Transcendents*, 23n15). Despite the version, however, this is the one clear example from the indigenous Chinese textual tradition of a woman who achieves a high level of religious transformation completely independent of any male kin, as she was abandoned as a child and raised in the wilderness.

20. Sailey, *Master Who Embraces Simplicity*, 143.

21. An overview of the idea of the Buddhist temples as a semipublic leisure is offered in Lewis, *China Between Empires*, 102–13.

22. Loukota Sanclemente, "Finding the Missing Nuns of Nuava."

23. Although the text says of itself that it was written by the monk Shi Baochang in the sixth century, this claim is suspicious since the text does not appear in Buddhist catalogs until the Song. Using these very catalogs, Tom DeRauw has raised a convincing case for doubting the attribution of the text to Baochang and concludes that we have no certainty who wrote the text, though it was likely written later than Baochang. See "Baochang," 203–18.

24. Hinsch, "Confucian Filial Piety," 49–75.

25. Hinsch, "Confucian Filial Piety," 54ff.

26. Hinsch, "Confucian Filial Piety," 55.

27. Tsai, *Lives of the Nuns*, 20. For a brief but informative study of the use of filial piety to justify one's practice of Buddhism, as seen in the early medieval period, see Wright, "Biography of the Nun An-Ling-Shou," 193–96.

28. In fact, such standards are still an issue in the lives of Buddhist women. In numerous places in the modern Buddhist world, such necessary communities for the further ordination of women have either died out or were never established, and women today are looking for a means of establishing legal ordination. An entire edited volume delas with this issue of women's ordination in various traditions. See Mohr and Tsedroen, *Dignity and Discipline*.

29. This struggle for ordination rights is detailed in Heirman, "Chinese Nuns and Their Ordination," 275–304. The story of this full ordination is found in the *Lives of the Nuns* in the biography of the nun Huiguo (364–433), who was a leading pioneer in the struggle (*T* no. 2063, 937b18–c7).

30. *T* no. 2059, 341a28–b9.

31. Heirman, "Buddhist Nuns: Between Past and Present," 605.

32. Chikusa, "Formation and Growth," 11–13.

33. Tsai, *Lives of the Nuns*, 21. This is biography of Zhixian (300–370 CE), who was stabbed more than twenty times for successfully resisting rape by the prefect Du Ba (*T* no. 2063, 935a26–b13).

34. Tsai, *Lives of the Nuns*, 27. This is the biography of Sengji (330–97 CE), who did not take food or drink once she had been betrothed, only relenting once her family allowed her to become a nun (*T* no. 2063, 936a13–26).

35. Tsai, *Lives of the Nuns*, 23. This is the biography of Miaoxiang (fourth century CE) who, by joining the community of nuns, divorced her husband because he did not undertake proper funerary rites after the death of his parents (*T* no. 2063, 935b14–28).

36. Lo, "Conversion to Chastity," 22–56.

37. Huan Wen's biography is in the *Book of the Jin* (*Jin shu* 98. 2568–83) and records that although he planned to overthrow the Jin he was not able to see that plan to completion, dying too early. However, his son Huan Xuan (369–404) succeeded where he left off, briefly usurping the Jin in the year 403 (*Jin shu* 99. 2585–2603).

38. Translation from Zhang, *Buddhism and Tales of the Supernatural*, 160–61.

39. Many of the biographies in the *Biographies of Exemplary Women* contain stories of women acting as political counselors. Those stories have been summarized and analyzed in Raphals, *Sharing the Light*, 27–60.

40. Although this text has been attributed to Tao Qian (365–427), that attribution has been seriously questioned (Zhang, *Buddhism and Tales of the Supernatural*, 76).

41. Zhang, *Buddhism and Tales of the Supernatural*, 161–62.

42. For a recent translation of the story of Subha, see Hallisey, *Therigatha*, 183–95. For Wilson's work on disgust as it relates to the female body, see Wilson, *Charming Cadavers*.

43. I have long been interested in the life and activities of Shi Sengzhi. Her story provides so many rare and important pieces of information on the lives and freedoms of Buddhist nuns in early medieval China. As such, I have published another article about her that contains many overlapping arguments with my discussion of her in this chapter. The article

also contains a fully annotated, complete translation of her entombed mortuary biography. The reader can find that article in the bibliography under Balkwill, "A Virtuoso Nun." Throughout this chapter, I also include translated sections of the bibliography, and when I do, I cross-reference them with the other publication. Similarly, when I engage with similar ideas and arguments in this chapter to the ones in the article, I also cross-reference.

44. On the Northern Wei forms, see Davis, *Entombed Epigraphy*, 290–306.

45. Other than those of Sengzhi and Gao Ying cited above, the other two are: (1) *The Entombed Biography of the Northern Wei Bhikṣuṇī Ciqing [Wang Zhong'er]*, dated the seventh day of the fifth month of the fifth year of the Reign of Gleaming Orthodoxy [June 23, 524 CE] (Wei gu biqiuni Ciqing (Wang Zhong'er) muzhiming [zhengguang wunian wuyue qiri]) (*Transcription: ZC* 146; *Image: ZW* 2.288); *Preface and Entombed Biography of the Bhikṣuṇī of the Yuan family from the Great Awakening Nunnery* (Wei gu cheji dajiang jun pingshu wending xing gong ji furen dajuesi biqiuyuanni muzhiming bingxu) (*Transcription: ZC* 261; *Image: B* 5.126).

46. Pang, "Eminent Nuns," 78.

47. Tsai, *Lives of the Nuns*, 81–83. *T* no. 2063, 943c25–944b5. Among the other stories about her political avoidance, this fascinating biography also tells us that Huixu looked and behaved like a man (944a1).

48. Wendi Adamek, *Practicescapes and the Buddhists of Baoshan*, see esp. chapter 7 for a discussion of women and their texts.

49. Chikusa, "Formation and Growth," 8.

50. Balkwill, "A Virtuoso Nun," 136–37.

51. The *Book of the Wei* records that Empress Dowager Ling lived in the Palace of Venerating the Teachings (*WS* 31.743). For more on this, see Balkwill, "A Virtuoso Nun," 136n17.

52. The "three capabilities" (*sancai*) are normally given as heaven, earth, and man. That Sengzhi is endowed with them suggests that she is of impeachable virtue (Balkwill, "A Virtuoso Nun," 136n18).

53. The term "seven governances" or *qizheng* is unstable throughout classical sources. The *Annals of the Historian*, for example, connects the seven governances to the stars of the Big Dipper (*Shiji. Tianshu guan.* 3), whereas the Great Commentary to the Shangshu names them as the four seasons along with heaven, earth, and man (*Shangshu dazhuan* 1.28). In any case, the usage is the same as in the "three capabilities" above in that the ascription of them to Sengzhi is for the purpose of showing the nun's universal virtue.

54. These are the powers that a highly advanced being on the path to buddhahood has attained through their practice and includes such capabilities as a divine eye.

55. The *Nirvāṇa-sūtra* (Da banniepan jing).

56. The *Lotus Sūtra* (Miaofa lianhua jing).

57. The *Lion's Roar Sūtra of Queen Śrīmālā* (Shengman shizi hou yisheng da fangbian fangguang jing).

58. For the biography of Empress Gao, see *WS* 13.336–37. For a study of this story, see Balkwill, "When Renunciation is Good Politics," 240–46. For a study of her entombed biography, see Pu, "Zigui musi de xiemu," 25–33.

59. For my more complete discussion of this story, see Balkwill, "When Renunciation is Good Politics," 250–55.

60. For a full philological explanation and interpretation of this name, see Balkwill, "A Virtuoso Nun," 147–48.

61. Yi, *Yungang*, 114–26.

62. *I* 01n0032, 82b05–6.

63. It is recorded that the text was preached to audiences of over a thousand people during the Liu-Song. On this, see Wayman and Wayman, *The Lion's Roar of Queen Śrīmālā*, 12.

64. For an expansion of this same argument, see Balkwill, "A Virtuoso Nun," 149–50.

65. McBride, "King Chinhŭng," 52.

66. Tsukamoto, "The Śramana Superintendent," 371.

67. Hurvitz, "Wei Shou," 53.

68. A complete study of this monk, his title, and his duties is found in Tsukamoto, "The Śramana Superintendent T'an-Yao," 363–96.

69. *WS* 114.3037. Translation is from: Declercq, "Wei Shu," 84. This is also cited, with the translation from Hurvitz, in Caswell, *Written and Unwritten*, 13.

70. For example, Caswell has shown that after the completion of the initial imperially sponsored strata at Yungang, the later stages of grotto building were funded by private donors who had become members of the Buddhist institution (*Written and Unwritten*, 29–40), a situation that speaks to the benefit that this relationship had for the Buddhist institution. For the court, their benefit comes from the reach over their populace that they gained in placing themselves as the supreme patrons of the Buddhist tradition, an important political move that will be discussed in detail in the next chapter.

71. *WS* 13.322.

72. Tseng, *Making of the Tuoba Northern Wei*, 29ff.

73. Miao Linlin's doctoral dissertation is a dedicated study of the women's ranks over time in the Northern Wei, wherein she argues that the system was one of established, formal ranks with associated regalia and reward, and that the women who held such ranks participated in an imperial system of esteemed ranks much like their male counterparts. See Miao, "Beiwei houguan zhidu yanjiu."

74. *WS* 13.321–22.

75. *Song shu* 41.1269–70.

76. Clarke, *Family Matters in Indian Monasticisms*, 144–46.

77. Chen Jinhua, "*Śarīra* and Scepter," 41n16.

78. Chen, "*Śarīra* and Scepter," 41n16.

79. The emperor's mourning is recorded in Ciqing's entombed biography cited above. What is particularly noteworthy is that he declares that she her funerary rites be taken in charge by the court—all of this despite her originally coming to the court in the menial service as the wife of a rebel leader (*Transcription*: Zhao 2008, 146: *Image #239*: Zhao 1975, vol. 2, p. 288).

80. *WS* 13.321.

81. Balkwill, "A Virtuoso Nun," 138.

82. I have translated *shenjing cheng* as "imperial city" based on other uses of *shengjing* from contemporary sources. For a full philological explanation, see Balkwill, "A Virtuoso Nun," 138n26.

83. The six palaces refer to the bedchambers of the king's principal wives (Hucker, *Dictionary of Official Titles*, s.v. "liugong").

84. The one dedicated study of Sengzhi's life that I have found is in the form of a Chinese-language critical edition and study of her entombed biography. See Wang, "Beiwei Sengzhi muzhi kaoyi," 87–107.

85. Balkwill, "A Virtuoso Nun," 139–40.

86. The very empress murdered by Empress Dowager Ling.

87. Wang Su's biography in the *Book of the Wei* can be found at *WS* 63.1407–13.

88. Jinling is modern-day Nanjing.

89. I believe that all these women sought refuge in the court's own nunnery, the Jade Radiance, which was said to be for the use of the widow of the court (*LYQLJ: T* no. 2092, 1003a01–a28).

90. The *Record of Buddhist Monasteries in Luoyang* relates that he built a nunnery for his first wife, Madam Xie, who was replaced and dejected when Wang Su came north to take a position in the Northern Wei and marry a Tuoba Princess. Much to Wang Su's embarrassment, the text tells us that the two women engaged in a public poetry battle over their shared man, and that this resulted in Wang Su building the nunnery for his first wife to live out her days in (*LYQLJ: T* no. 2092, 1011b09–c20).

91. *LYQLJ: T* no. 2092, 1003a17–18.

92. There seems to be no other reference to specific examples of funerary fires in the *Book of the Wei*. However, one biography of a high-level advisor to the Northern Wei, Gao Yun (390–487), may help us to establish whether or not this was a common practice. Gao Yun was advisor to many Northern Wei Emperors from Taiwu to Xiaowen, and having hailed from the Northern Yan, would have been familiar with Sinitic practices and hence was deeply involved in the Northern Wei's Sinification program and bureaucratic procedures. His biography attests to his attendance at Wencheng's funeral, his witnessing of Empress Dowager Wenming's attempt at self-sacrifice, and his opinions thereon. His biography reports the following: "Yun undertook the activities of regulating the collected ministers of Gaozong, and relied on the customs of old in so doing. The mourning rites of the women did not rely on ancient models and so Yuan remonstrated them, saying: 'In the previous courts, there was often put forth the bright edict that it was prohibited for women to make any merriment. On the day of the funeral procession, songs and ballads, drums and dancing, sacrificial animals, and the burning of the tomb—all of these are proscribed and cut off'" (*WS* 38.1073). What we may assume is that Yun took to regulating the mourning practices of imperial women as they were not in accord with those of prior Chinese dynasties and were perhaps customs of the northern steppe peoples, though the *Book of the Wei* says nothing more about this. Moreover, although Kurgan tumuli as far east as modern-day Mongolia have been excavated and show the existence of fire pits inside the tombs, and although there is evidence of Zoroastrian fire altars in the tombs of Sogdians in China from a similar time period (Lerner, "Aspects of Assimilation," 18), there is no evidence of fire in Serbi tombs in China. It is tempting to view mortuary fire, or the burning of the deceased body, in a Buddhist light; however, there is no evidence that this was practiced by Northern Wei courtiers. On the other hand, there is evidence of the Buddhist mortuary practice of placing the body in grotto niches. For example, grotto 7 at the Buddhist grotto site of Xiangtang shan in modern-day Handan, Hebei province, is the mortuary grotto of Northern Qi founding Emperor, Wenxuan (526–59) (Howard, "Buddhist Grotto Sculpture," 6–25).

93. Her biography in the *Book of the Wei* tells us the following: "When Gaozong died, so the story goes, the country was in great mourning and three days after his passing, all of the emperor's clothing, utensils, and belongings were burned and all of the hundreds of his empresses, courtesans, and ladies of the court were marked with tears while they surrounded the fire. The Empress screamed out in sorrow and threw herself in the fire. She was rescued by the [*zhaoyi* of the] left and the right and only revived after a long time" (*WS* 13.328).

94. Balkwill, "A Virtuoso Nun," 140–41.

95. Jonathan Silk argues that the weina is likely connected to the Sanskrit term *karmadāna* and he shows how both the weina and the karmadāna undertook the activities for daily running of the monastery. On this, see Silk, *Managing Monks*, 127ff. Petra Kieffer-Pulz agrees with Silks description of the tasks of the karmadāna/weina, but understands the meanings of the words differently (review of *Managing Monks*, 80).

96. The precise translation of *duweina* is difficult. I take it to be in two pieces, with the weina as described above and the *du* modifying it. As an adjective employed in military titles, the *du* can often mean "chief/head." Yet, in a number of courtly titles, it can also mean "region/area." The original meaning of the term, however, is "city/metropolis/capital." I have chosen to translate the title, here, as "metropolitan" because it appears that persons who held this name were aligned with regional administration through political connection to the central court. In agreement, the Song dynasty commentary on the *Annals on Buddhism and Daoism* (*WS* 114.3041) describes the different levels of regional and prefectural weina thought to have been employed in the dynasty. Furthermore, I prefer the translation of chief weina for a different title used in the period: *tongweina*. However, this translation is conjectural and much more work needs to be done on the foundation of such monastic titles under the Northern Wei.

97. *WS* 184.3043.

98. *WS* 184.3038.

99. Gu, "Huangfu gong," 90.

100. Balkwill, "A Virtuoso Nun," 144.

101. The translation "nirvāṇa carriage" is conjectural based on similar usage in other medieval Buddhist texts. For a full philological discussion, see Balkwill, "A Virtuoso Nun," 144n46.

102. *LYQLJ*: *T* no. 2092, 1004a02–7.

103. McNair, *Donors of Longmen*, 65.

104. McNair, *Donors of Longmen*, 66.

105. Lingley, "Lady Yuchi," 41–47.

4. A GIRL ON THE THRONE

1. Wang and Tsai, *Buddhist Stone Sūtras*, 164.

2. This inscription is titled *The Record on the Five parts of the Donation of a Religious Assembly of Brothers and Sisters for the Commissioning of an Image at Yellow Cliff* (*Huang-shiya zao xiang wuduan zhi fayi xiongdi zimei deng tiji*), which can be found in *B* 4.147. There is also a transcription of the inscription and a brief study of the site, available in Lai, *Shandong beichao Fojiao*, 5–7. See also Wang and Tsai, *Buddhist Stone Sūtras*, 182–87, where

a transcription, a photo, and a translation, and many missing characters that have been identified conjecturally, can be found.

3. Lingley, "Patron and Community in Eastern Wei Shanxi," 147.

4. The inscription is transcribed in Lai, *Shandong beichao Fojiao*, 6. An image of the inscription is available through Academia Sinica, accessed January 2, 2024, http://catalog .digitalarchives.tw/item/00/33/3c/41.html. The image, transcription, and a translation are also available (and have been consulted) in Wang and Tsai, *Buddhist Stone Sūtras*" 182–90.

5. Liu, "Art, Ritual, and Society," 17ff.

6. Wong, *Chinese Steles*, 43ff.

7. Hou, *Wu liu shiji*, 89ff.

8. Dorothy Wong made a similar argument almost twenty-five years ago in an article specifically dealing with the topic of women as art patrons in the Southern and Northern Dynasties period, which specifically asks the question of what Buddhism offered to women in this period. I owe much of my intellectual inspiration on this topic to her. See Wong, "Women as Buddhist Art Patrons."

9. Hao Chunwen. *Zhonggu shiqi sheyi yanjiu*, 273.

10. Characterized by Hou Xudong as one of the "great families" of the time, the Gao were the leaders of Dangmo, present-day Zhuoxian in Hebei province, and their name was the clan name that dominated the town itself (see Hou, "Rethinking Chinese Kinship," 31). Hence the inscription that remains of their family provides a unique opportunity to appreciate precisely how an elite family of the time would have presented themselves—as Buddhist, with female members of the clan taking charge of Buddhist affiliation more so than male members, and with those same female family members having names that either linked them with the ideal of concubinage or labeled them as concubines and courtesans connected to the Gao family of Dangmo.

11. *B* 3. 076. A digital image of the front side of the stele is available from Academia Sinica, accessed January 2, 2024, http://catalog.digitalarchives.tw/item/00/1b/fe/6f.html.

12. This word is often taken as a Chinese translation of the Sanskrit, *upāsaka*.

13. For an example of such transliterated names, see Zhang Qingjie and Li Biao, "Shanxi Lingqiu Bei Wei Wenchengdi 'Nan xun bei,'" 72. I owe knowledge of this source to Scott Pearce, who offers a fascinating overview of the writing of the Dai language in Sinographs in the early part of the dynasty (see Pearce, *Northern Wei*, 152–54).

14. Wang and Tsai, *Buddhist Stone Sūtras*, 172.

15. Hucker, *Dictionary of Official Titles*, s.v. "nü shangshu."

16. Miao "Beiwei hougong zhidu kaolun," 101.

17. If there is any doubt that a woman called "man" might exist, the *Book of the Wei* makes it clear that the job of "women's secretary" was a job for women (*WS* 13.321–22.).

18. Both the Jing River and the Long Mountain are located at the eastern edge of Gansu province, very close to the border with Shaanxi, which is also where Anding commandery is located.

19. According to the math in the biography, this would have been the year 459. In the year 459, the Northern Wei capital was still in Pingcheng (Datong) and Emperor Wencheng was ruling (r. 452–65). During this period, court ranks for women were considerably expanded and Wencheng's own empress was the first Northern Wei woman to hold the role of empress dowager, arguably also the first "empress" in a Sinitic cultural mode. That

Sengnan was at the court from 459 to her death in 521 is remarkable. She would have been among the longest-serving courtiers of the Northern Wei, serving five emperors and two empress dowagers and also relocating to Luoyang with the move of the capital there.

20. This refers to the brushes used by women in the inner chambers, which were themselves used for record keeping.

21. Jinyong is a city to the northeast of Luoyang, and the palace was first established to provide refuge for the imperial kin of the Kingdom of Wei (220–26). When the Northern Wei capital was moved to Luoyang, Emperor Xiaowen stayed there while construction on the Luoyang palace was being completed. This is recorded in the *Classic on Waterways* (*Shuijing zhu*) in its section on the river waters near Luoyang that join the Luo River (*Shuijing zhu* 16. Gu shui 25). I suspect that Sengnan was staying at Jinyong because of a palace coup d'état (520–25) in Luoyang that saw the empress dowager placed under house arrest.

22. Ch. *dongyuan miqi*: "The Secret Vessels of the Eastern Garden"—wherein the "Eastern Garden" is a euphemism for the imperial tomb and "secret vessel" is a euphemism for coffins and grave goods or both.

23. Ch. *wenliangche*; a type of funerary carriage akin to the modern-day hearse.

24. This refers to one of the stars in the constellation of the ox.

25. *The Biography of Feng Nülang, the Woman Secretary of the Palace of the Wei* (Wei gu gong yu zuo nü shangshu Feng Nülang zhi).

26. For more on the character of Mulan and her Northern Wei roots, see Kwa and Idema, eds., *Mulan*, xiff, 1–5. For those interested in an in-depth survey of the development of the Mulan story, Kwa and Idema's aforementioned *Mulan* indexes the major, Chinese-language literary and theatrical traditions from the medieval through the modern periods.

27. Chen, *Multicultural China in the Early Middle Ages*, 43.

28. Chen, *Multicultural China in the Early Middle Ages*, 51.

29. Chen, *Multicultural China in the Early Middle Ages*, 52.

30. Guilmoto and Tovey, "The Masculinization of Births," 211.

31. Tomášková, "Yes Virginia, There Is Gender," 109.

32. Bourland, "Queer Theory and the Shamanic Ideal," 8.

33. Bourland, "Queer Theory and the Shamanic Ideal," 14.

34. In modern-day China, the Evenki largely live in the region of Hulunbei'er in Inner Mongolia, which is the region of the Gaxian Cave. The main city in this territory is Jiagedaqi, where streets are named after the Northern Wei and where the local museum narrates the connection between the Evenki of today and the Taghbach of the Northern Wei.

35. By surveying these tombs, Zheng Wei argues that the Taghbach, in their early history, were merged with the Xiongnu (see "A Study of Xianbei Tombs," 164).

36. Safonova and Sántha, "Gender Distinctions in an Egalitarian Society," 124–25.

37. Safonova and Sántha, "Gender Distinctions in an Egalitarian Society," 127.

38. Safonova and Sántha, "Gender Distinctions in an Egalitarian Society," 122

39. Knapp, *Selfless Offspring*, 164, 178–81.

40. The most recent study of vengeful women, which engages with past scholarship, is Granger, "Violence, Vigilantism, and Virtue," 915–34.

41. In her study of Tang dynasty fashion, BuYun Chen documents images of cavalry-women and female court attendants from the early Tang that show women wearing pants suited to the task of riding. Since women commonly rode in the Northern Wei, and since

202 NOTES TO PAGES 109–137

the Northern Wei had a large impact on Tang culture, it stands to reason that the women of the Northern Wei wore similar pants while riding and working (see Chen, *Empire of Style*, 93–97).

42. Broadbridge, *Women and the Making of the Mongol Empire*, 2–3.

43. The "lion's roar" in Buddhist texts signifies the Buddha's own preaching voice and ability to convert beings. What makes the *Śrīmālā Sūtra* unique is that Queen Śrīmālā is the holder of the "lion's roar" and her teachings include the nature of the dharma body of the buddha, the nature of emptiness, and the superiority of the bodhisattva path over and above the paths of the arhats and the pratyekabuddhas who are the champions of the discriminatory and conditional teachings of the buddha—his skill-in-means teachings—but who have no understanding of the ultimate truth or unconditioned teachings of a buddha.

44. For an overview of some of this textual instability, see Balkwill, "Disappearing and Disappeared Daughters," in particular 260–63.

45. For this story, see Watson, *The Lotus Sutra*, 188.

46. For recent research that discusses the story of the Daughter of the Dragon King in its Japanese reception, see Abé, "Revisiting the Dragon Princess," 27–70.

47. For example, Diana Paul's translation of a section of the text, reads: "O Lord, those who first attained that stage [of nirvāṇa] were not ignorant of the Dharma and were not dependent upon others. They also knew they had attained the stages with remainder [through their own efforts], and would inevitably attain supreme, complete enlightenment (*anuttarā samyaksaṃbodhi*). Why? Because the śrāvaka (disciple) and pratyekabuddha vehicles are included in the Mahāyāna. The Mahāyāna is the buddha vehicle. Therefore, the three vehicles are the One Vehicle" (Paul and McRae, *The Sutra of Queen Śrīmālā of the Lion's Roar*, 29).

48. For a study of the formation of this text, which I have argued is a Chinese apocryphon, see Balkwill, "The Sūtra on Transforming the Female Form."

49. *T* no. 564, 0919a26–b17.

50. These details on the life of Bodhiruci are recorded in the *Extended Biographies of Eminent Monks* (Xu gaoseng zhuan: T no. 2060, 425c27–29).

51. Founded in the late Han dynasty, the White Horse Temple is traditionally considered the oldest Buddhist temple in China and can still be visited.

52. These details on the life of Buddhaśanta are also recorded in the *Extended Biographies of Eminent Monks* (*T* no. 2060, 429a09–13).

53. These details about the life of Gautama Prajñāruci are also recorded in the *Extended Biographies of Eminent Monks* (*T* no. 2060, 429b01–5).

54. The sacrifice of the physical body out of one's intense compassion for the plight of others is a common trope in Buddhist literature. Reiko Ohnuma has worked on the gift of the body in the specific story cited in this chapter ("The Story of Rūpāvatī," 103–46) and also, more generally, in *Head, Eyes, Flesh, and Blood*. James Benn discusses the gift of the body in various Chinese sources (*Burning for the Buddha*, 93–94).

55. For a brief overview of Prasenajit's patronage of the Buddha, see Lamotte, *History of Indian Buddhism*," 10–12.

56. For recent studies of such texts, see my other work in the bibliography: "The Sūtra on Transforming the Female Form"; "Disappearing and Disappeared Daughters"; "The Sūtra of the Unsullied Worthy Girl as Spoken by the Buddha."

57. For Bimbisāra, Prasenajit's brother-in-law, see Lamotte, *History of Indian Buddhism*, 12.

58. *T* no. 573, 946b17–21.

59. Chikusa, *Formation and Growth*, 19.

60. McNair, *Donors of Longmen*, 140.

61. Chen, *Informed Textual Practices*, 98.

62. Chen, *Informed Textual Practices*, 258–60.

63. McNair, *Donors of Longmen*, 67–68.

64. McNair, *Donors of Longmen*, 33–38.

65. Although there are neither dates nor epigraphs on the stele, Chen Qingxiang dates it to the Northern Wei period after the year 503, when Emperor Xuanwu was reigning. See Chen, "Maiji shan 133," 75.

66. These caves can be virtually visited at Digital Dunguang, accessed January 2, 2024, https://www.e-dunhuang.com/section.htm.

67. Hughes, *Worldly Saviors and Imperial Authority*, 8off.

68. McBride, "Why Did Kungye Claim to Be the Buddha Maitreya?" 36–60.

69. This association between Maitreya and the kings of Khotan is found in a Tibetan-language prophetic text about Khotan, *The Prophecy of the Li Country* (*Li yul luṅ-btsan-pa*), which is translated in Emmerick, *Tibetan Texts Concerning Khotan*, 405–9.

70. McNair, *Donors of Longmen*, 17.

71. Su, *Zhongguo Fojiao shikusi yiji*, 48.

72. Hughes, "Re-examining the *Zhengming Jing*," 14–16.

73. Tang, "'Mile wei nüshen jing' tanwei," 104–18.

74. The text that I am citing from here is popularly known as the *Great Cloud Sūtra*, though its full name and number in the Chinese Buddhist canon is *T* no. 387, *The *Mahāmegha-sūtra* [Ch. *Da fangdeng wuxiang jing*]. In a famous study, Antonino Forte reviews scholarship on the authenticity of the canonical text that I have cited above regarding a famous Dunhuang document with the prophecy of the birth of a female ruler. He suggests that the prophecy is contained in *T* no. 387 but that this might not have been the text presented at the court of Emperor Wu Zhao (Forte, *Political Propaganda*, 27–46).

75. *T* no. 387, 1098a02–09.

76. Forte, *Political Propaganda*, 87–146.

77. Rong, *Eighteen Lectures on Dunhuang*, 29–30.

78. Chen, *Informed Textual Practices*, 176–79.

79. Chen, *Informed Textual Practices*, 185.

80. Chen, *Informed Textual Practices*, 195.

81. Chen, *Informed Textual Practices*, 196.

82. On the uncertain and rare identification of pre-Tang manuscripts of the text, see Forte, *Political Propaganda*, 73–76.

83. Chen, *Informed Textual Practices*, 203.

84. Radich, "Problems of Attribution, Style, and Dating," 239–42.

85. Further details about Dharmakṣema in the *Book of the Wei* state that the reason the Northern Wei wanted Dharmakṣema is that the monk was known to have mastered secret sexual techniques that the then-Taghbach ruler, Taiwu or Taghbach Tao, also wanted to learn. According to this source, Dharmakṣema perfected these techniques with the women

of the Northern Liang court. For more information on this, see Chen, "The Indian Buddhist Missionary Dharmakṣema," 228.

86. Hao, "The Social Life of Buddhist Monks and Nuns," 83.

5. NO SALVATION IN BUDDHISM

1. Liu, "Ethnicity and the Suppression," 3

2. Liu, "Ethnicity and the Suppression," 15; Seiwert, *Popular Religious Movements*, 108–9.

3. Liu, "Ethnicity and the Suppression," 6.

4. Ownby, "Chinese Millenarian Traditions," 1513–30. For a thorough study of Prince Moonlight's character and his role in Buddhist messianism in early medieval China, see Zürcher, "Prince Moonlight," 1–75.

5. Ownby, "Chinese Millenarian Traditions," 1523ff.

6. Seiwert, *Popular Religious Movements*, 112.

7. I owe all these insights from the *Book of the Wei* to James Ware, who has dug through the book for references. For more information, see Ware, "Wei Shou on Buddhism," 172n3. Tsukamoto discusses this rebellion in greater detail in his section on these Buddhist rebellions in the Northern Wei (*Shina Bukkyō shi*, 269–90); as does: Seiwert, *Popular Religious Movements*, 111–14.

8. Seiwert, *Popular Religious Movements*, 112.

9. Although Cui Hao does not have a biography in the *Book of the Wei*, he is mentioned in many places. For example, in the "Annals on Buddhism and Daoism" we learn that he was put to death for the role that he played in the suppression of Buddhism under Emperor Taiwu (*WS* 114.3035) and we also hear much about his patronage of Kou Qianzhi throughout the "Daoism" section of that text.

10. The Northern Wei also famously patronized the tradition of Daoism during this time of the persecution of Buddhism (Mather, "K'ou Ch'ien-Chih," 103–22).

11. Kleeman, *Celestial Masters*, 199.

12. Ware, "The Wei Shu and the Sui Shu on Taoism," 237ff.

13. Mather, "K'ou Ch'ien-Chih," 110.

14. Mather, "K'ou Ch'ien-Chih," 111.

15. Lu Yuan is said to have been a trusted adviser of Emperor Wencheng's and Empress Dowager Wenming's. See his biography in the *Book of the Wei* in a biographical section that starts with his father: *WS* 47.1046–49.

16. A recent overview of the Yellow Turban revolt within the context of Daoist cults in the late Han, an overview that relies on accounts from the *Latter History of the Han*, can be found in Espesset, "Latter Han Religious Movements." As an introduction to her translation of the central text of the Yellow Turbans, the *Scripture on Great Peace* (Taiping jing), Barbara Hendrischke provides a thorough background to the movement, arguing that, more than simply being rebels, the Yellow Turbans had clear imperial ambitions and saw themselves as taking over heaven's mandate to rule from the Han House (*The Scripture on Great Peace*, 16–24).

17. *WS* 47.1048. Translation from Seiwert, *Popular Religious Movements*, 109.

18. The *Book of the Wei* reports that Faguo, the first "religious superintendent" of the Northern Wei was fond of saying, "Taizu has brilliant foresight and loves the Dao and is

none other than a Tathāgata in our times. As such, Śramaṇas must respond [to him] with all protocols" (*WS* 114.3031). The text further says that Faguo himself often revered the emperor. The question of whether or not the ruler should bow to the buddhas and the Buddhist community should be under the jurisdiction of the ruler was frequently debated in early medieval China. The contours of that debate have been summarized by Eric Zürcher and can be found in his work, *The Buddhist Conquest of China*, 106–10.

19. The term used here, *zhengjue*, is the term used in Chinese translations of Buddhist texts to represent the highest attainment of Buddhist awakening. Furthermore, the edict to release all birds of prey to a natural space with a pagoda is a clear reference to the empress dowager's Buddhist leanings.

20. *WS* 13.328.

21. Although falconry may have been introduced to China from Inner Asia or Mongolia, it appears to have been popular and widespread in China by the Han dynasty, with the earliest attestations of the practice dating from the Qin. The northern dynasties witnessed widespread interest in falconry, likely because of the predominance of northern peoples and northern rulers in the central plains. On this topic, see Schafer, "Falconry in T'ang Times," 295–97.

22. *WS* 114.3038. Translation from Declercq, "Wei Shu," 89. There is an alternate translation in Hurvitz, "Wei Shou," 77.

23. A survey of the changes that the Northern Wei made in its tax policy that includes useful tables indexing the different tax regions is found in Zhou, "Cong Beiwei Ji Ge Jun," 465–69.

24. McNair, *Donors of Longmen*, 63.

25. McNair, *Donors of Longmen*, 65.

26. For a reconstructed map of central Luoyang in the Northern Wei, see Lourme, *Mémoire Sur Les Monastères*, lii–liii.

27. This is likely a reference to the eight-fold path of Buddhist practice.

28. This is a reference to a doctrinal idea in the *Lotus Sūtra* that there is only one path of practice, not three, as is said to be the case in many other Buddhist writings.

29. *LYQLJ: T* no. 2092, 1003a17–20. Translation adapted from Wang, *A Record of Buddhist Monasteries*, 49.

30. McNair, *Donors of Longmen*, 62.

31. According to Wang, the *xian zhang* (immortal's palm) was an "ornament designed to collect dew as a gift of heaven, the consumption of which would promote longevity" (*A Record of Buddhist Monasteries*, 48 n181).

32. *LYQLJ: T* no. 2092, 1003a13–16. Translation adapted from Wang, *A Record of Buddhist Monasteries*, 48.

33. *LYQLJ: T* no. 2092, 1010b2–5.

34. *LYQLJ: T* no. 2092, 1010c19–22.

35. *Luoyang* and *Luoyang, Han Wei luoyang gucheng yanjiu*, 234.

36. *ZZTJ* 149.4646–49.

37. Zürcher, "Prince Moonlight," 45–46.

38. *WS* 22.591–92.

39. *ZZTJ* 158.67.

40. *Liji, Yueji,* 12.

41. Yang, "Making Sense of Messianism," 1.

42. Tang, *Han, Wei, liang Jin nanbeichao Fojiao shi*, 451.

43. As this was a hereditary title used exclusively in the Northern Wei, the biography in question is attached to that of the father, who held the same title, "Prince of Rencheng." Rencheng is located in modern-day Jining, Shandong province. See *WS* 19.461–89.

44. The memorial is in: *WS* 114.3044–47. The translation is from Declercq, "Wei Shu," 102–11. Alternate translation in Hurvitz, "Wei Shou," 92–99.

45. *WS* 114.3044–45. Translation from Declercq, "Wei Shu," 104–5; Hurvitz, "Wei Shou," 94.

46. *WS* 114.3045. Translation from Declercq, "Wei Shu," 106; Hurvitz, "Wei Shou," 94–95.

47. *WS* 114.3045. Translation from: Declercq, "Wei Shu," 108; Hurvitz, "Wei Shou," 96.

48. *WS* 114.3046; Declercq "Wei Shu," 106–9; Hurvitz, "Wei Shou," 95–96.

49. *WS* 114.3046; Declercq "Wei Shu," 110–11; Hurvitz, "Wei Shou," 98–99.

50. For example, these included a limit on the ordination of monks across the kingdom, the increased reliance on the *weina* to police the monastic community, the forbidding of the practice of ordaining slaves, and the punishment of officials involved in the private ordination of monastics (*WS* 114. 3043; Declercq "Wei Shu," 100; Hurvitz, "Wei Shou," 90).

51. *WS* 114. 3043. Translation from Declercq, "Wei Shu," 101; Hurvitz, "Wei Shou," 90.

52. *WS* 114.3048. Translation from Declercq, "Wei Shu," 113; Hurvitz, "Wei Shou," 103.

53. Stephen Bokenkamp has commented on a similar use of this term and argues that, although it is generally thought to signify destruction, it can also refer to the Celestial Master's rituals of repentance, called "mud and ashes" (*Early Daoist Scriptures*, 168 n†). Given that this is a memorial against popular religious practices, we may read the term similarly here.

54. *WS* 22.591–92.

55. Han Emperor Ling's biography is available in the *History of the Later Han* (*Hou Hanshu* 8. 327–60). A translation of the portions of the *Comprehensive Mirror to Aid in Government* that deal with Han Emperor Ling's rule is available in de Crespigny, *Emperor Huan and Emperor Ling*, 123ff.

56. For an updated discussion of the potential causes of the Yellow Turban Rebellion, see Farmer, "The Three Chaste Ones of Ba," 191–202.

57. Pearce, *Northern Wei*, 294–97.

58. Ware, "Wei Shou on Buddhism," 101. For the reference to Wei Shou's childhood name, "Fozhu," see *Bei Qi shu* 37.483.

59. Wei Shou's biography describes his talents and includes the story of a literary battle in which his senior rival, Xing Zicai, was fond of saying that "'Buddha Helper is the best of the court servants." This was not a complement. Wei Shou is said to have argued about his name with his adversary, likely because it was a childhood name given by his parents and may not have reflected how Wei Shou saw himself. At the end of the fight, Emperor Xuanwu scolded Zicai, saying, "Cai is not as good as Wei Shou" (*Bei Qi shu* 37.495).

60. *ZZTJ* 148.112.

61. *T* no. 2103, 104c9–10.

62. *T* no. 2103, 104c11.

63. *T* no. 2113, 604a09–14.

64. *T* no. 2113, 604a26–27.

65. This story is contained in two Tang-dynasty histories of the period in question, the *Book of the Zhou* (*Zhou shu* 37.658) and the *History of the Northern Dynasties* (*BS* 27.992), although it is not contained in the *Book of the Wei.*

66. *T* no. 2113, 604b09.

67. A new study of the *mingtang* provides perhaps the most detailed discussion of this hybrid symbology yet available (Xie, "Struggle on the Axis," 14–17).

68. Guisso, *Wu Tse-T'ien*, 46, 227n168.

69. The specifics of the building and destruction of the *mingtangs* can be found in Forte, *Mingtang and Buddhist Utopias*, 60–82.

70. I have made a similar argument in a different publication where I focus on the divergent meanings of the name "Ling" as understood by the empress dowager's court and her populace (Balkwill, "Metropolitan Buddhism vis-à-vis Buddhism at the Metropolis"). Here I make a similar argument although it is set in the context of the long *durée* of the fall of the dynasty.

71. *I* no. 1, 1.3b20.

72. The story of the rise of the Yellow Turbans and Han Emperor Ling's inability to suppress them or even control his court during the years of the rebellion is discussed at length in the emperor's biography in the *Complete Mirror of Governance* and chronicled from the years 183 to 185. The text describes how Han Emperor Ling was cautioned by his courtiers yet disregarded their cautions and, as such, the text has strong resonances with the stories of Empress Dowager Ling (de Crespigny, *Emperor Huan and Emperor Ling*, 174–98).

73. We have already seen such criticism in accounts of the empress dowager. For the Han emperor, see de Crespigny, *Emperor Huan and Emperor Ling*, 148–49.

74. These details of Han Emperor Ling's life, as retained in the *Complete Mirror of Governance*, can be found in De Crespigny, *Emperor Huan and Emperor Ling*, 135–74.

75. *HHS* 8.359.

76. Although one instance of the phrase "Became Ling" is found in the *History of the Later Han* and another instance is found in the *Book of the Wei*, the parallel is telling because the *History of the Later Han* was written during the Liu Song dynasty and so the language would have been similar to the contemporary usage in the Northern Wei.

77. *WS* 57.1259–63.

78. *WS* 57.1262.

79. *WS* 11.286.

80. *WS* 11.282.

81. For more on the background of the Erzhu and their dealings with Gao Huan, see Graff, *Medieval Chinese Warfare*, 99–103. Tang Zhangru also argues that references to the Jie peoples in the early medieval texts generally mean the different subgroups of the Xiongnu ethno-group, of which the Erzhu family belong. See Tang, "Wei Jin Za Hu Kao, 414ff.

82. Pearce, *Northern Wei*, 283.

CONCLUSION

1. Ooms, *Imperial Politics and Symbolics in Ancient Japan*, 164.

2. Carriere, *Silla Korea and the Silk Roads*, 178.

3. Lee and Leidy, *Silla: Korea's Golden Kingdom*, 123.

4. Carriere, *Silla Korea and the Silk Roads*, 94; McBride, "King Chinhŭng," 48–65.

5. In Uyghur sources, the name for China is *Tawyač* (variants *tawqač, tabyač*), which is taken from the word "Taghbach," which in Middle Chinese was presumably pronounced *t'ak-pat-* and was a rendering of the native ethnonym of the Northern Wei dynasty (Von Gabain, *Alttürkische Grammatik*, 181). The earliest Uyghur document where this appellation is found is the Tonyukuk inscription, dated to 716–25 (Geng, *Gudai Tujueyu Yufa*, 206).

6. Boodberg, "The Language of the T'o-Pa Wei," 223.

7. Miyake, review of *Translating Chinese Tradition*, 186.

8. Antonino Forte's study of the sūtra and its commentary remains the authoritative study of Emperor Wu Zhao's use of Buddhist literary precedents in her establishing herself as a cakravartin and as the future Buddha, Maitreya (Forte, *Political Propaganda*, 125ff).

9. Empress Wu had a team of political authors working under her that created her political opus. These so-called "scholars of the northern gate" or *Beimen xueshi* were recruited personally by Empress Wu because of their proven literary ability in working in various other parts of the government, but they were not an institutionalized sector within the court. Rather, they were brought in by the Empress for specific literary support. They are said to have produced more than one thousand scrolls of text and to have been responsible for the wording of imperial edicts (Twitchett, "'Chen Gui' and Other Works," 45–46). Yet the lives of these scholars of the northern gate were not very secure and by the time Empress Wu ascended the throne in her own name in 690 she had personally seen to the death of all but one of them, who had been killed by other means (Twitchett, "'Chen Gui,'" 53). The longest-enduring of these texts composed by Empress Wu through her scholars of the northern gate is the *Rules for Ministers* (*Chen Gui*), which replaced the *Laozi* on imperial examinations and is generally considered a part of a larger genre of texts detailing the proper actions and etiquette of court officials (Twitchett, "'Chen Gui,'" 57).

10. April Hughes has shown that the depiction of the ruler in the *Sūtra of Raining Jewels* resonates with that seen in canonical Maitreya sūtras, which depict Emperor Wu Zhao as a bodhisattva that "governs and converts the people" ("Re-Examining the *Zhengming Jing*," 3).

11. Forte, *Political Propaganda*, 205.

12. For a study of Emperor Wu Zhao's Buddhist rule, see Forte, *Political Propaganda*, 189–254. For a discussion of Empress Wu's campaign for the veneration of Buddhist relics, see Chen, "Śarīra and Scepter," particularly 56ff.

13. We do not know the precise birth and death dates for Wu Keji and Wu Juchang, though they would have lived in the sixth century. Emperor Wu Zhao's biography in the *New History of the Tang* records the three sets of posthumous honors that she awarded them: The first set of honors were granted in the year 684 (*Xin Tang shu* 10. 82), which was the first year of the Guangzhai era; the second set of honors were granted in the year 689 (*Xin Tang shu* 10. 88), which was the first year of the Yongchang era; and the third set of honors were granted in the year 690, which was the first year of her own independent reign in the Tianshou era of the Zhou dynasty (*Xin Tang shu* 10.90–91).

14. According to Chen Jo-shui, Empress Wu enacted traditional Han rituals for the empress and reconfigured them to stress the power of the empress as reigning matriarch ("Empress Wu and Proto-Feminist Sentiments," 77–116, esp. 79).

15. For a detailed description of her female bureaucracy, see Chen, "Empress Wu and Proto-Feminist Sentiments," 81ff.

16. The tomb of Wu Zetian's highest-ranking female assistant, Shangguan Wan'er (664–710) was recently excavated and an entombed biography was found. According to her biography, Wan'er held the rank of "lady of clear etiquette," which, as we have seen, was a high-ranking women's position at the Northern Wei court. It is something of an irony that when this inscription was found, it was highly publicized whereas the entombed biographies for Empress Dowager Ling's female staff have long been available and remain unstudied. For a translation of Shangguan Wan'er's entombed biography, see Rothschild, "Her Influence Great, Her Merit beyond Measure," 139–42.

17. Forte, *Political Propaganda*, 4.

18. The close relationship between Fazang and Emperor Wu Zhao is explored by Chen Jinhua in his study of the monk, see Chen, *Philosopher, Practitioner, Politician*, 132–63. For a book-length study of how Tang uses of Buddhism for political and military purposes gave rise to what is commonly called "esoteric Buddhism," see Goble, *Chinese Esoteric Buddhism*.

19. *T* no. 2073, 156b16–157c11.

20. Zhang, "Lingbian de shixiang yu xuxiang," 93–108.

21. Forte also goes through these classical Confucian arguments about the nature of the *Great Cloud Sūtra* that see the text itself as apocryphal, but he shows that the text was translated likely by Dharmakṣema a few hundred years earlier than it appeared in the court of Empress Wu (Forte, *Political Propaganda*, 3–54). Hence, although Empress Wu certainly utilized this Buddhist trope of buddhahood and leadership for women, she did not invent it.

22. Rothschild, *Emperor Wu Zhao*, 199.

23. Rothschild, *Emperor Wu Zhao*, 199.

24. This is discussed in: McBride, *Domesticating the Dharma*, 31; Vermeersch, *Power of the Buddhas*, 213–14.

25. This possibility is also raised by Joan Piggott in her discussion of Empress Suiko where she argues that the Buddhist ideal of the enlightened ruler, or cakravartin, was open to women and thus aided in Suiko's validation of her rule (*The Emergence of Japanese Kingship*, 95–96). Though brief, Piggott's argument links Empress Suiko with Buddhist texts of the time period that support the ideal of buddhahood and rule by women and thus makes a similar, though abbreviated, argument to the one I will make in the following pages. Michael Como has also explored the connections between female immortals of a Sinitic style and Sinitic notions of rule transplanted to the islands of Japan, though he does not discuss the Northern Wei case specifically (*Weaving and Binding*, 55–83).

26. *Shōmangyō gishou: T* no. 2185.

27. Although not a dedicated study of the empress, Bryan D. Lowe discusses her Buddhism in many places in his study of Buddhist scriptural practices (*Ritualized Writing*, 131, 187–88, 200–201).

28. Ooms, *Imperial Politics*, 13.

29. Lewis, *China Between Empires*, 1.

BIBLIOGRAPHY

PRIMARY TEXTS

Baoyu jing 寶雨經 [*Sūtra of Raining Jewels*]: *T* no. 660.

Bei Qi shu 北齊書 [*Book of the Northern Qi*]. 50 *juan*, decreed in 629. Compiled by Li Baoyao 李百藥 (565–648). Beijing: Zhonghua shuju, 1973.

Beishan lü 北山録 [*North Mountain Record*], *T* no. 2113.

Biqiuni zhuan 比丘尼傳 [*Lives of the Nuns*], *T* no. 2063.

Cefu yuangui 冊府元龜 [*Prime Tortoise of the Record Bureau*]. Edited by Wang Qinrou 王 欽若 (962–1025). Beijing: Zhonghua shuju, 1960.

Chamopodi shouji jing 差摩婆帝授記經 [*Sūtra on the Prophecy of Kṣemavati*], *T* no. 573.

Da fangdeng wuxiang jing 大方等無想經 [*The Mahāmegha-sūtra, The Great Cloud Sūtra*], *T* no. 387.

Da fang guang fo huayan jing 大方廣佛華嚴經 [*Flower Garland Sūtra*], *T* no. 278.

Da Wei gu zhaoxuan shamen datong ling fashi muzhiming 大魏故昭玄沙門令法師墓誌銘 [*The Northern Wei Dharma Master named Sengling, the Great Superintendent of the Śramaṇas who Clarifies Profundities*], *I* no. 32.

Dangchang gong huifu si bei 宕昌公暉福寺碑 [*Duke of Dangchang stele for Radiant Blessings Monastery*], *I* no. 1.

Dewugounü jing 得無垢女經 [*The Sūtra of Vimalī*], *T* no. 339.

Foshuo renwang bore boluomi jing 佛說仁王般若波羅蜜經 [*Prajñāpāramitā Scripture for Humane Kings, Spoken by the Buddha*], *T* no. 245.

Fo suoxing zan 佛所行讚 [*Acts of the Buddha*], *T* no. 192.

Foxing haizang zhihui jietuo poxin xiang jing 佛性海藏智慧解脫破心相經 [*Sūtra on the Nature of the Buddha, the Ocean-Store of Wisdom and Salvation, Which Shatters the Marks of the Heart*], *T* no. 2885.

Fozu tongji 佛祖統紀 [*Complete Chronicle of the Buddha and the Patriarchs*], *T* no. 2035.

Gaoseng zhuan 高僧傳 [*Biographies of Eminent Monks*], *T* no. 2073.

Guang hongming ji 廣弘明集 [*The Expanded Collection for the Proclamation and Clarification of Buddhism*], T no. 2103.

Huayan jing 華嚴經 [Flower Garden Sūtra]: T no. 279.

Huangshiya zao xiang wuduan zhi fayi xiongdi zimei deng tiji 黃石崖造像五段之法義兄弟姊妹等題記 [*The Record on the Five parts of the Donation of a Religious Assembly of Brothers and Sisters for the Commissioning of an Image at Yellow Cliff*], B 4.147.

Jin shu 晉書 [*Book of the Jin*]. 130 juan, decreed in 664, compiled in 646–48. Compiled by Fang Xuanling 房玄齡 (578–648) et al. Beijing: Zhonghua shuju, 1974.

Lunyu zhu zi suoyin 論語逐字索引 [*Concordance to the Lunyu*]. Edited by D. C. Lau, Ho Che Wah, and Chen Fong Ching. ICS series. Hong Kong: Commercial Press, 1995.

Lienü zhuan 列女傳 [Biographies of Exemplary Women]. In *Sibu congkan chubian* 四部叢刊初編 [*First Edition of the Four Categories of Books*]. Vols. 265–67. Shanghai: Commercial Press, 1929.

Ligou shinü jing 離垢施女經 [*The Sūtra of the Girl Vimaladattā*], T no. 338.

Liji in *Liji yizhu* 禮記譯注 [*The Annotated Book of Rites*]. Edited by Yang Tianyu 楊天宇. Shanghai: Shanghai guji chubanshe, 2004.

Luoyang qielan ji 洛陽伽藍記 [*Record of Buddhist Monasteries in Luoyang*], T no. 2092.

Nan Qi shu 南齊書 [*Book of the Southern Qi*]. 59 juan. Compiled by Xiao Zixian 蕭子顯 (578–648). Beijing: Zhonghua shuju, 1975.

Nü shangshu Wang shi wei Sengnan muzhi 女尚書王氏諱僧男墓誌 [*The Entombed Biography of the Woman Secretary "Saṃgha Man" from the Wang Clan*], ZW 124.

Puxian pusa shuo zhengming jing 普賢菩薩說證明經 [*Sūtra Expounded for the Bodhisattva Samantabhadra on Attesting Illumination*], T no. 2879.

Puyaojing 普曜經 [*Lalitavistara*], T no. 186.

Qianshi sanzhuan jing 前世三轉經 [*The Sūtra of the Transformations of the Three Prior Ages*], T no. 178.

Renwang huguo bore boluomiduo jing 仁王護國般若波羅蜜多經 [*Prajñāpāramitā Scripture for Humane Kings to Protect Their States*], T no. 246.

Runan wang xiuzhi guta ming 汝南王修治古塔銘 [*Inscription for the Refurbishment of an old stūpa by the Prince of Runan*]. In *Zhongguo gudai beizhi fashu fanben qingxuan* 中国古代碑志范本请选 [*Selections of Calligraphic Models from Stele Inscriptions from Ancient China*], edited by Tan Wenliang 谭文亮. Luoyang: Henan Meishu chuban she, 2017.

Shang shu 尚書 [*Book of Documents*]. In *Shisanjing zhushu* 十三經注疏 [*Thirteen Classics of Chinese Literature*], edited by Ruan Yuan 阮元 (1764–1849). Reprint, Beijing: Zhonghua shuju, 1980.

Shangshu dazhuan 尚書大傳 [*Great Commentary to the Book of Documents*]. Fu Sheng 伏生 (268–178 BCE). Hong Kong: Chinese University of Hong Kong Library.

Shi ji 史記 [*Records of the Historian*]. 130 juan. Sima Qian 司馬遷 (145–86 BCE) and Sima Tan 司馬談 (180–110? BCE). Beijing: Zhonghua shuju, 1959.

Shizong hou Gao Ying muzhi 世宗后高英墓誌 [*Tomb Memorial of Gao Ying, Empress to Shizong*]. Transcription, ZC 102. Image, ZW 1.35.

Shōmangyō gishou 勝鬘經義疏 [Commentary to the Śrīmala Sūtra], T no. 2185.

Song shu 宋書 [*Book of the Song*]. 100 juan. Compiled by Shen Yue 沈約 (441–513) et al. Beijing: Zhonghua shuju, 1995.

Sui shu 隨書 [*Book of the Sui*]. 85 *juan*. Compiled in 636–56. Compiled by Wei Zheng 魏徵 (585–643) et al. Beijing: Zhonghua shuju, 1961.

Taiping yulan 太平御覽 [*Imperial Readings of the Taiping Era*]. Completed in 983. Li Fang 李昉 (925–96). Edited by Wang Yunwu 王雲五 in 1935. Reprint, Taipei: Yangwu yinshuguan, 1980.

Tongzhi 通志 [*Comprehensive Records*]. Zheng Qiao 鄭樵 (1104–96). Beijing: Zhonghua shuju, 1995.

Wei gu biqiuni Ciqing (Wang Zhong'er) muzhiming (zhengguang wunian wutue qiri) 魏故比丘尼慈慶 (王鍾兒) 墓志銘 (正光五年五月七日) [*The Entombed Biography of the Northern Wei bhikṣuṇī Ciqing (Wang Zhong'er), Dated the Seventh Day of the Fifth Month of the Fifth Year of the Reign of Gleaming Orthodoxy (June 23, 524 CE)*] Transcription, *ZC* 146. Image, *ZW* 2. 288.

Wei gu biqiunitong fashi Shi Sengzhi muzhiming 魏故比丘尼統法師釋僧芝墓誌銘 [*The Entombed Biography and Eulogy of the Wei Superintendent of the Bhikṣuṇīs, the Dharma Master, Shi Sengzhi*], *ZZ* 20.

Wei gu cheji dajiang jun pingshu wending xing gong ji furen dajuesi biqiuyuanni muzhiming bingxu 魏故車騎大將軍平舒文定邢公繼夫人大覺寺比丘元尼墓誌銘并序 [*Preface and Entombed Biography of the Bhikṣuṇī of the Yuan Family from the Great Awakening Nunnery*]. Transcription, *ZC* 261. Image, *B* 5. 126.

Wei gu gong yu zuo nü shangshu Feng Nülang zhi zhi 魏故宮御作女尚書馮女郎之誌 [*The Biography of Feng Nülang, the Woman Secretary of the palace of the Wei*], *ZW*, 123.

Weimojie suoshuo jing 維摩詰所說經 [*Vimalakīrti-nirdeśa Sūtra*], *T* no. 475.

Xianyu Jing 賢愚經 [*Sūtra on the Wise and the Fool*], *T* no. 202.

Xin Tang shu 新唐書 [*New Book of the Tang*]. 225 *juan*. Compiled by Ouyang Xiu 歐陽修 (1007–72) and Qi Song 宋祁 (998–1061). Beijing: Zhonghua shu ju, 1975.

Xu gaoseng zhuan 續高僧傳 [*Extended Biographies of Eminent Monks*], *T* no. 2060.

Yili zhu zi suoyin 儀禮逐字索引 [*A Concordance to the Yili*]. Edited by D. C. Lau, Ho Che Wah and Chen Fong Ching. ICS series. Taiwan: Commercial Press, 1996.

Yinsenü jing 銀色女經 [*Sūtra of the Woman, "Silver Countenance"*], *T* no. 179.

Zhou shu 周書 [*Book of the Zhou*]. 50 *juan*. Compiled by Linghu Defen 令狐德棻 (583–666) et al. Beijing: Zhonghua shuju, 1971.

Zhuan nüshen jing 轉女身經 [*Sūtra on Transforming the Female Form*], *T* no. 564.

Zhuangzi zhu zi suoyin 莊子逐字索引 [*A Concordance to the Zhuangzi*]. Edited by D. C. Lau, Ho Che Wah, and Chen Fong Ching. ICS series. Hong Kong: Commercial Press, 2000.

SECONDARY SOURCES

Abé, Ryūichi. "Revisiting the Dragon Princess: Her Role in Medieval *Engi* Stories and Their Implications in the Lotus Sutra." *Japanese Journal of Religious Studies* 42, no. 1 (2015): 27–70.

Abramson, Marc S. *Ethnic Identity in Tang China.* Encounters with Asia Series. Philadelphia: University of Pennsylvania Press, 2008.

Adamek, Wendi. *Practicescapes and the Buddhists of Baoshan.* Hamburg Buddhist Studies 19. Bochum/Freiburg: Projekt Verlag, 2021.

Anālayo. "Women's Renunciation in Early Buddhism: The Four Assemblies and the Foundation of the Order of Nuns." In *Dignity and Discipline: Reviving Full Ordination for Buddhist Nuns*, edited by Thea Mohr and Jampa Tsedroen, 65–98. Somerville, MA: Wisdom, 2010.

Balkwill, Stephanie. "Disappearing and Disappeared Daughters in Medieval Chinese Buddhism: Sūtras on Sexual Transformation and an Intervention into Their Transmission History." *History of Religions* 60, no. 4 (May 2021): 255–86.

———. "Metropolitan Buddhism vis-à-vis Buddhism at the Metropolis: How to Understand the *Ling* in the Empress Dowager's Name." In *Buddhist Statecraft in East Asia*, edited by Stephanie Balkwill and James Benn, 24–47. Studies on East Asian Religions 6. Leiden: Brill, 2022.

———. "The Sūtra of the Unsullied Worthy Girl as Spoken by the Buddha." *Journal of Chinese Buddhist Studies* 34 (2021): 5–26.

———. "The Sūtra on Transforming the Female Form: Unpacking an Early Medieval Chinese Buddhist Text." *Journal of Chinese Religions* 44, no. 2 (2016): 127–48.

———. "A Virtuoso Nun in the North: Situating the Earliest-Known Dated Biography of a Buddhist Nun in East Asia." *Hualin Journal of Buddhist Studies* 3, no. 2 (2020): 129–60.

———. "When Renunciation is Good Politics: The Women of the Imperial Nunnery of the Northern Wei (386–534)." *Nan Nü: Men, Women, and Gender in China* 18, no. 2 (2016): 224–56.

Benn, James. *Burning for the Buddha: Self-Immolation in Chinese Buddhism*. Kuroda Institute Studies in East Asian Buddhism 19. Honolulu: University of Hawai'i Press, 2007.

Bokenkamp, Stephen R. *Ancestors and Anxiety: Daoism and the Birth of Rebirth in China*. Berkeley: University of California Press, 2009.

———. *Early Daoist Scriptures*. Berkeley: University of California Press, 1999.

———. "Record of the Feng and Shan Sacrifices." In *Religions of China in Practice*, edited by Donald S. Lopez, 251–60. Princeton, NJ: Princeton University Press, 1996.

Boodberg, Peter A. "The Language of the T'o-Pa Wei." *Harvard Journal of Asiatic Studies* 1, no. 2 (1936): 167–815.

Bourland, Joel. "Queer Theory and the Shamanic Ideal: Towards an Anthropology of Ecstasy, Affect, and Sexual Pluralism." *University of Toronto Art Journal* 6 (Spring 2018): 1–18.

Broadbridge, Anne F. *Women and the Making of the Mongol Empire*. Cambridge: Cambridge University Press, 2018.

Bryson, Megan. "Images of Humane Kings: Rulers in the Dali-Kingdom Painting of Buddhist Images." In *Buddhist Statecraft in East Asia*, edited by Stephanie Balkwill and James A. Benn, 87–118. Leiden: Brill, 2022.

Campany, Robert Ford. *Making Transcendents: Ascetics and Social Memory in Early Medieval China*. Honolulu: University of Hawai'i Press, 2009.

Carriere, Frederick F., ed. *Silla Korea and the Silk Roads: Golden Age, Golden Threads*. New York: Korea Society, 2006.

Caswell, James O. *Written and Unwritten: A New History of the Buddhist Caves at Yungang*. Vancouver: University of British Colombia Press, 1988.

Chaussende, Damien. "Être historien dans la Chine classique: un métier à risque." *Être historien dans la Chine classique: un métier à risque*. June 2010, 241–54.

Chen, BuYun. *Empire of Style: Silk and Fashion in Tang China*. Seattle: University of Washington Press, 2019.

Chen, Jo-Shui. "Empress Wu and Proto-Feminist Sentiments in T'ang China." In *Imperial Rulership and Cultural Change in Traditional China*, edited by Frederick P. Brandauer and Chun-Chieh Huang, 77–116. Seattle: University of Washington Press, 1994.

Chen Kaiying 陳開穎. *Xingbie, xinkou, quanli—Beiwei nüzhu zhuenzhi yu Fojiao* 性別，信仰，權力——北魏女主政治與佛教 [*Gender, Religion, Power: Politics and Buddhism for Empress Rulers in Northern Wei Dynasty*]. Zhengzhou: Zhengzhou daxue chubanshe, 2017.

Chen Jinhua. "The Indian Buddhist Missionary Dharmakṣema (385–433): A New Dating of His Arrival in Guzang and of His Translations." *T'oung Pao*, Second Series, 90, nos. 4/5 (2004): 215–63.

———. *Philosopher, Practitioner, Politician: The Many Lives of Fazang (643–712)*. Leiden: Brill, 2007.

———. "Śarīra and Scepter. Empress Wu's Political Use of Buddhist Relics." *Journal of the International Association of Buddhist Studies* 25, no. 1–2 (2002): 33–150.

Chen Qingxiang 陳清香. "Maiji shan 133 ku 10 hao zaoxiangbei de tuxiang yuanliu yu zongjiao neihan 麥積山133窟10號造像碑的圖像源流與宗教內涵" ["Origins and Religious Content in the Imagery of the Image Stele Number 10 in Cave 133 at Maiji shan"]. *Chung-Hwa Buddhist Journal* 18 (2005): 75–105.

Chen Ruifeng. *Informed Textual Practices?: A Study of Dunhuang Manuscripts of Chinese Buddhist Apocryphal Scriptures with Colophons*. PhD diss., McMaster University, 2020.

Chen Sanping. *Multicultural China in the Early Middle Ages*. Philadelphia: University of Pennsylvania Press, 2012.

Chen Shuguo. "State Religious Ceremonies." In *Early Chinese Religion. Part Two: The Period of Division (220–589)*, edited by John Lagerway and Lü Pengzhi, 1:53–142. Leiden: Brill, 2010.

Cheng, Bonnie. "Fashioning a Political Body: The Tomb of a Rouran Princess." *Archives of Asian Art* 57 (2007): 23–49.

Cheng Ya-ju 鄭雅如. "Hanzhi yu hufeng: zhongcai Beiwei de 'huang hou,' 'huang taihou' zhidu." 漢制與胡風：重探北魏的「皇后」、「皇太后」制度 ["Han System and Hu Style: Revisiting the System of 'Empress' and 'Empress Dowager' in the Northern Wei."] *Journal of the Institute of History and Philology at Academia Sinica* 90, no. 1 (2019): 1–76.

Chikusa Masaaki 竺沙雅章. *Chūgoku Bukkyō shakaishi kenkyū* 中国仏教社會史研究 [*Studies on Chinese Buddhist Organizations*]. Tōyōshi Kenkyū Sōkan. Kyōto: Dōhōsha shuppan, 1982.

Chikusa Masaaki. "The Formation and Growth of Buddhist Nun Communities in China." In *Engendering Faith: Women and Buddhism in Premodern Japan*, edited by Barbara Ruch and translated by Philip Yampolsky, 3–20. Ann Arbor: University of Michigan Press, 2002.

Chittick, Andrew. *The Jiankang Empire in Chinese and World History*. New York: Oxford University Press, 2020.

———. *Patronage and Community in Medieval China: The Xiangyang Garrison, 400–600 CE*. Albany: SUNY Press, 2009.

Choo, Jessey J. C. *Inscribing Death: Burials, Representations, and Remembrance in Tang China*. Honolulu: University of Hawai'i Press, 2022.

Clarke, Shayne. *Family Matters in Indian Monasticisms*. Honolulu: University of Hawai'i Press, 2014.

Como, Michael. *Weaving and Binding: Immigrant Gods and Female Immortals In Ancient Japan*. Honolulu: University of Hawai'i Press, 2009.

Davis, Timothy M. *Entombed Epigraphy and Commemorative Culture in Early Medieval China: A Brief History of Early Muzhiming*. Studies in the History of Chinese Texts 6. Leiden: Brill, 2015.

Declercq, Dominik. "Wei Shu 魏書, Chapter 114: Treatise on Buddhism and Taoism 释老志." In *Investigating Principles: International Aspects of Buddhist Culture: Essays in Honour of Professor Charles Willemen*, edited by Lalji "Shravak" and Supriya Rai, 45–133. Hong Kong: Buddha-Dharma Centre of Hong Kong, 2019.

———. *Writing Against the State: Political Rhetorics in Third and Fourth Century China*. Sinica Leidensia 39. Leiden: Brill, 1998.

de Crespigny, Rafe. *Emperor Huan and Emperor Ling: Being the Chronicle of the Later Han for the years 157 to 189 AD as recorded in Chapters 54–59 of the Zizhi tongjian of Sima Guang*. Canberra: Australian National University, Faculty of Asian Studies, 1989.

de Raschewiltz, Igor. *The Secret History of the Mongols: A Mongolian Epic Chronicle of the Thirteenth Century*. 2 vols. Brill's Inner Asian Library 7. Leiden: Brill, 2006.

de Rauw, Tom. "Baochang: Sixth-Century Biographer of Buddhist Monks . . . and Nuns?" *Journal of the American Oriental Society* 125, no. 2 (June 2005): 203–18.

———. "The Political Use of Buddhism by Emperor Wu of the Liang Dynasty (r. 502–549)." PhD diss., Ghent University, 2008.

Despeux, Catherine, and Livia Kohn. *Women in Daoism*. Cambridge, MA: Three Pines Press, 2003.

DiCosmo, Nicola. "Han Frontiers: Toward an Integrated View." *Journal of the American Oriental Society* 129, no. 2 (2009): 199–214.

Dien, Albert E. *Six Dynasties Civilization*. Early Chinese Civilization Series. New Haven, CT: Yale University Press, 2007.

Duthie, Nina. "The Nature of the *Hu*: Wuhuan and Xianbei Ethnography in the *San Guo Zhi* and *Hou Han Shu*." *Early Medieval China* 25 (2019): 23–41.

———. "Origins, Ancestors, and Imperial Authority in Early Northern Wei Historiography." PhD diss., Columbia University, 2015. https://doi.org/10.7916/D8NC601F.

Ebrey, Patricia. "Later Han Stone Inscriptions." *Harvard Journal of Asiatic Studies* 40, no. 2 (December 1980): 325–53.

Emmerick, R. E. *Tibetan Texts Concerning Khotan*. London Oriental Series 19. Oxford: Oxford University Press, 1967.

Espesset, Grégoire. "Latter Han Religious Movements and the Early Daoist Church." In *Early Chinese Religion: Part One: Shang through Han (1250 BC–220 AD)*, edited by John Lagerway and Mark Kalinowski, 1061–1102. Leiden: Brill, 2009.

Farmer, Michael J. "Jia Nanfeng." In *Biographical Dictionary of Chinese Women: Antiquity Through Sui 1600 B.C.E–618 C.E*, edited by Lily Xiao Hong Lee and A. D. Stefanowska, 302–7. New York, Routledge: 2017.

———. "The Three Chaste Ones of Ba: Local Perspectives on the Yellow Turban Rebellion on the Chengdu Plain." *Journal of the American Oriental Society* 125, no. 2 (June 2005): 191–202.

Faure, Bernard. "Les Cloches de La Terre: Un Aspect Du Culte Des Reliques Dans Le Bouddhisme Chinois." In *Bouddhisme et Lettrés Dans La Chine Médiévale*, edited by Catherine Despeux, 25–44. Paris: Éditions Peeters, 2002.

Foulks-McGuire, Beverly. "Playing with Karma: A Buddhist Board Game." *Material Religion: The Journal of Objects, Art and Belief* 10, no. 1 (2014): 4–28.

Forte, Antonino. *Mingtang and Buddhist Utopias in the History of the Astronomical Clock: The Tower, Stature and Armillary Sphere Constructed by Empress Wu.* Serie Orientale Roma. Rome/Paris: Instituto Italiano per il Medio ed Estremo Oriente/EFEO, 1988.

———. *Political Propaganda and Ideology in China at the End of the Seventh Century: Inquiry into the Nature, Authors and Function of the Tunhuang Document S. 6502, Followed by an Annotated Translation.* 2nd ed. Kyoto: Scuola Italiana di Studi sull'Asia Orientale, 2005.

Geng Shimin 耿世民. *Gudai Tujueyu yufa* 古代突厥语语法 *[A Grammar of Old Turkic].* Beijing: Zhongyang Minzu Daxue Chubanshe, 2010.

Goble, Geoffrey. *Chinese Esoteric Buddhism: Amoghavajra, the Ruling Elite, and the Emergence of a Tradition.* New York: Columbia University Press, 2019.

Golavachev, Valentin C. "Matricide among the Tuoba-Xianbei and Its Transformation during the Northern Wei." *Early Medieval China* 8 (2002): 1–42.

Graff, David A. *Medieval Chinese Warfare, 300–900.* London: Routledge, 2002.

Granger, Kelsey. "Violence, Vigilantism, and Virtue: Reassessing Medieval Female Avenger Accounts through the Study of Narratives about Xie Xiao'e." *Journal of the American Oriental Society* 142, no. 4 (2022): 915–34.

Gu Yanfang 顧彥芳. "Huangfu gong ku san bi kan xiang ji lifo tu kao 皇甫公窟三壁龕像及禮佛圖考" ["A Study on the Concave Images of the Huangfu gong Cave and the Buddha-worshipping Image"]. *Dunhuang Research* 敦煌研究, no. 4 (2001): 84–91.

Guilmoto, Christophe Z., and James Tovey. "The Masculinization of Births: Overview and Current Knowledge." *Population (English Edition, 2002–)* 70, no. 2 (2015): 184–243.

Guisso, R.W.L. *Wu Tse-T'ien and the Politics of Legitimation in T'ang China.* Bellingham: Western Washington University, 1978.

Hallisey, Charles. *Therigatha: Selected Poems of the First Buddhist Women.* Murty Classical Library of India 3. Cambridge, MA: Harvard University Press, 2015.

Hao Chunwen 郝春文. "The Social Life of Buddhist Monks and Nuns in Dunhuang during the Late Tang, Five Dynasties, and Early Song." *Asia Major* 23, no. 2 (2010): 77–96.

———. *Zhonggu shiqi sheyi yanjiu* 中古時期社邑研究 *[A Study of Lay Organizations in the Medieval Period].* Shanghai: Shanghai guji chubanshe, 2019.

Hendrischke, Barbara. *The Scripture on Great Peace: The Taiping Jing and the Beginnings of Daoism.* Berkeley: University of California Press, 2006.

Heirman, Ann. "Buddhist Nuns: Between Past and Present." *Numen* 58 (2011): 603–31.

———. "Chinese Nuns and Their Ordination in Fifth-Century China." *Journal of the International Association of Buddhist Studies* 24, no. 2 (2001): 275–304.

Hinsch, Bret. "Confucian Filial Piety and the Construction of Ideal Chinese Buddhist Women." *Journal of Chinese Religions* 30 (2002): 49–75.

Holcombe, Charles. "The Xianbei in Chinese History." *Early Medieval China* 19 (2013): 1–38.

Holmgren, Jennifer. *Annals of Tai: Early T'o-Pa History According to the First Chapter of the Wei-Shu.* Canberra: Faculty of Asian Studies in association with Australian National University Press, 1982.

———. "Empress Dowager Ling of the Northern Wei and the T'o-Ba Sinicization Question." *Papers on Far Eastern History* 18 (1978): 123–70.

———. "Family, Marriage and Political Power in Sixth Century China: A Study of the Kao Family of the Northern Ch'i, c. 520–550." *Journal of Asian History* 16, no. 1 (1982): 1–50.

———. "Lineage Falsification in the Northern Dynasties: Wei Shou's Ancestry." *Papers on Far Eastern History* 21 (1980): 1–16.

———. "The Northern Wei as a Conquest Dynasty: Current Perceptions; Past Scholarship." *Papers on Far Eastern History* 40 (1989): 1–50.

Hori Toshikazu 堀敏一. *Kindensei no kenkyū : Chūgoku kodai kokka no tochi seisaku to tochi shoyūsei* 均田制の研究:中国古代国家の土地政策と土地所有制 *[Research on the Equal Field System: Land Policy and the System of Land Ownership in the States of Ancient China].* Tokyo: Iwanami Shoten, 1975.

Hou Xudong 侯旭东. *Fotuo xiangyou: Zaoxiangji suojian beichao minzhong xinyang* 佛陀相佑：所见北朝民众信仰 *[The Buddha's Reciprocal Protection: People's Faith as Seen in the Northern Dynasties].* Beijing: Shehui kexue wenxian chubanshe, 2018.

———. "Rethinking Chinese Kinship in the Han and the Six Dynasties: A Preliminary Observation." Translated by Howard L. Goodman. *Asia Major* 3, no. 23 (2010): 29–63.

———.*Wu liu shiji beifang minzhong Fojiao xinyang (xiuding ben)* 五六世紀北方民众佛教信仰【修订本】 *[Buddhist Faith of Northern People in the Fifth and Sixth Centuries (Revised Version)].* Beijing: Shehui kexue wenxian chubanshe, 2015.

Howard, Angela F. "Buddhist Cave Sculpture of the Northern Qi Dynasty: Shaping a New Style, Formulating New Iconographies." *Archives of Asian Art* 49 (1996): 6–25.

Hucker, Charles O. *A Dictionary of Official Titles in Imperial China.* Stanford, CA: Stanford University Press, 1985.

Hughes, April. "Re-examining the Zhengming Jing: The Social and Political Life of an Apocryphal Maitreya Scripture." *Journal of Chinese Religions* 45, no. 1 (2017): 1–18.

———. *Worldly Saviors and Imperial Authority in Medieval Chinese Buddhism.* Honolulu: University of Hawai'i Press, 2021.

Hurvitz, Leon. "Wei Shou. Treatise on Buddhism and Taoism. An English Translation of the Original Chinese Text of Wei-Shu CXIV and the Japanese Annotation of Tsukamoto Zenryū." In *Unkō sekkutsu. Seireki go-seiki ni okeru Chūgoku hokubu Bukkyō kutsu-in no kōkogaku-teki chōsa hōkoku. tōyō bunka kenkyū-sho chōsa Shōwa jūsan-nen Shōwa nijūnen* 雲崗石窟.西暦五世紀における中國北部佛教窟院考古學的調査報告•東方文化研究所調査昭和十三年•昭和二十年 *[Yun-Kang: the Buddhist Cave-Temples of the Fifth Century A.D. in North China. Detailed Report of the Archaeological Survey Carried out by the Mission of the Tōyō Bunka Kenkyū-Sho 1938–45].* Vol. 16, Supplement. Kyoto: Jinbunkagaku kenkyū-sho, Kyoto University, 1956.

Ishimatsu Hinako 石松日奈子. *Beiwei Fojiao zaoxiang yanjiu* 北魏佛教造像史研究 *[Buddhist Images in the Northern Wei Period].* Translated by Shinohara Norio 筱原典生. Beijing: Wenwu chubanshe, 2007.

Janhunen, Juha, ed. *The Mongolic Languages.* Routledge Language Family Series. London: Routledge, 2003.

Janousch, Andreas. "The Aśoka of China: Emperor Wu of the Liang Dynasty (r. 502–549) and the Buddhist Monastic Community (Saṅgha)." *Frühmittelaltererliche Studien* 50, no. 1 (2016): 255–95.

———. "The Emperor as Bodhisattva: The Bodhisattva Ordination and Ritual Assemblies of Emperor Wu of the Liang Dynasty." In *State and Court Ritual in China*, edited by J. P. McDermott, 112–49. Cambridge: Cambridge University Press, 1999.

Kang Le 康樂. *Cong xijiao dao nanjia: Guojia jidian yu Beiwei zhengzhi* 從西郊到南郊國家祭典與北魏政治 [*From the Western Suburbs to the Southern Suburbs: Imperial Ritual and the Governance of the Northern Wei*]. Taipei: Daohe chubanshe, 1995.

Kieffer-Pulz, Petra. Review of *Managing Monks: Administrators and Administrative Roles in Indian Buddhist Monasticism*, by Jonathan Silk. *Indo-Iranian Journal* 53 (2010): 71–88.

Kinney, Anne Behnke, trans. *Exemplary Women of Early China: The Lienü Zhuan of Liu Xiang*. Translations from the Asian Classics. New York: Columbia University Press, 2014.

Kleeman, Terry F. *Celestial Masters: History and Ritual in Early Daoist Communities*. Harvard-Yenching Institute Monograph Series 102. Cambridge, MA: Harvard University Press, 2016.

Klein, Kenneth "Wei Shu." In *Early Medieval Chinese Texts: A Bibliographical Guide*, edited by Cynthia L. Chennault, Keith N. Knapp, Alan J. Berkowitz, and Albert E. Dien, 368–372. China Research Monograph 71. Oakland: University of California Press, 2014.

Knapp, Keith Nathaniel. *Selfless Offspring: Filial Children and Social Order in Medieval China*. Honolulu: University of Hawai'i, 2005.

Ko, Dorothy, JaHyun Kim Haboush, and Joan R. Piggott, eds. *Women and Confucian Cultures in Premodern China, Korea, and Japan*. Berkeley: University of California Press, 2003.

Kwa, Shiamin, and Wilt L. Idema, eds. *Mulan: Five Versions of a Classic Chinese Legend, with Related Texts*. Indianapolis: Hackett, 2010.

Lai Fei 賴非. *Shandong beichao Fojiao moya kejing diaocha yu yanjiu* 山東北朝佛教摩崖刻经调查与研究 [*Investigation and Study of the Buddhist Inscribed Sūtras and Carved Cliffs from Northern Dynasties Shandong*]. Beijing: Kexue chubanshe, 2007.

Lai, Chi-tim. "The Opposition of Celestial-Master Taoism to Popular Cults during the Six Dynasties." *Asia Major* 11, no. 1 (1998): 1–20.

Lai, Whalen. "The Earliest Folk Buddhist Religion in China: T'i-Wei Po-Li Ching and Its Historical Significance." In *Buddhist and Taoist Practice in Medieval Chinese Society: Buddhist and Taoist Studies II*, edited by David W. Chappell, 11–35. Honolulu: University of Hawai'i Press, 1987.

Lamotte, Étienne. *History of Indian Buddhism: From the Origins to the Śaka Era*. Translated by Sara Webb-Boin. Publications de l'Institute Orientaliste de Louvain 36. Louvain: Peeters, 1988.

Lee, Jen-der. "The Life of Women in the Six Dynasties." *Journal of Women and Gender Studies* 4 (1993): 47–80.

Lee, Soyoung, and Denise Patry Leidy. *Silla: Korea's Golden Kingdom*. Metropolitan Museum of Art. Metropolitan Museum of Art, 2013.

Legge, James. *The I Ching*. Vol. 16, *The Sacred Books of China*. 2nd ed. New York: Dover, 1963.

Lerner, Judith. "Aspects of Assimilation: The Funerary Practices and Furnishings of Central Asians in China." *Sino-Platonic Papers* 168 (2005): http://www.sino-platonic.org /complete/spp168_sogdian_funerary_practices.pdf.

Lewis, Mark Edward. *China Between Empires: The Northern and Southern Dynasties*. Cambridge, MA: Harvard University Press, 2009.

———. "Mothers and Sons in Early Imperial China." *Extrême-Orient Extrême-Occident*. Hors-Série, 2012. http://extremeorient.revues.org/226.

———. "Writing the World in the Family Instructions of the Yan Clan." *Early Medieval China* 13–14, no. 1 (2007): 33–80.

Li Zhengfen 李正奮. "*Wei shu yuanliu kao* 魏書源流考" ["Research on the Origins of the Weishu"]. *Guoxue Jikan* 國學季刊 2, no. 2 (1929): 362–82.

Lin Baocong 林寶琮. *Beiwei juntian zhidu zhi yanjiu* 北魏均田制度之研究 *[Research on the Equal Field System in the Northern Wei]*. Taichung: Taile chubanshe, 1989.

Lingley, Kate. "Lady Yuchi in the First Person: Patronage, Kinship, and Voice in the Guyang Cave." *Early Medieval China* 18 (2012): 25–47.

———. "Patron and Community in Eastern Wei Shanxi: The Gaomiaoshan Cave Temple Yi-Society." *Asia Major* 23.1 (2010): 127–72.

Liu Guoxiang 刘国祥 and Ni Runan 倪润安. "Gaxian dong yizhi de faxian ji xiangguang wenti tantao 嘎仙洞遗址的发现及相关问题探讨" ["An Investigation into Questions Related to Explorations of the Gaxian Cave"]. *Wenwu* 文物 [*Cultural Relics*], no. 11 (2014): 53–61.

Liu, Shu-fen. "Art, Ritual, and Society: Buddhist Practice in Rural China during the Northern Dynasties." *Asia Major* 8, no. 1 (1995): 19–49.

———. "Ethnicity and the Suppression of Buddhism in Fifth-Century North China: The Background and Significance of the Gaiwu Rebellion." *Asia Major*, 3rd ser., 15, no. 1 (2002): 1–21.

Liu Ts'un-Yan. *Selected Papers from the Hall of Harmonious Wind*. Leiden: Brill, 1976.

Lo, Yuet Keung. "Conversion to Chastity: A Buddhist Catalyst in Early Imperial China." *Nan Nü: Men, Women, and Gender in China* 10, no. 1 (March 2008): 22–56.

———. "Recovering a Buddhist Voice on Daughters-in-Law: The Yuyenü Jing." *History of Religions* 44, no. 4 (2005): 318–50.

Loukota Sanclemente, Diego. "Finding the Missing Nuns of Nuava: A Philological-Archeological Inquiry." Paper presented at Annual Conference of the International Association of Buddhist Studies, Seoul, August 2022.

———. "The Goods That Cannot Be Stolen: Mercantile Faith in Kumāralāta's Garland of Examples Adorned by Poetic Fancy." PhD diss., University of California Los Angeles, 2019.

Lourme, Jean Marie, trans. *Yang Xuanzhi: Mémoire Sur Les Monastères Bouddhiques de Luoyang* [*Luoyang qielan ji* 洛陽伽藍記]. [Yang Xuanzhi: Records of the Buddhist Monasteries of Luoyang]. Bibliothèque Chinoise 15. Paris: Les Belles Lettres, 2014.

Lowe, Bryan D. *Ritualized Writing: Buddhist Practice and Scriptural Cultures in Ancient Japan*. Kuroda Institute Studies in East Asian Buddhism 27. Honolulu: University of Hawai'i Press, 2017.

Luoyang shi wenwu ju 洛阳市文物局 and Luoyang Baima si hanwei gucheng wenwu baoguan 洛阳白马寺汉魏故城文物保管, eds. *Han Wei Luoyang gucheng yanjiu* 汉魏洛阳故城研究 *[Studies of the Imperial Cities of Luoyang from the Han to the Wei]*.

Luoyang wenwu yu kaogu 洛阳文物与考古 [*Cultural Artifacts and Archaeology of Luoyang*]. Beijing: Kexue chubanshe, 2000.

Mair, Victor H. "The Linguistic and Textual Antecedents of *The Sūtra on the Wise and the Foolish.*" *Sino-Platonic Papers* 38 (1993): 1–95.

———. Review of *Written and Unwritten: A New History of the Buddhist Caves at Yungang*, by James Caswell. *Harvard Journal of Asiatic Studies* 52, no. 1 (June 1992): 345–61.

Mather, Richard B. "K'ou Ch'ien-Chih and the Taoist Theocracy at the Northern Wei Court, 425–451." In *Facets of Taoism*, edited by Holmes Welch and Anna Seidel, 103–22. New Haven, CT: Yale University Press, 2002.

McBride II, Richard. *Domesticating the Dharma: Buddhist Cults and the Hwaom Synthesis in Silla Korea*. Honolulu: University If Hawai'i Press, 2007.

———. "King Chinhŭng Institutes State-Protection Buddhist Rituals." In *Buddhist Statecraft in East Asia*, edited by Stephanie Balkwill and James A. Benn, 48–65. Leiden: Brill, 2022.

———. "Why Did Kungye Claim to Be the Buddha Maitreya? The Maitreya Cult and Royal Power in the Silla-Koryŏ Transition." *Journal of Inner and East Asian Studies* 2, no. 1 (2004): 36–60.

McMahon, Keith. "Women Rulers in Imperial China." *Nan Nü: Men, Women, and Gender in China* 15, no. 2 (2013): 179–218.

McNair, Amy. *Donors of Longmen: Faith, Politics, and Patronage in Medieval Chinese Buddhist Sculpture*. Honolulu: University of Hawai'i Press, 2007.

———. "Ways of Reading and Writing in Medieval Chinese Relief Shrines: Examples from Guyang Grotto, Longmen." *Zurich Studies in the History of Art* 13/14 (July 2006): 186–205.

Miao Linlin 苗霖霖. "Beiwei hougong zhidu kaolun 北魏后宫制度考论" ["Investigation on the Structure of the Empress's Court in the Northern Wei"]. *Heilongjiang National Series* 黑龙江民族丛刊 2 (2016): 97–101. https://doi.org/10.16415/j.cnki.23-1021/c.2016.02.018.

———. "Beiwei houguan zhidu yanjiu 北魏后宫制度研究" ["Research on the System in the Palace in the Northern Wei Dynasty"]. PhD diss., Jilin University, 2011.

Miyake, Marc. " 'Budda Khan' in Korea and Japan." *Amaravati: Abode of Amritas* (blog), November 23, 2013. http://www.amritas.com/131123.htm#11232333.

———. Review of *Translating Chinese Tradition and Teaching Tangut Culture: Manuscripts and Printed Books from Khara-Khoto*, by Imre Galambos. *Cahiers de Linguistique Asia Orientale* 45 (2016): 184–90.

Mohr, Thea, and Jampa Tsedroen, eds. *Dignity and Discipline: Reviving Full Ordination for Buddhist Nuns*. Boston: Wisdom, 2010.

Morgan, Sue. "Theorising Feminist History: a Thirty-Year Retrospective." *Women's History Review* 18. 3 (2009): 381–407.

Ohnuma, Reiko. *Head, Eyes, Flesh, and Blood: Giving Away the Body in Indian Buddhist Literature*. New York: Columbia University Press, 2007.

———. "The Story of Rūpāvatī: A Female Past Birth of the Buddha." *Journal of the International Association of Buddhist Studies* 23, no. 1 (2000): 103–46.

Ooms, Herman. *Imperial Politics and Symbolics in Ancient Japan: The Tenmu Dynasty, 650–800*. Honolulu: University of Hawai'i Press, 2008.

Orzech, Charles D. "Metaphor, Translation, and the Construction of Kingship in the *Scripture for Humane Kings* and the *Mahāmāyūrī Vidyārājñī Sūtra.*" *Cahiers d'Extrême-Asie* 13 (2002): 55–83.

———. *Politics and Transcendent Wisdom: The Scripture for Humane Kings in the Creation of Chinese Buddhism.* Hermeneutics: Studies in the History of Religions. University Park: Penn State University Press, 2008.

Ownby, David. "Chinese Millenarian Traditions: The Formative Age." *American Historical Review* 104, no. 5 (December 1999): 1513–30.

Pang, Shiying. "Eminent Nuns and/or/as Virtuous Women: The Representation of Tang Female Renunciants in Tomb Inscriptions." *T'ang Studies* 28 (2010): 77–96.

Paul, Diana, and John McRae. *The Sutra of Queen Śrīmālā of the Lion's Roar / The Vimalakīrti Sutra.* BDK English Tripiṭaka. Berkeley, CA: BDK America, 2004.

Pearce, Scott. "A King's Two Bodies: The Northern Wei Emperor Wencheng and Representations of the Power of His Monarchy." *Frontiers of History in China* 7, no. 1 (2012): 90–105.

———. *Northern Wei (386–534): A New Form of Empire in East Asia.* Oxford Studies in Early Empires. New York: Oxford University Press, 2023.

———. "Nurses, Nurslings, and New Shapes of Power in the Mid-Wei Court." *Asia Major* 22, no. 1 (2009): 287–309.

———. "A Response to Valentin Golovachev's 'Matricide During the Northern Wei.'" *Early Medieval China* 1 (2003): 139–44.

———. Review of *Yungang: Art, History, Archaeology, Liturgy*, by Lidu Yi. *Early Medieval China*, 26 (2020): 110–14.

Piggott, Joan R. *The Emergence of Japanese Kingship.* Stanford, CA: Stanford University Press, 1997.

Pines, Yuri. *The Everlasting Empire: The Political Culture of Ancient China and Its Imperial Legacy.* Princeton, NJ: Princeton University Press, 2012.

Psarras, Sophia-Karin. "Han and Xiongnu: A Reexamination of Cultural and Political Relations (II)." *Monumenta Serica*, 52 (2004).

Pu Xuanyi 蒲宣伊. "Zigui musi de xiemu—(Wei yaoguang si ni Ciyi muzhiming) yanjiu 子貴母死的謝幕——《魏瑤光寺尼慈義墓志銘》研究" ["The Ending of the Policy of 'Killing the Mother if the Son is to be Enshrined': A Study on the Tomb Inscription of Nun Ciyi of the Yaoguang Monastery in the Northern Wei"]. *Wenxian* 文献, no. 02 (2019): 25–33.

Radich, Michael. "Problems of Attribution, Style, and Dating Relating to the 'Great Cloud Sutras' in the Chinese Buddhist Canon (T 387, T 388/S.6916)." In *Buddhist Transformations and Interactions: Essays in Honor of Antonino Forte*, edited by Victor Mair, 235–89. New York: Cambria Press, 2017.

Raphals, Lisa Ann. *Sharing the Light: Representations of Women and Virtue in Early China.* SUNY Series, Chinese Philosophy and Culture. Albany: State University of New York Press, 1998.

Rong Xinjiang. *Eighteen Lectures on Dunhuang.* Translated by Imre Galambos. Brill's Humanities in China Library 5. Leiden: Brill, 2013.

Rothschild, Harry N. *Emperor Wu Zhao and Her Pantheon of Devis, Divinities, and Dynastic Mothers.* Sheng Yen Series in Chinese Buddhist Studies. New York: Columbia University Press, 2015.

———. "'Her Influence Great, Her Merit beyond Measure': A Translation and Initial Investigation of the Epitaph of Shangguan Wan'er." *Studies in Chinese Religions* 1, no. 2 (2015): 31–48.

Sailey, Jay, trans. *Master Who Embraces Simplicity: A Study of the Philosopher Ko Hung, 283–343*. San Francisco: Chinese Materials Center, 1978.

Safonova, Tatiana, and István Sántha. "Gender Distinctions in an Egalitarian Society: The Case of Evenki People of the Baikal Region." *Anthropology of East Europe Review* 28, no. 2 (2010): 120–39.

Schafer, Edward H. "Falconry in T'ang Times." *T'oung Pao* 46, nos. 3/5 (January 1958): 293–338.

Schopen, Gregory. "On Emptying Chamber Pots without Looking and the Urban Location of Buddhist Nunneries in Early India Again." *Journal Asiatique* 296, no. 2 (2008): 229–56.

Schwartz, Wendy. "Revisiting the Scene of the Party: A Study of the Lanting Collection." *Journal of the American Oriental Society* 132, no. 2 (April–June 2012): 275–300.

Seiwert, Hubert. *Popular Religious Movements and Heterodox Sects in Chinese History*. Leiden: Brill, 2003.

Shimunek, Andrew. *Languages of the Ancient Southern Mongolia and North China: A Historical-Comparative Study of the Serbi or Xianbei Branch of the Serbi-Mongolic Language Family*. Wiesbaden: Harrassowitz Verlag, 2017.

Silk, Jonathan. *Managing Monks: Administrators and Administrative Roles in Indian Monastic Buddhism*. Oxford: Oxford University Press, 2008.

Slingerland, Edward. *Confucius, The Essential Analects: Selected Passages with Traditional Commentary*. Indianapolis: Hackett., 2006.

Song Qirui 宋其蕤. *Beiwei nüzhu lun* 北魏女主論. [*On Female Rulers of the Northern Wei*]. Beijing: Zhongguo shehuikexue chubanshe, 2006.

Soper, Alexander Coburn. "Imperial Cave-Chapels of the Northern Dynasties: Donors, Beneficiaries, Dates." *Artibus Asiae* 28, no. 4 (1966): 241–70.

Steinhardt, Nancy Shatman. *Chinese Architecture in an Age of Turmoil, 200–600*. Honolulu: University of Hawai'i Press, 2014.

Strong, John S. *The Legend of King Aśoka: A Study and Translation of the Aśokavādana*. Princeton Library of Asian Translations. Princeton, NJ: Princeton University Press, 1983.

Su Bai 宿白. *Zhongguo Fojiao shikusi yiji: 3 dao 8 shiji zhongguo Fojiao kaogu xue* 中国佛教石窟寺遗迹：3到8世纪中国佛教考古学 [*Remains of Chinese Buddhist Rock Cut Monasteries: Studies in Chinese Buddhist Archeology from the Third to Eighth Centuries*]. Beijing: Wenwu chubanshe, 2010.

Su Zhe 蘇哲. "*Yuan Yi Yuan Cha muzhi yu Beiwei xiaoming di chao de pengdang zhenzhi* 元懌元叉墓志與北魏孝明帝朝的朋黨政治" ["The Tomb Inscriptions of Yuan Yi and Yuan Cha and the Factional Politics of Emperor Xiaoming's Court in Northern Wei"]. *Journal of Archaeological Studies* 考古学研究 (1997): 111–15.

Sun Tongxun 孫同勛. *Tuobashi de Hanhua ji qita—Beiwei shilun wenji* 拓拔氏的漢化及其他—北魏史論文集 [*The Sinification of the Tuobas and Other Things—Studies in the History of the Northern Wei*]. Taibei xian Banqiao shi: Daoxian chubanshe, 2005.

Tang Jia 唐嘉. "'Mile wei nüshen jing tanwei' 《彌勒為女身經》探微" ["A Study on the Scripture of Maitreya as Being of a Female Body"]. *Journal of Guizhou University (Social Sciences)* 贵州大学学报 (社会科学版) 28, no. 02 (2010): 104–8.

Tang Yongtong 汤用彤. *Han Wei liang Jin nanbeichao Fojiao shi (zengdingben)* 汉魏两晋南北朝佛教史 (增订本) [*A History of Buddhism in the Han, Wei, Two Jin, and Northern and Southern Dynasties*]. Expanded ed. Dongfang Wenhua Jicheng—Zhonghua

Wenhua Bian 东方文化集成－中华文化编 [Integration of Eastern Culture—Chinese Culture Series]. Beijing: Kunlun chubanshe, 2006.

Tang Zhangru 唐長孺. "Wei Jin za hu kao 魏晉雜胡考" ["Investigation into the Various 'hu' in the Wei and Jin Periods"]. In *Wei Jin nanbei chao shi lun cong* 魏晉南北朝史論叢 [*A Collection of Studies on the History of the Wei, Jin, and Southern and Northern Dynasties Period*], edited by Tang Zhangru, 382–450. 2nd ed. Beijing: Sanlian shu chubanshe, 1957.

Teiser, Stephen F. *The Ghost Festival in Medieval China*. Princeton, NJ: Princeton University Press, 1988.

Tian, Xiaofei, and Kroll, Paul W. *Family Instructions for the Yan Clan and Other Works by Yan Zhitui (531–590s)*. Berlin: De Gruyter Mouton, 2021.

Tian Yuqing 田余庆. *Tuoba shitan xiudingben* 拓跋史探 (修订本) [*Exploration of Tuoba History*]. Emended ed. Beijing: Shenghua dushu xinzhi sanlian shudian, 2011.

Tomášková, Silvia. "Yes Virginia, There Is Gender: Shamanism and Archeology's Many Histories." In *The Archeology of Bruce Trigger: Theoretical Empiricism*, edited by M. Bisson and R. Williamson, 81–113. Montreal: McGill-Queen's University Press, 2006.

Traill, Henry Duff, ed. *The Works of Thomas Carlyle in Thirty Volumes*. London: Chapman and Hall, 1896–99.

Tsai, Kathryn. *Lives of the Nuns: Biographies of Chinese Nuns from the Fourth to Sixth Centuries, A Translation of the Pi-Ch'iu Ni Chuan, Compiled by Shih Pao-Ch'ang*. Honolulu: University of Hawai'i Press, 1994.

Tseng, Chin-Yin. *The Making of the Tuoba Northern Wei: Constructing Material Cultural Expressions in the Northern Wei Pingcheng Period (398–494 CE)*. BAR International Series 2567. Oxford: British Archaeological Reports, 2013.

Tsukamoto Zenryū 塚本善隆. *Shina Bukkyō shi kenkyū. Hokugi hen* 支那佛教史研究, 北魏扁 [*A History of Chinese Buddhism, Northern Wei Section*]. Tokyo: Kōbundō, 1942.

———. "The Śramana Superintendent T'an-Yao 曇曜 and His Time." Translated by Galen Eugene Sargent. *Monumenta Serica* 16, nos. 1/2 (1957): 363–96.

Twitchett, Denis. "'Chen Gui' and Other Works Attributed to Empress Wu Zetian." *Asia Major* 16, no. 1 (2003): 33–109.

Twitchett, Denis, and Herbert Franke. *The Cambridge History of China*. Vol. 6, *Alien Regimes and Border States, 907–1368*. Cambridge: Cambridge University Press, 1994.

Tung, Jowen R. *Fables for the Patriarchs: Gender Politics in Tang Discourse*. Lanham, MD: Rowman & Littlefield, 2000.

Vermeersch, Sem. *The Power of the Buddhas: The Politics of Buddhism during the Koryŏ Dynasty (918–1392)*. Harvard East Asian Monographs 303. Cambridge, MA: Harvard University Press, 2008.

Von Gabain, Annemarie. *Alttürkische Grammatik*. Leipzig: Harrassowitz Verlag, 1950.

Wang Chuanfeng 王傳丰. "Beiwei nüzhu he Fojiao—yi Ling taihou Hu shi wei zhongxin 北魏女主和佛教——以靈太后胡氏為中心" ["Female Ruler in the Northern Wei and Buddhism: Focusing on Empress Dowager Ling"]. Master's thesis, Nanjing Normal University, 2016.

Wang, Eugene. *Shaping the Lotus Sutra: Buddhist Visual Culture in Medieval China*. Seattle: University of Washington Press, 2005.

Wang, Robin, ed. *Images of Women in Chinese Thought and Culture*. Indianapolis: Hackett, 2003.

Wang Shan 王珊. "Beiwei Sengzhi muzhi kaoyi 北魏僧芝墓志考释" ["A Study and Explanation of the Tomb Inscription of Northern Wei Sengzhi"]. *Beida Shixue* 北大史学 13 (August 2008): 87–107.

Wang Xinrui 王鑫蕊. *Longdong beichao Fojiao yanjiu* 隴東北朝佛教研究" ["The Research on Buddhism of East Gansu in Northern Dynasties"]. Master's thesis, Lanzhou University, 2016.

Wang Yintian, Cao Chenming, and Han Shengcun. "The Mingtang Site at Pingcheng of the Northern Wei Dynasty in Datong City, Shanxi Province." *Chinese Archaeology* 2.1 (2002): 251–57.

Wang Yitong, trans. *A Record of Buddhist Monasteries in Lo-yang*. Princeton, NJ: Princeton University Press, 1984.

Wang Yongbo 王永波 and Tsai Suey-Ling 蔡穗玲, eds. *Zhongguo Fojiao shijing: Shandong sheng di san juan* 中國佛教石經•山東省第三卷. *Buddhist Stone Sutras in China: Shandong Province Volume 3*. Hangzhou and Wiesbaden: China Academy of Art Press and Harrassowitz Verlag, 2017.

Wang Yongping 王永平. *Qianluo yuanwei huangzu yu shizu shehui wenhua shilun* 迁洛元魏皇族与士族社会文化史论 *[The Review of Royal Family Who Migrated to Luoyang and Socioculture of Literati in Northern Wei]*. Beijing: Zhongguo shehui kexue chubanshe, 2017.

Wang Zhongluo 王仲荦. *Wei Jin nanbeichao shi* 魏晋南北朝史 *[History of the Wei, Jin, and Northern and Southern Dynasties]*. Zhongguo Duandaishi Xilie 中国断代史系列 [Series on the Eras of Chinese History]. Shanghai: Shanghai renmin chubanshe, 2008.

Ware, James. "The Wei Shu and the Sui Shu on Taoism." *Journal of the American Oriental Society* 53, no. 3 (1933): 215–50.

———. "Wei Shou on Buddhism." *T'oung Pao* 30, nos. 1/2 (1933): 100–181.

Watson, Burton, trans. *The Lotus Sutra*. New York: Colombia University Press, 1993.

Wayman, Alex, and Hideko Wayman. *The Lion's Roar of Queen Śrīmālā: Translation of the Lost Sanskrit Work Made from a Collation of the Chinese, Japanese, and Tibetan Versions*. New York: Columbia University Press, 1974.

Wilson, Liz. *Charming Cadavers: Horrific Figurations of the Feminine in Indian Buddhist Hagiographic Literature*. Chicago: University of Chicago Press, 1996.

Wong, Dorothy. *Chinese Steles: Pre-Buddhist and Buddhist Uses of a Symbolic Form*. Honolulu: University of Hawai'i Press, 2004.

———. "Women as Buddhist Art Patrons During the Northern and Southern Dynasties." In *Between Han and Tang: Religious Art and Archeology of a Transformative Period*, edited by Wu Hung, 535–66. Beijing: Wenwu, 2000.

Wong, Poh Yee. "Acculturation as Seen Through Buddha's Birthday Parades in Northern Wei Luoyang: A Micro Perspective on the Making of Buddhism as a World Religion." PhD diss., University of the West, 2012.

Wright, Arthur F. "Biography of the Nun An-Ling-Shou." *Harvard Journal of Asiatic Studies* 15, nos. 1/2 (June 1952): 193–96.

Xia Yihui 夏毅輝. "Beichao huanghou yu Fojiao 北朝皇后與佛教" ["Empresses of the Northern Dynasties and Buddhism"]. *Academic Monthly* 学术月刊, no. 11 (1994): 65–73.

Xie, Yifeng. "Struggle on the Axis: The Advance and Retreat of Buddhist Influences in the Political Axis of Capitals in Medieval China (220–907)." *Religions* 12, no. 984 (2021): 1–27.

Xiong, Victor Cunrui. "The Land-Tenure System of Tang China: A Study of the Equal-Field System and the Turfan Documents." *T'oung Pao* 85, nos. 4/5 (1999): 328–90.

Yang Fuxue 楊富學 and Du Doucheng 杜斗城. "Luoyang chutu de ji tong tangdai Anding Hu shi muzhi 洛陽出土的幾通唐代安定胡氏墓志" ["A Few Pieces of Tomb Inscriptions of the Anding Hu Family during the Tang Dynasty Excavated from Luoyang"]. *Wenxian* 文献, no. 03 (2003): 54–61.

Yang, Shao-yun. "Making Sense of Messianism: Buddhist Political Ideology in the Mahayana Rebellion and the Moonlight Child Incident of Early Sixth-Century China." Bachelor's thesis, National Singapore University, 2005.

Yao Ping. "Women's Epitaphs in Tang China (618–907)." In *Beyond Exemplar Tales: Women's Biography in Chinese History*, edited by Joan Judge and Ying Hu, 139–57. Berkeley: University of California Press, 2011.

———. "Women in Portraits: An Overview of Surviving Epitaphs from Ancient and Medieval China." In *Overt and Covert Treasures: Essays on the Sources from Chinese Women's History*, edited by Clara Wing-chung Ho, 34–61. Hong Kong: Hong Kong Chinese University Press, 2010.

Yi, Joy Lidu. *Yungang: Art, History, Archaeology, Liturgy*. New York: Routledge, 2017.

Zhang Jinlong 张金龙. *Beiwei zhengzhi shi* 北魏政治史 [*History of Northern Wei Governance*]. 9 vols. Lanzhou: Gansu jiaoyu chubanshe, 2008.

———. "Ling taihou yu Yuan Cha zhengbian 靈太后與元乂政變" ["Empress Dowager Ling and the Political Coup of Yuan Cha"]. *Journal of Lanzhou University (Social Sciences)* 兰州大学学报, no. 3 (1993): 95–101.

Zhang Qingjie 张庆捷 and Li Biao 李彪. "Shanxi lingqiu Beiwei Wenchengdi 'nan xun bei' 山西灵丘北魏文成帝《南巡碑》" ["Northern Wei Emperor Wencheng's 'Stele of the Southern Progress' from Lingqiu in Shanxi"]. *Wenwu* [*Cultural Relics*] 12 (1997): 70–80.

Zhang Wen-liang 張文良. "Lingbian de shixiang yu xuxiang—yi Fazang de 'Lingbian Zhuan' kaocha wei zhongxin 靈辨的實像與虛像—以法藏的《靈辨傳》考察為中心" ["The Truth and Fiction of Lingbian: Centered on Fazang's Biography of Lingbian"]. *Monograph of the Proceedings of the 2015 International Symposium of Huayan Buddhism* (2015): 93–108.

Zhang, Zhenjun. *Buddhism and Tales of the Supernatural in Early Medieval China: A Study of Liu Yiqing's (403-444) Youming Lu*. Sinica Leidensia 114. Leiden: Brill, 2014.

Zhao Wanli 趙萬里. *Han Wei nanbeichao muzhi jishi* 漢魏南北朝墓誌集釋 [*Collection and Explanation of Tomb Inscriptions from the Han, Wei, and Northern and Southern Dynasties*]. Taipei: Dingwen shuju, 1972.

Zheng Wei. "A Study of Xianbei Tombs." *Chinese Archeology* 12 (2012): 158–64.

Zheng Xiaoxiao 鄭曉霞 and Lin Jianyu 林佳鬱, eds. *Lienü zhuan huibian* 烈女傳彙編 [*Compilation of Biographies of Exemplary Women*]. 10 vols. Beijing: Beijing tushuguan, 2007.

Zhou Yiliang 周一良. "Cong Beiwei ji ge jun de hukou bianhua kan san chang zhi de zuoyong 从北魏几个郡的户口变化看三长制的作用" ["The Operations of the Three Elders System from the Perspective of the Changes in Several Hukou During the Northern Wei"]. In *Wei Jin nanbei chao shilun ji* 魏晋南北朝史论集 [*A Collection of Historical Studies on the Wei, Jin, and Southern and Northern Dynasties Period],* 460–75. Beijing: Shangwu yin shuguan, 2020.

Zhou Yin 周胤. "Beiwei Ling tai hou 'zhuanlun wang' yu 'fo' xingxiang de goujian 北魏灵太后'转轮王'与'佛'形象的构建" ["The Image Construction of 'Cakravartin' and 'Buddha' by Empress Dowager Ling of Northern Wei Dynasty"]. *Academic Forum of Nandu (Journal of the Humanities and Social Sciences)* 南都学坛 37, no. 06 (2017): 21–30.

Zhongguo she hui ke xue yuan kao gu yan jiu suo 中国社会科学院考古研究所 [The Institute of Archeology, Chinese Academy of Social Sciences]. *Beiwei Luoyang Yongning si, 1979–1995 nian kaogu fajue baogao.* 北魏洛阳永宁寺, *1979–1995* 年考古发掘报告 *[The Yongning Temple in Northern Wei Luoyang, Excavation in 1979–1994].* Beijing: zhongguo dabaike chuan su chubanshe, 1996.

Zürcher, Erik. "Buddhism in a Pre-Modern Bureaucratic Empire: The Chinese Experience." In *Studies in History of Buddhism*, edited by A.K. Narain, 401–12. Delhi: B. R Publishing Corporation., 1980.

———. *The Buddhist Conquest of China: The Spread and Adaptation of Buddhism in Early Medieval China.* 3rd ed. Leiden: Brill, 2007.

———. "'Prince Moonlight.' Messianism and Eschatology in Early Medieval Chinese Buddhism." *T'oung Pao* 68, nos. 1/3 (1982): 1–75.

FORDFOUNDATION

Working with Visionaries on the
Frontlines of Social Change Worldwide

⟶ movie on _____

Wendy by next
Wednesday

— Quebec first picks
for EU of
landscape

⟶ STSN D ~~acted~~ close
pix
_____

Teachings
⟶ _____
melting clock
scene

*Working with Visionaries on the
Frontlines of Social Change Worldwide*

FORDFOUNDATION

Working with Visionaries on the
Frontlines of Social Change Worldwide

CHARACTER INDEX

An Lingshou 安令首
Anding 安定

Baima si 白馬寺
bao taihou 保太后
baobian 襃貶
Baode si 報德寺
beimen xueshi 北門學士
beishen zuoyou 備身左右
biqiuni 比丘尼
biqiuni tong 比丘尼統
biqiuyuanni 比丘元尼
bixia 陛下
bude zizai 不得自在
Bukong 不空

Chang 常 (Madam)
Changyi 昌意
changqiu qing 長秋卿
chenghua shifu 承華世婦
Chinhŭng 真興
chonghua pin 充華嬪
chudi 出帝
Chuntuo 純陀
Ciqing 慈慶
cishi 刺史
Ciyi 慈義
Cui Guang 崔光
Cui Hao 崔浩

Dangmo 當陌
dao 道
Daohe 道和
daoren tong 道人統
Daoxuan 道宣
de 德
di 帝
dianxia 殿下
ding Han wang 定漢王
dongyang wang 東陽王
dongyuan miqi 東園祕器
Dou 竇 (Madam)
doutong 都統
Du Ba 杜霸
Dunhuang 敦煌
Duobao 多寶
duweina 都維那

ersheng 二聖
Erzhu Rong 尒朱榮
Erzhu Zhao 爾朱兆

Faguo 法果
Famen si 法門寺
fan 番
Faqing 法慶
fashi 法師
fayi 法義
Fazang 法藏

229

Founded in 1893,
UNIVERSITY OF CALIFORNIA PRESS
publishes bold, progressive books and journals
on topics in the arts, humanities, social sciences,
and natural sciences—with a focus on social
justice issues—that inspire thought and action
among readers worldwide.

The UC PRESS FOUNDATION
raises funds to uphold the press's vital role
as an independent, nonprofit publisher, and
receives philanthropic support from a wide
range of individuals and institutions—and from
committed readers like you. To learn more, visit
ucpress.edu/supportus.